# A Sociology of Work in Japan

What shapes the decisions of employees to work in Japan? The authors of this comprehensive and up-to-date survey of the relationship between work and society in Japan argue that individual decisions about work can only be understood by considering the larger social context. Many factors combine to affect such choices, including the structuring of labor markets, social policy at the national and meso level and, of course, global influences, which have come increasingly to impinge on the organization of work and life generally. The analysis asks why the Japanese work such long hours, and why they are so committed to their firms, if this is indeed the case. By considering labor markets, social policy, and relationships between labor and management, the book offers penetrating insights into contemporary Japanese society and glimpses of what might happen in the future. Underlying the discussion is a challenge to the celebration of Japanese management practices which has dominated the literature for the last three decades. This is an important and groundbreaking book for students of sociology and economics.

ROSS MOUER is Professor of Japanese Studies in the School of Languages, Cultures and Linguistics at Monash University. His publications include *Images of Japanese Society: A Study in the Construction of Social Reality* (1986).

KAWANISHI HIROSUKE is Professor of Sociology at Waseda University, Tokyo. He is the author and editor of many books including *Enterprise Unionism in Japan* (1991) and *The Human Face of Industrial Conflict in Post-war Japan* (1999).

Contemporary Japanese Society

Editor:
Yoshio Sugimoto, La Trobe University

Advisory Editors:
Harumi Befu, Stanford University
Roger Goodman, Oxford University
Michio Muramatsu, Kyoto University
Wolfgang Seifert, Universität Heidelberg
Chizuko Ueno, University of Tokyo

**Contemporary Japanese Society** provides a comprehensive portrayal of modern Japan through the analysis of key aspects of Japanese society and culture, ranging from work and gender politics to science and technology. The series offers a balanced yet interpretive approach. Books are designed for a wide range of readers, from undergraduate beginners in Japanese studies to scholars and professionals.

D. P. Martinez (ed.) *The Worlds of Japanese Popular Culture*
0 521 63128 9 hardback   0 521 63729 5 paperback

Kaori Okano and Motonori Tsuchiya *Education in Contemporary Japan: Inequality and Diversity*
0 521 62252 2 hardback   0 521 62686 2 paperback

Morris Low, Shigeru Nakayama and Hitoshi Yoshioka *Science, Technology and Society in Contemporary Japan*
0 521 65282 0 hardback   0 521 65425 4 paperback

Roger Goodman (ed.) *Family and Social Policy in Japan: Anthropological Approaches*
0 521 81571 1 hardback   0 521 01635 5 paperback

Yoshio Sugimoto *An Introduction to Japanese Society* (2nd edn)
0 521 82193 2 hardback   0 521 52925 5 paperback

Vera Mackie *Feminism in Modern Japan: Citizenship, Embodiment and Sexuality*
0 521 82018 9 hardback   0 521 52719 8 paperback

Nanette Gottlieb *Language and Society in Japan*
0 521 82577 6 hardback   0 521 53284 1 paperback

# A Sociology of Work in Japan

Ross Mouer
*Monash University*

*and*

Kawanishi Hirosuke
*Waseda University*

CAMBRIDGE
UNIVERSITY PRESS

CAMBRIDGE UNIVERSITY PRESS
Cambridge, New York, Melbourne, Madrid, Cape Town, Singapore, São Paulo

Cambridge University Press
The Edinburgh Building, Cambridge CB2 2RU, UK

Published in the United States of America by Cambridge University Press, New York

www.cambridge.org
Information on this title: www.cambridge.org/9780521651204

First published 2005

Printed in the United Kingdom at the University Press, Cambridge

*A catalogue record for this book is available from the British Library*

*Library of Congress Cataloguing in Publication data*
Mouer, Ross E., 1944–
A Sociology of Work in Japan / Ross Mouer, Kawanishi Hirosuke.
    p.   cm. – (Contemporary Japanese society)
Includes bibliographical references and index.
ISBN 0 521 65120 4 (alk. paper) – ISBN 0 521 65845 4 (pb.: alk. paper)
1. Industrial management – Japan.   2. Work – Japan.   3. Japan – Social conditions –
1945–   4. Japan – Economic conditions – 1989–   I. Kawanishi, Hirosuke, 1942–
II. Title.   III. Series.
HD70.J3M68   2005
306.3′6′0952 – dc22      2004054621

ISBN-13 978-0-521-65120-2 hardback
ISBN-10 0-521-65120-4 hardback
ISBN-13 978-0-521-65845-4 paperback
ISBN-10 0-521-65845-4 paperback

# Contents

**Part V:   The power relations shaping the organization of work in Japan**

**Part VI:   The future**

     *References*                                               264
     *Author index*                                             296
     *General index*                                            300

# Figures

# Tables

# Preface

This project began nearly ten years ago. At that time a huge literature existed in English on Japanese-style management. Most of it was favorably disposed to what was seen as being an approach to human relations and personnel management that had gone beyond the division of labor and regimentation associated with the Fordist paradigm. In particular there was an interest in how Japanese-style management had produced a highly motivated work force with an exceptionally strong work ethic and commitment to the firm and its goals. To get a better idea of the extent to which work was carried out autonomously in Japan, we felt it would be useful to shift attention from the cultural or ideational domain to the structuring of work choices at both levels, paying special attention to the consequences of not working "hard" for long hours. To provide a better understanding of the work ethic and the reasons for the long hours of work registered in Japan, we felt it was necessary first to set firm-level arrangements and choices about work in the context of the larger social parameters: the way external labor markets were structured, the overall mosaic of stratification and the provision of various kinds of social services, and the power relations between the labor movement and management at the national level. In our view these were the major structures which limited choice with regard to work at the firm level.

In our minds was the anecdote of the Japanese researcher who had traveled to Australia to investigate the country's unemployment insurance scheme in the early 1990s just as the unemployment rate in Japan was climbing to over 3 percent for the first time in nearly forty years. It soon became obvious that the researcher was looking for ways to tighten the system in Japan. His assumption was that tougher treatment of the unemployed would motivate them to resume work at a quicker pace. The assumption was perhaps reasonable, as Australia itself had had very low rates of employment until the early 1970s, and had then engaged in a discourse which referred to the unemployed as "dole bludgers" as the unemployment rate rose.

When he asked about the length of time for which unemployment benefits could be received, which at the time was only six months in Japan, he was greatly surprised to find that there was no time limit on receiving the benefits in Australia. Having ascertained that he was indeed being informed about the dole and not pensions or ongoing compensation for an incapacity owing to a work-related accident, he scratched his head and concluded that the work ethic in Australia was actually quite strong if roughly 90 percent of the labor force was still willing to work "voluntarily" without the compulsion of starving, whereas 3 percent of Japanese (or even more, considering disguised unemployment) chose not to work even with a very strong financial inducement to do so (i.e. to work or to starve after six months). This incident confirmed in our minds the need to tie ideas about why employees work as they do to broader structures limiting the conditions of possibility which confront each worker as he or she wrestles with several discourses about work in order to make decisions about where, when, and how hard to work.

Over the intervening years a number of correctives to the Japanese model began to emerge. As a result, many observers of Japanese-style management came to appreciate that, for whatever post-Fordist elements there might be, there were also ultra-Fordist features as well. More attention also came to be paid to the nature of the tiered subcontracting which was central to the functioning of just-in-time schemes and rested on a disaggregation or Balkanization of the labor market. Those inter-firm relationships injected into the organization of work another set of power relationships external to the firm. There was a growing appreciation that a large proportion of the labor force worked outside the large-firm sector in which the features commonly associated with the Japanese model were normally found. Rather than absorbing the casuals, part-timers, and subcontracted workers over time, it became clear that the large firms actually existed in a symbiotic relationship with them, dependent upon their very existence. A literature also emerged on attempts to implement Japanese-style management abroad, and other structural features began to be highlighted in terms of the considerable extent to which members of the core work force were regimented within the model companies themselves. While some writers attributed any friction which emerged to differences in cultural orientations, commenting that a managerial style suited for a conformist- or consensualist-oriented society would have difficulty in many of the more individualistically inclined societies of the West, the structural features designed to discipline the labor force still loomed large. From a slightly different perspective, the situation of working women had also become a popular topic for foreign researchers, and much of the English-language literature which resulted from this pointed to the structural weaknesses of Japan's 1986 Equal Employment Opportunity Law, which lacked the teeth to force change. In Japan itself attention was being given to the problem of *karoshi* and to the reasons employees felt compelled to overwork. With that there was a much broader concern with work patterns associated with the model which severely limited the opportunities for some of Japan's best-educated and dynamic male employees to be with their families and to take a greater interest in community affairs.

While valid, these critiques did not seem to present an integrated overview of the larger structural context in which workers made choices about work. Many of the critiques were set within a normative framework, albeit in critical terms which have no doubt served to nurture the belief that Japan needed to change. Few dealt with the changing power relations that shaped the structural context. Much of the change occurring in Japan was put down to the inevitability of universal forces or global patterns emerging elsewhere and explained in terms of how Japanese culture was "catching up." It seemed to be taken for granted that the collapse of Japan's union movement, especially in terms of its commitment to leftist political goals, was a logical outcome of having new levels of affluence. If there was a structured element, it was in the collapse of socialist regimes that heralded the end of the cold war (even while the Japan Communist Party continued to receive a healthy 10 percent of the popular vote at national elections). Many descriptions of work in Japan came to be characterized by a set of assumptions bound up in the view that the end of history as we knew it was now in sight in terms of the tensions produced by ideological and cultural differences.

The original idea for this volume was to present an alternative account which explained Japanese-style management not in terms of any uniqueness in cultural or ideological terms, but as a means of expropriating surplus within a specific superstructural framework that severely limited the choices available to workers and potential workers at the macro level. During the 1990s Japan drifted into a prolonged recession with rising unemployment and a growing awareness that the world outside was changing, as other nations were rapidly moving to find niches in the newly emerging global economy. In considering those changes, it seemed to us that a new superstructure was emerging which would increasingly shape the way work is organized in Japan. There was an awareness that the recession of the union movement was not unique to Japan. The aging of the population, the impact of Japan's affluence on the attitudes of its young people to work, the widening gap in the distribution of income, and many other changes in Japanese society could also be seen as universal phenomena. Successive financial scandals invited comparisons with the situation in other similarly developed societies. At the same time, out of those comparisons emerged a sense that international standards were coming increasingly to influence the way societies organized their economic, political, and social affairs (and, ultimately, their very cultures). Moreover, the north–south issues and Japanese investment overseas underlined ways in which the world is stratified and structured in terms of the global economy.

Given the above perspective, it became apparent to us that a full understanding of work in Japan would need to consider the labor process at three levels: the way work was organized in individual firms, the way societies were structured to allocate work through more broadly based labor markets, and the way the international division of labor was decided. The growing prominence of the extra-territorial factors has caused us to think of the global as a new world order that is now the macro level. To better articulate that way of sorting through our thoughts about work in Japan, we have come to use the term "meso level" when referring to structures, ideas, and events at the societal (particularly the national) level.

In considering the dynamics which result in decisions being made about the organization of work at each of these three levels, it seemed to us that the key variables relate to inequality of one type or another. The forces for change and those for the status quo can be found in the collectivities that have come to be organized in reference to those inequalities. The inequalities are most commonly defined by gender, occupation, organizational size, age, educational background, and spatial location. The role of these factors in accounting for inequalities will be obvious to most readers. Widened beyond a certain point, inequalities reveal objective contradictions. It is the awareness of those contradictions that produces tensions and creates pressure for change. In other words, it is the subjective assessment of those involved in working and in organizing work that is critical. In the past, unions have played a central role in influencing how workers felt about the objective inequalities which bounded their lives, and much of the employment relationship revolved around the attempts of labor and management to influence the way workers perceived the importance of those inequalities in their lives, the choices they had in managing inequality, and the tradeoffs that arose when inequality was multidimensional. Over time, other forces also came into play as the standard of living rose, and these seem to have become noticeably more conspicuous as Japan moved through the 1980s and 1990s.

The assessment of inequality is also tempered by an assessment of its relative importance in terms of the overall level of rewards received in the relevant society. Hence, a commonly heard argument from those seeking to justify having some measure of inequality is that it is better to be poor in a rich society than to be in the middle of a poor society. This view is often presented by those at the top of wealthy societies, and goes against the notions of mateship, comradeship, and to each according to his or her needs.

Once a view has crystallized about the dimensions of inequality and its overall importance in the larger scheme of things, the decision to act will be based on an assessment of the likely chances that change will occur and the likely sanctions that will be imposed should the push for change fail. Here the role of the state is central. Our search for the meaning of work in Japan is set in this context of objective inequalities, visions of inequality and the realities of power.

This volume seeks to examine how these three elements interact at the meso level. One of our working hypotheses is that individuals have already made an assessment of their chances and opportunities in the larger society before entering the world of work in a particular firm, and that a good deal of their behavior in the firm will result from decisions significantly shaped by that world view. This is a hypothesis we cannot test here, but the volume is written in part as a preparation for making such a test. While the media, increased travel, better education, the internet, and aspects of global consumption (e.g. international advertising) have served increasingly to draw individuals to the global level and have opened up opportunities to know more about the international division of labor and associated inequalities, and about local phenomena which are universal, it is our feeling that the minds of workers have been imprinted from that vantage point, but not yet to the extent that those impressions outweigh their impressions of the world from the meso level in shaping their assessment of the meso- or micro-level realities. This is another hypothesis to be tested, but not in this volume.

The major aim in writing this book was to draw a picture of the terrain on which work is organized at the meso level in Japan. There seems to be a general recognition that the old paradigms for organizing work in Japanese firms no longer hold. As the Japanese struggle to find ways to reinvigorate their economy, there is an active search for a model to replace that currently used for organizing work. There is a common recognition that the Japanese model – with all its structural features, as an important component of the Japanese economy (indeed, of Japanese society) – contributed immensely to the economic achievements of the 1960s and 1970s. The energy focused in accomplishing those achievements carried Japan forward to an economic apex during the "bubble years" of the late 1980s and early 1990s, when huge balance-of-payments surpluses were recorded and unrealistically high levels of lending occurred to finance further growth and non-growth projects alike. There is now a serious realization, however, that a replacement model is needed as one of the cornerstones, if not the keystone, in the building of a new Japanese economy. A study of the dynamics shaping labor process at the meso level will go some way toward highlighting the parameters likely to define the paradigm which emerges for work in Japan.

In trying to assess the way work is organized at the meso level we have sought to tell a story about how various objective facts relate to the way employees might see the world in subjective terms. We have tried to utilize a wide range of material, including academic opinion and some reference to scholarly research findings, government statistics, popular views in the media, and expositions in some of the popular encyclopedias. In the end we wanted a volume that would communicate not only to readers across several societies (i.e. an English-reading audience and a Japanese-reading audience), but also to those working at different levels in either society. Only time will tell whether we have been successful in doing this.

# Note on transliteration, romanization, and translation

A large number of Japanese terms are introduced in this volume. Several considerations have led us to their introduction. One is to overcome the tendency to think in terms of universals. The introduction of the terms, usually in parentheses following an English explanation, serves to remind us that many of the concepts used in writing about work in Japan have cultural *emic* dimensions (i.e. a set of connotations peculiar to the Japanese setting). The word *rodo kumiai*, for example, refers to an organization for and by workers in a generic or *etic* sense. However, when the term is used in Japan, its connotations for most Japanese suggest a particular approach to union organization, trends in unionization rates, a history of ideological struggle between left-wing and right-wing groups, an association with a broad range of citizens' movements, and a specific approach to organization at both the national level and the grassroots level. The term is also used to refer to a range of other self-help or mutual-help organizations, including credit unions and agricultural, consumer, or insurance cooperatives. Japanese terms are liberally inserted as a subtle reminder that there are real differences in meaning between the Japanese and English terms and the context in which people in different societies talk about similar matters.

A second reason for using Japanese terms is to facilitate communication by supplying readers with a basic list of key words that will immediately be recognized by the Japanese with whom they may wish to discuss issues raised in this volume. Consequently, references to "labor union" (*rodo kumiai*) serve to indicate that we use the term "labor union" as a rough equivalent for what we are really writing about (i.e., Japanese *rodo kumiai*). Conversely, reference to "*rodo kumiai*" (labor union) is made to indicate that the *rodo kumiai* we are writing about are fairly similar to "labor unions" in English.

As is common practice, all foreign words, including the large number of Japanese words introduced in this text, are italicized. The exceptions include proper nouns and official titles. The personal names of Japanese are given in the Japanese order, with the surname first. Exceptions are made for Japanese who live and work abroad and are generally known abroad by their given name followed by the surname. There are obviously cases in the gray area; an increasing number of Japanese move back and forth or have significant careers abroad before returning home to Japan. The decision in such cases can only be arbitrary.

Japanese words have been romanized in the Standard or Hepburn style. However, the macron or elongation mark has been omitted in transcribing long vowels for ordinary Japanese words. This is in line with common practice as noted by Neustupny (1991: 8), who suggests it is always inserted "in texts addressed to specialized Japanese studies audiences" but generally omitted from "more popular writings" for a broader audience. While purists in the use of the Japanese language might object, several considerations led to this decision. First, in percentage terms, a brief count of Japanese words mentioned in the text suggested that fewer than 10 percent had elongated vowels, and of those few were words where confusion would occur. An example of such confusion might be the name "Ohashi," which could consist of either the two characters meaning "big bridge" or the two characters meaning "little bridge." However, our feeling was that the majority of readers would be reading in English only and not reading the references. Second, dictionaries such as Kenkyusha's list words in romanized script so that all words which differ only in terms of the short and elongated vowel are listed together, and the choice of the right term is easy given the context, and the fact that an English translation is supplied in most cases.

In recent years the Japanese have absorbed a large number of foreign words which are sometimes more difficult to decode or to look up than native Japanese words. The origin of such words is denoted in Japanese by writing them in a designated script, *katakana*. For those words, we have indicated the elongated sound by repeating the double vowel in the roman script. Thus, the publication *Shukan Rodo Nyuusu* is the "Weekly News on Work." In trialing this approach with a small sample of postgraduate students, who were asked to transcribe back into English from romanized Japanese, it was found that the error rate in transcription was negligible. The experiment suggested that personal names were more difficult than ordinary words to transcribe back into Japanese, and that more errors occurred in transcribing items in the list of references than in the text. However, the purpose of the list is to allow readers to locate cited sources, and there are a number of ways to do that even with partial information (e.g. by looking up the title of the publication rather than the author's name), and again the demerits of omitting the elongation mark seemed small. In this regard, an effort was made to provide a list of references that was as detailed as possible.

This work has included small amounts of translation, mostly from the Japanese-language titles in the list of references for which both the romanized Japanese and an English translation are provided. Titles are short and tend to invite a direct translation. Because the direct translation is somewhat awkward or misleading in English when taken out of context, some liberty has been taken to provide a translation which best matches the overall thrust of each specific item. In translating longer passages, a number of arbitrary interpretive and stylistic decisions were made. These kinds of decisions rest on assumptions about the function the translation is to perform in the telling of the story. Which version is most appropriate can only be left to the reader's broader judgments about the story itself – judgments that are likely to vary from reader to reader. We can only ask for the reader's patience, tolerance, and understanding in this matter, and welcome all critical comments so that a better job of storytelling can be done next time.

# Abbreviations

| | |
|---|---|
| *ASC* | *Asahi Shimbun* (morning edition of a national daily newspaper) |
| *CPI* | Consumer Price Index |
| *GHQ* | General Headquarters (of the Allied occupation of Japan) |
| *ILO* | International Labor Organization |
| *JCP* | Japan Communist Party |
| *LDP* | Liberal Democratic Party |
| *LSL* | Labor Standards Law |
| *MITI* | Ministry of International Trade and Industry |
| *MNE* | multinational enterprise |
| *MSC* | *Mainichi Shimbun* (morning edition of a national daily newspaper) |
| *MWL* | Minimum Wage Law |
| *NGO* | non-government organization |
| *NKSC* | *Nihon Keizai Shimbun* (morning edition of the nation's leading financial daily) |
| *NPO* | non-profit organization |
| *QC* | quality control |
| *SRN* | *Shukan Rodo Nyuusu* (a weekly newspaper) |
| *WHO* | World Health Organization |
| *WTO* | World Trade Organization |
| *YSC* | *Yomiuri Shimbun* (morning edition of a national daily newspaper) |

*Part I*

# A context for studying work

# 1 The Japanese at work

## 1.1 Japanese-style management and the interest in Japanese at work

Over the last twenty years, a huge literature has emerged about work in Japan. The interest in Japan has followed that country's success as a national economy. Although economists had been aware of Japan's steady rise to economic prominence over the hundred years following the Meiji Restoration in 1868, from around 1970 Japan's large balance-of-payments surpluses drew wider attention to "the Japanese miracle." A number of books appeared to suggest that Japan had overnight become a new economic superstate that would challenge or even threaten Western economic supremacy. Their titles were often couched in ethnocentric terms that connoted not only warnings, but also condescending surprise, that a non-Western nation so severely beaten in 1945 could achieve so much within twenty-five years.

To explain Japan's sudden emergence as an economic superstate, many writers, including the futurologist Herman Kahn (1970), attached great importance to the Japanese mindset. They alleged that cultural remnants or feudalistic values – such as group loyalty, a motivation to achieve based on duty and the fear of shame or losing face, and Confucian frugality – and a special sense of community or national consensus were the wellsprings of Japan's economic success. Two underlying concerns marked much of that literature. One was a resentment of Japan's success in selling manufactured goods in the markets of the advanced industrialized economies. Many writers sought to assess the likelihood that Japan's success would be shortlived and not result in a long-term "threat." This focus underscored a fear and often encouraged a belief that there was a need for protective measures to counter the Japanese invasion. The second concern arose from the ideological position taken in many Western countries during the cold war. In the West a high value had been placed on free trade and there was a very real rationalist interest in how Japanese goods had become so competitive in terms of price and quality.

This emphasis served to counter the first concern and opened the door for the "Japan guru" and others associated with the "learn-from-Japan campaign" which emerged in the late 1970s.

As Japanese exports continued to make inroads abroad, and Japan's balance-of-payment surpluses ballooned in the 1980s, American and European managers began to visit Japan in large numbers to learn about quality control and bottom-up management techniques. An early stimulus to the interest in Japanese-style management was Dore's *British Factory – Japanese Factory* (1973). Taking the theory of late development as a starting point, Dore argued that Japan had leapfrogged ahead in the design of industrial relations systems because it had been able to circumnavigate many of the problems associated with earlier efforts to industrialize. He suggested that Japan had avoided the strong antagonistic class relations between workers and managers which had characterized the industrialization process in many Western societies. Dore argued further that corporate welfarism had resolved many of the social justice issues in Japan. In 1979 Vogel published *Japan as Number One*, in which he too argued that Japan had actually moved ahead of the US and many European countries in a number of critical areas. He praised the Japanese approach to organizing work, the maintenance of high levels of cultural cohesion and social stability, the functioning of a highly effective bureaucracy, and the achievement of generally high levels of literacy. By the early 1980s the "learn-from-Japan campaign" was in high gear. One book after another appeared which extolled Japanese approaches to maintaining law and order, to supplying high-quality education, to fostering meaningful social interaction, and to developing satisfying and productive industrial relations or management styles. It became fashionable for academic writers to conclude research reports on Japan with a chapter on lessons for others.

The interest in learning from Japan was quite pronounced in the area of management. Something about Japanese-style management was seen as accounting for high levels of productivity. The quality of Japanese products and the low level of industrial disputes were seen as evidence of the success of Japanese management, low levels of worker alienation, and a distinct work ethic. Ouchi's *Theory Z* (1981) and Pascale and Athos's *The Art of Japanese Management* (1981) were two of the earlier volumes seeking to explain Japanese-style management to English-speaking managers around the world. The 1980s saw an outpouring of volumes on all aspects of Japanese-style management. Throughout this period Japan's experience became a major point of reference for many who were writing about management and global capitalism. Writers such as Thurow (1983, 1992 and 1996) and Drucker (1993) typify this interest in Japan.

By the late 1980s many observers, such as Kenny and Florida (1993), were proclaiming that Japan had developed a truly post-Fordist or post-modern approach to organizing work.

Much of the literature on Japanese management assumed that the Japanese worker's commitment to work and to his place of work had been integral to the superior performance of the Japanese economy. That commitment was seen as overriding the adverse conditions which many workers had to put up with, including long hours and excessive regimentation. It was commonly argued that Japanese management had worked with and fostered a cultural paradigm that was quite different from the one found in most Western countries. The assumption was that Japanese culture resulted in workers and managers sharing similar values, which underpinned Japanese work practices and an unusually strong commitment to doing work. The conclusion was often that Western managers needed to alter their managerial style. The corollary was that a kind of cultural revolution was required in many Western societies so that antagonistic class relations formed during earlier stages of industrialization would give way to more cooperative relations at work and in society at large.

## 1.2    Reassessing Japanese-style management

Given the general enthusiasm for Japanese-style management, linked to the functional requisites for high productivity, other aspects of work organization have tended to be pushed aside. This was especially true outside Japan. North American scholarship had traditionally veered away from Marxist themes. As the cold war progressed, traditional perspectives on industrial relations which emphasized conflict and its resolution through power relations tended to give way to optimistic assessments concerning the manageability of human resources and the ability of progressive management to preempt conflict.

Countering that predilection, Kassalow (1983) argued that Japan's approach to industrial relations would not be a serious model for organizing work elsewhere unless three conditions were met. The first was that the system produced high levels of national economic competitiveness. Second was that all the stakeholders in Japan agreed the model was a satisfactory way of organizing work. Third was that members of the society generating the model desired to export it. The second and third conditions have been least satisfied and require close examination.

As for consensus, conservative governments and employers' associations have since the early 1950s attacked left-wing unionism and the Marxist-inspired scholarship associated with it. Two successive "oil shocks" in the 1970s fostered a renewed seriousness about national economic competitiveness and discipline at work. As socialist regimes abroad increasingly came to confront various contradictions in the 1980s, conservatives made headway and seemingly emerged victorious by the end of the 1980s, by which time militant left-wing unionism had also lost out in the unification of the labor movement. As the bubble years of the 1980s gave way to a new consumerism, dissident scholarship relevant to the understanding of work in Japan ebbed, and the interest in critiques of work organization in Japan waned. This gave the impression that consensus had been achieved and that the second condition seemed to have been met.

However, after Japan's economic bubble burst in the early 1990s, thirty-five years of conservative rule came to an end. In the 1990s successive financial crises, the frequent turnover of national governments, rising unemployment, multicultural pressures, and the incursion of foreign-made goods underlined the need for a fundamental questioning of the work-related institutions previously seen as the wellspring of Japan's postwar economic success. Many Japanese began to face a certain dilemma: three decades of hard work and Japan's very high per capita incomes had not produced a commensurately high standard of living. This led to questions about how hard to work and the even more basic question: how wealthy is wealthy enough?

By the 1990s many Japanese were feeling a great national tiredness and frustration in not knowing how to convert the nation's economic prowess into a better quality of life. There was a growing awareness that mammoth changes were required to alter a system that had been geared to putting production first. As Shimada (1995) put it, there were problems in having a system which produces more than can be consumed: Japan's huge balance-of-payments surpluses were symptomatic of serious economic anorexia. Japan's economy had come to be structured in ways that made it difficult for ordinary Japanese to enjoy the wealth it generated. It was an economy built on lean production. Such an economy, Shimada argued, had serious health problems.

Reflecting on this systemic problem, Sato (1993) wrote about Japan's new spiritual refugees who were migrating to Australia to escape the Japanese system. These Japanese differed from the economic emigrants who left Japan at the beginning of the twentieth century. At issue was the dysfunctioning of the Japanese system as a whole. For such Japanese the high material standard of living was offset by high levels of stress. This perspective is presented in the recent writings of Kumazawa (1996 and 1997) and by those who write about *karoshi* (death from overwork). Those writing about these aspects would argue that Kassalow's consensus was to be found more in the form of an awkward silence than in a resounding cheer for the benefits of Japanese-style management. Overseas, Japanese firms came to be known for their hostility to unionism, for their failure to incorporate local managers, women or the aged into the upper realms of management, for a lack of seriousness in dealing with certain social issues such as sexual harassment, for implementing just-in-time systems that overly disciplined workers in a vast array of hierarchically aligned sub-contractors, and for the tightness with which it withheld from the public information on in-house dealings and other socially relevant matters.

These considerations mark the extent to which official and unofficial interpretations diverge and the "labeling" by which certain ways of orga-nizing work are presented to the public as "respectable" and others are not. Because the engineering of work organization inevitably involves social change, management in leading firms must constantly engage in public relations exercises to implement change. For this reason, a full analysis of work in Japan requires that attention be paid both to the man-ifest and to the latent ways in which work is organized.

As for the third of Kassalow's conditions, Japanese management and the government have been equivocal about the transferability of Japanese-style management. Prior to 1980 most of Japan's investment overseas had been by small firms seeking to save on labor-intensive processes. From the late 1970s Japan's large firms began in a concerted manner to manufacture abroad within tariff-protected or regulated areas and to counter mounting criticism of the negative effects their large-scale exports from Japan were having on other societies. For this reason there was sensitivity to local work practices. However, as Japanese multinational enterprises (MNEs) became more confident in their own labor processes and more familiar with the foreign settings, many encouraged their leaner subcontractors to follow them abroad, and Japanese managers began to introduce some Japanese practices while leaving others at home.

On the home front, partly as a result of direct pressure through the Structural Impediments Initiatives that came to be built into US–Japan bilateral relations in the late 1980s, many Japanese became more aware of the benefits of aligning practices in Japan with those found in other major economies. Steps to deregulate the Japanese economy have also coin-cided with social changes in Japan over the past ten to fifteen years. New developments in global capitalism have made the export of Japanese-style management and Japanese-style industrial relations practices in toto less pertinent. Japanese who want to say no to Western demands are now much less likely to do so on cultural grounds or to invoke parochial notions of cultural relativism in order to justify the introduction of allegedly Japanese ways of managing.

As the evidence on Japanese-style management overseas accumulated during the 1980s, Japanese management increasingly came under the scrutiny of local communities. In North America and Europe many have a greater appreciation of the social consequences of Japanese-style management. Japanese managers now seem less enthusiastic about implementing the Japanese approach to industrial relations abroad. Another factor undermining the confidence of Japanese managers and depressing interest abroad in learning from the way work is organized in Japan has been the inability of the national economy to perform at levels achieved prior to 1990. During the 1990s the Japanese model lost its edge in meeting Kassalow's first criterion.

## 1.3     A general perspective on postmodernism and the organization of work: post-Fordist or ultra-Fordist?

The Japanese experience poses some hard questions about the nature of work. Four decades of rapid economic growth from the 1950s took Japan far beyond industrialization. In the late 1980s it was commonly argued that in becoming post-industrial Japanese society had also gone beyond modernization and the processes of rationalization which led to standardization, not just in work processes but also in life processes more generally. With the emergence of a national labor market and mass society, many came to the view that 90 percent of the Japanese identified with some amorphous "middle class." Nevertheless, although one can point to standardization in the education system, in the mass media, in the language, and in the rhythm of commuting, serious questions remain concerning the homogeneity of the Japanese in terms of a shared consciousness or ethos at work. These doubts were systematically detailed by Mouer and Sugimoto (1986). During the late 1980s and early 1990s debate focused on whether Japanese-style management actually represented a new post-Fordist system of production or was only a logical extension of the Fordist production system. Various contributions to that debate were later brought together in a volume edited by Kato and Steven (1993).

### 1.3.1     The dilemma of modernity

Modernization challenged social theorists with its emphasis on choice and liberation. Some time ago, Apter (1966) wrote that the essence of being modern lies in the willingness and the ability to make strategic choices. The dilemma of choice was especially apparent in societies that came late to industrialization and required disciplined efforts to "catch up." For them modernization became an exercise in the mobilization of entire populations to ward off outside control. This produced a tension between (i) the ability of individuals to make rational choices in their pursuit of individual freedom and autonomy, and (ii) the capacity of societies to make collective choices which were rational in terms of achieving self-sustaining development and national independence. Developmentalist ideologies sometimes blurred the distinction between internalized cultural values and politically supported policy objectives. Today some write about an Asian mode of democracy, whereby the national development needed to win new freedoms for Asian societies results in strategic restrictions being placed on the choices available to the individuals who constitute those societies.

The debate on Asian values highlights ambiguities and tensions created by modernity and by notions of universal economic rationality. Greater physical comfort and new standards based on universalistic principles are products of modernization and the drive for economic rationality. Beyond a certain point, however, further development requires more open flows of information that in turn allow individuals to disengage themselves from the state and its narrowly defined goals. This gives rise to postmodernity and to multiculturalist values that challenge many of the assumptions built into work when it is organized solely in the service of modernity and national development. As Japan continues to develop and the Japanese begin to enjoy the fruits of modernity, many of the tensions between modernity and postmodernity emerge at work.

For some time now, the nature of Japan's postmodernity has been debated. While the general consensus seems to be that Japan's culture has been able to incorporate contrasting elements, doubts remain about the extent to which Japan's social structures demonstrate a similar tolerance or flexibility. This was certainly the view of American policymakers intent on Japan removing various structural impediments in the late 1980s, and structured change did result in changed behavior and new patterns of consumption. Although structural inflexibility in the economy was highlighted by Japan's hesitancy to improve transparency in its financial sector, the Structural Impediments Initiatives also directed attention toward Japan's rigid system of centrally controlled education, segmented labor markets, and other facets of social organization. Change in these domains over the past decade reinforces the view that many structures in Japan have operated independently of a coherent national culture and can be further altered in response to political realignments of power relations.

## 1.3.2    The question of flexibility at work

From the early 1990s the flexibility of the Japanese system with regard to work has been questioned in three areas. One concerns questions of choice and multiculturalism at work. Here "multiculturalism" refers not only to the level of tolerance shown toward newcomers and Japan's different ethnic minorities, but also to flexibility in recognizing or accepting different work patterns to accommodate the handicapped, those with special family responsibilities, those at different points in their life, those with different sexual preferences, and those with different work–leisure ethics. Much of the discussion of these matters by business interests in Japan has correctly pointed out that this kind of flexibility is often very expensive in terms of a firm's economic competitiveness. Chapters 5 and 6 discuss the labor market and suggest that Japan's system for organizing work still appears to be rigidly modernist and assimilationist (i.e. monocultural), although internationalization and various internal forces for postmodernism seem to be producing greater flexibility at work than has been the case in the past.

A second area of concern involves the shift from the clearly defined and easily measured goal of income maximization and more national GDP per capita to the nebulous goal of improving the standard of living and lifestyles. Workers have come increasingly to reassess their goals at work, both materially and psychologically. Those in the modernist mode tend to conclude that the younger generation, spoilt by affluence, has lost the work ethic. Modernists may also push to widen the scope for individual choice, but relate workways and lifestyle to fairly predictable stages in life. However, the Japanese now access vast information about the outside world via the media and the internet. A growing number tour, study, and do business abroad, often accompanied by their families. During the bubble years many came to see irony in Japan having the highest GNP per capita and the most advanced electronic gadgetry in the world while many citizens experienced circumstances associated with the early stages of economic development: substandard housing, long hours of work, and poor infrastructure for leisure-time activities and for medical care.

The third set of choices relate to the nature of the work ethic, the commitment of the Japanese to their work organizations, and the balance between voluntarism and regimentation or between self-discipline and institutionalized discipline. The distinction between institutional structures and culture is important in assessing the extent to which the Japanese approach to work still relies on structures rather than on culture or shared values. This is odd, given that much of the literature on work in

Japan has traditionally placed heavy emphasis on uniquely Japanese cultural traits or values as major factors facilitating Japan's past economic achievements at the enterprise level. Structures exist at several levels, and behavior in the firm is often shaped by institutions at the national level, and increasingly by global arrangements.

### 1.3.3   Corporatism and the free market economy

Questions concerning the locus of power or decision-making in Japan have been at the center of debate on contemporary Japan for some time (e.g. Stockwin 1980). Numerous observers such as van Wolferen (1990) and McCormack (1996) have argued that decision-making in Japan is diffused in a complex network of interconnected interests. These descriptions, while sometimes intended as a means of delineating the peculiarity of Japan's approach to social organization, are often consistent with those found in writings about power elites and strategic elites in other societies. Pluralists (such as Sone 1989) point to a wide range of participants in Japan's political process. Contributors to Inagami (1995) describe work organization in corporatistic terms as a form of centralized democracy.

This view had appeared earlier in Okochi, Karsh, and Levine (1973), who argued that the organization of work in Japan and in other industrialized societies can usefully be understood in terms of the institutional framework earlier advanced by Dunlop (1958). They posited that work organizations are shaped by arrangements that incorporate and balance the interests of big business, big government, and big labor. This understanding was also the starting point for Kenny and Florida (1993), who saw Japan's strong union movement immediately after the war as a defining influence on work organization.

Developments of the past decade, however, lead one to question the corporatist framework. The influence of the national peak organizations for labor, including Rengo, has greatly declined. As noted below in chapter 9, the unionization rate has dropped considerably over the past two decades. Rengo's influence on social policy relevant to the wellbeing of many in Japan's labor force has also declined. Once the major political vehicle for organized labor in Japan, the Japan Socialist Party (now the Social Democratic Party) survives in a very shaky manner after a brief taste of coalition power with the Murayama cabinet (1993–6). As Shimizu (1997) and others have suggested, the inability of Japanese unions to affect policy has led many to question the need for Japanese unions to exist at all – a view at odds with the notion that there is a corporatist balance of power.

Such doubts are not new. Galenson and Odaka (1976) questioned whether Japanese unions were really free and meaningfully committed to the interests of their members. Kawanishi (1992a) described how many unions perform as an adjunct to management in the implementation of personnel policies designed by and for management. This is not to ignore the significant role some unions play in enhancing the wellbeing of their members at the firm level (cf. Kawanishi 1992a; Benson 1994 and 1996).

Another difficulty with the corporatist formulation is that the business–government relationship is less cosy and less predictable than in the past. The influence of the Ministry of International Trade and Industry (MITI) has waned considerably over the past fifteen to twenty years, and, despite amalgamation, the peak employer organizations such as Nikkeiren and Keidanren have come to have less sway over their members. In the 1980s Sugimoto (1988) noted a divergence between the forces for "emperor-first capitalism" and those for business-first capitalism. He posited that firms putting profits ahead of the national interest had become conspicuous in the 1980s. The tight linkage of corporate and bureaucratic interests through *shingikai* (government advisory councils) also weakened as radical unionism faded and old ministries were restructured by administrative reforms in the late 1990s. In 2001 the Ministry of Labor and the Ministry of Health and Welfare were merged. As the influence of the three main parties determining industrial relations waned, the corporatistic structuring of life also seemed to give way to less institutionalized market forces: a sign perhaps that a civil society was emerging in Japan.

This fits in with the views of a number of writers (e.g. Mouer and Sugimoto 1995 and 2003; Rifkin 1996; Garten 1997; Nikkei Bijinesu 1997) who suggest that the end of the cold war was accompanied by increased international competition and a new level of economic rationalism at the firm level. They point to fundamental ways in which a number of elements at the global level are coming to affect the organization of work as it evolves in Japan and elsewhere at the beginning of the twenty-first century. As the organization of work is restructured to incorporate advances in information technology and communications, it is perhaps useful to think of how labor process is being shaped simultaneously on three different, though overlapping, levels. In considering the future of work in contemporary Japan, the concerns mentioned in this section have shifted attention either up to the suprastructural factors at the international or global level or down to the firm and other factors at the local level. However, as the influence of big government, big business and big labor declines, there is a danger that other phenomena at the national level will be overlooked.

Without introducing the debate on the continuing significance of the nation state in the global era, this is, then, an argument that a thorough discussion of labor process must consider work relations at the *macro level* (used here to refer to factors shaping global standards and the international division of labor in terms of the world system), at the *meso level* (referring here to the many institutional arrangements influencing how work is organized at the national level), and at the *micro level* (referring primarily to how work is organized at the local level in specific firms and in regionally based industries). There is also a danger that the importance of institutional or structural differences will be downplayed as attention focuses on universal trends: the decline in permanent fixed-shift employment, falling unionization rates, the end to the long-term decline in the working hours of permanent employees, the multiculturalization of the labor force, the aging of the population, growing social inequality, and change in the family. Looking at fourteen nations around the world, the contributions to Cornfield and Hodson (2002) emphasize the continued importance of national differences in work organization while also acknowledging these common trends.

### 1.3.4    *The generation of surplus*

The fiftieth anniversary of the Marshall Plan in May 1997 drew attention to the importance of capital in the postwar economic recovery of Europe. The success of the Plan demonstrated a simple truth in the work of Rostow (1959) and others writing about economic development: ongoing capital accumulation is a sine qua non for economic growth. They argued that societies progressed through a series of stages with the rate of savings increasing to a critical level where economies "took off," and then to even higher levels in periods of very high growth, before dropping back to levels necessary to sustain high productivity.

Continuing to present this simple truth, writers on the advanced economies over the past few decades have come to recognize that surplus for capital formation is a necessary but not always sufficient condition for growth to occur. The lower rates of productivity found in many Western nations during the 1970s and 1980s were attributed to excessive spending, some of which was by the state for social welfare and social justice. In some countries, military spending has also eroded savings. Subsequent efforts to constrain public spending in such areas has shifted attention to the microeconomic level and to what private firms can achieve when unfettered by taxes and regulations. Here, certain aspects of Japanese-style management (e.g. just-in-time arrangements and enterprise bargaining) have been featured as ways in which firms can achieve higher levels of productivity. Massive restructuring in large economic organizations has not stopped simply with the removal of waste. The overall belt-tightening in firms has resulted in more careful regulation of labor inputs and the intensification of work among those who remain in permanent employment. This has obviously affected the way work is organized in Japan.

Many writers suggest that the new advances in information technology now drive a new kind of industrial revolution. Less prominently noted is the fact that these changes in the economy's technological base are requiring new levels of capital accumulation for another takeoff and for the sustained growth that is meant to follow. Accordingly, for the foreseeable future, work organization is likely to be characterized by the ongoing change needed to sustain a process of capital formation and accumulation. The changes required for the necessary savings to be achieved may be seen in various social developments. One is the growing inequality in the distribution of income. This trend needs to be understood not only in each of the advanced economies of the world, but also in terms of the growing gap between the rich and the poor nations as world production systems come to institutionalize divisions of labor on a global scale (Korzeniewicz and Moran 1997).

Japan is again a key case. Huge investments are required if the Japanese economy is to transform itself in the high-tech era in order to improve its competitiveness in world trade. Already Japan feels pressured by China's emergence as an economic powerhouse. Central to Japan making the transition will be the mechanisms for generating surplus. Doubt since the 1990s about whether Japan's financial institutions will perform well in this regard has caused many of Japan's most dynamic enterprises to push for labor market deregulation. The demand for freedom to maneuver their labor force more flexibly focuses attention on how the Japanese state will balance efforts to generate economic surplus with the need to provide economic security to citizens at work. While some writers have indicated that work organization will have to change fundamentally in more globalized economies (Rifkin 1996; Lipietz 1997), some such as Kumazawa (1996 and 1997) have noted that this transition is already producing in Japan various mechanisms to squeeze labor further. This is consistent with the view that Japanese-style management in the 1970s and 1980s had become an accentuated form of "ultra-Fordism" rather than the harbinger of "post-Fordism." The earlier debate on Fordism reminds us that an understanding of how work is organized in Japan must include a careful consideration of how labor process at the micro level functions within the broader context of labor process at the meso (national) and macro (global) levels.

## 1.4    Work ideology in the changing world system

To develop further a sociology of labor in Japan, attention needs to be given to how the new technologies are shaping interaction between labor processes on the global, national, and local levels, as individuals, organizations, and states seek to generate economic surplus. Work intensification, casualization, and changes in the wage system have been markedly shaped by power relations between the "big three." As new forces emerge at the local and international levels and the fundamentals of ownership change, especially as they relate to industrial property (i.e. the production, movement, and control of information) and to citizenship, further tensions will emerge from the clash between ideologies pushing for the modern and those advocating the postmodern. Following the cold war, attention shifted away from the East–West divide and from comparisons of how capitalist or market economies stacked up against socialist or command economies. However, even though socialism is now widely seen as a failed blueprint for economic development, if not for social development more generally, it is difficult to conclude that we will see the end of ideology as predicted by Bell (1960) over forty years ago, or Fukuyama (1993) more recently. Hampden-Turner and Trompenaars (1994) argue that there are at least seven cultures of capitalism. As the competition between capitalist nations intensifies, debate will likely come to revolve around the superiority of specific approaches to capitalism.

The "Look East policies" of Malaysia and Singapore in the 1980s and early 1990s combined ideas about work organization in Asia with assumptions about Asian modes of democracy. Mahathir and Ishihara (1994) and others argue that Asian values require a different approach to social organization. Although the final outcome may be a move toward global standards, it will likely be some time before we see the ultimate capitalist system combining best capitalist world practice in all spheres of economic and social activity. The experience with national systems of industrial relations has been that complex institutions have a life of their own and that such institutions are revamped only every fifty to a hundred years. It is thus important to consider the extent to which Japan's institutions at the national level accommodate or compromise "global standards."

To understand the forces shaping the future of work in advanced capitalist economies, it is useful to assess how the debate on different capitalisms is shaping the world system. Much of the recent discussion of trade strategies in international forums is about the balance to be struck between working and living. Two general categories of concern are central to any assessment of competing brands of capitalism. One is the way work is organized and relates to the right, the privilege, the opportunity, and/or the duty to work. The other involves the goals to be achieved through work.

## 1.5    Toward a superior work ethic?

Several yardsticks are used to evaluate competing economic models. Some time ago Wilcox (1966) identified eight criteria for the task. Here two are considered: efficiency and the freedom to choose.

### 1.5.1    *Efficiency*

The first criterion is whether one system of production is more efficient than another. The focus on efficiency is largely about the ability of systems to export and to generate balance-of-payments surpluses. That ability was mentioned above as a major reason why national systems of industrial relations become widely accepted as models for other societies. The importance of this criterion will be enhanced by moves to more open trade through the World Trade Organization (WTO). With freer trade in capital, technology, ideologies and culture accompanying the more market-oriented approach of the WTO, the competitive advantage of many local areas may not go much beyond the productivity of locally based labor. Microeconomic reform is about making those workers more efficient and testing their efficiency through competition (e.g. deregulated labor markets).

Most assessments of Japan, beginning with two OECD reports on the Japanese system of industrial relations in the 1970s, have rated highly the contributions of Japanese labor to Japan's overall economic competitiveness. Japan is now confronted by the need to squeeze from its labor force further productivity while maintaining higher levels of commitment. By choosing to further deregulate Japan's labor markets, policymakers are challenging established understandings about the rewards and incentives previously seen as keys to motivating the Japanese labor force. The issues raised by this dilemma are addressed at various points throughout this volume as central to any assessment about the peculiarities that might distinguish Japanese capitalism from other versions.

### 1.5.2    *Choice and free trade*

A key issue arising out of the commitment to free trade is how to conceive of the right to compete in the free trade of goods and services. These concerns link back through time to questions of colonialism, economic imperialism, and economic dependence. Do workers in industrialized countries really wish to compete on a level playing field with workers in the non-industrialized world? If so, what are the rules that define notions of fair competition, and who makes those rules? How legitimate are sweat shops? How legitimate as a means of competing is social dumping in the form of lower wages, longer hours of work, poorer housing, and environmental degradation? The consequences of winning or losing the game of national economic competition are such that citizens in many countries can easily be persuaded that various deprivations are a reasonable price to pay for national economic independence.

### 1.5.3    Human rights and the right to compete

Unbridled competition between work organizations ultimately raises questions about human rights and cultural style. Time lags in development often invite accusations of hypocrisy from the less-developed nations. Why were sweat shops or child labor acceptable in eighteenth-century England but are not in twenty-first-century Bangladesh? Why does the coverage given to the Olympics and to many other international sporting events by the Western-dominated media legitimate one kind of child labor that later leads to stardom in the entertainment industry while the same media condemn child labor when it occurs in a factory?

While these kinds of issues seldom surfaced in Japan–US trade disputes, assumptions about which structural arrangements for work are "fair" or "unfair" did. Many Japanese continue to be resentful of what they see as American attempts to impose its inconsistent norms as "global standards." Such attempts are seen ultimately as abrogating the right to compete and limiting the right of nations to set and to control working conditions in line with the wishes of their citizens. As a means to an end, the right to compete is the right to work, and that is in turn the right of workers to accept regimentation to achieve national goals. In contemporary Japan *karoshi* (death from overwork) has been seen as a serious problem (Karoshi Bengodan Zenkoku Renraku Kaigi 1991), but if the Japanese wish to pay that price, do most Europeans, Australians, or North Americans still wish to compete? Free trade arrangements for financial services and the flow of investment have come increasingly to mean that the price of failure could well be selling off "the farm" or a nation's cultural assets to more competitive foreign interests. Another consideration is the fact that the amount of effort required to gain independence often appears to be greater than that necessary to maintain a competitive advantage once this has been achieved. A third is that workers in more competitive economies often become "embourgeoised" once an affluent lifestyle is achieved.

The challenge is more starkly stated when translated into hours of work. Japan's annual average of 2,100–2,200 hours *circa* 1990 contrasted sharply with the 1,500–1,600 hours recorded in many European countries. While the extra leisure enjoyed by many Europeans might be regarded as a kind of reward for superior efficiency, a free trade regime will, *ceteris paribus*, result in Japan's longer hours of work putting pressure on workers in those societies to follow suit. Similarly, still longer hours and lower labor costs in China are seen as pressuring Japanese workers. Given the general acknowledgment that many Japanese workers are doing "service overtime" (unrecorded, and therefore free, overtime for their employers), some between 500 and 800 hours a year, it is not idle to speculate about mechanisms in Japan that might ensure that Japanese workers cannot be prodded into working 2,500 hours a year in order to improve their international competitiveness.

Although the Japanese model now draws less interest, Japanese views on these matters are relevant to policymakers elsewhere. Leaving aside the very public contribution of Japanese commentators to Australian thinking about its levels of industrial disputation at the end of the 1970s, and less obvious Japanese influence contributing to the introduction of enterprise bargaining, one might speculate about how the publicity given to Japanese perceptions at the end of the 1980s that Australians were all "large, lazy and lucky" (Ormonde 1992) facilitated work intensification and the rise in the hours of work in Australia over the 1990s. Because hours of work fell remarkably in Japan during the 1990s, and Japan is no longer so different in this regard, the Japanese experience is relevant to the management of international competition and to assessments of Asian values and propositions that the appropriateness of certain social arrangements (including regimentation at work) is determined by overall levels of productivity and what a society (and its individuals) can reasonably afford. Japanese policymakers continue to grapple with the trade-offs between efficiency and social justice and with how best to motivate younger workers with a diverse range of interests. In order to assess that tradeoff, a fuller appreciation of the factors shaping the Japanese "commitment" or "willingness" to work long hours is needed.

Central to any evaluation of the long hours of work recorded in Japan at the beginning of the 1990s is an assessment of how voluntarily Japanese workers work. If the long hours of work recorded in Japan are just a reflection of a culturally ordained work ethic (i.e. the joy of working as much as possible), the appropriate response in societies wishing to compete may simply be to exhort their own workers to work longer or harder or with more commitment. If, however, Japanese work habits are seen to be the product of structures which reward and penalize workers for differences in hours worked, then there are questions about human rights at work, about the desirability of having international standards, and about the tradeoff between hours of work, productivity, and voluntariness.

## 1.6    Toward an understanding of work in Japan

The preceding discussion suggests there are competing visions of how work is organized in Japan. This should not be surprising; Japan is a complex society. Its economy consists of large and small firms, male and female employees, those with more education at elite institutions and those with less education at mediocre schools, various industries and geographic regions, unionized and non-unionized workers. For persons positioned differently in the Japanese economy, work will obviously mean different things and result in different understandings. These variations will be most apparent at the micro level.

This volume tries to capture some of the context or milieu in which the Japanese make choices about work. As indicated above, the context for work can be conceived on three levels: the macro or international, the meso or national, and the micro, firm-specific, or local. Workers and management interact most at the micro levels. Many studies, including a number of good ethnographies, have thrown light on how work is organized at the firm level.

At the other end of the spectrum, few workers or managers have much input on the international stage. Decisions there are often made beyond the boundaries of most states. The extent to which Japan as a nation state or the Japanese as private citizens are able to affect decisions at the global level increasingly deserves careful attention as global civil society emerges. At the national level, individual workers also have little direct input, although some may have a collective input through their unions. Managers at large firms, however, are probably more likely to affect arrangements for work at the national level in Japan. They most often do so through industrial federations and have an input into the formation of industrial policy. Management at medium-sized and smaller firms and representatives of regional economic interests may have varying amounts of influence. In democracies like Japan individuals can and do compete to support political parties with quite different social agendas at the national level. Out of that competition (or lack of it) emerges the overall framework structuring inequality, social welfare and redistributive mechanisms, education, and the political balance of power. The mosaic of institutions, legislation, practices, and political alliances which emerges at this level very much colors the milieu in which each worker makes choices in their own world of work. The outcomes at the national or "meso" level set parameters limiting the choices available to individuals when they think about their work.

The literature on industrial relations and labor law in Japan at the meso level is abundant. It tends to be framed largely in terms of how institutions function from the point of view of policymakers. Less emphasis has been placed on how that framework delineates the choices confronting workers on an everyday basis. This volume considers how the meso level impinges on those choices and affects labor process in Japan's external labor markets.

This book does not seek to provide a definitive introduction to all aspects of work in Japan. In focusing on the meso or national level, it has left discussion of in-house concerns at the firm level for another volume. Such a volume would also consider more carefully the everyday life concerns and the ways work and individual life courses are conceptualized within the context of the family. Although work organization is increasingly coming to be influenced by international bodies (such as the WTO or the ILO) and by the diffusion of international standards across a wide range of domains (including social welfare, education, skill classifications, working conditions, and labor market reform), these influences are also beyond the scope of this book.

Written as an introduction to the world of work in Japan, this volume is conceived as an eclectic exercise. Several disciplines deal with work. The sociology of work has been greatly enriched by reference to a wide range of competing paradigms. An effort was made in writing this volume to introduce a range of paradigms providing insight into how work is organized in Japan, and the views of those in industrial relations, management studies, the organizational and administrative sciences, philosophy, anthropology, and psychology are incorporated.

The study of work also embraces a concern with comparative issues. Here it is important to balance an emphasis on Japan's uniqueness with an awareness of the universal. Japan is a society with a long social history. Over many centuries various traditions and practices developed which continue to shape the organization of work in Japan and the vocabulary for talking about work. While Wigmore's volumes on commercial practices in Tokugawa Japan (1969–75) suggest that it would be wise to eschew gross generalizations about work, even when referring to traditional Japan, a discernible rhythm to work in contemporary Japan nevertheless distinguishes it from work elsewhere. Knowledge of that ethos provides a general mindset or common ground for the Japanese to exchange views about work. At the same time, the way work is experienced in contemporary Japan varies greatly as a result of one's positioning in a complex and very segmented labor market. Moreover, the organization of work is increasingly being shaped by the logic of production technologies found elsewhere and by developments in the global economy.

Over the years, the debate on convergence and divergence has centered on Japan because it was the first Asian nation to industrialize (e.g. see Cole 1971; Rohlen 1974). Social scientists and other observers were interested in whether Japan's Asianness or its industrialization would be the more influential factor shaping social life in Japan. Those believing in convergence (such as Cole 1971) argued that Japanese society would gradually become more like Western societies as it adopted similar industrial technologies. They saw convergence as a logical outcome of the push to modernize. Other scholars (such as Rohlen 1974) argued that Japanese society would remain culturally and socially distinct, reflecting Japan's different history and its unique culture. Rather than being dominated by the logic of industrialism, they argue, Japan has achieved new levels of economic choice which will allow it increasingly to articulate its difference in economic terms and in the way work is organized.

A third position was taken by Dore (1973), who argued that reverse convergence might occur, a position which seems reasonable given the overseas interest in Japanese-style management in the 1980s. A fourth, less optimistic, scenario would be that associated with Huntington's (1992) notion of civilizations tenaciously fighting to survive and constantly jostling for position in the new world order. Whatever the process of cultural diffusion and social change might be, the preceding discussion in this chapter has underlined the importance of considering the Japanese experience with work in a comparative perspective and in terms of its linkages to the experiences of other countries.

The continuing debate on convergence and divergence raises interesting and challenging questions about the nature of social change. The debate has also injected into discussions of work in Japan the important distinction between function and form. Cole's (1971) discussion of functional equivalents allows us to see similarities in terms of the overall functioning of society, while cultural differences remain in terms of forms.

## 1.7    The structure of this volume

This chapter has provided a broad context in which the political economy of work links hours of work to the nation's economic competitiveness. The next chapter introduces the Japanese literature on work, focusing on the sociology of work and its attention to the paradoxical coexistence of high levels of commitment to work and high levels of alienation born out of the harsh conditions under which many Japanese have labored. It discusses eight streams of scholarship dealing with work and tells the story of the uncovering of a dual consciousness among Japan's employees. On the distributive side, the poor working conditions and the constraints imposed by management at the place of work are mentioned. The other concern has been with efficiency – the dictates of the market and the realities of the firm as a socioeconomic entity. Although it is the acceptance of "managerial wisdom" that is usually associated with paternalism and Japanese-style management, traditional concerns with social justice and the associated *emic* vocabulary in the union movement still surface in the everyday lives of employees and their families.

Chapter 3 develops further the framework beginning to take shape in chapter 2. It identifies four paradigmatic approaches for considering work in contemporary Japan, and then introduces four influential figures writing about work in contemporary Japan. It concludes by presenting a multilevel framework for considering work organization in Japan.

Chapter 4 presents data on hours of work in Japan, the aspect of workways in Japan most commonly cited in the literature on Japan's international competitiveness as setting Japan apart from advanced industrialized economies. As mentioned above, some cite long hours of work as evidence of a strong commitment to the firm and to an especially strong work ethic in Japan. For others, the same long hours symbolize the extremes of unbridled competition and the excesses of an ultra-Fordist approach to regimenting work. While the chapter concludes that hours of work in Japan are probably long compared to those in many other similarly industrialized societies, it also recognizes the long-term trend toward shorter hours of work, and eschews a tendency to exaggerate the extent to which work in Japan is characterized by excessively long hours.

The remaining chapters focus on the meso-level milieu in which choices about work are made by most Japanese individuals in the context of their families. They describe a milieu in which many Japanese choose to work or feel impelled to work long hours. They identify as the main reason for the continuing trend toward a shorter work year in Japan the gradual loosening of structural constraints rather than changing cultural values per se. Chapters 5 and 6 consider how the labor market is structured. Chapters 7 and 8 consider how labor law and redistributive social policies provide parameters shaping industrial relations and civil minimums for Japan's workers. Chapters 9 and 10 provide brief overviews of management organizations and labor unions which, along with the government and bureaucracy of Japan, share power in determining those parameters and minimums.

The volume concludes with a look to the future, commenting on how the elements go together and on the issues that have begun to surface at the beginning of the twenty-first century as the economy and society of Japan continue to internationalize in the face of globalization. Returning to some of the issues raised in this chapter, the conclusion comments on tensions currently shaping discussions about the future of work in Japan.

As an introduction to understanding work in Japan, this volume is written with two principal audiences in mind. The first consists of students who are informed about industrial relations and the sociology of work but who do not have a knowledge of work in Japan. The second consists of students who possess a basic knowledge of Japanese society but do not have a full grasp of issues concerning work.

In providing an introduction to the world of work in Japan, the authors seek to provide a perspective useful in considering the following questions:

(1) Why have the Japanese worked longer hours in the postwar period?
(2) How do meso-economic, political, and social environments limit the choices Japanese employees have regarding their work?
(3) Who are the major actors shaping the choices which Japanese workers have at the meso level?
(4) How much variation is there in the environments in which Japanese workers find themselves?
(5) In what meso-level context are workways practiced in Japan, and how does the Japanese context differ from those found elsewhere in other similarly advanced economies?
(6) How are certain interests served by the competing perspectives on the above questions?
(7) What forces exist to change the way work is presently conducted in Japan?

While no chapter will deal with all of these questions, it is the authors' earnest desire that the volume as a whole will assist readers in formulating their own answers to the questions listed above. As in any introductory treatment, the brushstrokes are necessarily broad; significant details and some issues have been glossed over. Nevertheless, the authors have endeavored to provide a snapshot that will capture the complexities characterizing work organization in Japan. They welcome any feedback and hope there will be an opportunity to revise their thinking in future writings on work in Japan.

# 2 Toward a sociology of work in postwar Japan

## 2.1 Perspectives on work in Japan

Scholars researching the organization of work in Japan can be characterized in terms of their interaction with eight scholarly traditions. Each grouping has had its own traditions, professional associations, and publishing outlets. Many scholars have worked across several of these traditions in their efforts to understand how work is organized in Japan and what the resultant processes have meant for Japan, for the Japanese firm, and for the individual Japanese worker. Although one can delineate a number of coherent intellectual approaches as distinct streams of scholarship, one must also recognize that they overlap.

This chapter has three aims. One is to introduce eight streams of research on work in Japan and to indicate how the insights of each bear on our understanding of how work is organized in Japan. The second is to trace some of the main arguments that have emerged in the attempt to grasp how individual workers have come to develop a work ethic. These overviews are presented as a means of encouraging readers to develop multiple perspectives when formulating their views on the work ethic in Japan.

The third aim is to have readers think about the methodology of studying work. Compared with the approach taken to studying work by many scholars in North America and Europe, Japanese intellectuals have been reluctant to engage in participant observation or extended participation. Rather, they have conducted in-depth interviews with broad cross-sections of workers. Exceptions include Kamata (1973 and 1982), a journalist who worked at a subsidiary of the large automobile manufacturer, Toyota. Another would be Shimizu (1996), a novelist who has drawn on earlier work experiences to portray the workplace and its inhabitants. Although a small number of labor sociologists in Japan have shown an interest in methodologies which result in interaction with working people, the paucity of close encounters with the workplace and its inhabitants in Japanese studies of work contrasts with the heavy reliance on such approaches by foreign scholars studying work in Japan. The studies by Cole (1971), Rohlen (1974), Clark (1979), the contributors to Plath (1983), Kondo (1990), Dalby (1985), and others rely on participant observation or other methods of close interactive observation and stand out in this regard.

The next section of this chapter provides a brief overview of various competing paradigms or streams of research that provide insight into how work is organized in Japan. The development of the sociology of labor is then discussed, with a focus on worker motivation. The following section considers four paradigmatic approaches used by contemporary writers on work in Japan.

## 2.2 Eight intellectual traditions focused on understanding work in Japan

Although there is much overlap, meaningful distinctions can be drawn between the approaches to studying work organization in terms of (a) the phenomena on which each focuses, (b) the sense of relevance and the outcome most commonly sought, (c) research methodology, and (d) the unit of analysis most frequently used. An overview of the major approaches is presented in table 2.1. A full list of the main persons associated with each of the streams would show that many individuals have been active in more than one stream.

The world of work has generated debate among Japanese academics and other intellectuals over the past hundred years. One concern has been with understanding how new technologies alter organizational requirements and power relations in ways that fundamentally influence work culture and practices, the social stratification matrix, and the lines of cleavage that fragment or segment the labor force and the larger society. Another focus has been the mobilization and melding of the labor force to achieve the aims of the state. A third has been the effect of new products and services on Japan's consumer culture and on the work ethos of ordinary citizens as they attempt to mesh their work life (on the production side) with family life and a certain standard of living (on the consumption side). Over the years attention has focused on what appears to be the paradox of the Japanese work ethic: the general tendency of Japanese to accept long hours of work and other forms of discipline without the full returns or the rewards generally associated with having done concomitant work in many other advanced economies.

The discussion tends to progress from a consideration of approaches most concerned with the social context in which work occurs to those more focused on individual outcomes. A loosely chronological order is

Table 2.1 Approaches to understanding labor processes and the organization of work in Japan

| | A. Social policy | B. Studies on the labor movement | C. Industrial sociology/ anthropology | D. Industrial relations | E. Human resource management (Japanese-style management) | F. Labor economics | G. Sociology of work (Labor sociology) | H. Science of work |
|---|---|---|---|---|---|---|---|---|
| Japanese term | Shakai seisaku ron | Rodo undo ron (roshi kankei ron) | Sangyo shakaigaku Sangyo jinruigaku | Roshi kankei ron | Nihonteki keiei ron | Rodo keizaigaku | Rodo shakaigaku | Rodo kagaku |
| Intellectual origins | Germany | England Japan | England America | America | Japan | America | England France America Japan | Germany |
| Phenomena most concerned with | Workability of state policies concerning work arrangement | Labor unions and labor movement | Institutions which structure and facilitate the organization of work at the firm level | System for the regulation of the collective (organized) interests of the state, employers, and workers | Personnel management strategies | Workings of the labor market as it determines the composition of the work force, labor mobility, wages, and other working conditions | Labor process The workers' consciousness Union behavior | Physiology of work and fatigue Poverty (household expenditures and the uses of time) |
| Significant outcome sought from research | Social unity (fairness and integration of worker into society) maximizing social efficiency | A more effective labor movement which better serves the interests of workers vis-à-vis the interests of monopoly capital | Understanding of work organization The management of alienation generated by work arrangements | Economic development | Effective personnel management | More effective labor market and allocation of labor in terms of having an efficient economy | A more egalitarian society for workers and managers A more effective union movement | Healthy work force |
| Main methodology | Government policy Documents and statistics | Interviews with labor leaders Union documents | Attitudinal and behavioral surveys | Government policy documents Government statistics | Case studies based on interviews with management Company documents | Government and industry-based survey data and statistics Enterprise surveys | Interviews with workers (Participant) observation of the workplace | Physiological experiments Observation of the workplace |

| | The state and national policy | The union | Employee and interpersonal relations | Case studies based on interviews with key players | Management organization | Surveys of individuals | Historical documents | Analysis of household records and time sheets |
|---|---|---|---|---|---|---|---|---|
| Major unit of analysis | The state and national policy | The union | Employee and interpersonal relations | System disputes | Management organization / Culture | The individual and mechanisms | Division of work / The worker / The union | Body |
| Main Japanese writers associated with the approach | OKOCHI Kazuo / KOSHIRO Kazutoshi / HANAMI Tadashi | TOTSUKA Hideo / YAMAMOTO Kiyoshi / HYODO Tsutomu / SHIRAI Taishiro / FUJITA Wakao | MATSUSHIMA Shizuo / MANNARI Hiroshi / OKAMOTO Hideaki | NAKAYAMA Ichiro / KOSHIRO Kazutoshi / HANAMI Tadashi | TSUDA Masumi / IWATA Ryushi / NAKAYAMA Ichiro / HAZAMA Hiroshi | KOIKE Kazuo / SANO Yoko / ONO Akira / SHIMADA Haruo | ODAKA Kunio / MATSUSHIMA Shizuo / HAZAMA Hiroshi / KAWANISHI Hirosuke / KAMATA Satoshi / KUMAZAWA Makoto / SHIMIZU Ikko and similar novelists | FUJIMOTO Takeshi / SHIMOYAMA Fusao / KAGOYAMA Kyo / KAROSHI Bengodan |
| Major academic associations | Shakai Seisaku Gakkai | Rodo Undo Kenkyusha Shudan | Nihon Roshi Kankei Kenkyu Kyokai | Nihon Roshi Kankei Kenkyu Kyokai | Soshiki Gakkai / Kei-eishi Gakkai | | | |
| Major journals | *Shakai Seisaku Gakkai Nenpo* | *Gekkan Rodo Mondai* | *Nihon Rodo Kenkyu Zasshi* | *Nihon Rodo Kenkyu Zasshi* | *Soshiki Gakkai Nenpo* / *Kei-eishi Gakkai Nenpo* | | | *Rodo Kagaku* |
| Major research organizations | | | Nihon Rodo Kenkyu Kiko | Nihon Rodo Kenkyu Kiko | | | | Rodo Kagaku Kenkyujo |
| Main writers in English to consult | Sheldon Garron / Ehud Harari | Joe Moore / Andrew Gordon / Matthew Allen | Robert Cole / Ronald Dore / Rodney Clarke / Thomas Rohlen | Solomon Levine / Ronald Dore | Richard Pascale / William Ouchi / Robert Ballon / Ronald Dore | Robert Evans / Koji Taira / KOIKE Kazuo | Jon Woronoff / Robert Cole | |

followed to provide the reader with some sense of how each intellectual milieu and ethos has evolved. A cursory examination of the competing intellectual traditions reveals that their development reflects not only stages in Japan's industrial development, but also distinct periods in the political and social economy of Japan and the Japanese state.

### 2.2.1    The Social Policy School (Shakai Seisaku Gakkai)

As an urban working class began to emerge at the end of the nineteenth century, the "labor problem" (rodo mondai) (the tensions arising out of poor or exploitative working conditions and the need for intervention to protect many in the labor force) began to draw the attention of policy-makers and those with a serious interest in the directions in which the nation was heading. Leaders in late developers like Japan and Germany knew from the experience of early developers like the United Kingdom that serious social unrest could easily result from the dislocations associated with industrialization. In Germany the Society for the Study of Social Problems was formed in 1872 to promote studies facilitating the state taking an active role in regulating work and industrial relations, so that the nation could develop and modernize as quickly as possible. Soon afterwards the Japanese government began sending students to study social policy in Germany, with the expectation that it too would develop policies to expedite Japan's modernization and industrialization by carefully dealing with a range of problems emerging from the dislocation and poor working conditions experienced by its labor force. If not managed properly, it was held, the tensions produced by rapid social and economic change could seriously delay or even derail Japan's efforts to develop.

The Japanese state at that time was being structured around an imperial ideology that promoted and legitimated paternalistic approaches to work organization. To implement that ideology, policies were developed to repress independent labor unionism. In that climate, the study of labor unions and the working class was beyond the imagination of those who formed Japan's Society for the Study of Social Policy (Shakai Seisaku Gakkai) in 1896. The Society's first national conference in 1907 focused on "The Factory Law and the Labor Problem" and supported the ameliorative approach being taken by "responsible" leaders at that time. The Society was blatantly pro-capitalist, although its early thrust was reformist rather than revolutionary. Following World War I an increasing number of the Society's members began to criticize the social policy approach from a Marxist class-based perspective, and schisms within the Society made it difficult for it to continue as an effective forum.

After the Pacific War, Professor Okochi Kazuo from Tokyo University played a key role in reconstituting the Society for the Study of Social Policy. Japan's defeat left the prewar imperialists discredited. The right to dissent came to be recognized, and trade unions were legalized for the first time. The years immediately after the war were characterized by militant unionism and open conflict in much of Japanese industry. While there seemed to be a general agreement that the government needed to intervene so that minimal standards and a safety net could be established to ensure the welfare of the ordinary worker, as described in Okochi (1970) and Kazahaya (1973), debate focused on the essence of social policy. One group led by Okochi argued that social policy should be driven by the needs of progressive capitalism. Another group gathered around Professor Kishimoto Eitaro (Kyoto University) and Hattori Eitaro (Tohoku University). It argued that a basic conflict of interest existed between workers and capitalists, and that the different needs of the two classes could not be ascertained simply by enlightened government policy. Its view was that power relations between the two were central to any understanding of workgroups.

While that debate was occurring, Okochi, Sumiya Mikio, and Ujihara Shojiro led a group of scholars at Tokyo University's Social Science Research Institute (Shakai Kagaku Kenkyujo, which is commonly referred to as "Shaken") in developing a number of empirical studies on the union movement and on the actual state of work in postwar Japan. Their research shifted attention to the worker and took the understanding of work organization in Japan to new levels (see Ujihara 1966). It dealt with various aspects of labor market segmentation (focusing on temporary and casual employment, on small and medium-sized firms, and on women workers), working conditions (pay levels, the wage system, and hours of work), livelihood issues (related to economic security, household budgets, housing, welfare and leisure), and industrial relations.

From the late 1970s, the union movement declined markedly, and the state came increasingly to be concerned with (i) international pressures for liberalizing the economy, and with (ii) the need for Japanese firms to internationalize in order to maintain their competitiveness in an increasingly globalized economy. Accordingly, social policy has often been treated within the broader confines of economic policy. A look at the membership of the Society for the Study of Social Policy will reveal that economists, labor law specialists, and scholars with specialized and/or practical knowledge of specific aspects of work organization have come to play a dominant role in various academic associations. Many of its members have served on one or more of the government's many consultative committees (*shingikai*). (Oddly enough, political scientists have played only a minor role in the Society, and have tended to focus on labor policy.) Although the Society has moved away from an emphasis on pure basic research and philosophically reflexive concerns, the Society continues to be an influential professional body that brings together those interested in the organization of work at the macro level in Japan.

### 2.2.2    Theories of worker–capitalist relations (roshi kankei ron)[1] and the union movement (rodo undo ron)

For the first thirty postwar years economists and labor law specialists were strongly influenced by Marxist thinking. Their starting point was often the inevitable contradictions between the working and capitalist classes. As the Society for Social Policy came increasingly to focus on the development of ameliorative labor policies for a conservative government bent on economic development at all costs, a small group of scholars at Tokyo University's Social Science Research Institute focused their work on the inferior working conditions of Japanese workers (their excessively low wages and exceedingly long hours of work) as major factors shaping class relations in prewar Japan. Viewing the relations between workers and capitalists in Japanese society as inherently exploitative, they tended to sympathize with workers as the underdogs and felt morally compelled to volunteer their knowledge and expertise as advisers to various leftist elements in the union movement (which was itself rather factionalized). Their views and research were regularly published in the journal *Gekkan Rodo Mondai* (the Labor Problem Monthly).

As the major national center for organized labor on the left, Sohyo (the General Council of Trade Unions of Japan) came under increasing pressure from conservative governments, management groups, and the more conservative national labor center, Domei (the Japanese Confederation of Labor), in the 1960s and 1970s. Totsuka Hideo, Hyodo Tsutomu, Nakanishi Yo, and Yamamoto Kiyoshi responded by forming the Labor Movement Researchers' Group (Rodo Undo Kenkyusha Shudan) in October 1976. Twice a year they published important summaries of their research and views in special issues of *Gekkan Rodo Mondai*, and called for union organizers to participate in the search for a new leftist-oriented theory of the union movement. However, the union

---

[1] The term *roshi kankei* is written in two ways in Japanese. One uses the character for *shi* which indicates *rodosha-shihonka kankei* (the relations between workers and capitalists). The other uses another character for *shi* which indicates *rodosha-shiyosha kankei* (labor–management relations). The literature cited in this section tends to come from the tradition that uses the first term; the literature in section 2.2.4 continues a tradition that tended to use the second term.

movement continued to move to the right in the 1970s and the interest in radical unionism faded. *Gekkan Rodo Mondai* folded late in 1981, and the group disbanded shortly afterwards. However, a number of scholars (e.g. Nitta Michio and Saguchi Kazuro) have continued the survey tradition developed at the Institute, and some outstanding case studies have been published on unions in Japan, on industrial relations at the plant level, on industrial disputes, and on the introduction of new techniques.

### 2.2.3    Labor economics (rodo keizaigaku)

By 1960 the debate on the essence of social policy had petered out. Looking for a new framework which could explain working conditions (e.g wages and hours of work) and the overall positioning of individuals in the labor market, Sumiya and Ujihara argued that attention should be shifted from normative pronouncements on what *should be* the goals of the policy to the forces actually shaping behavior at work. Sumiya (1954) had earlier argued that attention should be shifted from the doings and thoughts of capitalists and management to the actual lives of workers. In 1960 and 1965 he elaborated further with the proposal that research should bridge the two domains in which the wage worker lived: the economic domain in which his labor was sold in the labor market as an economic commodity and the social domain in which he existed (as a member of the working class). To realize these ambitions a number of younger scholars were sent to study labor economics in America. By the mid-1960s Ujihara (1966: 2–19) was arguing that labor economics (*rodo keizaigaku*) ought to develop as a social science focused on understanding the worker as "economic man" (*keizaijin to shite no rodosha*).

By the late 1960s nearly all economists with an interest in labor and work had shifted to the study of labor economics, reflecting a widespread feeling that the social policy approach would not contribute much more to the understanding of work behavior. The development of labor economics in Japan from the Marxist and classical perspectives gave labor economics in Japan its own characteristics. Nevertheless, the American influence was dominant, and that approach to labor economics is summarized in column F of table 2.1. The approach was explicitly comparative in its orientation; it introduced sophisticated statistical analysis and eschewed engagement with those interested in labor process.

Most prominent in developing the American brand of labor economics (with an emphasis on the economics of education) was the Keio group, which included Obi Keiichiro, Tsujimura Kotaro, Nishikawa Shunsaku, Sano Yoko, Ishida Hideo, and Shimada Haruo (see Nishikawa 1980). Also well known was Koike Kazuo. These scholars analyzed aggregate government survey data, and made inferences about the thinking and behavior of those in the labor force based on choices in the labor market. The approach assumed that workers were autonomous actors. Much of their research was commissioned by the Ministry of Labor or other government agencies. Some obtained quantitative data from a range of historical documents to advance theories about the development of Japan's labor force over the past 100–300 years.

### 2.2.4    Industrial relations (roshi kankei ron)[2]

As Japan entered nearly two decades of high economic growth from the late 1950s, the oligopolization of the economy became more pronounced. The Miike struggle at the Mitsui Mines in Kyushu at the end of the 1950s signaled not only a shift in power from labor to management but also a greater willingness by the government to use the industrial relations machinery to contain disruptive disputes in key industries while leaving the determination of working conditions to collective bargaining and the balance of power between labor and management at the enterprise level.

In 1958 the government passed legislation to establish the Japan Institute of Labour (JIL) (*Nihon Rodo Kyokai*). In 1968 the Japan Industrial Relations Research Association (JIRRA) was formed and the Institute came to house its secretariat. Under the leadership of Nakayama Ichiro (second president of the Institute from 1961 to 1980), JIRRA developed an explicitly comparative agenda, and its members have been active within the International Industrial Relations Association (IIRA) (Sumiya was president of the IIRA from 1979 to 1983). In line with the institutional approach developed by Dunlop (1958), Japanese scholars working in industrial relations in the 1960s and 1970s tended to shift attention from individual choice to the role of institutions in channeling Japan's labor–management relations in directions conducive to Japan's long-term development (see Sumiya 1969; Nakayama 1974 and 1975). While Dunlop referred to the study of the government–management–labor nexus as "industrial relations" (*sangyo kankei*), in Japan "*roshi–kankei*" became the standard term for "labor" management relations.

With its focus on institutions, Japan's industrial relations scholarship overlapped with the social policy framework. Both traditions have shown

---

[2] The character *shi* used here refers to management (i.e. upper-level employees) and shifts attention from questions of ownership which were prominent in the late 1940s and 1950s when the character for *shi* meaning capital (and implying that exploited wage labor stood in opposition to the interests of management and the owners of capital) was widely used in writings about work. From 1960 there is a sharp decline in the characters for labor–capitalist relations and today only the characters for "labor–management relations" are used.

an ongoing interest in labor law, the social welfare system, the machinery for settling disputes, corporatism, and education. Many scholars have participated actively in both groupings. From the early 1970s Shirai (1983), Koike (1988 and 1995), and many others (e.g. Nishikawa 1980) came to integrate (i) quantitative government data and (ii) data from their own customized questionnaires. There have been few careful on-the-ground case studies. The Japan Institute of Labor has come increasingly to be seen as a policy research center for the management of labor and issues relevant to the organization of work.

### 2.2.5    *Japanese-style management (*nihonteki keiei ron*)*

High economic growth and the reestablishment of managerial prerogatives gave Japanese conservatives the confidence to question the extent to which many Japanese intellectuals had come to associate American-style democracy with economic success and all prewar Japanese practices with feudalism, economic backwardness, and Japan's defeat in the Pacific War.

In the 1960s a number of scholars began to emphasize the merits of a paternalistic "Japanese-style" approach to management. Without careful comparative work, they argued that Japan's work practices had been born out of Japan's unique culture that attached an especially strong value to hierarchy, to group or organizational solidarity, and to consensus. Many saw those values embodied in seniority wages, lifetime employment, and enterprise unionism. Writers such as Hazama (1964, 1971, and 1997a), Morikawa (1973), Tsuda (1976, 1977, 1982, and 1987) and Iwata (1974, 1975, 1980, and 1982) argued that Japanese-style management provided a superior form of organization that blended mechanisms promoting economic rationalism with humanistic structures. The detailed work of those scholars, which was both historical and ethnographic, documented the vocabulary used by employees in managing affairs within their firms and provided a humanistic approach to human resource management. In presenting the dynamics of ideological control as culture, some writers came to impose on management an idealistically democratic model by ascribing to it the moral essence of being Japanese.

The interest in Japanese-style management as a cultural phenomenon both at home and abroad contributed to a worldwide interest in corporate identity and commitment, and to a shift in the late 1980s and early 1990s in emphasis from meso-economic to micro-economic reform with quality assurance, just-in-time requirements, *kaizen*, and downsizing. Ironically the ready adoption of many "Japanese" techniques abroad ultimately undermined many assumptions associated with the culturalist arguments. An appreciation of the structural elements grew as those techniques came under increasingly rigorous scrutiny when they were adopted or transplanted abroad. A comparative perspective was fostered: an outlook which brought with it a growing awareness that "Japanese-style" management had precedents abroad (i.e. that it might not be uniquely Japanese) and that it conformed to certain fairly universal principles of management philosophy which had existed for long periods in other countries as well. This requestioning initiated the debate on whether Japanese-style management was post-Fordist or ultra-Fordist (as seen in Kenny and Florida 1993 and in Kato and Steven 1991).

Once assumptions about cultural uniqueness were largely dispelled, many propositions about the allegedly unique cultural underpinnings of Japanese-style management lost their appeal. As an approach to understanding the organization of work in Japan and elsewhere, however, the value of this tradition can now be seen in its emphasis on ethnographic case studies. Although its adherents continue to focus on formal organization and on manifest functions rather than discussions of power relations at work, they developed a methodology firmly based on the management ethos and *emic* vocabulary found on the shop and office floor. In doing so they have clearly demonstrated the importance of paying close attention to the *emic* vocabularies used to motivate workers in many large Japanese firms.

### 2.2.6   *Industrial sociology (*sangyo shakaigaku*)*

Industrial sociology was introduced to Japan from the US by Odaka Kunio (who had come into contact with American sociologists stationed in Japan after the war). Industrial sociology in America had grown out of Elton Mayo's famous Hawthorn experiments, and had developed around the use of interviews and observation to ascertain the state of interpersonal relations on the shop floor. Odaka, however, relied heavily on questionnaires to gauge the extent to which workers were satisfied with management and their unions. Odaka (1952) concluded that most workers felt loyalty both to the firm and to the union.

Odaka's work provided the methodological foundations for much research on workers in postwar Japan. Those following in his footsteps have relied heavily on the questionnaire and sophisticated statistical procedures. They have frequently been commissioned to carry out large-scale surveys for the government and its agencies. With the greatly enhanced capacity of computers, Japan's sociologists have refined this technique. Critics point to the tradeoffs between reliability (high) and validity (low), and emphasize the need for more involvement or contact with the workers being studied.

Superior examples of this approach have appeared in the monthly journal of the Japan Institute of Labor, *Nihon Rodo Kenkyu Zasshi* (formerly the *Nihon Rodo Kyokai Zasshi*), *Rodo Kenkyu Shoho* published by Tokyo's Research Centre (Tokyo Toritsu Rodo Kenkyujo), the series of research reports (*Kenkyu Hokoku Shiriizu*) produced by the Sogo Seikatsu Kaihatsu Kenkyujo (a think tank affiliated with Rengo [the Japanese Trade Union Confederation]) and *Rodo Chosa* which is published by the Rodo Chosa Kyogikai (Association for Surveying Workers). Many union and management federations at the industrial level have research divisions that conduct surveys of attitudes and opinions on a regular basis. Such surveys provide a useful basis for gauging changes in the consciousness and everyday behavior of unionists, employees, and managers in Japan.

### 2.2.7   The sociology of labor (rodo shakaigaku)

In the mid-1950s Matsushima Shizuo and Kitagawa Takayoshi led a group of scholars who did not feel the industrial sociologists' questionnaire method had adequately grasped the underlying realities that characterized work organization in Japan. They argued for a case study approach that firmly situates the worker and his choices within a social context defined by employment status, social class and interorganizational relations (e.g. between large and small firms). They rejected the optimistic methodological individualism built into most survey research. The structural approach of the labor sociologists emphasized the preeminent importance of considering power relations. This contrasted with the dominant ideology which tended to see collective behavior as the sum total of individual choices, an attitude reinforced by the consumeristic outlook associated with new choices resulting from Japan's rapid economic growth and the neo-nationalistic confidence born out of that success. As the influence of the industrial sociologists became more prominent in the 1970s and 1980s, structure came to be the preserve of those in industrial relations and labor law at a time when it was fashionable to set structures wholly within a cultural context. Those extolling the virtues of Japanese-style management in the late 1970s and 1980s also shifted attention from structures to culture. In the context of Japan's prosperity it became increasingly difficult politically to talk about the power relations and the processes which shifted economic surplus from workers to management, and labor sociology came to be seen as the sociology of the "unrespectable." Young researchers were drawn to consider how workers could best be managed in structural-functionalistic terms. The more unsavory aspects of laboring (*rodo modai*) came to be overlooked.

To reinvigorate the tradition of labor sociology, Kamata Toshiko, Kawanishi Hirosuke, and others established the Japan Association for Labor Sociology (Nihon Rodo Shakai Gakkai) in 1988. They sought a sociology that would tell the "real story" of workers laboring under Japanese-style management, based on intensive interviews of workers and detailed case study material that could be gleaned only by getting dirty on the shop floor. Another aim was to train young scholars in that tradition and its methodology. A number of economists (such as Kumazawa Makoto) and industrial sociologists (such as Mannari Hiroshi) have been associated with this grouping and the Association's membership stood at 290 members in 2003.

### 2.2.8   The science of labor (rodo kagaku)

The science or physiology of labor developed in response to the prewar priority placed on having a reliable supply of healthy workers physically and mentally fit to serve the needs of national socialism and the state. This tradition has incorporated the work of physiologists and psychologists. The Institute of Labor Science (Rodo Kagaku Kenkyujo) was formed in 1921 to direct research on fatigue, labor productivity, and morale. It integrated sociological perspectives with the findings of natural scientists on the physiology of work. The prewar studies of Ando (1941 and 1944) investigated the number of calories required to do manual work. The wartime studies of Matsushima compared attitudes toward work in Japan's villages and cities and were published in 1951. In the early postwar years that kind of research was linked to studies on poverty and on the minimum household expenditure needed to support a working adult (cf. Rodo Kagaku Kenkyujo 1943, 1954 and 1960). The famous *densangata* wage system (which was common in many industries from the late 1940s until the mid-1950s and remains influential as a model even today) was one outcome of such research in Japan's electric power companies during the war.

The Institute contributed greatly to the postwar understanding of poverty, civil minimums, and the need for safe working conditions (Kagoyama 1953; Fujimoto *et al.* 1965). However, this tradition of scholarship lost some of its urgency as Japan's affluence gave way to a belief in the efficacy of corporate welfarism in the 1980s. In recent years the Institute's research has centered on fatigue and the relationship between work and physical strength, body type, nutrition, health, intelligence, housing, clothing, and other aspects of the workers' daily lifestyle or culture.

## 2.3 Human networks and the sociology of work in postwar Japan

In the preceding discussion two motifs should have been apparent. One is the central role played by academics at Tokyo University. The other is the ongoing interest in issues related to the consciousness of workers as they relate to management and their unions. This section deals with the former and the following section considers the latter.

From 1945 to 1965 a small group at Tokyo University developed comprehensive taxonomies and theoretical frameworks for systematically describing and explaining work in Japan in terms of its labor markets, competing union movements, labor–management relations, industrial disputes, and technological change. The Tokyo University scholars initiated a large number of empirically based case studies and large-scale surveys that still constitute the benchmark for research today. Some intellectual traditions emphasized aspects allegedly peculiar to Japan, and highlighted the *emic* vocabulary for describing work in Japan: *dekasegi-gata rodo* (migrant labor), *kigyobetsu kumiai* (the enterprise union), *nenko-gata romu seido* (seniority-based personnel practices). Many experimented with several of the approaches introduced above. The Tokyo scholars engaged in vigorous debate among themselves and integrated new theoretical perspectives from overseas. Over time this gave way to a growing interest in some of the more universal processes associated with industrialization, economic development, and modernization more generally. Koike's work in the 1980s on external and internal labor markets would be an example of that trend. Nevertheless, reflecting their strong policy orientation, a delicate balance was maintained between conclusions that work practices and attitudes would inevitably be Westernized and those pointing to other paths Japan might follow.

There were several groupings at the University of Tokyo. One was centered in the Faculty of Economics and the closely aligned Social Science Research Institute. Okochi Kazuo was the senior mentor who had begun his career before the war and later served as president of Tokyo University from 1963 to 1968. The first generation of scholars under Okochi included Professors Sumiya Mikio (later the third president of the Japan Institute of Labor from 1980 to 1988, president of Tokyo's Women's College, and president of the IIRA in the early 1980s), Ujihara Shojiro (head of the Social Science Research Institute), and Shirai Taishiro (later professor of economics at Hosei University). The second generation included Totsuka Hideo, Hyodo Tsutomu, Nakanishi Yo, Yamamoto Kiyoshi, Takanashi Akira (later professor of economics at Shinshu University and fifth president of the Japan Institute of Labor from 1996 to 2001), and Koike Kazuo (later professor of economics at Hosei, Nagoya, Kyoto, and again at Hosei). The third generation would now consist of Nomura Masami (professor of economics at Tohoku University), Saguchi Kazuro (professor of economics at Tokyo University), Mori Tetsushi (professor of economics at Tokyo University), Niita Michio (professor of economics in the Social Science Research Institute at Tokyo University), Kamii Yoshihiko (professor of economics at Saitama University), Inoue Masao (professor of economics at Rikkyo University), and Ishikawa Akihiro (professor of sociology at Chuo University).

The Law Faculty of Tokyo University produced the leading experts in labor law over the same period: Ishikawa Kichiemon, Hagisawa Kiyohiko, Fujita Wakao (professor of labor law at the Social Science Research Institute and later at the International Christian University), and Hanami Tadashi (professor of labor law at Sophia University and currently the sixth president of the Japan Institute of Labor). In the university's Department of Sociology (in the Faculty of Letters), Professor Odaka Kunio led a number of investigations into the nature of workplace culture, occupations, and occupational mobility. Many students who studied aspects of work at Tokyo University later occupied important positions in the ministries of Labor and Social Welfare and in many government-funded research institutions such as the Japan Institute of Labor.

Two other centers rate a special mention. Hitotsubashi University and Keio University accelerated the shift from the somewhat normatively oriented policy framework to that of the labor-market-oriented one. Before becoming the second president of the Japan Institute of Labor (1961–80), Nakayama Ichiro too had been a distinguished professor of economics. A contemporary of Okochi, he was president of Hitotsubashi University from 1949 to 1956 and had served as head of the Central Labor Relations Commission from 1949 to 1960. In that role he had practical experience in the famous Miike dispute.

Hitotsubashi's Economic Research Center housed a number of Japan's leading authorities on Japan's economic growth (e.g. Okawa Kazuo and Tsuru Shigeto). By the early 1960s Hitotsubashi was at the forefront of research on the history of Japan's economic growth since the middle of the previous century. Central to explanations of that growth were studies of the labor market. In addition to its quantitative labor economists (e.g. Umemura Mataji and Ono Akira), Hitotsubashi could also boast of having Japan's foremost expert on Japanese-style management, Tsuda Masumi (a product of Okochi's group at Tokyo University). His tradition of scholarship has been maintained by one of his students (Hayashi Hiroki), while another of his students (Sato Hiroki) is currently a professor of sociology at Tokyo University. Odaka Konosuke (son of

Odaka Kunio) is a professor of economics at Hitotsubashi. Kato Tetsuro (a student of Maruyama Masao at the University of Tokyo) has been one of the few political scientists writing about work organization.

The other early center of excellence was Keio University. Its labor economists, many of whom were mentioned above, came to the fore in the 1970s. One of their leaders, Tsujimura Kotaro, became the fourth president of the Japan Institute of Labor from 1988 to 1996. Iida Kanae and Komatsu Ryuji were known for their studies of unions; Chubachi Masami was known for his work on household finances and their relationship to the motivation to work.

As Japan moved through the 1960s and 1970s, the number of private universities expanded rapidly. The postwar baby boom and the higher standard of living produced by Japan's economic growth resulted in an inflated demand for tertiary education. At the same time, Japan's economic successes, especially in the export of manufactures, stimulated substantial public interest in the organization of work, and graduates from the above-mentioned universities were soon found in a large number of "lesser" universities where they trained their own students and prepared them for further study overseas (mainly in North America). Accordingly, from the mid-1970s research on work in Japan is characterized by a greater diversity in style, problem consciousness, and ideological orientation.

The 1970s was a watershed in terms of the fortunes of the main divisions in scholarship on the organization of work. In the early 1960s the schism between a democracy-first grouping on the left and those with an efficiency-first orientation on the right became pronounced. The former was critical of the shift in the union movement from militant confrontation to outright cooperation with management. The second group felt that the interests of the workers were maximized through cooperation with management to lift productivity and thereby each employee's material standard of living. In general the left had boasted close ties with the union movement, and its position was greatly undermined when the Japan Council of the International Metalworkers' Federation gave priority to productivity. As a peak labor organization to the left of center, Domei tacitly supported the determined efforts of successive conservative governments to destroy strong left-wing unions (such as the Japan Teachers' Union or the several unions organizing workers from the Japan National Railways).

While many of the leading scholars of the 1950s (such as Okochi, Sumiya, and Matsushima) had felt free to work across a number of paradigms, movement between or across the streams decreased as the schisms deepened in the 1970s and 1980s. By the early 1980s those working in the conservative social policy framework, labor economics, industrial sociology, and industrial relations had come to be the dominant group. A loose group of dissenting scholarship was formed by those concerned with the detrimental effects of social policy, relations between workers and managers as the guardians of capital, the union movement per se and how to reverse its decline, labor process and labor sociology, and the older traditions of the science of labor. Those emphasizing the cultural uniqueness of Japanese management have largely remained on their own. The last project attempting to bring scholars from the two major groups together was led by Ujihara in the late 1970s, but the fundamental differences remained and were reflected in the resultant volume of unwieldy papers (Roshi Kankei Chosakai 1981).

While the conservative group was able to move ahead with research money and support from the government, conservative unions, and businesses, the other group seemed to fade before the glitter of the economy's bubble years and the neo-nationalist sentiments of the 1980s. After the bubble burst in the early 1990s, however, there seems to have been a renewed interest in critical scholarship on the nature of work and society, as ordinary citizens began to question the disparity between their high average per capita income and their less salubrious standard of living, and to worry about their vulnerability in terms of job security and retirement needs.

## 2.4    Early postwar studies of workers as a community

Studies of working life immediately after the war include the research led by Odaka Kunio (1948) at the traditional Izumo iron works in Shimane Prefecture in 1945 and the research done by Matsushima Shizuo (1951) at various mines in 1947 and 1948. During the war Odaka had researched religious customs among Chinese leather workers on Kainan Island. An officer in the Japanese Army, Matsushima had been responsible for personnel management. Although Odaka had written a volume introducing a sociology of occupations (*shokugyo shakaigaku*) in 1941 and another about changing notions of work in 1944, the research at Izumo presented him with his first opportunity to empirically test this sociological perspective for understanding work. Prewar sociologists had focused largely on kinship, village life, and neighborhood interaction, leaving the formation of communities among workers to the economic historians and business economists.

Going beyond the economist's narrower functional concerns with production and cost considerations, Odaka revealed (a) the extent to which the skilled workers (*shokunin*) were tied together by a social network of mutual obligations which encompassed their families, (b) the rigid status delineations among occupational categories based on notions of skill, (c) a work ethos which incorporated various beliefs which were part of the workers' folk religion, and (d) a strict set of rules by which workers collectively regulated their own behavior. Although the research was based on a partial recording of interviews with only the aged workers, and thus provided a static snapshot of the work organization in the *emic* vocabulary of those who were interviewed, it nevertheless documented the extent to which workers had independently formed a community of their own that could influence the way work was organized.

As a new graduate, Matsushima traveled from railway station to railway station, getting off at a number of places where mines existed in Ibaraki and Akita Prefectures. He too became critical of the economic analyses that did not go beyond the formal organization of work. He argued that the community life of workers determined the way work was actually performed, and documented the terrible working conditions and the strong desire of the workers to escape from their poverty. He reported on how the miners had formed their own self-help relief organizations (called *tomoko*) and identified a complex network of fictive kin relationships which formed the basis of the workers' community and everyday life. He noted the *oyabun-kobun* relationships at the individual level. Those were the fictive kin terms used by those in the paternalistic boss system of employment later described in the work of Bennett and Ishino (1963). The boss system structured labor exchange and provided occupational training. Although the mines soon closed, Nakano (1956) and others found the same *oyabun-kobun* relationships in their studies of an iron casting town (Kawaguchi). They argued further that such relations were vital not only in explaining work in manufacturing, but also for understanding how unions and other associations functioned as living organisms in contemporary Japan.

Similar studies linked this sense of community to the dynamics of poverty. In their efforts to establish a baseline for conceptualizing poverty, researchers were influenced by American scholarship and they soon came to rely on surveys to capture the consciousness of workers. Consequently, the amount of interaction between researchers and the researched declined considerably. The first survey of worker attitudes (*rodosha ishiki chosa*) was carried out in 1947 by the Department of Sociology (Shakaigaku Kenkyushitsu) at the University of Tokyo (Odaka 1952). The economists at the Social Science Research Institute (Shakai Kagaku Kenkyu Jo 1950) conducted a similar survey among unionists to assess the state of the labor movement. The first study concluded that the workers had not themselves produced the demands for change that were being promoted by the union movement (Odaka 1952: 277). Although the survey methodology positioned researchers outside the phenomena they were studying, the economists accepted the union movement as an existing reality that needed to be seen through the eyes of those involved, and were prepared to accept that workers had the will to change social relations (Okochi 1956).

The industrial sociologists sought to view the worker from a distance in a detached manner by sending him surveys, interpreting the results based on a priori assumptions not only about what the workers were thinking but also about what they were (culturally) capable of thinking. Here we can see the culturalist view emerging. A kind of cultural determinism closed off the possibility that workers could change either their thinking about the world or their willingness to accept the status quo and their harsh working conditions. Some have criticized the sociologists for reaching their conclusions before the research started, for then choosing a biased sample, and for using loaded questions to obtain findings in support of their beliefs or ideological positions. Kawanishi (1979: 205; 2001: 24) noted that the survey was distributed to workers in eighteen very small firms in industries that had no unions and only minimal leadership to move in the direction of change. Workers in the heavily unionized sectors (such as the electric power industry, the print media, and the public service) were not surveyed. This was the beginning of a methodological approach that dominated industrial sociology for the next thirty to forty years and reinforced the role of sociologists in creating self-fulfilling prophecies.[3]

The next large project launched by the Tokyo University group of scholars was the "Imono no Machi" survey (Odaka 1956). The research team set out to study the iron (*imono*) workers at Kawaguchi's iron foundries. With the exception of the research by Nakano (1956), which utilized intensive interviews, the research at Kawaguchi was carried out through surveys. A battery of three surveys was distributed to each worker to ascertain his (i) consciousness regarding work, (ii) morale at work, and (iii) socioeconomic characteristics. The inclusion of (ii) reflected an interest in the Hawthorn studies in America and the fact that Odaka had been considerably influenced by Max Weber's work on the ethos of

---

[3] The worst examples of the survey approach can be seen in the generation of the myth of middle-class consciousness whereby Japanese respondents were invited to tick boxes to show they were middle class almost as a reflex action, without any thought as to what 'middle' might actually mean, simply because they had come to read and/or hear from the mass media that they were in the middle class.

work.[4] The concern with stratification resulted from Odaka's reading of Warner's *Yankee City* series (Nakano 1956: 71–2). The first two surveys became the core for the dual consciousness surveys (*niju kizoku ishiki chosa*) which were administered eleven times to a mammoth sample (for the times) of about 20,000 persons between 1952 and 1962. Although the findings appeared to support the view that most workers identified with both their firm's management and their union (Odaka 1956), the research was later criticized by Hazama (1967) (who at the time of the research was a young scholar working under the direction of Matsushima) for (i) yielding little more than a series of cross-tabulations and for (ii) giving ideological approval to the findings.

The third survey in the dual consciousness project became the basis for the famous SSM (social stratification and mobility) surveys that have been conducted every ten years since 1955. Under the leadership of Odaka's successor, Tominaga Ken-ichi, the research came to be dominated by sophisticated statistical analysis that kept it in step with the most recent studies of such phenomena in the US. Although the findings have come to provide extremely important clues to understanding Japanese society, as we note below in chapter 7, the approach took research a long way from the place of work and the milieu which colored the everyday thinking and interactions of workers on the shop floor.

In 1955 Matsushima returned to intensive fieldwork in the mining areas he had first visited in 1947 and 1948. He was critical of those who sought to avoid the issues of social class, and argued that the sociology of labor ought to be concerned primarily with the contradictions that emerge at work as a result of conflicting class interests (Matsushima 1956a and 1956b). Though the contradictions he wrote about were reflected in the dual consciousness surveys, his research "on the ground" provided a basis for linking that split consciousness to the objective realities surrounding work. In their hand-to-mouth existence, he argued, workers sought to survive economic adversity by forming horizontal *tomoko*-type associations, including unions, whose very existence was linked directly to the workers' need for livelihood guarantees (*seikatsu hosho*). Such unions provided a safety net and a minimal amount of economic security. At the same time, he believed that the employees' dependence on the firm created a

---

[4] A number of Weber's writings had been translated into Japanese at about the same pace as they were becoming available in English. *The Protestant Ethic and the Spirit of Capitalism*, for example, was translated into Japanese by Kajiyama Tsutomu and became available from Yuhikiku in 1937, only seven years after Talcott Parsons' English translation appeared in 1930.

need to cooperate with management and to demonstrate overt loyalty to the work organization. His conclusion was that the two consciousnesses were inextricably linked to the objective realities delineating the choices confronting workers.

Matsushima joined with Kitagawa Takayoshi and Hazama Hiroshi to conduct the famous Hitachi mine study in the early 1960s. Their research yielded a portrait of how the workers' consciousness was shaped by the fact that Hitachi Mining had built a company town into a living community by looking after all aspects (as distinguished from all needs) of the employees' everyday lives. The company provided the housing, the bathhouse, the barbershop, recreation and sporting facilities, the school, and the hospital. To appeal to workers, unions had to obtain credit either for establishing social minimums at the national level or for obtaining various fringe benefits at the enterprise level. The first approach left them on grounds that were too abstract for workers living on a day-to-day basis. The second left them disadvantaged because they could not control financial resources to the extent that management could. However, while left-wing economists and union activists saw the emerging enterprise unions as the end of effective unionism, the research at the Hitachi mine documented ways in which enterprise unions could effectively win from management various forms of welfare and concessions on how the labor process was organized.

While noting the importance of the union in fighting for social welfare at the national level, Hazama and Matsushima argued that workers found in the enterprise union a most rational way (*jisshitsu gorisei*) to improve their situation given the circumstances. They averred that it was the way unions functioned, not the form of unionism, that mattered. Seeing the conflict of interest between labor and management primarily in terms of livelihood guarantees (*seikatsu hosho*) for the workers (i.e. in terms of the allocation of monies coming into the firm), they did not investigate the form, role, or process of labor disputes either at the enterprise level or on the shop floor. Hazama and Kitagawa (1985) noted how management sought the ideological high ground by presenting livelihood guarantees in ways which management could manipulate as company benefits aligned with sociocultural values. They suggested that workers were being indoctrinated to believe (i) that honest work required them to be extra thrifty, hard-working, and non-complaining and (ii) that such behavior was an inborn cultural trait. Their view was that any push by workers individually or collectively for better conditions could be presented as selfish or anti-social behavior. This ideology, they argued, was seen as legitimating management's efforts to contain wages, expenditures on safety, and other labor-related costs.

This point is crucial to understanding Hazama's later writings. Although he has often been interpreted as having successfully (and approvingly) substantiated that that group-oriented culture of self-denial, hard work and strong commitment to the firm was culturally ordained (e.g. see the interpretations given by Motojima 1965 or Okamoto 1964),[5] it is important to remember that Hazama's starting point was the assumption that Japan's workers were always economically insecure and had always had an ethos which encouraged them to act strategically, cognitive of their own interests and interested in taking positive steps to maximize those interests. Commenting on the formative period when a Japanese management ideology for personnel management was emerging after World War I, Hazama clearly states (1964: 16) that it would be absurd to dismiss the Japanese worker as leading a passive slave-like existence. Morale was obviously high among workers in Japan's most advanced industries, which were rapidly introducing new technologies after the war. He has also expressed his skepticism for cultural theorists who tried to explain the worker's consciousness simply by reference to a special Japanese work ethic.

The problem for Hazama was how to explain such high morale among workers given their extremely poor working conditions. Hazama felt that important answers would be found in the way management organized the work force and in the paternalistic ideology it used to legitimate various labor processes. Hazama was quite clear that work ideology was management driven and controlled. He is less clear as to the techniques used to maintain the ideology, the treatment of those who spoke out against it, and the system of remuneration used to reward those who supported it. Rather, Hazama focused on how the vocabulary of the family or *ie* had been employed to lock management and workers into a world view circumscribed by the firm and its interconnected (extended-family) firms (*keiretsu kigyo*). As the economy continued to grow, the firm came to be seen as a successful model. Hazama's original problem consciousness and his belief in the intellectual independence of the worker were given little attention by others as the focus on economic organization in Japan shifted to the firm as a fully integrated holistic entity. This had two

---

[5] Perhaps this was partly owing to the title of his mammoth work, *Nihon Romu Kanri Shi Kenkyu* (Research on the History of Personnel Management in Japan) (1964). In any case, many people have read that volume as a study of the personnel management system and the history of its formation in Japan. The term *nihonteki romu kanrii* (Japanese-style personnel management) – as opposed to *nihon romu kanri* (personnel management in Japan, without reference to its uniqueness) – later came to be used by those who read and adapted Hazama's research findings for their own uses, and the popular term *nihonteki keiei* (Japanese-style management) was later picked up and used inadvertently by Hazama himself.

effects. One was to legitimate the ideology and transcribe it as a "true cultural" norm in a way that often occurs with self-fulfilling prophecies. The second was to blur further the distinction between "real" and "false" consciousness. Returning to Kassalow's (1983) formulation, the need to project Japanese-style management as a viable alternative model no doubt increased as Japanese exports made inroads into other economies, because suspicions about social dumping were aroused and doubts about the consciousness of Japanese workers and the nature of their work ethic persisted.

## 2.5     Modernization theory and the culturalist reaction

Following defeat in 1960 at Miike and in their struggle to stop the renewal of the Mutual Security Treaty with the US, militant unions and other citizens' movements began to lose confidence in their cause. Both struggles involved the mass mobilization of whole communities (*machigurumi*), with families and friends protesting in the streets and on barricades. As workers lost confidence, the belief of researchers in the autonomous ethos of the working classes waned. The nation's attention soon shifted to the meaning of rapid growth for Japan as it continued to industrialize and the material standard of living improved considerably. The Japanese media subjected its audiences to daily comparisons of per capita GNP figures for the major countries of the world as the Japanese economy climbed from insignificance to being the world's second-largest economy.

In the 1950s and 1960s Japanese intellectuals were influenced by a cold-war regime that posed questions about the world in terms of the choice between socialism and the market system. Modernization theory provided perspectives ideologically favorable to the interests of American policymakers and portrayed America as "Number One." Many Japanese intellectuals were drawn into the modernization mode of thinking by the "Princeton series."[6] With regard to the organization of work, Totten (1967) and Levine (1967) adopted the structural-functionalist framework

---

[6] The Princeton series consisted of six volumes on Japan published by Princeton University Press. Known also as the "Modernization Project on Japan," the series brought together many of America's foremost scholars with expertise on Japan with the explicit purpose of undermining Marxist or conflict-oriented perspectives. The project was seen as an American attempt to assist Japanese scholars to see Japan in much more holistic, structural-functionalistic terms, geared to the promotion of economic development through market mechanisms. For a short account of that research and references to other discussions of the Princeton series see Mouer and Sugimoto (1986: 27–32 and 47–9). A number of Japanese were involved in the project and the series received considerable attention in Japan.

of the modernization theorists in explaining what was happening in Japan's industrial relations.[7] They and others predicted that many unique features of work organization in Japan (especially the familial ideology, lifetime employment, and seniority wages) would gradually fade as Japan industrialized further. This was the crux of what came to be known as the debate on convergence and divergence.

Hazama and other Japanese scholars quickly came to have serious doubts about the suitability of modernization theory as an explanation for what was happening in Japan. Taking technology as the major independent variable, he conducted some case studies to examine how personnel management practices were affected by the importation of Western technologies. He looked at firms that had been newly created to implement those new technologies and at the more established firms that were also absorbing such technologies at a rapid rate. He then distinguished between (i) the early stages during which the technologies were introduced and (ii) the next stage when they had been fully adapted to the needs of the Japanese firm. The study considered how personnel practices in Japan were altered to accommodate technological requirements, and the extent to which technologies were adapted to accommodate existing Japanese management practices. He found that different personnel practices were adopted in the first stage, but that in the second stage the earlier practices were reinstated. He further argued that over time traditional practices became more entrenched rather than being undermined (Hazama 1964). Hazama (1962 and 1963) had clearly come to the opinion that the Japanese experience could not be adequately explained by the theories generated by Western experience, and at that point he seemed happy to conclude that the practices were *nihonteki* (uniquely Japanese).[8]

Debate soon focused on whether and in what ways, if any, convergence was occurring in a wide range of social organizations, from the

---

[7] This is not to say that either author subscribed fully to the tenets of modernization theory. Each did, however, fulfill the brief – to test the usefulness of modernization theory in explaining labor–management relations in postwar Japan. Both probably concluded that to some extent "modernization" and the accommodation of worker and management interests were occurring as Japan industrialized.

[8] Hazama's view was that workers had a certain view of the world, and could not be forced by management to work in a new way simply because a new technology had come along. While management may have created an ideology to control labor costs and raise morale, he argued that managers were then also bound to that same ideology by the workers, who would act based on what made sense to them. Missing from his historical analysis in 1964, however, was an account of how militant workers had taken the initiative in institutionalizing "Japanese-style management" for all workers in the late 1940s and early 1950s. That link was later supplied by one of his students (Kawanishi 1977), through his studies on the large industrial union in the electric power industry (Densan) and its position in the labor movement immediately after the war.

work domain to the family domain. One of the early non-Japanese contributions to the debate was provided by Cole (1971). He argued that the working class would eventually become like working classes elsewhere, and that the relatively unsophisticated and docile workers who had come into Japan's urban factories from rural agricultural areas would gradually become cynical and politically astute. He concluded that the consciousness linking workers horizontally would eventually override more traditional notions of loyalty to their firm's management. And, to be sure, as late as the early 1970s Japan still had a quite militant union movement, and the political outcomes in terms of how work would be organized were not obvious.

Following on from the growing interest in the merits of Japanese-style management, Dore (1973) provided an interesting twist to the convergence position. He held not only that Japan had caught up with the West industrially, but also that it had done so at such a rapid pace that it had leapfrogged over many Western nations. The result, he argued, was a state of affairs in which Japanese management was leading the pack with a kind of postmodern mix of elements that ideally suited it for organizing work in the post-industrial era. He predicted a kind of reverse convergence. This was later disseminated through Vogel's *Japan as Number One* (1979), a volume which extolled the virtues of Japan's postwar successes and exhorted Americans to adopt various organizational approaches from Japan.

The growing appreciation of the merits of Japanese-style management was greatly reinforced by two OECD reports on Japan's manpower planning (1972 and 1977). Outside Japan a plethora of books appeared that described and praised various features of Japanese-style management. By the early 1970s Japanese scholars had tied together a number of independently observed features of work organization in Japan into the codified formula which treated lifetime employment, seniority wages, and enterprise unions as three inextricably linked phenomena. Known euphemistically in Japanese parlance as the *sanshu no jingi* (three sacred treasures) of Japan's industrial relations, these practices were soon presented overseas in the popular tracts on Japanese management as keys that would unlock the secrets of Japan's economic success at the firm level (e.g. Pascale and Athos 1981; Ouchi 1981; OECD 1977). Soon a new genre of writings about corporate identity, worker commitment, and human resource management had been created, and perhaps that has been Japan's great contribution to our understanding of how work is organized, not only in Japan but in many other advanced economies as well.

This volume seeks to counter depictions of work organization in Japan that rely heavily on cultural explanations, and it is important to note, along with Hazama, Matsushima, and many of their contemporaries, that those who emphasized the uniqueness of Japanese-style management worked mainly on Japanese social phenomena. Without comparative data, they usually accepted at face value Western theories about work in the West, assuming that Westerners knew about the West. Accordingly, though a great deal had been written about company towns and paternalism in Western societies, those dealing with Japanese personnel practices and ideology began to report on such phenomena in Japan as somehow being *nihonteki* (peculiarly Japanese).[9] Reflecting on the research of the 1960s that eventually gave way to the infatuation with Japanese-style management, it is important to note that the research of Matsushima and Hazama had been based on the assumption that relations at work were ultimately based on a conflict of interest between management and its labor force. Kitagawa (1956: 237–8) had argued that the use of surveys had shifted attention away from the labor union as an important social fact. He suggested that attention needed to be directed away from management, a theme also taken up by Sumiya (1954). Kitagawa stressed the need to research the possibility that workers and labor unions might develop an ideology different to the one described by Hazama – one which could successfully counter the paternalistic rhetoric generated by management. As mentioned above, there was a feeling that surveys had come by and large to be administered through management to employees as employees (*jugyoin*) rather than being distributed directly to the workers as workers (*rodosha* or *romuin*) or as unionists (*kumiaiin*).

Kitagawa (1956: 240–1) pointed to another methodological challenge. He believed that conflict between labor and management needed to be treated as an ongoing and ever evolving phenomenon. He noted that it would be difficult to discern the true nature of labor–management relations as long as one side held the upper hand, even though *on the surface* it might appear that all conflicts had been resolved. According to Kitagawa (1965), the new technologies would be introduced in an effort to reinforce management's ideological control (*shiso kanri*). He predicted that the company-oriented consciousness based on a sense that there was a living community of workers (*seikatsu kyodotai* or *shokuba shudan*) would be undermined whenever a new labor process was tried. As

---

[9] Readers are referred to a similar account in Mouer and Sugimoto (1986: 60–2 and 147–8) of how Nakane Chie came to see an emphasis on vertical relations as the distinguishing feature of Japanese society. They argued that much of the literature in the 1970s on Japanese-style management as a manifestation of peculiarly Japanese cultural traits needs to be understood in terms of a Japanese society that was at the time questioning its sense of national identity as Japan's place in the world changed. Just as Japan was again becoming a player on the international stage, a new world order was beginning to reveal itself and the Japanese had good reason to think about their place in the sun.

workers came to feel sure that they would always have food on their tables, personnel management (and union policies) based on notions of securing the workers' livelihoods would no longer be effective. The changes in the consciousness of workers that would accompany affluence – the type of transformation which would later be picked up by Goldthorpe and his colleagues in their studies of the affluent worker in Britain (1968 and 1969) – were foreshadowed. Much later the introduction of IT would lead to other questions about the ability of unions and management to compete ideologically.

### 2.6     The coming challenge to the sociology of work in Japan

By the mid-1970s references to the study of work organization had become mainstream across the curriculum at many universities in Japan. Economic growth was driving society. In foreign and domestic policy it was economics first, and the agendas of large Japanese corporations had become the business of Japan. With the two reports by the OECD on work in Japan in the 1970s, Japan's approach to work organization, industrial relations, and human resource management came to occupy a central place in explanations of Japan. It is not surprising that university courses incorporating those views were popular across all faculties.

The 1970s was a decade when research on all aspects of work burgeoned. Scholars were especially concerned with mapping out the future of work in Japan in terms of incomes policy, human resource development, participation in management, the quality of working life, and other trendy perspectives. However, in the 1980s the very success of Japan's large corporations in competitive industries, and the collapse of Japan's left-wing unions, resulted in work being dropped from the political agenda. By the early 1990s academic and student interest in the organization of work had waned considerably, perhaps reflecting a growing conviction among many that Japan had solved the major work-related issues confronting capitalist societies. Based on a belief that high levels of work commitment had been achieved without the alienation found in other advanced capitalist societies, and that high levels of employment had been achieved without the stagflation plaguing many other advanced competitor economies, some observers even came to suggest that bodies such as the Ministry of Labor had no real function to perform in Japanese society. Given these changes, few were surprised when the Ministry of Labor and the Ministry of Welfare were merged in 2001.

# 3 Competing models for understanding work in Japan

## 3.1 Toward an appreciation of competing models

The sociology of both work and industrial relations is multidisciplinary and multiparadigmatic. Introductory textbooks in those traditions often begin by describing several competing paradigms. Deery, Plowman, and Fisher's *Australian Industrial Relations* (1981), for example, identifies four distinct approaches to industrial relations: the unity approach, the pluralist approach, the Marxist approach, and the systems approach. In writings about work in Japan the delineations are slightly different, as indicated in the preceding chapter, but at least four major frameworks stand out. Although a single paradigm seldom covers all aspects of work, taken together a fairly comprehensive grasp of the major issues is attained. This volume presents four perspectives, and then looks at the contributions of four major writers on work in Japan.

### 3.1.1 *The conflict approach*

In the early 1900s some Japanese came to be interested in socialism and other ideologies that focused on social inequality and advocated social change to alter the relations of production. Peasant uprisings and other disturbances in pre-Meiji Japan occurred sporadically and were easily put down by a very centralized system that controlled the instruments of repression. New ideologies in Europe, including Marxism, presented Japanese dissidents with a new and more systematic vocabulary for expressing concerns about inequality. Anarchism attracted a following, and journalists exposed horrific working conditions and other inequities. The spread of democratic socialism and the formation of the Japan Communist Party in 1921 further emboldened those holding such views. These developments were severely repressed by conservative forces within society, including the government, although there appears to have been a period of progressive liberalism in the 1910s and 1920s. Many critical of power relations in Japanese society were forced underground by the

51

upsurge of ultra-nationalists and militarists who came to dominate public life in Japan from the early 1930s.

After the war, the public reacted against the "fascist forces." Under the Occupation many leftists were released from jail, and left-wing unionists and scholars critical of fascist elements came to have considerable influence. Focusing on the wrongs of the prewar and wartime regime, they utilized social class as a key concept for understanding Japanese society. Many Japanese came to adopt a Marxist framework in which conflict was assumed to be an integral part of industrial relations in capitalist societies. For them the outcomes of work-related disputes were determined largely by the relative amount of power the working class could generate.

Much of the scholarship on work and industrial relations in Japan during the 1950s and 1960s reflected these concerns. Okochi, Ujihara, and the scholars around them wrote profusely about the labor movement in Japan, the plight of day laborers and the urban poor, ongoing conflicts in firms and industries, and the "ganging-up" of government and management groups on employees. They attached special importance to the superstructures which ordered labor process at the meso or national level: the absence of safety nets, the segmentation of labor markets and its accompanying dualities, the "red purges," the packing of government "advisory" bodies with conservatives, and government policies designed to counter radical industrial unionism in the public sector.

Writers such as Hidaka (1984) have written about consumerism and the embourgeoisement of Japan's working class and salaried employees. Important questions were raised about alienation and motivation; they argued that choices at work were increasingly coming to be circumscribed by a new capitalist regime. Much of that questioning continues to be relevant as the Japanese assess the merits of Japan's economic growth over the past fifty years. These perspectives continue to provide important understandings of the backdrop against which work is performed in many firms. While a huge Japanese literature was produced in this vein, little of it has appeared in English. Exceptions can be found in the research of Moore (1983) on the Japanese union movement immediately after the war, the translation of Kamata's (1982) diary about life as a worker in the automobile industry, Woronoff's reports (1982 and 1990) on alienation and various contradictions at work, Chalmers' report (1989) on work in Japan's small firms, Kawanishi's large volume (1992a) on enterprise unionism in postwar Japan, and Kumazawa's essays (1996 and 1997) about the pressures of work in a society dominated by the business firm. Today many of the scholars working in this tradition are affiliated to the Japan Association for Labor Sociology (see table 2.1).

### 3.1.2    The institutional approach

Although the United States was instrumental in democratizing Japan immediately after the war, it shifted its stance as the cold war began to take shape. Conservative Japanese authorities were allowed to dilute early reforms, and the Occupation came to support successive conservative governments from the early 1950s (when Japan regained its independence). The US government invited numerous young industrial relations scholars to American universities for training in American theories of industrial relations. During the 1960s the systems approach of John Dunlop and others focused attention on the role of institutions that managed industrial conflict and balanced the power of labor, management, and government.

Some of those young scholars returned to Japan and became affiliated with the Japan Institute of Labor (JIL) which had been established by the Japanese government in 1958. Their work focused on institutions shaping industrial relations in Japan and carefully examined the way in which management organizations and labor unions were structured and interacted in various public forums. Hanami would be one of the outstanding scholars associated with this approach. This perspective also appears in English in many of the contributions to *Workers and Employers in Japan*, a large volume edited in the mid-1970s by Okochi, Karsh and Levine. These scholars provided a systematic overview of the legal framework in which employment relations occurred. Those affiliated to the Institute often had privileged access to bureaucrats who administered relevant legislation and gathered relevant data. However, this approach tended to limit analyses to Japan's unionized sector (i.e. employees mainly in Japan's large firms and some public sector industries and the civil service).

### 3.1.3    The behavioralist approach

By the mid-1970s a new brand of American-trained scholars was coming to the fore. They formed a third grouping loosely affiliated with the JIL. Many had completed postdoctoral work in the US, and were skilled in statistical analysis. Their comparative perspective began to influence discussions of work from the early 1970s. Several in that group were labor economists who commented on wage determination, hours of work, and labor turnover. Sano's regression analysis became the basis for predicting outcomes of the Spring Wage Offensive. Koike's work on the nature of the seniority wage system is also well known. Koshiro was another scholar associated with this approach. Their work appeared in volumes edited by Nishikawa (1980) and Shirai (1983).

The behavioralists utilized surveys and other techniques to study the way workers perceived their experiences at work. Whitehill and Takezawa (1968) used surveys that were administered in the late 1960s and then again in the late 1980s to capture change over time (Takezawa 1995). Inagami was another well-established researcher in this mode. Today many young scholars are trained in this approach and actively engage in survey research.

### 3.1.4    The culturalist approach

A fourth approach focusing on the allegedly unique features of work organization in Japan has highlighted the role of a distinctly Japanese culture in shaping the main institutions that structure how work is organized. Its adherents distinguish between the official legal framework and the actual practices shaping work on the shop floor. Abegglen (1958) and Bennett and Ishino (1963) were early writers presenting that view of work in Japan. Numerous Japanese scholars traced the origins of Japanese work practices to the early twentieth century, arguing that they grew out of the Japanese cultural preference for group-oriented forms of social organization. They argued that Japanese culture had given the Japanese a special attachment to vertical social linkages (which were contrasted to horizontal emphases believed to exist in an individualistically oriented West). A notable volume edited by Ballon (1969) puts forward this orientation.

This view of work was common in many of the more popular English-language depictions of work organization in Japan in the 1980s and early 1990s. Its emphasis on lifetime employment, seniority wages, and enterprise unionism became the basis for the attention given to such practices as bottom-up consensual decision-making, humanistic management, and corporate welfarism. This approach to understanding work in Japan is best assessed in the context of more general holistic interpretations of Japanese society known as *nihonjinron*, an orientation which came under heavy criticism during the 1980s as unsubstantiated ideology (e.g. see Mouer and Sugimoto 1986 and 1995). Nevertheless, it is still the framework that appears most frequently in popular discussions of Japanese management. In Japan established academics such as those in Hamaguchi (1993) and the Research Project Team for Japanese Systems (1992) continued to emphasize the unique Japanese cultural context as a major factor spawning the group-oriented employee as a corporate actor quite distinct from his more individualistically programmed counterpart overseas.

While this volume is generally critical of the culturalist viewpoint, its authors see in the writings of the culturalists a good deal of the *emic* vocabulary that is indispensable when tapping into Japanese discussions of work. It would be difficult to discuss work organization in Japan without reference to *nenkoteki chingin* (seniority wages) as a uniquely Japanese phenomenon, even though similar age-wage profiles exist in many other advanced economies where the term "seniority wages" is not part of the day-to-day vocabulary of most workers. In English a number of ethnographies continue to be an important reference to the vocabulary of everyday Japanese and will be cited where relevant. Accordingly, this volume introduces a range of Japanese terms commonly used in sophisticated discussions of work in Japan.

## 3.2    Some competing perspectives

Paradigms are created in a political context. For writings about work in Japan, the 1970s was a watershed. In the late 1960s and early 1970s, workers in many North American and European countries seemed suddenly to revolt against the over-regimented structures of Taylorism. Absenteeism, drugs, and the distraction of affluence seemed to be factors undermining the productivity of firms. Then came the successive "oil shocks," stagflation, and the continuing high levels of unemployment. The Japanese economy seemed to emerge unscathed, and was soon generating huge balance-of-payments surpluses with what appeared to be an unbeatable productive capacity. While some saw that capacity as something to be feared, others agreed that Japan might have some organizational lessons for other societies. They explained Japan's success in positive terms, and encouraged Western managers to visit Japan and learn those lessons. Such adulation later gave way to more critical appraisals in the 1990s.

Four Japanese writers are introduced here to indicate how thinking on work in Japan has evolved over the past two decades. Particularly important is the move away from culturalist theories as the labor economists come to the fore, and a concerted effort is made to understand social change in Japan in terms of the more universal processes involved in industrialization/post-industrialization, modernization/post-modernization, and, more recently, globalization.

### 3.2.1    Koike Kazuo and the environment conducive to skill formation

Perhaps the Japanese writer on work best known overseas is Koike Kazuo. He has been prolific not only in Japanese (1977, 1978, 1991, and 1994), but also in English (1983a, 1983b, 1988, 1989, 1995, and 1997). He is one of the few Japanese scholars who have worked within an explicitly comparative framework. His early research (1977) examined the role of the union on the shop floor in American and Japanese manufacturing firms. He then (1978) shifted his attention to participation in management in West Germany, the United Kingdom, Sweden, France, and Japan. He is best known today for his work on skill formation and reward structures within the framework of the economics of education and internal labor markets.

Koike's theory of worker motivation has three major components. The first is the behavioralist assumption that workers are independent economic rationalists who behave in order to maximize their own economic well-being (Koike 1989). He sees the Japanese system of management as cleverly conceived to maximize the benefits flowing from the employee's own rationalism. He believes that workers see benefit for themselves when they acquire skills, and that the system can be transferred to other societies because the conditions for skill formation lie largely in the institutions that any society can institute.

Job placement, promotion, and job security are seen as important for the economic wellbeing of all employees. In Koike's view, a developed internal labor market provides all three. Labor turnover is seen by labor and management as undermining such markets. Larger firms have more robust internal labor markets that make possible long-term career progression for each worker through on-the-job training and job rotation. The result is an internalized career (*naibuka shita kyaria*) as intellectual skills (*chiteki jukuren*) become deeper and more broadly based. To the extent that all employees gain skills and promotion through the firm's internal labor market, the entire labor force is constantly being upgraded and the employee's economic wellbeing comes to be tied directly to the prosperity of the firm. The Japanese are seen as working diligently for their employer not out of a culturally ordained work ethic or desire for paternalistic care, but for their own economic advantage. They are accommodated within win–win relationships for the worker and for management.

Within this framework that places productivity first, the worker's pay is seen as being a function of his intellectual skill (*chiteki jukuren*) (as opposed to manual skills). These skills result from carefully structured promotions (*shoshin*) and job rotations (*haichi tenkan*) so that employees have the necessary opportunities for skilling. While recognizing a certain universality in the internal labor markets for white-collar workers in large firms, Koike emphasizes the extent to which Japanese firms, especially large ones, institute personnel systems that "white-collarize" large segments of the blue-collar labor force. Koike believes career paths are most developed within Japan's internal labor markets.

The third element in Koike's vision is the way unions function on the shop floor. A union's most important functions are guaranteeing that opportunities for skilling exist for its members and limiting the arbitrariness with which management makes decisions that most affect the process by which skills are formed. His feeling is that the enterprise union is the form of unionism that will best ensure that internal labor markets function smoothly. He contrasts three types of union: (i) the American-Japanese type, in which the union has a solid formal organizational structure embracing all members at the shop-floor level, (ii) the British type, in which unionists are bound together by informal organizational structures, and (iii) the German type, in which all employees are members of a works' council. For Koike, the way a union functions on the shop floor is more important for skill formation than union activities at the industry or national level. The Japanese approach to participation in management is also important. Koike distinguishes (i) participation in the top management decision-making bodies from (ii) participation through feedback at the factory and firm level and (iii) participation through ownership and profit sharing. He posits that the second form of participation is most important for skilling since it allows employees to influence matters concerning promotion, placement, and job security. While conceding that enterprise unions are not always as vocal in expressing the views of their members as unions in some other countries (e.g. the Anglo-Saxon countries), he feels they are on a par with unions in West Germany and Sweden, and stronger than their French counterparts. Any weakness of the enterprise union is offset by the existence of very strong work groups (*sagyo shudan*) that function as fairly autonomous units and assert the views of their members. One outcome is management flexibility when it comes to job placement, job security, and other issues related to skilling.

Koike seems to assume the Japanese approach to work organization is based on universal elements in the human psychic makeup. He sees skill formation as a critical concern of all workers. Accordingly, rather than restricting the competitiveness of Japanese firms and any tendency to social dumping, Koike argues that firms in the other advanced countries need to become more competitive by adopting the Japanese approach. He sees no need to apologize or to use cultural arguments and the principle of cultural relativism when defending practices he sees as characterizing work organization in Japan.

### 3.2.2  Inagami Takeshi, the affluent worker, and corporatistic arrangements

The sociologist Inagami Takeshi has also been a prolific writer with a clear view of worker motivation (1981, 1988, and 1994; Inagami and Kawakita 1988). His early work was based on in-depth interviews with members of Doro (the Union of Train Engineers), a strong left-wing union that organized train drivers working for the Japan National Railways. That research clearly established that a strong work group existed which was similar to the shop-floor mateship-based groups in the United Kingdom.

Inagami has conducted a large number of questionnaire-based research projects dealing with the consciousness of workers, many commissioned by the government through the Japan Institute of Labor, the Labor Survey Association (Rodo Chosa Kyogikai) and various unions such as Denki Roren, Tekko Roren, and Zendentsu. The general conclusion which emerged from that research was that affluence was not having the same effects in Japan as elsewhere. The theoretical and comparative base informing the surveys and his conclusions was the series of reports on the affluent worker in Britain issued by Goldthorpe and his colleagues (1968 and 1969).

The British study identified three basic outlooks among workers in the UK. One was a materialistic view whereby work was seen wholly as a means of obtaining the income necessary to enjoy a certain lifestyle away from work. Semi-skilled and unskilled blue-collar workers formed the core of those subscribing to this view. Those in this category were seen as being rather self-interested and calculating in dealing with their firm, the union, and political parties. Their main interest was in relationships outside work rather than in advancement with their employer. A second type of consciousness was found among white-collar workers focused on career advancement within bureaucratically structured organizations. They served their firms, unions, and political interest groups to progress in their careers. Promotions were seen as being linked to larger incomes and higher status. The third type was found among workers in the traditional trades where the culture of worker solidarity was strongly entrenched. Work was conceived as part of a living social community which linked the shop floor and family life. For those with this consciousness, work was not divorced from the rhythm of daily life. Goldthorpe and his colleagues predicted that workers possessing the first type of consciousness would increase with rising levels of affluence.

Based on his extensive surveys, Inagami came to a different prediction for Japan. He concluded that affluence would result in workers coming to adopt the second consciousness. His view of worker consciousness in Japan was based on an assessment of several aspects of work organization. First was the advanced level of white-collarization among blue-collar employees. He argued that the difference between white-collar and blue-collar workers was minimal in terms of wages, participation in decision-making, and lifestyle. This view was consistent with the notion that 90 percent of Japanese formed a broadly based middle-class society. The white-collarization of blue-collar work into internalized careers meant that the traditional worker had largely disappeared. Rather than striving to protect vested interests tied to traditional ways of laboring, Japan's workers recognized the need for change and accepted that ability and performance should be the basis for promotion and the ordering of work. He stressed that the attitudes and thinking of Japan's blue-collar workers were converging with those of Britain's white-collar employees. In asserting that Britain's blue-collar workers would catch up with the intellectual outlook and attitudes of their Japanese counterparts, his views were similar to those of Koike.

Unlike in other countries where the identity with one's enterprise evolved out of a normative attachment to an egalitarian ethos emphasizing mateship, notions of social justice, and mutual assistance, he claimed that the Japanese sense of community was more in terms of a shared economic fate. The outlook of each employee was tied not only to the fate of other employees but also to the fate of their enterprise. The emphasis was on each individual's contribution to the wellbeing of the firm rather than egalitarian treatment. Whereas workers in Britain were seen as increasingly coming to see their private life apart from (and more important than) their life at work, Japanese workers tended to believe their private lives depended upon the success of their firm and were influenced by the productivity of social relationships and organizational arrangements at work. Inagami concluded from his data that this orientation became stronger as Japanese employees progressed through internal career structures.

The third critical element in Inagami's vision of work was informal organization at the shop-floor level and the inclination of workers to become involved in the work of others in their shop. This meant that work could be flexibly organized at this level, with workers having ample opportunity to expand their skills and responsibilities at work. The foreman played a key role as the intermediary between more senior management and the ordinary employee. As a representative of the workers, one of his roles was to ensure that the shop functioned semi-autonomously. Perhaps because of job rotation, the sense of identification with the work group in the shop (*shokuba kyodotai*) was more ambiguous than that which bound the workers to the firm as a community (*kigyo kyodotai*). Inagami evaluated highly the contribution of the quality control (QC) circle (*shoshudan*) to the sense of productive spontaneity. In addition to activating the talents of the most skilled workers, it also promoted the "gray-collarization" of the blue-collar work force, assisted workers in internalizing the goals of their firm, improved personal interaction, and allowed each employee to feel that they were tangibly helping to enhance their firm's performance.

Inagami saw the union as less important on the shop floor than did Koike. He found that many unionists did not identify with their union and disapproved of the way their union was managed. Most workers in his study wanted more opportunities for involvement in the union's decision-making and some form of direct democratic participation. Because the union was not seen as active at the shop level, Inagami's workers were more likely to present their grievances to the foreman than to the union representative. By participating in management on the shop floor, workers were able to identify with management's goals of achieving higher productivity. As the structures supporting internalized careers expanded, Inagami predicted, the enterprise union would increasingly have to find ways to strengthen the competitive position of the firm that employed its members.

Both Inagami and Koike saw the enterprise system as central to understanding the outlook of Japanese workers. However, whereas Koike saw economic self-interest and the ability of the individual to make economically rational choices as key ingredients, Inagami tended to take a structural-functionalist perspective. For Koike work organization in Japan was a clever device that could harness the energy of rational workers. Inagami tended to see the enterprise system as antecedent, existing before the Japanese worker was employed and socializing workers who came into its world.

Although Koike and Inagami arrive at similar conclusions from different starting points and using different methodologies, both share similar shortcomings. Both are based on observations of regular employees in Japan's large-scale sector, whereas 60 percent of the labor force is in firms with less than a hundred employees. Many in Japan's large firms are not regular employees. Both have gathered their data from firms in the advanced automated sectors in Japan's economy – electrical machinery, steel, and automobiles – or from workshops in which career-linked skill progressions are most noticeable. There is considerable variation between industries in this regard, and even within some industries, where subcontracting is prevalent. Finally, neither pay much attention to women, part-timers, and others who form Japan's peripheral work force.

### 3.2.3   *Nomura Masami: skilling and the segmentation of work*

Critical of the views espoused by Koike and Inagami, Nomura Masami (1993a, 1993b, and 1994) has focused on (i) weaknesses of the enterprise union, (ii) the extent to which management can arbitrarily structure work arrangements and command labor, (iii) the skills-linked segmentation of the labor market and the extent to which skilling is conceived in terms of management prerogatives rather than the interests of employees, and (iv) the use of the wage system as a mechanism for social control.

Nomura introduces a sociology of knowledge perspective, and argues that Koike's theories about skill may be seen as speculative ideology arising from the general intellectual milieu of the 1980s (Nomura 1993b: 55). He characterizes the 1980s as a period of rising neo-nationalist confidence in the superiority of all things Japanese, when the strong yen allowed Japanese interests to acquire cultural assets overseas. Nomura argues that productivity results not just from the skilling of Japan's workers; it also depends upon the overall level of technology in each industry, the cost of raw materials, the price elasticity of what is sold, and market-distorting monopolistic arrangements. Moreover, Nomura doubts the extent to which Japan's production workers are more skilled, suggesting that they have low-level all-round skills and perhaps a limited array of specialized skills.

Nomura attaches importance to the role of the traditionally skilled worker (*senmonko*) in Japan. He feels that writers like Koike overlook such workers and the fact that the skills they possess are very similar to those acquired by their counterparts overseas. Central to work organization in Japan, he argues, is the division of the labor force into those doing repetitious and monotonous work and those who are allowed to do the skilled work. He criticizes Koike for not being clear about the type of workers that support the allegedly superior Japanese approach to skilling workers. Although Koike is quick to note differences in the types of workers in American and European firms, Nomura argues that Japanese workers are not all incorporated within Koike's white-collarization process. Nomura is particularly concerned with developing a framework that can incorporate women and other workers who tend to be left outside standard treatments of the labor force.

Nomura's view is that the power relationship between labor and management is critical. He does not see the wage system as being driven by the market or by some mutually agreed-upon arrangement designed to stabilize each firm's internal labor market, and calls on Koike to provide evidence on how wages are decided. That the age-wage profile is consistent with the view that there are economic returns to education and to skilling does not mean it is designed only to provide those returns. Averaged curves do not show individual variation. Nomura pays attention to the use of personnel appraisals to establish wage differentials between employees. In arguing that the differentials heighten competition among employees, a similarity with Inagami and Koike emerges: all three see the employee's commitment to their firm as being based on self-centered materialism. However, Nomura sees such competition in zero-sum terms which compel employees to compete with workmates. Nomura posits that power relations are also reflected in the general weakness of the enterprise union. He criticizes Koike for not supplying facts showing that the influence of Japan's enterprise unions is on a par with that of management councils (*Betriebsrat*) in West Germany. He avers that the enterprise union is outspoken on few issues of vital importance to its members. He notes the limits placed on union involvement in meaningful managerial decision-making. For these reasons he does not see the workplace as a community in which workers spontaneously take the initiative to skill themselves or to work with management to enlarge the pie. He feels that the contribution of QC circles and the *kaizenhan* (progressive change groups) to significant change is frequently orchestrated, with the traditionally skilled worker (*senmonko*) and supervisory staff (*kantokusha*) taking the lead. These perspectives move the discussion more into the framework of labor process.

### 3.2.4    Kumazawa Makoto and the inordinately competitive society which is the Japanese firm

Unlike the preceding three scholars, who come from the Tokyo area and are committed to empirically based research, Kumazawa represents the Kyoto penchant for speculative scholarship. A professor of economics at Konan University, he is best known for his case study approach to oral and intellectual histories of work. Rather than relying on observations and systematic interviews or surveys on the shop floor, Kumazawa's contact with the workplace comes from his involvement as an activist defending the human rights of workers and from the feedback he receives at his frequent public-speaking engagements. As a result his arguments tend to fall back on anecdotes and impressions; his style is journalistic. An English translation of his work (1996) brings together chapters selected from his earlier work in 1981 (five chapters) and 1986 (four chapters). Much of his thinking over the past twenty years is brought together in a very readable paperback (1997).

Kumazawa's main message is that Japan's enterprise society (*kigyo shakai*) needs to be revamped if work life in Japan is to become more humane. His point of departure can be found in his writing (1983) about the decline of the British union movement and the British Labour Party in the 1960s. Another influence has been Beynon's *Working for Ford* (1984). He seeks to provide an explanation for the relative weakness of the Japanese union movement and the absence of the strong sense of mateship which, he believes, characterizes workplace social relations in the UK.

In examining the ethos and milieu of the workplace in the postwar Japanese enterprise, he is struck by the strong desire of workers to achieve an average standard of living, a kind of "keeping up with the Watanabes or the Tanakas." Kumazawa searches for the intangible qualities that distinguish individual volition from corporate culture. Aware of the control mechanisms which regulate work and the lives of Japan's employees, he seems to indicate that workers have been socialized or goaded into accepting that control.

Kumazawa cites two factors as contributing to the behavior of employees. One is the set of structures and the corporate ideology that foster competition among workers. He contrasts reward systems in Western countries that explicitly give weight to skill and job responsibilities with those used in Japan that are tied to a more total evaluation not only of performance but also of more nebulous criteria such as potential, attitude, and character. While the Japanese system may be a fairer system in some ways, it also keeps employees in the dark and constantly on their best behavior. The result is a kind of self-censorship and excessive self-discipline. Individuals choose to focus on immediate tasks and conceal their own shortcomings from colleagues. The results are stress, workmates in constant competition, and a tension-producing system in which one's best efforts are never good enough. Kumazawa argues that *kaizen* practices, quality control circles, and other group activities need to be understood within that context. Although such activity manifestly functions to produce solutions that make work easier, it also invariably functions latently to intensify work and competition. Kumazawa believes the resulting atmosphere is inherently alienating, and much of his writing focuses on individual accounts and anecdotes of how the system has drained the life-blood of employees. He describes a system in which there are no safety nets or social compacts to protect the individual from overwork and the tragedy of being constantly fatigued.

Although Kumazawa provides a more sanguine assessment of work organization, he tends, like Koike and Inagami, to focus on elite male salaried employees in Japan's large firms. Although all of them write about women, minorities, the handicapped, and others in the peripheral labor force, for the most part they remain outside those visions of enterprise society. For Kumazawa their presence is a constant source of the fear felt by core employers at the thought of downward mobility. While there are methodological problems which make it difficult to generalize from Kumazawa's account, he provides acute insight into some of the contradictions which influence the way many Japanese think about work. He also begs a fundamental question about work in Japan: if Japan's elite employees face problems, how much more trying is the environment in which Japan's non-elite employees labor?

### 3.3     Toward a framework for understanding work and labor process in contemporary Japan

The discussion in chapters 1–3 raises several issues that must be incorporated into any vision of work in Japan. First is dual consciousness of workers. While it is impossible to assess Japanese employees as autonomous and rational actors, one can be aware of the context in which workers have to choose at work. Many accounts of work in contemporary Japan draw attention to power relations at work, but few present a systematic framework for assessing the effect of those relations on notions of political correctness, self-censorship, and rational choice.

When arguing that power relations are taken as a starting point for analysis, it may be useful to stand back from the majority of analyses of work in Japan that focus on what happens within the enterprise. At the enterprise level many writers have approached the workplace through behavioralist formulations (e.g. by surveying individuals) developed out of managerial perspectives. Those who have entered the workplace have been more inclined to deal with labor process and the ways in which work allocation relates to power relations. It is necessary to return to some of the concerns of the more traditional industrial relations and social policy scholars. Their research provides a view of the larger socioeconomic context that is characterized by variation at work. Although the most coherent views of work are those which focus on the elite white-collar male permanent employee in Japan's large firms, critics note that such employees are heavily subsidized by a much larger number of less-privileged workers (including women and those in various forms of casual employment and/or in smaller firms).

In this volume labor process at the meso level is considered in terms of factors that segment or stratify the labor market and limit the plausible outcomes for each entrant. Japan's labor market is not a pool of homogeneous labor. Despite a huge body of literature on cultural and social homogeneity in Japan, the Japanese enter the labor market on an unequal footing and that inequality has consequences in terms of their bargaining power and their choices with regard to work. This volume rests on the premise that consequences of labor process at the micro level within the firm can only be understood once labor processes at the meso level are understood. Many researchers interview workers without considering carefully the consequences of higher-level processes, even though these are often taken for granted by the workers being studied. Power relations at the micro level often depend upon the structure of the external labor market and the opportunities to walk out of a given place of work. Those conditions are often defined at the meso level. For example, many women put up with sexual harassment and discrimination at work because the opportunities elsewhere are limited. For this reason chapters 5–10 focus on the labor market, labor policy, and the power relationship between organized labor and management groups. Only upon that foundation can the everyday life processes which link the worker to his or her family and to the local community be meaningfully discussed in terms of the choices they make at work.

*Part II*

The commitment to being at work

# 4    Hours of work, labor-force participation and the work ethic

## 4.1    How hard do the Japanese work?

Well into the 1990s many foreigners and Japanese alike perceived that the Japanese were working harder than their counterparts in other advanced economies. This view was held not only by critics of Japan (who felt that Japanese worked too much), but also by advocates of the Japanese model who saw in long hours of work enviable levels of commitment to an employer. Many who associated long hours of work with high levels of motivation saw in Japan an approach to management that would take human resource management in Japan and other advanced societies into the twenty-first century.

Most assessments of how hard the Japanese work are implicitly comparative. To the extent that Japanese workers are perceived as working very hard, workers overseas come to be seen as not working hard enough. Lincoln and Kalleberg (1996) cite the short working hours of German employees as a major concern for Japanese managers stationed in that country. Japanese managers in Australia have been quick to fault Australians for not working hard enough (Meany et al. 1988; Mizukami 1993: 23). "Large, Lucky and Lazy" was the title of one study of Japanese managers who criticized Australian workers for their reluctance to work overtime or at the weekend (Ormonde 1992). Managers in other countries have taken such views on board, arguing that their employees should adopt what the managers see as being a superior work ethic.

The assumption that the Japanese do work harder than others begs key questions about the motivation of the Japanese to work. In setting the agenda for a discussion of work in Japan, this chapter asks: how hard do the Japanese really work? The question is comparative, and some key concepts require careful consideration. One approach equates hard work with effort. Most societies acknowledge that the amount of effort required to accomplish the same work varies significantly according to the work environment. Hardship allowances are compensation for the additional effort required to work in extreme heat or cold, with noxious fumes,

69

or with deafening noise. These adjustments often give some sense of fairness to workers within a particular society. However, the comparisons and resultant compensations more often than not remain internal to a single firm or industry. For the most part, they do not extend across national boundaries. Workers in a Toyota plant in Bangladesh are not in a position to claim hardship simply because their Japanese counterparts work in more comfortable conditions. A further difficulty with the focus on effort is that employees are often compensated for earlier investments of time and resources. The return to education is well documented. The acquisition of many skills, physical fitness, and social capital yields similar returns.

Even more vexing is the notion of output. As experience with piecework has shown, finished work is often of uneven quality, meaning that the same work is seldom performed by any two workers. With increasingly higher levels of specialization and the international division of labor, meaningful comparisons of individual productivity within and across societies become more problematic over time. The factors affecting the productivity of any given individual in a plant are considerable. Many connect holistically to all other aspects of the production process, but are external to the workers themselves. Differences in equipment, in layout, in the goods produced or the services provided, in raw materials used, and in various other factors all impact upon the physical work requirements, the work environment, and the output that can reasonably be expected in many jobs.

## 4.2    Hours of work: comparisons and trends

References to the Japanese work ethic invariably come with data showing that the Japanese work longer hours than other people. However, the most simple comparison of hours of work in manufacturing in five countries provides ambiguous results at best. Table 4.1 presents figures on average weekly hours of work for five countries at five-year intervals for the forty years up to 1995. Japan would seem to record the highest number of hours worked per week in manufacturing in five of the eleven years: 1960, 1985, 1990, 1995, and 1999. Moreover, the trends in Japan, the US, and the UK seem to move together, suggesting that perhaps some common underlying cross-national dynamic may be at work in those societies. Some time ago, Koike (1969) argued that the hours of work registered in Japan might better be understood in terms of the overall process of economic development. He suggested that hours of work had been longer and that work had been more arduous in the UK and many other advanced societies when they were in the early stages

Table 4.1 *International comparison of weekly hours of work for production workers in manufacturing*

| Year | Japan | USA | UK | France | Germany |
|------|-------|-----|----|--------|---------|
| 1956 | 47.5[e] | 40.4[e] | 48.2[e] | 45.6[e] | 47.8[e] |
| 1960 | 48.1[e] | 39.7[e] | 47.4[e] | 45.7[e] | 45.6[e] |
| 1965 | 44.3[e] | 41.2[e] | 46.1[e] | 45.6[e] | 44.1[e] |
| 1970 | 43.3[d e] | 39.8[d e] | 44.9[d e] | 44.8[d e] | 43.8[d e] |
| 1975 | 38.8[d] | 39.5[b d] | 42.7[b d] | 41.7[b d] | 40.4[b d] |
|      | 38.6[b] | | | | |
| 1980 | 41.2[a b c d] | 39.7[a b c d] | 41.9[b d] | 40.7[a b c] | 41.6[a b c d] |
|      | | | 42.3[c] | 40.6[d] | |
| 1985 | 46.2[a] | 40.5[a] | 43.7[a] | 38.6[a] | 40.7[a] |
| 1990 | 45.7[a] | 40.8[a] | 44.3[a] | 38.7[a] | 39.5[a] |
| 1995 | 43.5 | 41.6 | 42.2 | 38.7 | 38.3 |
| 1999 | 42.7 | 41.7 | 41.4 | n.a. | n.a. |

*Notes:* The definitions used by each country vary slightly:

Japan: hours actually worked by males and females in firms with 30+ employees.

USA: hours paid for males and females in firms of all sizes.

UK: hours actually worked by males aged over twenty-one in firms of all sizes (later becoming figures for adult males and females).

France: hours actually worked by males and females in firms with 10+ employees.

Germany: hours paid for males and females in firms with 10+ employees.

*Sources:* (1) All of the figures for 1995 and 1999 are from Kosei Rodo Sho Daijin Kanbo Tokei Joho Bu (2002a), p. 327.

(2) The other figures are from one or more of the following sources:

a Rodo Daijin Kanbo Seisaku Chosa Bu (1995), p. 333;
b Rodo Daijin Kanbo Seisaku Chosa Bu (1985), p. 266;
c Rodo Daijin Kanbo Seisaku Chosa Bu (1996a), p. 257;
d Rodo Daijin Kanbo Tokei Joho Bu (1982), p. 219;
e Rodo Daijin Kanbo Tokei Joho Bu (1976), p. 337.

of development, later falling as GNP per capita lifted. Figures from the Ministry of Labor's monthly survey (*Maitsuki Kinro Tokei Chosa*) (begun in 1944) reveal that there has been a long-term trend toward shorter hours as Japan has developed economically over time (Ogura 1996: 46).

International comparisons of hours of work are not straightforward; nations collect such statistics in different ways. For a long time, the UK collected figures only for males aged over 21. Few countries collect figures throughout the year (as Japan does); most use the first full week of work in certain months or at the beginning of each quarter, and do not capture institutionalized fluctuations that characterize the annual rhythm of work. Firms of different sizes are surveyed, and in some instances individuals

Table 4.2 *Annual hours of work in twelve countries, 1988–99*

| Country | 1988 | 1991 | 1992 | 1997 | 1999 |
|---|---|---|---|---|---|
| Japan | 2,152 | 2,139 | 2,017 | 1,942 | 1,942 |
| America | 1,898 | 1,847 | 1,957 | 2,005 | 1,991 |
| UK | 1,938 | 1,835 | 1,911 | 1,934 | 1,942 |
| Belgium | | 1,628 | | 1,517 | |
| Italy | | 1,622 | | | |
| France | 1,657 | 1,619 | 1,682 | 1,677 | |
| Australia | | 1,595 | | | |
| Denmark | | 1,571 | | | |
| Sweden | | 1,568 | | | |
| Holland | | 1,560 | | | |
| Norway | | 1,540 | | | |
| Germany (West Germany until 1991) | 1,613 | 1,499 | 1,567 | 1,517 | |

*Sources:* 1988 Kusaka (1989), p. 65.
1991 German Research Center as reprinted in Osono (1995), p. 153.
1992 NHK Kokusai Kyoku (1995), p. 99.
1997 Kosei Rodo Sho Daijin Kanbo Tokei Joho Bu (2001), p. 247.
1997 and 1999: Kosei Rodo Sho Daijin Kanbo Tokei Joho Bu (2002a), p. 247.

rather than firms are surveyed. Some governments survey for the hours paid (including paid leave), while others survey only for the hours actually worked. None record unofficial work – overtime, training, and networking that is done outside the place of work and not recorded.

Despite these and other difficulties in making international comparisons,[1] rough comparisons with adjusted figures point to the likelihood that annual hours of work vary considerably from country to country and that they have until recently been considerably longer in Japan than in other comparably developed economies (table 4.2). Most countries can be placed in one of three categories: those with relatively short hours of work, those with relatively long hours of work, and those in between (table 4.3). Sano (1988: 248) suggested that annual hours of work in Japanese firms with over thirty employees rose to 2,111 hours in 1987. She argued that this was roughly 200 hours above the levels recorded

---

[1] For example, the conversions between weekly, monthly, and annual hours of work (the most commonly used timeframes when statistics are collected and compared) are difficult to decipher. Apparently conflicting figures appear even in the different publications of the Japanese Ministry of Labor, as is evidenced when comparing the figures in its White Papers (the *Rodo Hakusho*) with those in its Annual of Labor Statistics (the *Rodo Tokei Nenpo*) and those in its handbook of labor statistics (the *Rodo Tokei Yoran*). The conversions to, and the measuring of, hours of work over a lifetime are fraught with even greater difficulties.

Table 4.3 *International groupings by annual hours of work*

| Country group | Countries | Annual hours of work |
|---|---|---|
| Countries with relatively short hours | Italy<br>France<br>Germany | 1,500–1,650 |
| Countries with medium number of hours | Australia<br>UK<br>United States<br>Japan (circa 2002) | 1,800–1,950 |
| Countries with relatively long hours | Japan (circa 1990) | over 2,100 |

for American and British workers and some 500 hours above the levels recorded for their German and French counterparts. Recognizing this fact over a decade earlier, another noted economist, Tsujimura (1980: 67), observed for 1970 that:

Although the difference of several hours per week may not seem like much, the weekly difference of 5.6 hours between Japan and the United States means an annual difference of 291 hours per worker . . .This means that annually the Japanese are working four to six weeks more than their counterparts overseas. A difference of more than one month per year is not insignificant.

It is easy to see logic in the commonly voiced complaint that Japanese employees were working 14–15 months a year while their Italian and French counterparts were keeping to 12 months. There may have been a competitive advantage in the ability of Japanese firms to lower labor costs, to honor delivery times, or to secure contracts with a "last-minute push" and more overtime.

While official data on weekly and annual hours of work in Japan (e.g. in tables 4.1 and 4.2) led to different conclusions, the national public broadcaster's exhaustive survey on how the Japanese use their time supports the view that working hours in Japan have been very long. Using a sample of nearly 160,000 Japanese with a return rate of 75 percent, the survey provides valuable insight into how time is used on weekdays, Saturdays, and Sundays. The figures in table 4.4 are for 1990 and 2000. They represent the average time spent working by all Japanese on different days of the week. Breakdowns are given for six different age groups. When viewing the figures, it is important to remember that the hours of work are averages for all in that age group – including both those who are working and those who are not working. In other words, the average hours worked by those who are actually employed would be even longer

Table 4.4 *Hours of work based on the NHK surveys on the uses of time in Jap*

| A Age group | Hours of work for all males | | | | F Total weekly hours worked by women | G Female hours of work as a percentage of male hours (100F/E) | H Total an hours of for men |
|---|---|---|---|---|---|---|---|
| | B Weekdays | C Saturdays | D Sundays | E Total (5B+C+D) | | | |
| | | | | | | | **1990** |
| 20–29 | 7:30 | 5:37 | 2:30 | 45.6 | 30.3 | 66.4 | 2,371.2 |
| 30–39 | 9:03 | 6:17 | 2:36 | 54.1 | 20.9 | 38.6 | 2,813.2 |
| 40–49 | 8:42 | 6:07 | 2:40 | 52.3 | 29.5 | 56.4 | 2,719.6 |
| 50–59 | 8:08 | 6:05 | 3:11 | 49.9 | 26.6 | 53.3 | 2,594.8 |
| 60–69 | 5:10 | 4:28 | 2:40 | 33.0 | 17.9 | 54.2 | 1,716.0 |
| 70+ | 2:25 | 2:24 | 1:57 | 16.4 | 7.6 | 46.3 | 852.8 |
| | | | | | | | **2000** |
| 20–29 | 7.42 | 5.26 | 3.20 | 47.3 | 33.3 | 70.4 | 2,459.6 |
| 30–39 | 9.40 | 5.10 | 2.22 | 55.9 | 22.6 | 40.4 | 2,906.8 |
| 40–49 | 9.01 | 5.45 | 2.30 | 55.3 | 25.4 | 47.7 | 2,771.6 |
| 50–59 | 8.45 | 4.59 | 2.37 | 51.4 | 26.4 | 51.4 | 2,672.8 |
| 60–69 | 4.37 | 3.35 | 2.05 | 28.8 | 12.8 | 44.4 | 1,497.6 |
| 70+ | 1.26 | 1.52 | 1.20 | 10.4 | 6.6 | 63.5 | 540.8 |

*Note:* (1) The figures in columns B, C and D are given as hours and minutes, "7:30" meaning 7 hours and 30 mi. represented as "7.5."

(2) The figures are averages for the entire population in a given age group, including individuals not

*Source:* NHK Yoron Chosa Bu (1992), pp. 350–7.

NHK Hoso Bunka Kenkyu Jo (2002), pp. 350–7.

than the figures given in table 4.4. Moreover, the figures do not include the time the Japanese spend commuting to work.

Three conclusions may be drawn from the NHK findings. First, annual hours of work are exceptionally long for men (over 2,500 hours), confirming the view that there is probably a good deal of unreported overtime in Japan that is not captured in official figures. Second, despite their relatively high labor-force participation rate, Japanese women are less involved in work *outside the home* than men, reflecting the peripheralization of their involvement in the labor force on a part-time basis. As the figures in columns I–K of table 4.4 show, Japanese women engage in a lot of housework. Adding that to work done outside the home, women's contribution to hours worked for the household economy looms large. Third, despite a nominal retirement age in the early sixties for many men, in 1990 males in their sixties were still working a weekly *average* of 33 hours, and then an *average* of 16.4 hours every week of the year for the rest of their lives after the age of 70. This is a far cry from the

*) and 2000*

| annual of work men | J Weekly hours of housework done by men | K Weekly hours of housework done by women | L Annual hours of housework done by men (52J) | M Annual hours of housework done by women (52K) | N Total annual hours of all work done by men (H+L) | O Total annual hours of all work done by women (I+M) | P Ratio of annual hours of work by women to those of men (O/N) |
|---|---|---|---|---|---|---|---|
| 6 | 3.6 | 22.6 | 187.2 | 1,175.2 | 2,558 | 2,751 | 4.08 |
| 8 | 4.6 | 43.6 | 239.2 | 2,267.2 | 3,052 | 3,354 | 1.10 |
| 0 | 3.9 | 35.6 | 202.8 | 1,851.2 | 2,922 | 3,385 | 1.15 |
| 2 | 4.1 | 34.0 | 213.2 | 1,768.0 | 2,808 | 3,151 | 1.12 |
| 8 | 7.2 | 34.0 | 374.4 | 1,768.0 | 2,090 | 2,699 | 1.29 |
| 2 | 8.5 | 27.3 | 442.0 | 1,419.6 | 1,295 | 1,815 | 1.40 |
| 6 | 3.8 | 17.2 | 197.6 | 894.4 | 2,657 | 2,262 | 0.99 |
| ,2 | 4.6 | 40.5 | 239.2 | 2,106.0 | 3,146 | 3,281 | 1.04 |
| 8 | 5.4 | 36.5 | 280.8 | 1,898.0 | 3,052 | 3,219 | 1.05 |
| 8 | 3.7 | 31.8 | 192.4 | 1,653.6 | 2,865 | 3,026 | 1.06 |
| 6 | 4.6 | 34.3 | 239.2 | 1,783.6 | 1,737 | 2,449 | 1.41 |
| 2 | 7.8 | 24.8 | 405.6 | 1,289.6 | 946 | 1,633 | 1.73 |

gures in columns E through O are given as hours and fractions of hours, with 7 hours and 30 minutes being

orce and those on any form of leave.

cultural norm described some time ago by Kaneko (1980: 106–10), who portrayed the ideal for each worker's declining years as a golden interlude when they could expect to enjoy a comfortable retirement in a home that they owned. The figures in tables 4.1 and 4.2 nevertheless suggest that work hours continue to fall, and that the gap between Japan and other advanced economies closed considerably during the 1990s.

How do the Japanese work those hours that they do work? How is their decision to work structured? Before turning to answer such questions in the remaining chapters of this volume, however, the statistics on hours of work can take us a little further in our understanding of the situation. When considering the subtleties of organization and the thoughts and outlooks which employees take to work, the statistics are important because they point to two sorts of structural difference. One is in terms of labor-force participation and the temporal organization of work. The other is in terms of variation. Japanese do not all do the same amount of work, and the patterns in the amount of work performed by different types of individuals provide important clues as to how work is structured in Japan.

## 4.3    Labor-force participation and the organization of time: some comparisons and trends

How are hours of work constituted in Japan? How much discretion do Japanese workers have in organizing their life at work? These important questions require answers before levels of motivation and the level of commitment in Japanese firms can be assessed. This section considers how workloads are assembled.

### 4.3.1    The two-day weekend

Notions of work can be deconstructed by looking at the spread of work across the week and "after hours." The figures in tables 4.4 and 4.5 suggest that Japan's workweek is spread out a fair bit and a good deal of work is done on Saturdays and Sundays. In the early 1970s the government began to respond to foreign criticism of Japan's long hours of work. One corrective was the two-day weekend, and large firms took the initiative (see table 4.5). Shorter hours of work in larger firms tended to attract the more able graduates. Many less able graduates and others not employed by the larger firms have had to labor at weekends in Japan's smaller firms. Although established institutional arrangements, intertwined with various traditions and cultural proclivities, mediated the introduction of the five-day workweek, the main determinant was productivity. Tsujimura (1980) demonstrated that productivity correlated inversely with hours of work. Firms had to alter organizational molds built around the five-and-a-half-day workweek. Many did so by shifting a half day of work from Saturdays back into the week (albeit with longer hours during the week). Taking commuting and preparation time into consideration, that small shift freed up a whole extra day each week for many employees. The increased amount of usable leisure time resulted in a much greater appreciation of its value. By the 1990s most employees had the two-day weekend in some form (table 4.5).

### 4.3.2    Overtime

Overtime is another practice involving not only the hours worked, but also the discretion of employees in planning for time outside normal hours of work. Numerous writers have mentioned the extent to which the willingness to work overtime has been reflected in the *hyotei* (the evaluation of employees which management in many Japanese firms uses to decide on promotions and other decisions ultimately affecting the earning potential of each employee within the firm). Table 4.6 reveals that recorded

Table 4.5 *The implementation of the two-day weekend by firm size: 1994*

| Firm Size | Firms with two-day weekends every week | | Firms with two-day weekends every three weeks | | Firms with two-day weekends twice every month or once every other week | | Firms with two-day weekends once every month | | Firms with other arrangements including a weekday off | | Percentage of employees in firms with a system which allows for flexible working hours |
|---|---|---|---|---|---|---|---|---|---|---|---|
| | Percentage of firms | Percentage of employees | Percentage of firms | Percentage of employees | Percentage of firms | Percentage of employees | Percentage of firms | Percentage of employees | Percentage of firms | Percentage of employees | |
| 1,000+ | 70.1 | 80.8 | 17.3 | 12.0 | 9.4 | 15.8 | 1.4 | 0.7 | 1.1 | 0.5 | 46.4 |
| 300–999 | 44.9 | 48.5 | 28.2 | 28.5 | 19.5 | 40.7 | 4.0 | 3.3 | 4.4 | 2.4 | 38.1 |
| 100–299 | 30.9 | 33.3 | 20.3 | 20.3 | 34.6 | 41.2 | 7.2 | 6.9 | 6.7 | 5.3 | 28.9 |
| 30–99 | 18.7 | 19.8 | 15.8 | 17.5 | 35.6 | 34.7 | 16.0 | 14.3 | 13.6 | 12.3 | 26.7 |
| Average | 24.3 | 53.9 | 17.6 | 17.6 | 33.7 | 18.9 | 13.0 | 5.0 | 11.1 | 4.0 | 37.9 |

*Source:* Rodo Daijin Kanbo Seisaku Chosa Bu (1995), pp. 254 and 263.

Table 4.6 *Monthly standard hours of work, overtime, and total hours of work in Japan, 1960–2001*

| Year | Standard hours | Overtime | Total hours worked | Percentage of overtime |
|------|----------------|----------|--------------------|------------------------|
| 1960 | 180.8 | 21.9 | 202.7 | 10.8 |
| 1965 | 176.4 | 16.5 | 192.9 | 8.6 |
| 1970 | 169.9 | 16.7 | 186.6 | 8.9 |
| 1975 | 161.4 | 10.6 | 172.0 | 6.2 |
| 1980 | 163.0 | 12.7 | 175.7 | 7.2 |
| 1985 | 161.0 | 14.6 | 175.6 | 8.3 |
| 1986 | 160.8 | 14.4 | 175.2 | 8.2 |
| 1987 | 161.1 | 14.8 | 175.9 | 8.4 |
| 1988 | 160.2 | 15.7 | 175.9 | 8.9 |
| 1989 | 158.2 | 15.8 | 174.0 | 9.1 |
| 1990 | 159.0 | 13.0 | 172.0 | 7.6 |
| 1991 | 156.3 | 12.3 | 168.6 | 7.3 |
| 1992 | 154.7 | 10.5 | 165.2 | 6.4 |
| 1993 | 150.5 | 9.5 | 160.0 | 5.9 |
| 1994 | 149.8 | 9.4 | 159.2 | 5.9 |
| 1995 | 149.6 | 9.6 | 159.2 | 6.0 |
| 1996 | 149.7 | 9.7 | 159.9 | 6.1 |
| 1997 | 147.3 | 10.3 | 157.6 | 6.5 |
| 1998 | 146.8 | 9.6 | 155.9 | 6.2 |
| 1999 | 143.8 | 9.5 | 153.3 | 6.2 |
| 2000 | 144.6 | 9.8 | 154.4 | 6.3 |
| 2001 | 143.6 | 9.4 | 153.0 | 6.1 |

*Notes:* The figures for 1980–98 are for firms with thirty or more employees. The figures for all other years are for firms with five or more employees.
*Sources:* 1960–80: Rodo Daijin Kanbo Tokei Joho Bu (1982), p. 161.
        1980–89: Rodo Sho (1995), p. 384.
        1985–91: Rodo Daijin Kanbo Seisaku Chosa Bu (1992), p. 95.
        1991–96: Rodo Sho (1999), p. 590.
        1997–2001: Kosei Rodo Sho Daijin Kanbo Tokei Joho Bu (2002a), p. 113.

overtime has fluctuated somewhat, but shows the same long-term decline as is seen in the normal workweek and the days at work each month. Overtime continues to be used by firms to adjust their labor force and to regulate labor costs. Studies following the oil shocks in the mid-1970s estimated that the actual unemployment rate in Japan rose to perhaps 6–8 percent, but that increase did not show up in the official statistics because it was spread across the labor force through across-the-board reductions in overtime.

### 4.3.2.1    Overtime and the wage system

The relatively high percentage of overtime worked in Japan partially reflects the fact that salary systems are institutionalized for regular employees in Japan's more established firms. Florida and Kenny (1993) suggest that this is one benefit won for workers by a very powerful union movement following the war. Unions strove to abolish the status system that had explicitly divided workers into white-collar employees (on guaranteed salaries) and production workers (on fluctuating wages which were directly linked to the number of hours or days worked). Salaries tend to fix labor costs and to divorce remuneration from work performed and other considerations of labor productivity. For this reason management in many firms has striven to restructure their remuneration systems in ways that enhance their ability to adjust labor costs.

One technique has been to keep the standard workweek well within the hours of work needed and to institutionalize overtime. While this may initially increase the costs of labor by a small amount (the legally prescribed rate or premium for overtime being only 25 percent), it greatly increases the discretion management has over the overall supply and cost of labor.[2] Although working conditions are generally much better and the overall number of hours worked is lower in larger firms, overtime as a proportion of all hours worked actually increases with firm size (table 4.7).

### 4.3.2.2    Overtime and the bonus system

Another device to regulate labor costs is the deferred payment of a considerable portion of the employee's wages. Bonuses are dependent on the

---

[2] The following example might help to clarify the workings of such an arrangement. A firm which must pay ¥100,000 to employ a worker for forty hours a week might go about arranging its workweek of fifty hours in two different ways. One way would have a standard workweek of fifty hours. The cost would be another ¥25,000 in salaries for the additional ten hours per week. However, a cutback to forty hours if business declined would not be accompanied by a drop in average costs, as all workers would be on a salary of ¥125,000. The second approach would be to set the standard workweek at forty hours and pay separately for ten hours of overtime. This would cost the firm an additional 25 percent for those ten hours, bringing the total cost of labor to ¥131,250. However, labor costs would drop to ¥100,000 when weekly hours fell to forty. Aware of the extra income involved, unions in the 1960s and early 1970s often included a demand for a shorter standard workweek in the annual Spring Wage Offensive. However, it has been argued that unions did not want shorter hours of work but a reduction in the standard workweek so that more of their hours would qualify for the overtime rate and incomes would be increased for their members. The tradeoff for the unions and the bonus for management was that management then had a free hand to regulate up to 20 percent of their wage costs for the initial payment of a 5 percent differential for the additional ten hours required of workers. Because overtime has actually been in the realm of 10–15 percent of standard hours (as appears in table 4.6), the number of hours that could be adjusted and the premium paid by management would have been smaller than shown in this example.

Table 4.7 *Total annual hours of work and the percentage worked as overtime by firm size: 1960–2000*

| Firm Size | 1960 | Percentage of overtime | 1970 | Percentage of overtime | 1975 | Percentage of overtime | 1980 | Percentage of overtime | 1985 | Percentage of overtime | 1990 | Percentage of overtime | 1995 | Percentage of overtime | 2000 | Percentage of overtime |
|---|---|---|---|---|---|---|---|---|---|---|---|---|---|---|---|---|
| 500+ | 1,987 | 12.5 | 2,225 | 11.5 | 1,999 | 6.5 | 2,093 | 10.0 | 2,102 | 10.9 | 2,066 | 11.9 | 1,912 | 8.4 | 1,898 | 9.1 |
| 100–499 | 2,027 | 10.0 | 2,236 | 8.9 | 2,063 | 6.6 | 2,090 | 7.7 | 2,101 | 8.6 | 2,054 | 9.3 | 1,914 | 7.4 | 1,852 | 7.7 |
| 30–99 | 2,070 | 9.9 | 2,254 | 7.4 | 2,106 | 5.5 | 2,134 | 6.5 | 2,117 | 6.9 | 2,042 | 7.5 | 1,912 | 6.5 | 1,850 | 6.7 |
| 5–29 | n.a. | n.a. | 2,351 | n.a. | 2,192 | n.a. | 2,214 | n.a. | 2,173 | n.a. | 2,081 | 5.5 | 1,914 | 4.5 | 1,844 | 4.8 |
| 1–4 | n.a. | n.a. | 2,570 | n.a. | 2,410 | n.a. | 2,312 | n.a. | 2,234 | n.a. | n.a. | n.a. | n.a. | n.a. | n.a. | n.a. |

*Source:* 1960–75 Rodo Daijin Kanbo Tokei Joho Bu (1982), pp. 162–3.
1980–2000 Kosei Rodo Sho Daijin Kanbo Tokei Joho Bu (2002a), pp. 113–15.

Table 4.8 *Bonus payments as a multiple of monthly salaries in non-agricultural industries excluding services, 1955–2000*

| Year | Firms with thirty or more employees | | | Firms with five or more employees | | |
|------|-----------------|-----------------|-------------------|-----------------|-----------------|-------------------|
|      | Summer bonus | Year-end bonus | Total of bonuses | Summer bonus | Year-end bonus | Total of bonuses |
| 1955 | 0.71 | 0.91 | 1.62 |      |      |      |
| 1965 | 0.95 | 1.24 | 2.19 |      |      |      |
| 1970 | 1.15 | 1.34 | 2.54 |      |      |      |
| 1975 | 1.39 | 1.72 | 3.11 |      |      |      |
| 1980 | 1.55 | 1.78 | 3.33 |      |      |      |
| 1990 | 1.51 | 1.79 | 3.30 | 1.24 | 1.46 | 2.70 |
| 2000 | 1.31 | 1.44 | 2.75 | 1.13 | 1.20 | 2.33 |

*Sources:* Rodo Daijin Kanbo Tokei Joho Bu (1982), p. 96.
Rodo Daijin Kanbo Seisaku Chosa Bu (1992), p. 120.
Kosei Rodo Sho Daijin Kanbo Tokei Joho Bu (2002a), p. 130.

company's overall performance (i.e. its ability to pay). Many firms, especially large and well-established ones, pay bonuses twice a year equivalent in total to 2–6 months' salary (table 4.8). A payment of bonuses equivalent to two months' salary twice a year means that one-fourth of a firm's labor costs can be tied to its productivity. Many employees in Japan's larger firms depend upon overtime pay and bonuses to cover mortgage repayments and other large obligations. Together these might account for 40 percent of annual income if 10 percent of working hours are overtime and biennial bonuses total six months' salary. Many mortgage contracts establish a repayment schedule requiring that two large lump-sum repayments be made at bonus time. Because bonuses are linked to (a) the company's overall profitability, (b) what is recorded in each employee's *hyotei* (the permanent record of management's evaluation of an employee's contributions and attitude) and (c) the employee's position in the firm (which results from *hyotei*-based promotion), many employees have difficulty refusing overtime.

### 4.3.2.3   Free overtime
Many employees feel the need to provide the firm with unpaid overtime (known as "service overtime" [*sabisu zangyo*] in Japan). The provision of such labor is not captured in Ministry of Labor surveys (which are completed by firms rather than by workers themselves). This may well explain a good part of the sizable difference between the estimates provided by the Ministry of Labor and those from the NHK survey. One

internal document from Zen Shokuhin Domei (National Federation of Food Industry Workers' Unions) estimated that its members performed huge amounts of unaccounted and unpaid labor in 1993: an average of 500 hours annually on top of the 2,400 hours officially reported by the industry.

Large amounts of overtime and *sabisu zangyo* tell us not only a story of employees' commitment to their work or their firm (in the ordinary sense of the work ethic), but also a tale about the extent to which ordinary employees battle to keep their heads above water financially. Kawanishi (1992a) tells of one employee in a Hiroshima firm who was cynically referred to by his workmates as *ofurokakari* (the bath captain) because he felt that he had to stoke the bath heater at the home of his immediate supervisor in order to maintain his position in the firm. While that is an extreme example, Japan's popular culture provides many examples of the pressures put on employees to work those extra hours. That culture includes the business novels by Shimizu Ikko (1987 and 1996), Hirose Niki (1983 and 1989), Takasugi Ryo (1992 and 2000), and others. The stress flowing from such impositions is also a major theme in the work of Kumazawa whose writings were introduced in chapter 3.

### 4.3.2.4   Overtime away from the place of work

A good deal has been made of the after-hours demands placed on Japanese employees, either for *tsukiai* – entertaining clients – or for socializing with workmates (Atsumi 1979). Such hours have been the subject of considerable controversy. In this regard, it is interesting to note that very little time is reported as being spent in such activities in the NHK data (which shows considerably less than an hour a week being used for socializing with one's workmates). This suggests that the publicity given to a small number of elites who visit classy cabarets and bars on unlimited expense accounts in the large urban centers might have resulted in the creation of an urban legend about a lifestyle that many young male employees might aspire to (but seldom achieve). One might add to this the demands made by some small and medium-sized firms that young employees participate in weekend training camps. Every now and then reports of excessive bullying and physical hardship inflicted on employees appear in the media. Such practices remind one of the rigid training schedules imposed by many high school and university sporting clubs on their members during holiday periods, phenomena not too distant from pledging and other rites of passage associated with group membership in the US several decades ago.

Table 4.9 *The average number of hours spent commuting, 1990*

| A<br>Age group | B<br>Weekly hours men spend commuting | C<br>Weekly hours women spend commuting | D<br>Annual hours men spend commuting (=52B) | E<br>Annual hours women spend commuting (=52C) |
|---|---|---|---|---|
| 20s | 5.5 | 4.1 | 270 | 213 |
| 30s | 5.7 | 1.8 | 296 | 94 |
| 40s | 5.9 | 2.2 | 307 | 114 |
| 50s | 5.6 | 2.0 | 291 | 104 |
| 60s | 3.1 | 0.7 | 161 | 36 |
| 70s + | 0.7 | 0.2 | 36 | 10 |

*Source:* NHK Yoron Chosa Bu (1992), pp. 350–7.

### 4.3.3    Time spent commuting

Although stopping off at a bar or at other such establishments is not covered by the Law on Workers' Compensation for work-related injury, time spent in commuting between the place of work and home is, although such time is not normally counted in hours of work. Tables 4.9 and 4.10 show that considerable time is spent commuting. Obviously, this time is greater for office workers in the larger cities than for those in less urbanized areas, production workers in factories on the outskirts of large cities, and the unemployed. Still, commuting adds another 250 hours to the annual hours given for men in table 4.4.

### 4.3.4    Hours of work and family life

Visitors to Japan often comment on the number of Japanese sleeping on the train. The long hours consumed by activities related to work have resulted in a fatigue which must surely affect the ability of many employees to work creatively and take active pleasure in their work. It would seem likely that the time demands of work undermine the quality of family life (Mouer 1995). Over the last decade many Japanese have started to consider why the quality of their own lives remains so impoverished amidst affluence, while a growing number of observers have commented on the fatherless family as a major characteristic shaping social life and the nature of interpersonal relationships in postwar Japan. Kumazawa (1996: 249–54) argues that long hours of work are both a source and an outcome of the stress which comes from "working like mad to stay in place" simply to maintain an average standard of living.

Table 4.10 *Percentage distribution of the labor force by commuting time in twelve countries, 1988*

| Country | 0–30 minutes | 30–60 minutes | 60–90 minutes | 90–120 minutes | Over two hours |
|---|---|---|---|---|---|
| Japan | 55.6 | 28.9 | | 14.3 | |
| Into Central Tokyo: 1975 | 3.4 | 39.0 | 40.0 | 14.7 | 2.9 |
| Into Central Tokyo: 1985 | 2.7 | 35 | 41.0 | 17.0 | 3.5 |
| All EC countries | 75 | 15 | | 5 | |
| Belgium | 72 | 20 | | 8 | |
| West Germany | 73 | 25 | | 2 | |
| Denmark | 82 | 16 | | 2 | |
| France | 74 | 18 | | 8 | |
| Ireland | 70 | 26 | | 4 | |
| Italy | 78 | 20 | | 2 | |
| Luxembourg | 81 | 17 | | 2 | |
| Holland | 81 | 15 | | 4 | |
| UK | 75 | 20 | | 5 | |

*Source:* Based on data from the Prime Minister's Office (Somucho Tokei Kyoku), the Ministry for International Trade and Industry (Tsusan Sho) and the Ministry for Transportation and Communications (Unyu Sho) as provided in Osono (1995), p. 129.

### 4.3.5    Working away from one's family

A different form of commuting further highlights the powerlessness of the employee in Japan's corporate world: the phenomenon known as *tanshin fu-nin*, when a parent is given a work assignment requiring him or her to live apart from their family for an extended period in order to have a career in the corporate world. This occurs primarily in Japan's larger firms. While size allows a firm to provide its employees with higher wages and with a measure of social status, it also brings an extensive internal labor market and offices at distant locations. Those transferred far away by their employer are mostly men.

Another group similarly situated consists of those stationed overseas. For a good while, especially before 1970 when foreign exchange restrictions were still in place, many employees were sent on overseas assignment as *kaigai fu-ninsha*. While the number working abroad who are accompanied by their families has increased dramatically over the past twenty years, Tsuchiya (1995: 169–75) writes that family separation has posed serious problems for some employees, and that a number of cases of "abnormal behavior" can be attributed to enforced "bachelorhood" abroad. He goes on to indicate that many firms have started to relax restrictions on family members joining fathers on their overseas assignments, and that some firms have even encouraged them to reside abroad with the employee. The point to be made here is that firms only accommodate the interests of their employees when it is largely in the interest of the firm to do so. A careful reading of the literature on this phenomenon will reveal that companies link decisions on these kinds of matters to considerations of productivity. Management often expects its employees to adjust their lifestyle to accommodate the interests of the firm.

Associated with the overseas posting of businessmen are the problems of the *kaigai-kikoku shijo* (children overseas and returnee children). Having received considerable attention in the 1980s and early 1990s (Mabuchi 2001), the barriers confronting these children in the education system have steadily receded, and many returnees now find themselves advantaged in some ways when it comes to obtaining entry to a good university (Goodman 1992). While one might conclude that this reflects the spread of more multicultural values, as more Japanese come to appreciate the merit which flows from being proficient in other languages and familiar with other cultures, many of the changes have resulted from the pressure placed by Japanese management on "the system." Managers have used the vocabulary of "internationalization" (*kokusaika*) and "living together in the world community" (*kyosei*) to press for changes in the system of education that will primarily benefit their own offspring. Mabuchi (2001) has argued that the dynamics of social class have been overlooked in much of the discussion on the *kaigai-kikoku shijo*.

### 4.3.6    Absenteeism

Numerous writers on worker motivation have used low absenteeism as a measure of high commitment to work and the work organization (e.g. Whitehill and Takezawa 1968; Azumi and Hull 1982; Marsh and Mannari 1976). However, several features contribute to historically low levels of absenteeism in Japan. Japanese firms do not have a recognized system for sick leave. Employees do not have a right to phone so many mornings a year and simply report without documentation that illness is keeping them from work. To the extent that firms acknowledge the need for such time off, it is granted more in the form of compassionate leave. This contrasts to some European countries where employees have abused their use of "sickies" by claiming RSI or other injuries in order to take a holiday. Japanese firms also take a much stricter approach to lateness. In the past a considerable slice of the day's pay has often been deducted for undocumented lateness.

Table 4.11 *International comparison of working days lost to industrial disputes in the early 1990s*

| Country | Days lost per 1,000 employees |
| --- | --- |
| Japan | 2.26 |
| USA | 46.14 |
| UK | 66.59 |
| France | 21.74 |
| Germany | 12.21 |
| Italy | 217.72 |

*Source:* The figures were calculated by the authors from figures on days lost in 1993 owing to industrial disputes and the number of persons in each labor force in 1990 as appeared in Rodo Daijin Kanbo Seisaku Chosa Bu (1995), pp. 334 and 336.

Table 4.11 reveals considerable variations among nations in working days lost owing to industrial disputes. Kumazawa's data (1996: 5–6) clearly shows, however, that these differences among countries narrowed considerably between 1970 and the early 1990s. Sugimoto's (1977) comparison of industrial disputes in Japan and Australia in the 1950s and 1970s showed a long-term decline in both countries. Kumazawa argues that the global trend is for days lost to decline when liberal governments sympathetic to labor are in power, noting that Japan is an exception, with disruptive action declining under a firmly entrenched conservative government. Global movements in ideology and a general spread of the conservative, anti-unionist ideologies associated with Thatcherism and Reaganomics have probably been a more important factor behind the long-term decline in disputes. Free-market ideology enjoyed a long-term ascendancy as the cold war progressed and was eventually won by the forces for capitalism. Such ideologies were further legitimated by the Western attention given to the Japanese miracle and the subsequent "learn-from-Japan boom" that accompanied the decline of socialist systems in the 1970s and 1980s. These changes also accompanied the decline in unionization rates in most of the advanced economies.

### 4.3.7   Underutilization of accrued annual leave

Another facet of low absenteeism in Japan is the underutilization of annual leave. Teruoka (1990: 119) presents data collected by Zenkoku Kensetsu Kanren Rokyo (the National Federation of Construction Workers' Associations) in the late 1980s showing that workers feel compelled to save

Table 4.12 *The accrual and use of annual leave, 2001*

| Firm size (number of employees) | A<br>Average number of days of annual paid leave accrued | B<br>Average number of days of annual paid leave actually used | C<br>Leave consumption rate (100B/A) |
|---|---|---|---|
| 1,000+ | 19.4 | 10.6 | 54.6 |
| 300–999 | 18.2 | 8.7 | 47.6 |
| 100–299 | 17.1 | 7.7 | 45.4 |
| 30–99 | 16.4 | 7.3 | 44.6 |

*Source:* Kosei Rodo Sho Daijin Kanbo Tokei Joho Bu (2002a), p. 122.

accrued annual paid leave for a rainy day. Forty percent of the workers in that survey reported that they used some of their paid annual leave entitlement for illness; 30 percent did so for days they were simply too tired to get out of bed; and another 30 percent did so to look after family members. Although the law provides for menstruation leave, it is unpaid, and 17 percent of the women in the survey said they took annual leave on days when they had severe menstrual pain. Only 30 percent replied that they used annual leave for leisure or recreation. Twenty percent said they used annual leave to take care of legal matters, to attend a wedding, and to deal with other official matters. Only 2 percent answered that leave was used for community or organizational activities. Teruoka (1990: 120) also cites a Ministry of Labor Survey showing a steady decline in the willingness of workers in firms with thirty or more employees to use their annual leave. The consumption rate dropped from 62.1 percent in 1970 to 50.2 percent in 1987 and then from 54.1 percent in 1990 to 49.5 percent in 2000, albeit with an increase over that same period in the absolute number from 14.4 days accrued in 1980 to 18.0 days in 2000 (Rodo Daijin Kanbo Tokei Joho Bu 1982: 176; and Kosei Rodo Sho Daijin Kanbo Tokei Joho Bu 2002a: 123).

Table 4.12 reveals sizable differences in the amount of paid annual leave accrued by workers in Japan's large and small firms. It also highlights two other facts. First, employees in all firms generally use only half of their accrued leave. While this is often interpreted as evidence of a strong work ethic, the institutional constraints explained above in section 4.3.6 need to be considered. Second, even in consuming only half of their annual leave, many employees in Japan's large firms still take close to ten days a year, roughly equivalent to the situation in many American firms where the practice of providing only two weeks of annual paid leave to all employees is fairly well entrenched.

## 4.4    Labor-force participation

Consideration of labor-force participation provides another perspective linking the work ethic, social structure, and the economy's overall performance. For the economy to grow, competitive sectors with high productivity must expand their labor force. More skilled labor is drawn to those sectors by recruiting new employees from outside the labor force or by shifting workers from activities with low returns to activities with high returns. The likelihood of getting persons to shift jobs and change firms is enhanced when replacements can be found for those lower down the productivity chain. The first wave of replacements was brought from agricultural activity to secondary industry at a frantic pace in the 1950s and 1960s. Thereafter came the expansion of part-time and other forms of casual employment.

A number of mechanisms facilitated the shift of workers from sunset industries to sunrise industries. The spread of part-time work accompanied the movement of women into the labor force, although care needs to be taken in making this argument, as the labor-force participation for women has remained remarkably stable at around 50 percent for some time. The long-term impact of the Douglas-Long-Arisawa effect (the propensity of married women to withdraw from the labor force as their husband's salary increases over time) seems to have been offset by the desire of households to achieve the ever more expensive lifestyles associated with the upper middle class. Obi (1980) observed this in the early 1970s. Since then many women have shifted from full-time employment with *relatively* poor working conditions to part-time work with *relatively* better conditions, thereby maintaining income while also limiting the opportunity costs accruing to the household when a family member works outside.

Many countries have overcome "labor shortages" by importing workers, either as guests (e.g. in Germany and Japan) or as new members of the body politic (e.g. in multicultural Australia or in the American "melting pot"). Japan's reliance on outside labor has been negligible; most additions to its labor force have come from within (e.g. as part-time workers [housewives], as contracted sessionals [older workers over the nominal retirement age], or as *arubaito* [students]). Though Japan generally failed to absorb large numbers of refugees from Vietnam in the late 1970s, the bubble years were accompanied by a tightening of the labor market. The high aspirations spawned by the bubble years lowered the willingness of many Japanese to do work characterized by "the three Ds" (danger, dirt, and difficulty) (known as "the three Ks" in Japan: *kitanai, kikenna,* and *kitsui*). The strong yen also drew many foreigners to Japan to work both legally and illegally. By the late 1990s over one million foreigners were living in Japan, and one out of every forty persons living in Tokyo was a foreigner with permanent residency. This is an important fact not only when considering the directions in which Japanese society is moving in terms of its internationalization and multiculturalization, but also when considering hours of work and the work ethic in Japan.

Much has been written over the last decade about the changing values of the Japanese. Some have argued that a new generation has brought a different outlook to the workplace. Many catchphrases have been used to capture the essence of the new attitudes: *yawarakai kojinshugi* (soft individualism), *shinjinrai* (the new humanism), etc. However, the percentage of men aged between 15 and 64 who are working has remained remarkably stable over time. So too has the percentage of women, although there has been a slight rise in the participation rate of women in the middle age groups.

Despite the apparent shifts in the lifestyle and perhaps the thinking of many Japanese over the past ten to twenty years with regard to work, other factors have also been important. One of these has been the changing age profile of the population. Although the labor-force participation rate of those aged 15–64 has been rather stable over that period, the proportion of the population constituting that age group has grown throughout the postwar period. Moreover, a good number of people aged over 65 are working. As a result, the percentage of the total population gainfully employed grew by three percentage points between 1980 (47.29 percent) and 2000 (50.79 percent) (Kosei Rodo Sho Daijin Kanbo Tokei Joho Bu 2002a: 20 and 30). As items I and J in table 4.13 indicate, considerably more Japanese were gainfully employed in the early 1990s than were their counterparts in several other advanced economies. While five out of every ten Japanese were actually working to produce goods and services, only four out of ten persons in Italy and France were doing so. From the point of view of the national economy, this means that each working person in Japan was supporting one other person, whereas in the other two countries every person was supporting 1.5 other people. Arguments about productivity aside, the consequences for national savings and their contribution to economic productivity should be obvious. These considerations move key reference points even further from simple notions of labor productivity in terms of the hourly output of individual workers.

Another consideration here is unemployment. Until the 1990s Japan had exceptionally low unemployment. One benefit to economies with low unemployment is that fewer persons drain surplus from the economy while not making any contribution to it. Japan's approach to managing unemployment has reaped other benefits as well. These include

Table 4.13 *Comparative figures on labor-force participation for six countries in the early 1990s*

| | Japan 1993 | USA 1993 | UK 1993 | France 1993 | Germany 1992 | Italy 1991 |
|---|---|---|---|---|---|---|
| **1. Overall labor-force participation rates** | | | | | | |
| A. Total population (in millions) | 124.7 | 259.4 | 57.2 | 57.5 | 64.7 | 57.1 |
| B. Labor force (in millions) | 66.2 | 129.5 | 28.8 | 25.7 | 31.9 | 24.2 |
| C. Number of persons in the military: 1992 (in millions) | 0.246 | 1.914 | 0.294 | 0.432 | 0.246 | n.a. |
| D. Civilian labor force (in millions) | 65.9 | 127.6 | 28.5 | 25.3 | 31.6 | n.a. |
| E. Percentage of the population aged over 15 in the labor force | 63.8 | 63.3 | 62.4 | 55.0 | 58.3 | 50.1 |
| F. Percentage of total population in the labor force ($=100\mathbf{B/A}$) | 53.1 | 49.9 | 50.3 | 44.7 | 49.3 | 42.5 |
| G. Percentage of total population in the civilian labor force ($= 100\ \mathbf{D/A}$) | 52.9 | 49.2 | 49.8 | 44.0 | 48.9 | n.a. |
| H. Unemployment rate (%) for (**B**) above | 2.5 | 6.8 | 10.4 | 10.8 | 6.7 | 10.9 |
| I. Percentage of the total population actively employed when corrected for unemployment [$=\mathbf{F} \times (100-\mathbf{H})$] | 51.8 | 46.5 | 45.1 | 40.0 | 46.0 | 37.9 |
| J. Percentage of the total population actively employed in the civilian labor force when corrected for unemployment [$=\mathbf{G} \times (100-\mathbf{H})$] | 51.6 | 45.9 | 44.4 | 39.2 | 45.6 | n.a. |
| | Japan | USA | UK | France | Germany | Italy |
| **2. Labor-force participation rates by age group and gender** | | | | | | |
| Males 15–19 | 19.0 | 39.8 | 61.1 | 9.8 | 39.4 | 32.2 |
| Females 15–19 | 17.4 | 38.4 | 58.0 | 6.7 | 34.3 | 19.3 |
| Males 20–64 | 90.3 | 80.5 | 85.5 | 74.6 | 82.2 | 83.0 |
| Females 20–64 | 58.2 | 66.8 | 66.8 | 60.5 | 59.5 | 44.0 |
| Males 65+ | 37.7 | 15.2 | 7.4 | 2.5 | 4.9 | 8.1 |
| Females 65+ | 15.9 | 7.5 | 3.5 | 1.3 | 2.0 | 2.2 |

*Note:* Some figures may appear to be slightly out as the raw figures with more significant digits were used for some calculations.

*Sources:* Rodo Daijin Kanbo Seisaku Chosa Bu (1995), pp. 332 and 334.

Yano Tsuneo Ki-nenkai (1993), p. 562 (for row **C** only).

the maintenance of social order and an incidence of crime lower than in some societies with institutionalized poverty. Some have argued that Japan's lower unemployment rates were accompanied by high levels of compulsion to work and the associated stress. The unemployment system still adopts a rather punitive and coercive approach that makes the dole an unattractive option for most Japanese. While benefits paid to the unemployed may be satisfactory and training is provided in a positive manner, the fact remains that the benefits for many stop after a maximum of 180 days. The fact that the unemployed in Australia could until recently receive quite generous benefits for an unlimited time is very difficult for many Japanese business persons and policy makers to comprehend. This meant that with a 10 percent unemployment rate Australia was a society in which over 90 percent of the relevant population worked without any compulsion, whereas in Japan 2–3 percent of that population chose not to work even though considerable pressure to do so was exerted. Put this way, it is not so obvious that Japanese have had the better work ethic, despite the fact that a larger percentage of their population was in some way employed. Another factor to consider is the relationship between the centrally determined living wage and the unemployment rate. Management and government advisers in Japan tend to argue that higher minimum wage rates contribute to higher unemployment. Although Japan enacted minimum wage legislation in 1958, the rate has always been below the going rate in the open labor market and has not served as a safety net for anyone. This points to tradeoffs which need to be recognized not only in evaluating work organization in Japan in normative terms, but also in considering the weight to be given to cultural factors when looking for explanations.

Returning to consider Japan's savings rate and general economic competitiveness, one might also note the small number of resources Japan devotes to defense. This is not simply a matter of shifting expenditure from military to investment goods. It is also a matter of how the labor force is assigned to spend its time. Large powers like the US, Russia, and China – and a few highly mobilized societies such as Israel or the Koreas – have large numbers of people in the military. Japan has a small military, and a larger proportion of its work force is employed in factories and offices. This adds to the percentage of the population that is gainfully employed in ways linked to the production of GNP and the economy's international competitiveness.

When adjustments are made for those in the military and for those who are unemployed (rows C and H in table 4.13), substantial differences emerge in terms of the percentage of the entire population which is working (row J). Japan has a larger working population (though not necessarily

Table 4.14 *Real difference in hours of work per person in the population, circa 1992–3*

| Country | A<br>Percentage of population in the civilian labor force who are actively employed (Row J in table 4.13) | B<br>Annual hours of work in 1992 (from table 4.2) | C<br>Index with Germany set at 1.00 | D<br>Hours worked in economic production per person in the population [=(A×B)/100] | E<br>Index with Germany set at 1.00 |
|---|---|---|---|---|---|
| Japan | 51.6 | 2,017 | 1.29 | 1,041 | 1.46 |
| USA | 45.9 | 1,957 | 1.25 | 898 | 1.26 |
| UK | 44.4 | 1,911 | 1.22 | 848 | 1.19 |
| France | 39.2 | 1,682 | 1.07 | 659 | 0.92 |
| Germany | 45.6 | 1,567 | 1.00 | 715 | 1.00 |

*Source:* The figures in this table have been taken from tables 4.2 and 4.13.

one with a more developed work ethic). The figures on annual hours of work in table 4.2 and those on labor-force participation in table 4.13 have been brought together in table 4.14 to provide a further perspective on the different amounts of labor Japanese and Western Europeans put into their respective national economies on a per capita basis for the entire population (as opposed to just the gainfully employed). The differences in the early 1990s were not negligible.

Japanese management has continued in public forums to lament that the work ethic of the younger generation has declined and to exhort employees to work harder. Older employees have romanticized their long hours of work in the past. On the other hand, younger employees have been enthusiastic for more leisure-time activity. These generational differences are not unique to Japan. They generally fit into a Mannheimian framework, and more sanguine observers look to the demographic profile to explain these perspectives. A 1997 study by the Kokuritsu Shakai Hosho Jinko Mondai Kenkyujo (National Institute for the Study of Social Welfare and the Population) indicated that the Japanese population will likely drop from the 2010s onwards, but notes that the number of persons aged between 15 and 64 (an age group that increased throughout the postwar period) will drop even more dramatically (*Nihon Keizai Shimbun* [*chokan*], 28 March 1997, pp. 1 and 3). This means that Japan will come to have a population with proportionally fewer people working and an increasingly large group of dependent individuals unless the already high labor-force participation rate for those over 65 increases further.

These changes will slow down the Japanese economy and result in attention shifting from the alleged work ethic of the Japanese. At the same time, the drive to secure good-quality labor will be reflected in the way the organization of work is revamped in Japan over the next ten to twenty years. That will in turn impact significantly on how Japan internationalizes. With regard to bringing in foreign labor, Japan is likely to follow a path between the American and the Australian experiences. The melting pot approach of the US has allowed successive waves of migrants to flow in at the bottom of the labor market to do work characterized by the three Ks and then to be "bumped up" the occupational ladder as newer arrivals replace them in the bottom labor markets. The multicultural approach of Australia has been somewhat more careful in targeting skilled persons, with migrants from a broader spectrum of social classes integrating into society. The costs associated with the enculturalization of newcomers are not insignificant, and the tradeoffs between productivity and reformulated notions of social justice will likely alter perceptions of the work ethic in Japan.

*Part III*

# Processing labor through Japan's labor markets

# 5    Change and challenge in the labor market

Today is May Day, eighty some years on from the first May Day in 1920 . . . It has been a bleak year for labor. This year's Spring Offensive resulted in no gains for most, and even a cut in wages for some. Job security, a traditional priority for Japan's unions, has been undermined by corporate lay-offs . . .

There is also positive news in signs of an economic recovery. However, real economic growth, meaning restructuring, is needed. More effort must be put into creating . . . opportunities for students to acquire the new IT technology that can be immediately used at work. Steps need to be taken to implement work sharing. Changes are needed so that demand for nursing care and other services can be met. Employers must stop forcing workers to put in unpaid overtime . . . The gap in working conditions for regular and part-time workers must be closed . . . Without movement in these directions, new ways of working will not emerge (editorial in the *Tokyo Shimbun* [morning edition], 1 May 2002, p. 4).

## 5.1    The winds of change

The decision of many Japanese to work as they do is fundamentally shaped by their options in a very segmented labor market that tends to lock each individual into a clearly delineated niche. A number of dualities characterize Japan's labor market. Internal labor markets are also differentiated. Educational histories determine entry into the labor market and entrenched hierarchies influence job choices in the segmented labor market. The 2002 May Day editorial above argues that Japan is being challenged to replace that labor market. As China displaces Japan's role as a major manufacturing center, labor market reform will be crucial to any plan to revitalize Japan's economy.

Figure 5.1 shows how Japan's labor market has been structured over the past forty to fifty years. It compares the situation in Japan with that in Australia. Mobility in Japan is primarily downward or laterally out of the privileged large-scale sector. Some time ago Koshiro (1982b) wrote

**A. Labor market flows in Japan**

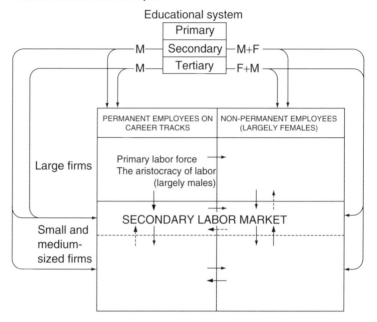

**B. Labor market flows in Australia**

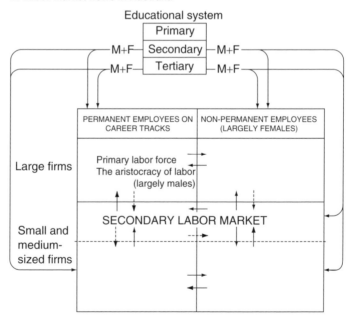

Figure 5.1 The structuring of the labor market in Japan, entry into its segments and the paths for downward mobility (circa 1990).
*Source:* Mouer (1989), p. 118.

about the scarcity of good jobs and the difficulty of gaining employment in the privileged sectors of Japan's labor market.

Many Japanese focus on how they and others are positioned in a number of cross-cutting labor markets. Graduates compete hard to get into the best-placed market and then strive to avoid slipping into a less well-positioned one. Entry into the elite market of Japan's largest and most prestigious firms has traditionally been reserved for male graduates from Japan's better universities and a few select high schools and technical institutes.

For many Japanese competition for the superior jobs began in middle school and this has shaped a good deal of the behavior in postwar Japan: examination hell, the cramming and various psychological ploys associated with entrance examinations, the annual round of hiring ending in March each year, internal politics in many firms, *amakudari* (the practice of well-positioned bureaucrats being allocated sinecures in the private sector after a career in the public sector), and the maneuvering for promotion in private firms in order to secure the best post-retirement positions in affiliated firms. The sagas of the *moretsu shain* (the gung-ho company employee) unfolded in firms large enough to have internal markets and competitive jostling was the basis for a whole genre of business novels as discussed by Tao (1996). Authors such as Shimizu Ikko, Shiroyama Saburo, and Takasugi Ryo come immediately to mind. When firms came under financial pressure they simply demanded more of their employees, and the phenomena associated with *karoshi* (death from overwork) emerged.

This chapter describes multiple ways in which Japan's labor market is segmented, the tiering of markets, the difficulty of moving from lower to higher markets, and the consequences of cascading down the tiers when someone does not live up to expectations. In the 1990s Japan's labor markets were altered by a number of changes: increased international competition owing to globalization, government policies deregulating the labor market, industrial restructuring, rising unemployment, a record number of bankruptcies, a greater willingness of individuals (especially young people) to critically assess options in the labor force, and new corporate strategies to adapt to these kinds of changes. New levels of affluence and the appreciation of the yen presented Japan's youth with options altogether outside the labor market.

This chapter looks briefly at Japan's rising unemployment rate and then at the legal framework that delimits the labor market in Japan. After discussing the organization of internal and external labor markets, the chapter examines the markets for new graduates, women, employees in foreign firms, and the growing number of foreign workers.

## 5.2     The overall dimensions of the labor market

As discussed in chapter 4, Japan has a fairly high labor-force participation rate. Table 5.1 shows the participation rate falling for males aged over 14 from around 85 percent in the mid-1950s to just over 75 percent at the turn of the century. It fell for women from 55 percent in 1955 to just under 46 percent by 1975, but it has risen to hover around 50 percent since 1990. Table 5.1 also reveals a steady shift between 1955 and 1995 in the distribution of the labor-force toward employment and away from entrepreneurial engagement. For women the movement has also been away from family-run businesses to which they contributed without formally being remunerated. The gross figures do not reveal the extent to which employment has been casualized. The other major change has been the rising unemployment rate during the 1990s.

The labor-force participation rate of those aged over 65 stands out. Table 5.2 shows how labor-force participation varies by age. First, there is very little gender difference for those aged 15–24. Nearly everyone becomes employed upon graduation (at 18 for most school leavers and for most tertiary graduates). Second, labor-force participation drops off markedly for females aged over 60. Third, the M-shaped labor-force participation curve for women has begun to flatten out. The dip still exists, but it is now much less pronounced than in the early 1970s. Women aged 25–35 have noticeably increased their participation. Several changes account for this. The curve for women with higher education is rounded upwards without the dip; the traditional M-shaped curve now fits only those with a senior high school education. The postponement of marriage and childbirth has spread out the absence of women from the labor force so that the dip is less pronounced for women in their early thirties.

Table 5.2 shows that the participation rate for Japanese aged over 65 is high by international standards. Policymakers in contemporary Japan have frequently commented on the falling ratio of the working population to the dependent population as society ages. They are concerned about Japan's ability to support its retired labor force adequately. The proportion of the population aged over 65 has increased from 7.9 percent in 1975 to 16.7 percent in 1999, while the proportion of the population aged under 15 (for which the participation rate is zero) has dropped from 24.3 percent to 14.8 percent and the number of Japanese of working age between 15 and 65 have increased from 67.7 to 68.5 percent (Yano Tsuneta Ki-nenkai 2001: 43). As the aged population continues to expand, any downward shift in the currently high labor-force participation rate among Japan's older population will require a major adjustment in a range of social institutions.

Table 5.1 *Labor-force participation for males and females in Japan, 1955–2000*

| | | 1955 | 1965 | 1975 | 1985 | 1995 | 1996 | 1997 | 1998 | 1999 | 2000 |
|---|---|---|---|---|---|---|---|---|---|---|---|
| **M** | Number in the labor force (in 10,000 s) | 2,455 | 2,884 | 3,270 | 3,503 | 3,843 | 3,858 | 3,892 | 3,858 | 3,831 | 3,817 |
| **A** | Labor force as a % of total population | 56 | 59 | 59 | 58 | 62 | 62 | 63 | 62 | 61 | 61 |
| **L** | Participation rate as a % of population aged 15+ | 86 | 82 | 81 | 78 | 78 | 78 | 78 | 77 | 77 | 76 |
| **E** | Unemployment rate | 2.6 | 1.1 | 2.0 | 2.6 | 3.1 | 3.4 | 3.4 | 4.2 | 4.8 | 4.9 |
| **S** | Distribution of gainfully employed as employees | 52 | 69 | 76 | 79 | 84 | 84 | 84 | 84 | 84 | 84 |
| | as self-employed | 32 | 23 | 20 | 18 | 14 | 14 | 14 | 14 | 14 | 14 |
| | in family employment | 16 | 8 | 4 | 3 | 2 | 2 | 2 | 2 | 2 | 2 |
| **F** | Number in the labor force (in 10,000s) | 1,740 | 1,903 | 1,987 | 2,367 | 2,701 | 2,719 | 2,760 | 2,767 | 2,755 | 2,753 |
| **E** | Labor force as a % of total population | 38 | 38 | 35 | 38 | 42 | 42 | 42 | 42 | 42 | 42 |
| **M** | Participation rate as a % of population aged 15+ | 57 | 51 | 46 | 49 | 50 | 50 | 50 | 50 | 50 | 49 |
| **A** | Unemployment rate | 2.3 | 1.3 | 1.7 | 2.7 | 3.2 | 3.3 | 3.4 | 4.0 | 4.5 | 4.5 |
| **L** | Distribution of gainfully employed as employees | 31 | 48 | 59 | 67 | 78 | 79 | 79 | 79 | 80 | 81 |
| **E** | as self-employed | 16 | 14 | 14 | 12 | 8 | 8 | 8 | 8 | 8 | 8 |
| **S** | in family employment | 53 | 36 | 25 | 20 | 12 | 11 | 11 | 11 | 11 | 11 |

*Source*: Taken from successive reports of the *Rodoryoku Chosa* (Labor Force Survey) which has been conducted monthly since 1947 and is now administered by the Statistics Bureau of the Ministry of Public Management, Home Affairs, Posts and Telecomunications. The figures in this table have been transferred and processed from the Labor White Paper for 2001 (Kosei Rodo Sho 2001a), pp. 234–6.

Table 5.2 *Male and female labor-force participation rates by age group, 1990 and 2001*

| Age group | Males | | Females | |
|---|---|---|---|---|
| | 1990 | 2001 | 1990 | 2001 |
| 15–19 | 18.3 | 17.9 | 17.8 | 17.5 |
| 20–24 | 71.7 | 71.9 | 75.1 | 72.0 |
| 25–29 | 96.1 | 95.4 | 61.4 | 71.1 |
| 30–34 | 97.5 | 97.2 | 51.7 | 58.8 |
| 35–39 | 97.8 | 97.8 | 62.6 | 62.3 |
| 40–44 | 97.6 | 97.7 | 69.9 | 70.1 |
| 44–49 | 97.3 | 97.2 | 71.7 | 72.7 |
| 50–54 | 96.3 | 96.3 | 65.5 | 68.2 |
| 55–59 | 92.1 | 93.9 | 53.9 | 58.4 |
| 60–64 | 72.9 | 72.0 | 39.5 | 39.5 |
| 65+ | 36.5 | 32.9 | 16.2 | 13.8 |
| Americans aged 65+ | | 16.9 | | 8.9 |
| Germans aged 65+ | | 4.5 | | 1.6 |

*Note:* The data for America and Germany are for 1999.
*Source:* The figures for Japan are taken from successive reports of the *Rodoryoku Chosa* (Labor Force Survey) which has been conducted monthly since 1947 and is now administered by the Statistics Bureau of the Ministry of Public Management, Home Affairs, Posts and Telecommunications. The figures in this table have been transferred and processed from the 2001 White Paper on the Labor Economy (Kosei Rodo Sho 2001a), pp. 234–6. The figures for America and Germany are from the ILO's *Yearbook of Labor Statistics* as published in the 2001 Welfare and Labor White Paper (Kosei Rodo Sho 2001b), p. 43.

## 5.3 Unemployment

After four decades of extremely low unemployment rates, the situation deteriorated considerably in the 1990s. The unemployment rate doubled from just over 1 percent in the 1960s to just under 3 percent in the 1980s. It then surpassed 3 percent in 1995, 4 percent in 1998 and 5 percent in July 2001. Considering how narrow the definition is for counting the unemployed in Japan's statistics and the downward adjustments made in overtime, the situation is likely to have a greater impact on ordinary people than is shown in the statistics. The oil shocks of the 1970s reminded policymakers that a good deal of unemployment was disguised as a result of across-the-board reductions in overtime. In the 1990s employers were more willing to concentrate unemployment on a few individuals rather than spreading it across their entire workforce.

It is interesting to note that about 40 percent of women leaving jobs did so for personal reasons (*jihatsuteki rishoku*). Only a quarter of female separations involved the women being "pushed out" (*hijihatsuteki rishoku*) as opposed to about 40 percent for men. These patterns have been fairly stable over the past two decades. However, the statistics are blurred by the practice of recruiting large numbers of "voluntary" retirees (*kibo taishokusha*) for whom the pain of separation may be eased by the use of an early retirement scheme. The statistics also do not include as involuntary separations many others who receive no package but are informally tapped on the shoulder and told their time is up (a practice known as "*katatataki*").

It is important to note that the definition of unemployment used in producing Japan's official statistics is very narrow. To be counted as unemployed in the monthly Labor Force Survey, a respondent must have been completely unemployed but actively looking for work during the last week of the preceding month. Those who have worked as little as one hour in the last week after being completely unemployed over the first three weeks of that month are not counted as unemployed. The "employed" include unpaid family workers, those on various forms of leave, and those doing no work but still on an employer's payroll. Those who are so unemployable that they have given up actively looking for work through the Employment Security Office are not counted as unemployed. Japan's narrow definition of unemployment contrasts to that used in America where all who have looked for work over the past month are counted as unemployed. In Germany and France the unemployed are those who have received unemployment benefit during the period covered by the survey.

Given the difficulty of making international comparisons, one cannot simply conclude that Japan's unemployment rate has been low. Some time ago Nakamura (1995: 59 and 165) suggested that a distinction should be drawn between full employment and total employment. Japan has traditionally been good at having large numbers employed (total employment) in non-productive activity that resulted in considerable underutilization (less than full employment). This situation was noted recently in a survey of the Japanese economy undertaken by the OECD (2001: 44–7) which commented on the variation in total factor productivity between various sectors of the Japanese economy.

## 5.4    Structural change and insecurity

The recent increase in Japan's official rates of unemployment reflects larger changes accompanying Japan's integration into the global economy. The work culture of Japan was for a long time cast in terms of the country's prodigious manufacturing sector. However, Japan's competitive edge in manufacturing was challenged in the 1990s. In Japan's established auto industry Matsuda decided in 2001 to release 2,210 employees. Isuzu followed with 740; and then Mitsubishi Motors with 1,382. Sony announced plans to close fifteen of its seventy factories in Japan (*ASC* 25 August 2001: 7). A succession of established firms followed: Fujitsu (16,000 persons), NEC (4,000), Aiwa (a Sony subsidiary) (400), Toshiba (20,000), and Matsushita (5,000). The new economy offered little certainty even for employees in Japan's largest and most elite firms. The above companies all had well-established reputations for providing employment security above all, in line with the founder of Matsushita/ Panasonic Matsushita Konosuke's outspoken promotion of paternalistic management and his rhetoric fully embracing all employees even in the worst economic downturn. The prestige associated with the unions at these firms had also rested on the perception that they had successfully fought to protect their members' jobs above all else. The symbolism of those layoffs for ordinary Japanese was not lost: employment was no longer guaranteed in any segment of the labor market.

Japan's financial crisis in the early 1990s contributed significantly to fracturing the understandings and the confidence upon which old ways of doing business had been based. Although direct foreign investment began in the early 1970s, when small manufacturers in textiles and other light industries began to move operations overseas following the floating of the dollar in August 1971, the rising costs of domestic production, the demand for greater accountability financially and environmentally, the advantages of producing on the other side of tariff barriers, rapidly accumulating reserves of foreign exchange, and further appreciation of the yen motivated many of Japan's larger manufacturers to step up the transfer of production to overseas sites.

The effects of these trends were recently summarized by the president of Nihon Densan (Japan's top manufacturer of small precision motors):

Manufacturing today is characterized by a labor surplus in some areas and by marked shortages in others. While we face high labor turnover among newly employed graduates, we are also stuck with a good proportion of middle-aged employees who are being paid more than their productivity warrants. The problem is that in terms of skills and seniority we have some serious mismatches [in the labor market] (*ASC*, 4 September 2001: 13).

The loss of Japan's competitiveness in manufacturing is now a big concern in Japan. From late 2001 the media has suggested that Japan is at a crossroads. The influential *Asahi Shimbun*, for example, ran a series entitled "The Strength of Manufacturing: The Cornerstones for Recovery" (29 April – 4 May 2002). It acknowledged China's unbeatable competitive edge in labor-intensive areas, and noted the drop in Japan's overall international competitiveness, citing European research which indicated that Japan had dropped from first position in 1991–3 to thirteenth in 2002 (3 May: 11). The series concluded with an emphasis on the need for business leadership to motivate Japan's labor force (4 May: 7). Nissan's three-year 108 Plan calls for the company to open a joint venture in China (*NKSC*, 10 May 2002: 3; *ASC*, 10 May 2002: 3). Mitsubishi's plans to cooperate with Germany's Daimler to manufacture in China have also attracted attention. Another special feature article in *Nikkei Bijinesu* (6 May 2002) questioned whether small businesses, the backbone of the Japanese economy, would survive. Many, such as Yoshida (2001), a distinguished professor of economics at Osaka and Kyoto universities, recognize that Japan has somehow fallen behind and that the change necessary to catch up is going to be particularly painful for those in Japan's labor force.

Globalization has also worked to free up Japanese markets to imports. In 2002 most observers predicted that there would be continuing pressure on firms to restructure. In their special report for the *Far Eastern Economic Review*, Kruger and Fuyuno (2002) describe how cheap Chinese imports have undercut the centuries-old ceramics and textile industries in Gifu with labor costs that are one-tenth to one-thirtieth those in Japan. For a long time Japanese believed they were manning the factory of the world; now China has taken over that mantle. At the same time large-scale retailers muscle in with more cheaply produced goods from China. Such competition cannot be met by the myriad of small shops which constitute station shopping areas (*shotengai*) throughout Japan. Reports in 2002 that Wal-Mart might soon be opening outlets in Japan is disturbing news for Japan's retailers. At all levels economic life is being rationalized.

The Ministry of Welfare and Labor distinguishes between structural unemployment owing to friction or mismatching in the labor market (resulting from long-term shifts in the market for goods and services) and unemployment owing to a drop in demand for a specific product or service (because of short-term cyclical fluctuations). Reflecting wider recessionary conditions during the 1990s the contribution of structured unemployment to overall unemployment fell from over 90 percent to under 80 percent. However, long-term unemployment continues to result from the difficulties labor markets are having in shifting labor to more productive activities, as businesses attempt to recast Japan's industrial structure in the face of globalization. These difficulties are one measure of how effectively Japan's various labor markets are functioning. While internal labor markets, tiered subcontracting and the use of multiple employment statuses have enhanced the leverage of management in dealing with labor, inefficiencies in Japan's labor markets have been exposed by global competition – not just in terms of individual firms but also in terms of the national economy. Reacting to this situation, large-scale players in the private sector have pushed hard to deregulate the labor market.

In the past firms adjusted costs by cutting off subcontractors, by altering conditions, by not hiring part-time or other non-regular workers on annual contracts, and by regulating overtime. (In this discussion, it is important to remember that reductions in hours worked do not reduce costs for most of Japan's regular employees, white-collar and blue-collar, who are on a salary.) Although each of these strategies reinforces the sense of economic insecurity among non-permanent employees, they do not seriously alter patterns of labor market segmentation. Permanent employees are still permanent employees, and their market in the large-scale sector still attracts an army of hopeful aspirants who work hard to position themselves as best they can in the education system as a prelude to entering into one of the tiered labor markets.

Until the 1990s, much of the structural change was in terms of small shifts in demand (requiring, for example, either a change in the volume produced or an alteration to products already being produced). These shifts required a relatively simple expansion (or contraction) of the labor force. This could be managed by hiring (or releasing) non-regular employees and subcontractors who provided duplicate labor, by "multiskilling" or "reassigning" employees through elaborate job rotation schemes, or by adjusting the working hours (e.g. the overtime or scheduling) of regular employees who did duplicate or repetitive work. Globalization has come to require (a) a more complex or sophisticated mix of employees who are more differentiated and specialized than in the past, and (b) a much shorter turnaround time. This has meant a lower ratio of (i) permanent (core) employees in supervisory positions and in more inflexible forms of employment to (ii) non-permanent staff doing repetitive work whose relationship with management can be altered much more easily, and to (iii) more individually specialized professionals whose labor could also be regulated more easily.

Many core employees now need a much greater range of conceptual and interpersonal skills at much higher levels than on-the-job training or other in-house schemes can provide. Staff who do repetitive work are also being required to acquire higher levels of proficiency in very specific, often technical, sets of skills that firms find difficult to impart and then use elsewhere when operations change. Accompanying the shift from importing technology to creating their own as a means of gaining competitive advantage, professionals are being asked to be more adventurous in producing new ideas. Professionals who concentrate their efforts on developing new technologies increasingly bear the risks when their efforts do not succeed – something that management is now less willing to do. Strategies designed to meet challenges faced by the Japanese economy as a whole add new dimensions to the external labor market. By the late 1990s Japanese firms recognized the need for labor market flexibility beyond that provided by attrition and the slow process of multiskilling associated with traditional Japanese approaches. International competitiveness in the modern world encourages firms to hive off operations that are not economical to parties better prepared to make them profitable, and to acquire operations they can revitalize. Whether buying or selling, the speed and the ability to be decisive at the right moment are critical. Long-term employment practices compromise a firm's ability to reduce the labor costs associated with having a large coterie of salaried professionals.

With greater transparency in personnel matters, Japan's large firms have been more willing to rely on external labor markets. While this no doubt reflects the influence of economic rationalism as an international ideology, conservative Japanese businessmen have in the main always subscribed to such a philosophy. This has been reflected in the policies advocated by Nikkeiren (the Japan Federation of Employers' Associations) at times such as the Spring Wage Offensive. Management has long acknowledged the importance of labor process at the meso and the micro levels as a means of maintaining the bottom line and expropriating today's labor surplus for tomorrow's investment (and for managerial remuneration).

The last quarter of a century has seen the balance of power between organized labor and organized management shift to the latter. As chapter 8 indicates, the reasons for the decline in the political influence of Japanese labor unions, especially left-wing unions, are complex. Many of these reasons are not peculiar to Japan. They include domestically driven restructuring, casualization, and the changing aspirations of new graduates entering the labor force. Without concrete evidence to the contrary, it would seem likely that the development of highly networked global communications has initially helped management more than labor unions in Japan. More knowledge about why that is so is critical for any prognostication about the future of work in Japan. The dissemination of new international vocabularies has given Japan's management groups a means of repackaging the rhetoric for expressing old concerns. Although some Japanese workers have enjoyed the fruits of globalization, especially as consumers, there is also considerable disquiet among certain segments of the labor force, and it cannot be assumed that they will continue to benefit from globalization in net terms.

It is still too early to know how the more disciplined use of Japanese labor will impact upon labor markets. As long as firms remain committed

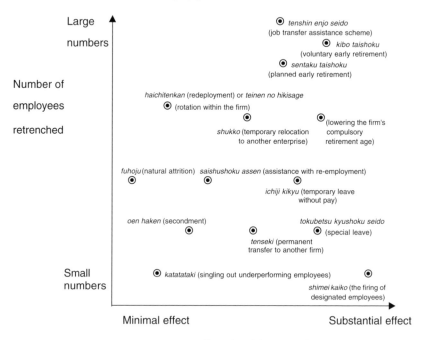

Figure 5.2  Strategies used by firms to reduce labor costs by the severity of the recession and the number of employees needing to be retrenched. *Source:* Shibata (1988), p. 54.

to old patterns of adjusting labor inputs, fundamental change is not likely. Figure 5.2 shows fourteen strategies listed by Shibata (1988) that Japanese firms have commonly used to reduce labor costs. The more drastic means are located in the upper right-hand corner of the diagram. While tight comparisons are difficult, results from a survey of firms in four other advanced economies are shown in table 5.3. The reduction of overtime is the first line of action in all four countries. The major difference setting Japan apart from the US and France (and presumably Britain and Germany, although information was not collected for those countries on the same categories) is the use of job sharing. With regard to firings and temporary layoffs, OECD data (Kosei Rodo Sho 2001a: 181 and A74) suggests that Japanese firms rank only in the middle among twenty-six OECD countries in terms of employment security. Using an index derived by quantifying over a dozen separate measures, the study indicates that firms in the US and the UK are more likely than Japanese firms to let employees go, whereas those in Italy, Germany, and France are less likely to do so.

Table 5.3 *Percentage of firms using different means of reducing their labor costs in four countries in the late 1990s*

| Means of reducing labor costs | America (1997) | France (1998) | UK (1996) | Germany (1996) |
|---|---|---|---|---|
| Cutting overtime | 82.1 | 82.0 | 85.0 | 89.6 |
| Letting casual employees go | 76.4 | 63.0 | 77.0 | 62.7 |
| Relocation | 76.4 | 82.0 | 87.5 | 63.7 |
| Cutting back on hirings | 74.7 | 69.0 | 80.5 | 88.6 |
| Job sharing | 72.5 | 69.0 | n.a. | n.a. |
| Layoffs | 57.2 | 50.0 | 59.0 | 49.8 |
| Cutting back on the standard workweek | 51.1 | 77.0 | 48.0 | 48.3 |
| Moving workers to affiliated firms | 48.0 | 54.0 | 56.5 | 52.7 |
| Promoting early retirement | 47.6 | 80.0 | 78.5 | 66.2 |
| Firing regular employees | 30.1 | 37.0 | 34.0 | 46.8 |
| Demoting regular employees to temporary or casual status | 6.6 | 49.0 | n.a | n.a. |

*Source:* This table has been compiled using data provided in an ILO study, *Kaigai Rodo Jijo Chosa Kekka Hokokusho* (Report on a Survey of Work Overseas) and cited in the 2001 White Paper on Japan's labor economy produced by the Kosei Rodo Sho (2001a), p. 181 and p. 74 of the Appendices.

It is difficult to sort the voluntarily retired from the involuntarily retired. When Japanese firms offer early retirement packages, more employees apply than are wanted. Behind that behavior is a psychology of fear. Employees know they are likely to be in an even worse situation if they wait. The offer of a package is seen by many employees as a veiled warning. The *Asahi Shimbun* (*ASC*, 25 August 2001: 3) reported that Matsuda had 2,210 applicants on the first day when it asked for 1,800 employees to take an early retirement package in 2001. Of the 1,588 successful applicants living in the same prefecture, 16 percent already had other jobs waiting. Mitsubishi Motors advertised 1,200 packages but had 2,028 applicants before applications closed. Firms offering such inducements have had to bear the added expense of (i) offering more packages than originally budgeted for and filling unexpected vacancies, or (ii) coming up with a plan to allocate a fixed number of packages in a manner which appears to be fair in order not to undermine further the morale of the employees they retain. As for the cost, many firms have had to offer benefits equivalent to twice the normal retirement benefit. While packages seem to provide attractive financial inducements to employees suffering from work intensification, older employees have more difficulty than younger ones in finding suitable reemployment, and many aged over 65 need to supplement their pension benefits with employment income.

Job sharing has recently received attention in Japan as a means of spreading employment (and unemployment). However, management has not been enthusiastic. It is still attached to the idea that it can simply cut the hours put in by regular staff and have that work done more cheaply by casuals or by outsourcing. Japanese firms have been unwilling to have employees on a shared basis. Rather than lowering costs, as outsourcing and casualization do, job sharing results in the same unit cost for labor. Firms must cover additional welfare benefits and pension contributions and make their health and recreational facilities and other fringe benefits available to greater numbers. Of more serious concern, job sharing would lead to a blurring of the separate labor markets that have clearly differentiated between regular and casual employment over the past half-century. Changing this arrangement would fundamentally alter power relations between firms and employees and among different groupings in the labor market. Employees who worked a standard week of 40 hours plus 10 hours of unpaid overtime might start to work half-time for only 20 hours to fully benefit from the job share, thereby leaving the firm to hire one more half-time employee (and pay 25 percent more in labor costs for the same work) to make up the difference of 40 hours.

Such change would force managements to be much more transparent in justifying their expropriation of labor surplus. The sense of total control was much clearer in the past when management could force workers, in military fashion, to sing company songs, recite company mottos, and listen to morning pep talks. This is not to argue that management has the upper hand in all of its dealings with labor. It too is responding to wider events it cannot control. With a much higher standard of living than in the past, potential workers, particularly Japan's young consumers, are able to withhold or to withdraw their labor in a way that could only be dreamed about in the past. Thus, if ordinary Japanese must compete for scarce jobs, as Koshiro suggests, firms too must compete to recruit good staff. More will be said about this below, but farreaching changes on the supply side of the labor market cannot be ignored.

## 5.5    Deregulation of the labor market

In the 1990s, management groups pushed the Japanese government into deregulating the labor market. In the past Nikkeiren has been torn between members supporting deregulation and those arguing that social stability and order at work could best be maintained by honoring a kind of social contract with the labor force (Nihon Kei-eisha Dantai

Renmei 1995). After the bubble years, Nikkeiren and the government sought to regain Japan's industrial competitiveness. Two sorts of reform were critical to management's ability to command labor. One was to enhance management's right to have employees work at its own convenience. The other concerned the ease with which work could be outsourced. The opposition of organized labor to the proposed changes resulted in amendments to the Labor Standards Law being delayed in the Diet for more than a year, with passage not occurring until September 1998. Disagreement between labor and management over this legislation was pronounced on four points.

**A designated work system (*sairyo rodo seido*)**   The proposed legislation allowed for work to be delegated to employees against a nominal time standard. Essentially a return to piecework, it allowed employees to complete their designated tasks faster or slower than the standard time (i.e. without reference to the actual time required). Although the law had allowed for this to occur in very limited areas, management had pushed vigorously for employers to be able to allocate work in this manner to all white-collar employees. Labor unions argued that this would only promote competition among such employees and result in labor intensification and an increase in *karoshi* (deaths from overwork). Implemented from September 1999, the legislation fully incorporated the views of management.

**Restrictions on overtime**   In the past the Labor Standards Law of 1947 allowed labor and management to negotiate at the firm level limits on the amount of overtime employees could be required to work, with no set upper limit on overtime. Labor and management in many firms had agreed, however, that employers could require male employees to do overtime up to 15 hours per week, 45 hours per month, and 360 hours per year. Management pushed to remove all legal constraints. Labor wanted the legal limit on annual overtime set at 360 hours for male employees, dropping to 150 hours for all employees once the amendments to the Male-Female Equal Employment Opportunity Law came into effect in April 1999 (thereby removing the annual limit of 150 hours of overtime applying only to women). The final outcome was that the 360-hour limit was legislated, with the 150-hour limit for women being extended to April 2002. Nevertheless, as mentioned in chapter 4, the standard workweek has dropped from 176 hours in 1965 to 143 in 2000. Even with considerable overtime, the total workweek for most people today would be shorter than the standard workweek of their parents.

Table 5.4 *The effects of introducing a variable workweek scheme on wage costs: some hypothetical cases*

| Case | Standard Workweek | Weeks worked | Hours worked per week | | Total hours worked for the year | | | Labor cost | | |
|---|---|---|---|---|---|---|---|---|---|---|
| | | | Standard | Overtime | Standard | Overtime | Total | C1 salary for period | C2 cost of overtime with 25% loading | C3 total cost C1 + C2 |
| **A** | 48 | 26 | 48 | – | 1,248 | – | 1,248 | 2,600 | – | 2,600 |
| | | 26 | 48 | – | 1,248 | – | 1,248 | 2,600 | – | 2,600 |
| | Totals | 52 | 48 | – | 2,496 | – | 2,496 | 5,200 | – | 5,200 |
| **B** | 48 | 26 | 48 | 12 | 1,248 | 312 | 1,560 | 2,600 | 553 | 3,153 |
| | | 26 | 36 | – | 936 | – | 936 | 2,600 | – | 2,600 |
| | Totals | 52 | | | 2,184 | 312 | 2,496 | 5,200 | 553 | 5,753 |
| **C** | 48 | 26 | 48 | 12 | 1,248 | 312 | 1,560 | 2,600 | – | 2,600 |
| | | 26 | 36 | – | 936 | – | 936 | 2,600 | – | 2,600 |
| | Totals | 52 | | | 2,184 | 312 | 2,496 | 5,200 | – | 5,200 |
| **D** | 40 | 26 | 40 | | 1,040 | 312 | 1,352 | 2,600 | 975 | 3,575 |
| | | 26 | 28 | | 728 | – | 728 | 2,600 | – | 2,600 |
| | Totals | 52 | | | 1,768 | 312 | 2,080 | 5,200 | 975 | 6,175 |
| **E** | 36 | 26 | 36 | 12 | 936 | 312 | 1,248 | 2,600 | 1,083 | 3,683 |
| | | 26 | 24 | | 624 | – | 624 | 2,600 | – | 2,600 |
| | Totals | 52 | | | 1,560 | 312 | 1,872 | 5,200 | 1083 | 6,283 |
| **F** | 40 | 26 | 40 | 12 | 1,040 | 312 | 1,352 | 2,600 | 975 | 3,575 |
| | | 26 | 28 | | 728 | – | 728 | 1,820 | – | 1,820 |
| | Totals | 52 | | | 1,768 | 312 | 2,080 | 4,420 | 975 | 5,395 |

*Cases:* A Employee with no overtime in firm without a variable workweek scheme when the standard workweek is 48 hours and the employee is on a monthly salary.

B Employee with heavy overtime for six months offset by light workload for six months at a firm without a variable workweek scheme when the workweek is 48 hours and the employee is on a monthly salary.

C Employee with heavy overtime for six months offset by light workload for six months at a firm with a variable workweek scheme when the standard workweek is 48 hours and the employee is on a monthly salary.

D Employee with heavy overtime for six months offset by light workload for six months at a firm with a variable workweek scheme when the standard workweek is 40 hours and the employee is on a monthly salary.

E Employee with heavy overtime for six months offset by light workload for six months at a firm with a variable workweek scheme when the standard workweek is 36 hours and the employee is on a monthly salary.

F Employee with heavy overtime for six months offset by light workload for six months at a firm with a variable workweek scheme when the standard workweek is 40 hours and the employee is on an hourly wage.

*Notes:* (1) It is assumed that all salaried employees are paid a monthly salary of ¥100,000.

(2) It is assumed that all employees are paid overtime pay at 1.25 times the normal hourly rate of pay.

(3) The hourly wage for the employee in case F was calculated as one fortieth of the salary of the other employees for whom the standard workweek is 40 hours.

(4) The cost of overtime in column C2 was calculated as being equal to $[C1 \times (B2/B1)] \times 1.25$.

*Comments:* (1) Comparing Cases B and C, the cost per employee for the firm not using a variable work system scheme is 10.63 percent.

(2) Comparing Cases B, C, and D, when the standard workweek is lowered from 48 to 40 hours and then again to 36 hours, the cost of not using a variable workweek scheme jumps to 18.75 percent and then climbs further to 20.8 percent.

(3) Comparing Cases D and F, the cost to Japanese firms with a salary system and a variable workweek scheme spreading overtime over the year is still 3.75 percent lower (at ¥5,000) than the cost of such labor for firms (overseas) which use a wage system (¥5,395).

**The standard workweek and the standard work year**     Management pushed for the right to extend the variable workweek (*henkei rodo jikan seido*) so that overtime would be calculated in terms of overtime for a standard work year. By giving time off equivalent to the amount of overtime worked during busy periods, management has in the past been able to have employees work up to 10 hours a day and 52 hours a week for up to three months without paying overtime rates. After three months the limits were set at 9 hours and 48 hours respectively. Management wanted employees to work the 10 hours a day and 52 hours a week for more extended periods without being liable for overtime. Unions wanted the 40-hour standard workweek respected every week. The revisions to the Labor Standards Law fully incorporated management's demands.

Given that the overall number of hours worked remains the same, this may seem like a small point. However, as the hypothetical example in table 5.4 shows, the difference of paying for overtime can be as much as 10 percent when the standard workweek is 48 hours and employees are utilized fully for 12 hours of overtime each week for half the year and are not utilized for 12 of their 48 hours during the other half. Moreover, when the standard workweek shrinks to 40 hours, the cost savings for management are more pronounced. It is not surprising, then, that an increasing number of firms have introduced variable workweek schemes over the past fifteen years (table 5.5).

**Length of the employment contract (*rodo keiyaku kikan*)**     Previously the legal maximum length of time for a labor contract was one year. Regular employees, however, without a long-term contract worked on the basis of an informal agreement with management recognizing their firm's policy of having a fixed retirement age. (In the late 1970s and early 1980s courts began to rule that firms could not set different standards for males and females.) The debate on labor contracts mainly concerns two groups of workers. One consists of casual employees hired as part-timers, *arubaito*, *shokutaku*, *rinjiko*, or other temporary help. Management has argued that such employees would be able to organize their own everyday affairs at home with more certainty were they on longer contracts of up to five years. This of course would mean that management could "lock in" its casual labor force and have its own measure of certainty. It also meant that the distinction between the labor markets for regular and non-regular employees would be reinforced. Behind this there was also perhaps the idea that many regular employees in highly technical or professional jobs might in the future be hired on such contracts. This certainly seemed to be the suggestion in the above-mentioned paper issued by Nikkeiren in 1995. It is too early to know how this will play out, but

Table 5.5 *Change in the percentage of firms using a variable workweek scheme, 1989–2000*

| Year | Percentage of firms with a variable workweek system | Percentage of firms balancing out variations over a one-month period | Percentage of firms balancing out variations over a one-year period | Percentage of firms having flexi-time arrangements |
|------|------|------|------|------|
| 1989 | 7.0 | 6.0 | 0.1 | 0.8 |
| 1990 | 9.8 | 8.4 | 0.3 | 1.2 |
| 1991 | 13.2 | 10.7 | 0.6 | 2.2 |
| 1992 | 18.1 | 14.8 | 1.0 | 2.7 |
| 1993 | 27.7 | 23.3 | 1.5 | 3.5 |
| 1994 | 27.4 | 22.7 | 1.6 | 3.9 |
| 1995 | 31.3 | 21.2 | 7.6 | 3.6 |
| 1996 | 30.4 | 18.3 | 8.7 | 4.3 |
| 1997 | 40.5 | 22.4 | 15.1 | 4.8 |
| 1998 | 54.4 | 16.3 | 35.9 | 4.4 |
| 1999 | 54.8 | 17.5 | 34.3 | 5.1 |
| 2000 | 53.00 | 16.6 | 33.3 | 5.7 |

*Source:* Kosei Rodo Sho Daijin Kanbo Tokei Joho Bu (2002a), p. 125; and Rodo Sho (1998), p. 241, and p. 118 of the Appendix.

there is the possibility that the dual market arrangement will give way to a triple market arrangement whereby repetitive labor stays on one- or two-year contracts, professionals and skilled technicians have medium-term contracts, and only a small number of managers enjoy the benefits of longer-term employment and career-track employment in Japan's large firms. The new law lifted the limit for contracts from one year to three. It is clear that management will in the future be much more selective in deciding who to hire as regular employees.

The other legislation of particular relevance to the labor market is the Law for Dispatching Workers. First passed in 1986, the law provided for certified companies to supply labor to cover (temporary) shortages in thirteen highly specialized occupational categories. In its implementation the number of such categories was increased to sixteen. In 1994 Nikkeiren called for categories to be opened up, and the number was raised to twenty-six in 1996. After further lobbying by Nikkeiren, the supply of such labor was in principle opened up for all occupations in December 1999, and a system of longer-term job placements through temporary assignments (*shokai yotei haken seido*) was established in 2000.

While organized labor has been able to slow deregulation in some areas, management's push to deregulate has made headway overall; further changes will likely follow. Like management elsewhere, management in

Japan prefers self-regulation without punitive measures. Business pushed hard for the first equal employment opportunity legislation in the mid-1980s to impose on management the obligation only to *endeavor* to remove discrimination without any penalty for not doing so. The leadup to this legislation in the late 1990s provides an interesting insight into how international public opinion was used by progressives in Japan to get light penalties built into the new legislation. Nikkeiren has also argued for the abandonment of the cumbersome industry-by-industry and prefecture-by-prefecture approach to setting minimum wages, provisions in the Labor Standards Law for the eight-hour workday, and restrictions on private job placement providers and dispatchers of temporary help.

## 5.6     Looking to the future

Organized labor has not responded to these kinds of proposals. Its continued emphasis on increasing penalty rates for overtime suggests it still gives priority to increasing the income of its members. However, the failure to obtain any increase at all in the 2001 and 2002 Spring Offensives underlines the difficulty of their position in the face of increased international competition and the prolonged recession. Unlike the bubble years when firms had plenty of resources, reports in the new media and the shelves in bookstores early in 2002 suggest that the public mood had become very somber. The feeling is that Japan must somehow restructure its industries and find a new formula for restoring Japan's international competitive edge. Many acknowledge that Japanese are somehow better off having a cheap Chinese labor force taking over responsibility for running the world factory. "Being responsible for the world factory" is seen as a source of the stress experienced by many Japanese workers over the past three decades. At the same time globalization has brought a deep uneasiness in terms of the loss of control over the nation's destiny and, by extension, an individual's own future. Japanese are slowly opening up to the possibility that multiculturalism may add an important dynamic to the search for solutions. Carlos Ghosn, the Frenchman who is president of Nissan, was a national hero before becoming head of the entire Nissan group on 31 May 2002. Given the yearning for economic leadership in Japan today, there is a vacuum that a more dynamic labor movement could fill with its own vision. However, unions will not be seen as having leadership material as long as they simply argue that management should be forking out for wage increases and carrying underutilized employees.

# 6    Segmentation of the labor market

## 6.1    Employment status, firm size, and labor market segmentation

The efforts to deregulate the labor market shifted some portions of the labor force from the market for full-time regular employees to other markets. Data from the *Shugyo Kozo Chosa* (Survey of Employment Structure) indicates that the percentage of male workers casually employed as non-regular employees (*hiseiki koyosha*) rose from 9.0 percent in 1992 to 10.1 percent in 1997. For women the figures rose from 37.3 to 42.2 percent (table 6.1). Using a different categorization, the 2000 Labor White Paper (Kosei Rodo Sho 2000: 110 and p. 63 of the appendix) informs us that the number of *hiseishain* (those not considered to be company employees) was 27.5 percent in 1999. The Labor Force Survey (*Rodoryoku Chosa*) yields yet another figure: the percentage of employees who are ordinary operatives (*joyo koyosha*), indicating that the number of *rinjiko* and *hiyatoi*, who are on daily wage rates or on contracts of less than one year, rose from 5.4 percent of all employees in 1990 to 7.1 percent in 2001 (Kosei Rodo Sho Daijin Kanbo Tokei Joho Bu 2002a: 35). (This data includes nearly all part-timers as ordinary employees because they are on one-year contracts.) Whichever data is used, however, the evidence is that casualization is advancing, and surveys of management indicate that it is occurring in order to contain labor costs and to enhance the discretion of management in the use of labor (see the results of a survey taken by the Sanwa Research Institute in 2000 in Kosei Rodo Sho 2001a: 167–70, and in the appendix on pp. 68–9).

A recent White Paper on small and medium-sized businesses (Chusho Kigyo Cho 2001: 26–8) argues that these changes open up opportunities for smaller entrepreneurs. It states that the employment of non-regular employees, for example, is disproportionately large in smaller firms, but shows that the increase is occurring across all sizes of enterprise (see table 6.2). The figures on the composition of the labor force by firm size and the number of firms in each size grouping (table 6.3) underline the

Table 6.1 *The percentage distribution of private sector employees by employment status, 1992 and 1997*

| Year | Gender | Employees in managerial positions | Regular employees (*seiki no shokuin/ jugyoin*) | Non-regular employees | | | | |
|------|--------|-----------------------------------|------------------------------------------------|-----------|----------|--------------------|-----------|-------|
| | | | | Part-timer | *Arubaito* | Dispatched workers | *Shokutaku* | Other |
| 1992 | Male | 9.6 | 81.4 | 1.0 | 4.0 | 0.2 | 1.8 | 1.9 |
| 1997 | Male | 9.0 | 80.9 | 1.3 | 5.0 | 0.2 | 1.8 | 1.8 |
| 1992 | Female | 4.4 | 58.3 | 27.5 | 6.0 | 0.6 | 1.5 | 1.9 |
| 1997 | Female | 4.0 | 53.8 | 30.0 | 7.7 | 0.6 | 1.7 | 1.9 |

*Source:* Data is from the *Shugyo Kozo Kihon Chosa* (The Survey of the Employment Structure) which is conducted every five years. Kosei Rodo Sho Daijin Kanbo Tokei Joho Bu (2002a), p. 47.

Table 6.2 *Growth in the number of non-regular employees in the non-agricultural private sector by firm size, 1996 and 2000*

| Firm size | The percentage of all employees who are non-regular employees | |
|---|---|---|
| | February 1996 | August 2000 |
| 1–29 | 30.0 | 34.7 |
| 39–99 | 23.8 | 34.8 |
| 100–499 | 19.5 | 24.8 |
| 500+ | 14.6 | 19.1 |

*Note:* The term "non-regular employee" used here is a translation of "*hiseiki jugyoin.*"
*Source:* Chusho Kigyo Cho (2001), p. 26.

Table 6.3 *The distribution of establishments and the number of employees by firm size, 1978, 1986, and 1999*

| Firm size by number of employees | The percentage distribution of firms | | | The percentage distribution of employees | | |
|---|---|---|---|---|---|---|
| | 1978 | 1986 | 1999 | 1978 | 1986 | 1999 |
| 1–4 | 64.2 | 60.3 | 57.2 | 13.0 | 7.7 | 7.8 |
| 5–29 | 32.0 | 33.9 | 36.5 | 34.1 | 38.1 | 39.3 |
| 30–99 | 4.5 | 4.6 | 5.1 | 33.3 | 24.0 | 24.7 |
| 100–499 | 1.0 | 1.0 | 1.1 | 18.5 | 19.5 | 19.3 |
| 500+ | 0.1 | 0.1 | 0.1 | 12.0 | 10.8 | 8.9 |

*Source:* Rodo Daijin Kanbo Tokei Joho Bu (1982), pp. 28–31.
Rodo Daijin Kanbo Tokei Joho Bu (1992), pp. 34–6.
Kosei Rodo Sho Daijin Kanbo Tokei Joho Bu (2002a), pp. 50–2.

importance of including employees in Japan's small firms in any discussion of work organization. At the turn of the century 71.8 percent of Japan's labor force worked for firms with less than 100 employees. Less than 10 percent of Japan's entire labor force is employed by firms with more than 500 workers. Given the vastly different working conditions in large and small firms, firm size differentials continue to define the most important way in which the labor market is segmented in Japan. The downsizing of employment in Japan's largest firms can only mean that Koshiro's scarce jobs are becoming scarcer.

Japan's large-scale sector is delineated by a number of characteristics. The most readily apparent signifier is found in working conditions. Table 6.4 shows that remuneration is vastly superior in the large firms, and

Table 6.4 *Variation in working conditions by firm size in 2001*

| Firm size | A Monthly take-home pay | B Bonuses received | C Hours of work | D Percentage of firms with a two-day weekend every week | E Days of annual leave actually used | F Percentage of firms giving over 120 days off a year | G Percentage of firms guaranteeing employment until age 65 |
|---|---|---|---|---|---|---|---|
| | 2001 | 2001 | 2001 | 2001 | 2001 | 2001 | 2000 |
| 5,000+ | | | | | | | 3.7 |
| 1,000–4,999 | 379.8 | 131.3 | 156.9 | 79.3 | 10.6 | 50.6 | 5.0 |
| 500–999 | | | | | 8.7 | 39.5 | 6.2 |
| 300–499 | | | | 62.2 | | | |
| 100–299 | 315.7 | 93.1 | 153.3 | 40.2 | 7.7 | 23.2 | 13.8 |
| 50–99 | | | | | | | |
| 30–49 | 276.0 | 66.9 | 153.5 | 31.2 | 7.3 | 14.7 | 27.9 |
| 5–29 | 245.2 | 44.4 | 151.6 | | | | |
| Source | H-136 | H-136 | H-113 | H-121 | H-122 | H-123 | M-85 |

*Sources:* The following letters were used in the last row to indicate the sources, with the page number following the hyphen:
H Kosei Rodo Sho Daijin Kanbo Tokei Joho Bu (2002a).
M Miura (2001).

that monthly hours of work do not vary much by firm size. While social norms tend to regulate notions of the normal workday (as opposed to the normal workweek), the organization of time varies by firm size. More large firms have implemented the two-day weekend and allow more paid annual leave. Large firms are much less likely to guarantee employment to age 65, but more likely to have secondment (*shukko*) and other schemes in place for the redeployment of employees who become redundant. Large firms have a complex network of subcontractors and affiliated firms into which their employees can be channeled, and a higher proportion of large firms have early retirement schemes (column A in table 6.5). Larger firms offer more fringe benefits and a much smaller risk of injury at work. The firm-size segmentation of the labor market is reflected in three other institutionalized differences: the extent to which large firms have a first claim on graduates, unionization rates, and the level of benefits flowing from health plans and pension schemes. The discussion on firm-size segmentation is extended here because these dualities color all other forms of segmentation in one way or another.

The market for non-regular employees continues to grow. One submarket is for "part-timers." This nomenclature can be misleading in that many part-timers actually work a full week. While part-time work used to be associated with women, it should be noted that 24.6 percent of male graduates became employed on a part-time basis in 1998 (as opposed to 30.3 percent for women) (Kosei Rodo Sho 2000: 182 and p. 90 of the appendix). A 2001 White Paper (Kosei Rodo Sho 2001a: 44) indicated that part-timers (*paatotaimu rodosha*) earned an average of ¥95,226 per month as compared with ¥421,195 for ordinary employees (*ippan rodosha*). However, the difference in the average number of hours worked was much smaller. The overall differential of 1.0 to 4.423 contrasted to a differential of only 1.0 to 1.73 per monthly hour actually worked (97.3 hours for part-timers and 168.8 hours for ordinary workers) (Kosei Rodo Sho Daijin Kanbo Tokei Joho Bu 2002c: 238). On an hourly basis this means ordinary workers earned over 2.5 times the remuneration paid to part-timers.

Most statistical presentations distinguish the part-timers' market from that for *arubaito*. Whereas part-timers usually work under contract and have traditionally been housewives earning secondary income and having the freedom to look after some of the household's daily business, *arubaito* are still enrolled in school or university and work for pocket money without a formal contract. Without the practice of work sharing or fractional appointments, women (like men) have a choice between (i) regular employment (with the expectation of long hours and secondments away from home for those wishing for a career in

Table 6.5 *Variation in working environment by firm size in 2000*

| Firm size | A Percentage of firms with scheme for early retirement | B Percentage of firms with retirement age for executives | C Index indicating frequency of work-related accidents | D Index indicating severity of work-related accidents | E Percentage of firms with special safety practices for workers aged over 50 | F Unionization rate | G Percentage of firms reaching early agreement to employ university graduates |
|---|---|---|---|---|---|---|---|
| | 2000 | 2000 | 2000 | 2000 | 2001 | 2000 | 2000 |
| 5,000+ | 58.2 | 35.8 | | | | | 92.1 |
| 1,000–4,999 | 43.0 | 34.6 | .47 | 0.07 | 61 | 54.2 | 81.4 |
| 500–999 | | | .89 | 0.10 | 57 | | |
| 300–499 | 24.3 | 26.3 | 1.94 | 0.15 | 43 | 18.8 | 63.7 |
| 100–299 | 10.1 | 19.1 | 2.52 | 0.25 | | | 33.8 |
| 50–99 | | | | | 34 | | |
| 30–49 | 3.0 | 10.1 | 3.52 | 0.23 | | 1.4 | 8.8 |
| 5–29 | | | | | 30 | | |
| Source | M-83 | M-83 | Y-257 | Y-257 | H-200 | K-486 | Y-55 |

*Sources:* The following letters were used in the last row to indicate the sources, with the page number following the hyphen:
H Kosei Rodo Sho Daijin Kanbo Tokei Joho Bu (2002a).
M Miura (2001).
Y Kosei Rodo Sho Daijin Kanbo Tokei Joho Bu (2002c).
K Kosei Rodo Sho Roshi Kankei Tanto Sanjinkan Shitsu (2002).

the internal labor market) and (ii) part-time work with greatly reduced pay.

Obi (1980) noted some time ago that decisions concerning the labor-force participation of secondary earners in Japan (and elsewhere, based on the research of Douglas and Long) depend not just on the wage rate, but also on the opportunity cost (the value) attached to the time that is shifted from other activities important to the overall wellbeing of the family. This has meant that part-time work for women has been an attractive and rational economic option for many households. Part-time work allows someone to concentrate on concretely defined work tasks without the responsibilities and hassle that go with being a regular employee. In this sense, part-time work is not necessarily exploitation.

Since Obi was writing, several longer-term changes have reinforced the increase in part-time work. They include the decline of three-generational households from 19.7 percent in 1968 to 10.6 percent in 1999, the increase in the number of single-person households from 19.8 to 23.6 percent, and the decline in the proportion of all families with children under the age of 15 from 41.2 to 34.4 percent over the same period. The percentage of single-parent households has remained fairly constant at 5.3 percent (Tominaga 2001: 246).

Graduates who go into part-time work in large numbers and then stay in that kind of employment are known as *furiitaa* (meaning freelance workers). The term is used for both male and female dropouts from high school and university and for secondary and tertiary graduates who have not taken on a full-time permanent job. Those who decide to make a career or lifestyle of *arubaito*-type employment often work just enough to save money for overseas travel or some other recreational activity (sometimes related to a serous interest in surfing, photography, painting, music, etc.). Working-holiday arrangements between governments allow some to continue their *furiitaa*-type lifestyle abroad.

The *furiitaa* are not a new phenomenon. The Special Labor Force survey indicates that there were 500,000 *furiitaa* in 1982, and 790,000 in 1987. With one million in 1992 and 1.5 million in 1997, the figure continued to rise to 1.93 million by 2000. The government's data in table 6.6 excludes people over 34 years of age and married women from the *furiitaa* category, but may include married men. There seems to be a presumption that at 35 individuals will marry or become part-timers, although it is unlikely that a lifestyle and its associated values and outlook subscribed to for ten or fifteen years by males or females in their thirties will easily be scuttled.

There is not much research on the *furiitaa*, but one study in 2001 by a group at the Japan Institute of Labor concluded from its survey of

Table 6.6 *The number of* furiitaa *in August 2000*

| Age | Men | Women (who are not married) | Total (in 10,000s) |
|---|---|---|---|
| 15–24 | 45 | 53 | 98 |
| 25–34 | 38 | 57 | 95 |
| Total | 83 | 110 | 193 |

*Source:* Nihon Rodo Kenkyu Kiko (2001b), p. 2.

*furiitaa* that 39.2 percent were the *moratoriamu* types (social dropouts), first identified as a substratum of the population by Okonogi (1978) in the late 1970s. Another 33.0 percent claimed they were *furiitaa* because they could not find permanent work, and 27.8 percent claimed they were pursuing a dream. Although many were anxious about their future, few had plans to acquire skills that would lead to a stable career in a field of interest to them (Nihon Rodo Kenkyu Kiko 2001b). A survey of firms by the Ministry of Welfare, Labor and Health in 2001 indicated that about one-third of firms saw the *furiitaa* experience as negative for job applicants, while only a few saw it as positive (Kosei Rodo Sho Daijin Kanbo Tokei Joho Bu 2002a: 80).

Yamada (1999) has recently identified another group as "parasite singles" – those who are able to maintain a comfortable lifestyle even on relatively poor wages because they depend on their parents to subsidize their freedom. Here some interesting parallels might be drawn between the lifestyle of many *furiitaa* and that of several anti-heroes. Tora-san was the very likable but restless character who could not settle down to full-time employment and tramped around Japan unable to settle down through a well-known series of forty-four movies produced by Yamada Yoji, and starring Atsumi Kiyoshi and Baisho Chieko, from the late 1960s until the mid-1990s. Over the years many Japanese have identified with this sort of character. Two other examples from the samurai past might be Zato Ichi, the blind mendicant *ronin samurai*, and another *ronin*, the famous swordsman Miyamoto Musashi. *Enka* (a genre of melancholy music reminiscent of early country and western music in North America) also serves to make this lifestyle attractive but attaches opprobrium to those who seem unable to fit in with the changes imposed by the increased materialism which has spread with rapid economic development, modernization, and internationalization.

The economic prospects of those choosing the *furiitaa* lifestyle appear bleak as they age. Few have the medical and pension benefits associated with stable patterns of employment. Many will feel pinched once they begin to think about having a family and about the responsibilities that implies, or to experience the ailments associated with advanced middle age or the onset of old age. Even if the male *furiitaa* later decides to seek steady employment on "settling down" to the responsibilities of family life, opportunities outside the peripheral labor market are limited. At the same time, there still seems to be prejudice against unmarried middle-aged males in the dominant labor market, especially regarding promotion. While this results partially from a perception that married men are more willing to take group/corporate responsibility, there may also be a general aversion to homosexuality in the masculine culture found in Japan's large firms. However, growing recognition of its acceptance in other industrialized societies, more "coming out" in Japan, and the entry of women into the male preserve will tend to soften attitudes toward the *furiitaa*. The fact that some *furiitaa* do acquire a highly marketable skill by pursuing a serious interest, and are able to advance themselves significantly in the secondary labor market, is already evidence of a certain openness. One key to the future of work in Japan will be the extent to which management in major firms will see work-related value in the skills acquired through such a lifestyle.

Just as the employment practices in Japan's large-scale firms serve as a model whose relevance extends far beyond that sector, so too the lifestyle of the *furiitaa* strikes a chord with many who would normally have been channeled into traditional employment. Unlike the part-timer who is perceived as someone supporting the family system, the *furiitaa* challenges what has always been seen as the stable pattern of employment for both males and females. Here the gradual long-term decline in male labor-force participation should not be overlooked. The shifts are small, but are reinforced by a growing appreciation of the need to have fathers more involved in child rearing and providing some relief to spouses (e.g. Masataka 2002). Fewer males will want to sacrifice family life to the extent demanded by Japan's large employers in the past, and employers will respond flexibly to this change in values. The shift has already taken place abroad (Phillimore 2002), and it is likely that these trends will, with a time lag, also appear in Japan. It is also likely that the opportunity cost of some women not working in the labor force as regular employees will be greater than that of their husbands, and that the same household logic that once made it profitable for women to enter part-time work will in the future see some husbands turn over to their wives the role of being the main breadwinner.

Although still episodic at this stage, Hanami, Mitsuhashi, and Tachigi (2002) report on three new developments in the labor market. One is the use of traditional franchising arrangements (known as *noren wake*, literally, the dividing of the shop's front curtain) to allow outstanding employees to set up independently their own place of work. (To be sure, some large manufacturers in the past assisted skilled workers to establish their own firms, but such employees formally became retirees and almost always remained in a subcontracting power relationship with their previous employer and very much tied to that employer's technology.)

Second is the rapid expansion of teleworking. The Japan Association of Teleworkers estimates that the number of teleworkers has grown from 810,000 in 1996 to 2.46 million in 2000, and projects that there will be 4.45 million such workers (about 7–8 percent of the labor force) by 2005 (Hanami *et al.* 2002: 31). The estimates of the Japan Institute of Labor's researchers (as reported in Kosei Rodo Sho 2001b: 443) are much more modest. They suggested that the figure in 1997 was 174,000 (of which 70 percent were women with children) and that nearly 8 percent were aged over 60. However, the establishment of the privately funded SOHO Think Tank serves to indicate that the trend to teleworking will continue (SOHO Shinku Tanku 2001; *ASC*, 7 May 2002: 12). Many work on a freelance basis. These developments fit in with the push of management to introduce task-based pay (*sairyo rodo seido*) which was mentioned above. The percentage of firms allowing employees to do work outside their premises increased from 6.1 percent in 1996 to 9.2 percent in 2000, when nearly 20 percent of the firms with over 1,000 employees were doing so compared with 6 percent of firms with 30–99 employees (Kosei Rodo Sho Daijin Kanbo Tokei Joho Bu 2002: 124).

Third is the increasing number of people giving up pressured employment in profit-driven businesses for more meaningful engagement with a non-profit organization (NPO). With the change in legislation allowing for donations to many NPOs to be tax deductible, the number of registered NPOs has increased from less than 20,000 organizations in 1998 to over 90,000 by 2000, with the number of Japanese involved growing from less than two million to about seven million over the same period (Keizai Kikaku Cho 2001: 14). In 2001 the Economic Planning Agency (Keizai Kikaku Cho 2001: 15–19) noted that Japanese lagged far behind other nationalities in this regard, with only 25 percent of Japanese (mostly women aged over 35) engaged in such activity, somewhat below the 55.5 percent recorded in America and the 48 percent recorded in the UK. This finding was confirmed in a survey by the Nomura Research Institute (Nomura Sogo Kenkyu Jo 1999: 79–82). The findings indicate that male patterns of full-time regular employment prevent men from being as involved during their working years. The White Paper further noted that for housewives the level of interest varied directly with their level of education and with household income (p. 51), reflecting the realities of the Douglas–Long–Arisawa effect mentioned above.

On the employment front, a survey of NPOs by the Keizai Sangyo Kenkyu Jo (Institute for Economic and Industrial Research) revealed that NPOs themselves predicted an increase in the numbers they employ from 176,000 in 2000 (only 0.3 percent of the labor force, of which 80,000 were full-time professionals in regular employment) to 418,000 (0.6 percent) by 2010. Although differing estimates and assessments have been reported by various parties, all are consistent in documenting a concerted move away from the more regimented approaches to work organization associated with the *kaisha shakai* (the enterprise-based society) which has dominated thinking about work choices in postwar Japan. The coverage given these issues in the media has increased exponentially over the past ten or fifteen years (Keizai Kikaku Cho 2001: 6–9 and 237–8), and Japanese have come to accept these changes as a normal part of civil society (Nomura Sogo Kenkyu Jo 1999: 71–8). At the same time, there is a spreading perception that government cannot meet all the needs of the community and that the quality of life is immensely improved by the work of volunteers (Keizai Kikaku Cho 2001: 9). If Japanese industry is to regain its international competitiveness, employers will have to nurture a highly motivated and creative labor force by responding to the spread of this consciousness among Japanese youth.

Technically counted as ordinary employees, with the dispatching firm paying their wages, these employees have more than doubled in number during the 1990s, reaching 1.068 million in 1999. Most observers see this as a growth sector. The December 1999 legislation was designed to promote the transfer of temporary workers into permanent employment after a year. Firms wishing to retain the services of a dispatched temporary worker beyond one year to do the *same work* are expected to take them on as regular employees. Some critics argue that the same work clause may be abused, but it is too early to discern its effects on the relative bargaining power of individuals and firms in the labor market.

Labor unions are ambivalent regarding deregulation. The use of dispatched workers undermines the job security of regular employees. However, the wages of their members are maintained by reducing costs. Unions generally serve Japan's privileged employees in the large-scale sector. A recent study in 2000 showed that 43 percent of unions surveyed wanted even further relaxation of the restrictions on dispatching, while 27 percent wanted the present arrangements to stay (*SRN*, 23 April 2001). Another finding from that survey was that union leaders tended to see dispatching as a device mainly for wives, mothers and "career women" aged over 30. Japan's enterprise-based union movement is democratic in

Table 6.7 *Percentage of students who become employed upon graduation, 1996–2000*

|  | 1996 | 1997 | 1998 | 1999 | 2000 |
|---|---|---|---|---|---|
| Senior high school | 24.3 | 23.5 | 22.7 | 20.2 | 18.6 |
| Technical college | 71.8 | 69.6 | 66.2 | 63.0 | 59.7 |
| Junior college | 65.7 | 67.9 | 65.7 | 59.1 | 56.0 |
| University | 65.9 | 66.6 | 65.6 | 60.1 | 55.8 |
| Graduate school | 66.7 | 67.7 | 79.3 | 64.9 | 62.9 |

*Source:* Kosei Rodo Sho Daijin Kanbo Tokei Joho Bu (2002c), p. 47.

responding to the demands of its members from Japan's aristocracy of labor. However, as it continues to serve that membership it is also alienating workers positioned elsewhere in the labor market. The shrinking size of that aristocracy and its privileged treatment will further isolate the union movement from mainstream Japanese, thereby reducing the likelihood that it will produce the economic leadership seen as being in short supply in present-day Japan.

## 6.2     The market for new graduates

A quite distinct market has traditionally existed for new graduates. Firms competed for the best graduates, and then encouraged them to work as hard as possible for wages below their productivity. In theory, the new employees would later be rewarded above their productivity as they progressed up a seniority-driven earnings curve. Firms that could somehow siphon off older employees when their productivity fell below the rate of remuneration did better. The more able graduates generated larger surpluses early in their employment and it was less likely that their productivity would ever fall below their remuneration as they gained seniority in their firm.

Today there is a very real shortage of graduates. Data from the *Basic Survey of Schools* (Gakko Kihon Chosa) shows that the percentage of graduates employed upon graduation has fallen (Table 6.7). The drop for senior high school and technical college graduates reflects the fact that more of the better graduates are going on for further education as their cohort shrinks in size and more places remain vacant at Japan's tertiary institutions. However, for graduates of junior colleges, the rate of continuation to further education has not changed over this period of time, while there has been a real decline in their labor-force participation.

Table 6.8 *Percentage of firms reaching informal agreements to hire March 2001 graduates before they graduated*

| Firm size (number of employees) | High school graduates | Technical college graduates | Other training schools graduates | Junior college graduates | University and graduate school graduates |
|---|---|---|---|---|---|
| 5,000+ | 57.9 | 31.5 | 30.3 | 50.9 | 92.1 |
| 1,000–4,999 | 42.3 | 19.6 | 25.9 | 40.5 | 81.4 |
| 300–999 | 38.8 | 11.5 | 19.1 | 25.1 | 63.7 |
| 100–299 | 28.4 | 5.6 | 7.8 | 11.3 | 33.8 |
| 30–99 | 11.2 | 2.5 | 5.1 | 2.2 | 8.8 |

*Source:* Kosei Rodo Sho Daijin Kanbo Tokei Joho Bu (2002c), p. 55.

The figures from the same survey also show a considerable dropout rate from Japan's senior high schools. Whereas in March 1996, 96.8 percent of 1,545,270 middle school graduates entered senior high school that April, only 1,362,682 (91.1 percent) graduated from high school in 1999. For the 1997 cohort the figures were 96.8 and 90.9 percent, respectively (Kosei Rodo Sho Daijin Kanbo Tokei Joho Bu 2002c: 47). A large proportion of dropouts became professional *arubaitaa*.

The figures for university students are harder to assess, as there are numerous paths of entry and progression, but one estimate would be that the dropout rate is roughly similar or slightly higher. In 2000, 45.1 percent of Japan's senior high school graduates reported they would continue into further education, up from 39.0 percent in 1996. However, only 95.6 percent of the 605,619 high school graduates reporting an intention to go on to further education in April 1996 actually enrolled, and only 93.01 percent of that cohort graduated (Mombu Kagaku Sho 2002: 30–3). These figures represent a tightening up of the market for graduates, and there is concern that firms will not have a sufficient number of skilled employees to generate the surplus on which they depended in the past. The dropout problem is exacerbated by the fact that only 55.8 percent of university graduates and 18.6 percent of high school graduates entered the labor force in 2002, down from 81.0 and 41.1 percent in 1990. At the same time, the demand for new graduates has shifted to those with work experience. Thus unemployment rates for workers aged 35–55 were lower than for any other age group under 65 (Kosei Rodo Sho 2002a: 18).

The market for graduates is dominated by Japan's large firms. Table 6.8 shows that university students are a much-sought-after commodity. In order to protect university students in this tight market from excessively aggressive recruitment practices, in 1996 representatives from Japan's universities, business, and government tried for the third time to hammer out an accord. The agreement was that firms would not give students informal commitments that they would hire them upon graduation (*naitei*) before the 1 October preceding their graduation in March. However, firms would not keep to the agreement, and once one firm broke ranks, other firms had to follow suit. Since the collapse of the third accord, the market has opened earlier and earlier for Japan's university students, who now begin their discussions with employees in October of their third year at university. In many cases the market closes in May of the student's fourth year.

One result of this early activity in the labor market for graduates is that students end their serious study some time toward the end of their third year. Another is that many students who are committed to their studies and not ready to commit themselves to an employer miss out. A third is that the market remains very volatile; firms or industries seen as attractive by potential graduates (i.e. third- or fourth-year students) one year often lose favor in subsequent years. For graduates in the social sciences and humanities, only one company in the top ten of sought-after employers in the 1990s was still there in 2000. For engineers and science students, only four of the top ten preferred employers remained there over the decade (H. Suzuki 2002: 10). While the change in part reflects the ongoing crisis in the financial sector, with banks, insurance companies, and various other financial service providers losing favor in the 1990s, there is also a feeling that students are signing up with firms based on images generated in the media rather than a careful assessment of the work they are likely to be assigned and its match with their own abilities, aptitudes, and interests.

Many newly graduated employees now change jobs within the first three years of being employed. The cajoling, bluffing, bargaining, and other pressures that are associated with *shushoku katsudo* (job hunting) probably work to compromise the judgment of students when they commit themselves to informal agreements with employers. Moreover, the pressurized examination system, the demands of extracurricular activity (such as sports clubs), and expectations that students will complete their university education within the standard four years, limit the time that students have to engage in meaningful employment before they agree on their first firm. Summer internships are not common in Japan. One study of university students in twelve countries revealed that 96.8 percent of male and 98.3 percent of female university students in Japan had never taken time off from their studies to experience a full-time work environment, whereas just over half of their counterparts in Europe had done so (Nihon Rodo Kenkyu Kiko 2001a: 10). The study suggested that the European students were much more active in looking for and creating employment-linked opportunities, and much more likely to see casual employment as having a value far beyond the cash it brought in. The same study also revealed that about half the graduates in Europe found what they had learned at their university useful in their work, whereas only about a quarter of Japanese graduates did so. In this regard, a gradual shift seems to be occurring among university administrators in Japan, who are now beginning to see the value of complementing the strongly conceptual and theoretical orientation traditionally emphasized in Japanese universities with a more practical emphasis (*SRN*, 27 November 2000: 3; and 18 December 2000: 3).

One further development among university graduates is the interest in venture businesses, and in recent years some observers have talked about the "venture business boom" (*kigyoka buumu*). However, the requirements of Japanese banks make it difficult for new graduates to raise the necessary capital. A recent study by the OECD of IT strategies in its thirty member countries found that Japan ranked twenty-fifth in the league table when it came to investing in venture capital (*ASC*, 6 May 2002: 5). Many graduates do not want to work in what they believe are stifling conditions in Japan's corporate world. Rather, they want to challenge their own abilities, even if it means failing, and to engage in work that will hold and further ignite their interests. The pressure for change exists on both the supply and the demand side, as economic leaders realize Japan will not be able to satisfactorily restructure (e.g. find new profitable niches) in the context of globalization unless the country's capacity to develop venture businesses is rapidly expanded.

## 6.3    The market among foreign firms

During the 1990s foreign firms came to be seen as attractive employers. This perhaps reflected media coverage given to globalization and the prolonged recession in Japan over the last decade. A survey by Recruit Research of 13,000 fourth-year university students in 1997 and 1998 revealed that the popularity of such firms rose rapidly in the late 1990s (*ASC*, 6 June 1998: 14). Graduates used to prefer Japanese employers because they provided more security and because foreign firms often required additional language skills. However, restructuring over the last decade and increased international competition has weakened the confidence of graduates in the ability of Japanese firms to supply the same security in the future. Moreover, the number of students studying and traveling abroad increased significantly in the 1990s.

In March 2002 the Ministry of Welfare, Labor and Health released findings from a survey of 529 foreign-owned companies operating in Japan (*SRN*, 9 April 2001: 4). The findings revealed that foreign firms hired mainly people with work experience whose productivity could be utilized immediately. The firms had a fairly high labor turnover, but often provided shorter working hours and better leave. Foreign-owned firms had a unionization rate above the national average for Japan (though below that for Japan's large firms) and more disputes than local firms (not surprising, perhaps, given the opportunity for cross-cultural misunderstandings to occur). Two-thirds had workweeks under 38 hours, whereas only one-fifth of Japanese firms did so. Similar proportions hold for the number of firms giving employees sick leave and more than 120 days off per year.

These comparisons are difficult to make and to assess. The foreign-owned company is usually part of a large multinational operation, and tends to adopt the parent organization's approach to international standards. This makes comparisons with Japan's large-scale sector appropriate, and it is often with this sector that foreign firms compete for Japan's good labor. At the same time, most operate as independent units having their own bottom line in Japan. They usually employ a small number of locals, and for this reason the comparison with overall averages is appropriate. In any case, they often lead Japanese firms in introducing progressive practices and, as English becomes less of a barrier and more graduates have experience abroad, more university graduates seem willing to work for foreign firms. Many appreciate the shorter hours and the responsibility they are given without waiting until they are older, as would normally occur in most Japanese firms. These changes suggest that thinking about choices in the labor market is evolving. As the lines around this market blur, prejudices faced by Japanese students raised abroad (*kaigai kikoku shijo*) or those who work abroad for foreign firms are being replaced by respect for the skills and perspectives gained through such experience. Increasingly those attributes will be put to good use by Japanese firms as they accommodate the globalizing environment.

### 6.4    The labor market for women

As they have moved from being unpaid family workers into the ranks of the employed, the proportion of women among Japan's employees has steadily risen from 31.7 percent in 1965 to 40.0 percent in 2000. Sizable numbers became employed as part-timers; in 1999 the number of women employed part-time surpassed the number in regular employment. One outcome of the restructuring process is that firms seeking to contain labor costs prefer to hire women on a part-time basis (*ASC*, 2 April 2001: 20). At the same time, the government's White Paper on Working Women recorded that the average tenure of women working for the same firm has risen from 7.2 years in 1989 to 8.8 years in 2000. This compares with 12.4 years in 1989 and 13.3 years in 2000 for men (Kosei Rodo Sho Koyo Kinto-Jido Katei Kyoku 2001: appendix, p. 37). The same source (p. 38) indicates that women still accounted for less than 10 percent of those in managerial positions at the end of the century, although that percentage is slowly rising. The percentage of divisional managers who were women was up from 1.0 percent in 1980 to 2.2 percent in 2000; section chiefs were up from 1.3 to 4.0 percent; and supervisors were up from 3.1 percent to 8.1 percent. In a system that still emphasizes experience and on-the-job training for managers, the shorter tenure of women and their part-time status must be seen as keeping many from advancing into management.

The M-shaped labor-force participation curve is gradually becoming a mound-shaped curve which fails to reach the same height as the male curve and tapers off more quickly with aging. The labor-force participation behavior of female high school graduates still follows the M-shaped curve, peaking at around 20, dropping for marriage, childbirth and child rearing, and then swinging up for a second peak when those women reach their mid-forties. For female university graduates, however, the peak associated with their highest labor-force participation rate comes some years later, and tapers off more gradually as they postpone marriage and childbirth in order to follow a career. These women no longer have a second peak; the curve continues to slope downwards, revealing that, as they enter their forties, this cohort of women seems to "give up" on their chances of a meaningful career in the labor force and seeks other outlets for their creative urges. The reasons for their apparent despondency have to do with the limited prospects for promotion (Wakisaka and Tomita 1999: 3). While women's take-home pay was only 65 percent of men's pay in 2000 – low among developed economies – the differential has slowly narrowed from 59 percent in 1980 (Kosei Rodo Sho Koyo Kinto-Jido Katei Kyoku 2001: 26–7), and much of it can be explained by the different distributions of men and women in terms of employment status, job content, firm size, and industry. If and when women move into predominantly male domains, the differential will likely narrow dramatically.

In this context the Male-Female Equal Employment Opportunity Law of 1985 should be mentioned. Implemented from April 1986, the law was seen as a Japanese response to international pressure that was brought to bear on domestic politics by various women's groups. The law forbade gender-based discrimination in recruiting, hiring, pay, and promotion, but was immediately criticized by feminists for not imposing penalties on firms that did not comply. Although the law was not designed to force change in such a heavy-handed manner, its advocates felt it was a means of increasing public awareness of the issue and promoting a gradual, but more lasting, cultural change, and the more modest goal of putting gender on the corporate agenda was achieved.

The effectiveness of the legislation is difficult to assess. Some (e.g. Owaki, Nakano and Hayashi 1996; Asakura and Konno 1997) conclude that the changes fostered by the legislation would have occurred anyway, owing in part to continuing internationalization and the increased awareness of changes abroad. Such change is also consistent with the view of those participating in the Asian values debate who see the way to a more civil and egalitarian society as requiring a progression to higher levels of affluence and the concomitant stages of economic development rather than a change in Asian values per se (Mouer and Sugimoto: 2003). The legislation seems to have opened doors for more articulate women in the professions, with less impact on the world of work in factories, the distribution system, and much of the traditional service sector where part-time work is prevalent. While shifts in public consciousness are hard to assess in an area dominated by political correctness, today there is less bandying about of hackneyed phrases which referred to women as "office wallflowers" (*shokubano hana*) or as "leftover Christmas cakes" (suggesting that a woman's use-by date was passed if she had not married by the age of 25). The use of the term "OL" (office lady) also seems to have declined.

The labor-force behavior of women is clearly different from that of men; and women are treated differently in the work force. Do those differences constitute a different labor market? If one sees the treatment as preceding the behavior, the answer could be "yes." If behavioral choice precedes the treatment, the answer could be "no." Those who follow a line of thinking similar to that of Obi (1980) would tend to say "no." The "yes" camp would probably focus more on the process whereby firms create surplus by "exploiting" a good source of quality labor and maintaining their ability to do so through their power relations with women in the labor market. The institutionalization of practices for treating men and women differently would tend to suggest that their markets and certainly their career chances are different. However, the choice of whether to enter the "girls' market" as part-timers (where men can also be employed) or the open market still exists, and there is little gender difference in the growing market for the *furiitaa*.

Women are choosing to marry later, to have their first child later, and to have fewer children. The data in Ninomiya (2001: 40) shows that the percentage of women not yet married aged 30–34 increased from 7.2 percent in 1970 to 19.7 percent in 1995; the figures are 5.8 and 10.0 percent for women aged 35–39. For men the corresponding increases have been even more dramatic: up from 11.7 to 37.3 percent and from 4.7 to 22.6 percent. Isa (2002) presents data showing that the percentage of women aged 30–34 having their first child doubled from 16.8 percent in 1975 to 35.3 percent in 2000; those aged 35–39 doing so has tripled from 3.3 to 10.6 percent over the same period. Isa attributes this to a conscious decision by women to balance carefully the risks of raising children before they have had some experience of life and the biological risks of waiting too late.

A recent White Paper (Kosei Rodo Sho 2001b: 50–100) reports not only that women still do the bulk of the housework and the child rearing, but also that Japanese males are much less likely to perform those tasks than their counterparts abroad. However, the same report shows clearly that thinking about the division of labor at home is quickly changing. Surveys by the Office of the Cabinet reveal that those who do not agree with the proposition that the primary responsibility of men is to work and that of women is to look after the home and children increased from 27 percent in 1987 to 48 percent in 2000 (p. 59). The White Paper suggests that a growing number of women aspire to a life combining work *and* family, and that fewer women now want or plan for a family-centered existence. This varies from the position taken by Ninomiya (2001: 41–2), who argues that women want to have children but find it increasingly difficult to do so because of the realities of household finances that cause them to stay in a labor market which discriminates against them.

On the demand side, globalization will push firms to change to maintain their competitiveness in product markets. Firms are likely to be increasingly driven by the rather universalistic logic of global capitalism, and sensitivity to international standards will further weaken the notion that there should be two gender-based markets. As firms move to build clever teams of highly motivated individuals, these changes will be further supported. Firms that continue to conceive of their competitive edge in a mechanical manner focused on hours of work and on the strict surveillance and command of the salaried employee's time will slow the dissolution of the two markets.

### 6.5    The market for foreign workers

The changing power relationship between more fussy Japanese suppliers and cost-conscious buyers is reflected in the evolution of the labor market for foreign workers. It is estimated that the combined total of legal and illegal entrants working in Japan number in the vicinity of 700,000. While the term "foreign worker" used to connote prostitutes, dancers, and other female entertainers brought in from the Philippines and other Southeast Asian countries to service the lower end of the recreation industry, from the mid-1980s foreign workers came increasingly to be employed in menial work characterized by the "three Ks." In the early years the majority of these workers came by different routes from China, Korea, Southeast Asia, and Iran. Many Chinese nominally came as students but worked illegally in order to send money home to their families. Others, particularly those from Southeast Asia, came as on-the-job trainees on schemes organized through foreign aid programs. In this regard, some Japanese firms have been criticized for being more interested in the cheap labor supplied by the interns than in their training per se.

The Japanese government was caught between concerns about a perceived threat to social stability (in terms of the disruptiveness caused by migrant labor in many European countries) and the economic reality that migrant labor was underpinning the Japanese economy in ways that removed bottlenecks in areas where Japanese would no longer work. During the bubble years the Japanese government let the dual (legal and illegal) markets for foreign workers coexist. Government figures showed a sudden growth in legal immigrants in the 1980s. Their number tripled from 106,000 to nearly 300,000 between July 1989 and May 1993 (Kuwahara 2001: 8). However, the recession and rising unemployment in the early 1990s stimulated a backlash against foreign workers. The media seemed to highlight the most prominent tensions in terms of those who were most different visually and culturally (e.g. those from Islamic nations such as Iran, Pakistan, and Bangladesh). The government sought to tighten its control over immigration, and the number of legal migrant workers began to drop slightly; the proportion from the Islamic nations dropped from 20–25 percent to about 10 percent. While the overall effect of the recession was to close the door to more foreign workers, it did not result in a large exodus, and economic recovery is likely to be accompanied by further increases.

Kuwahara's (2001) study of small employers in the Hamamatsu area suggests that employers completely accept the inevitability of having foreign workers. This is also a stance described in a volume by Miyajima and Kajita (2000), which reports on field research in Toyohashi and Kawasaki. Komai (2001), even more optimistically, suggests that Japan's new migrant population is reaching a critical mass whereby multiculturalism will flourish. He predicts that the ideas of people with a different cultural background will add an important dynamic to Japanese society. Y. Suzuki (2002: 135–79) argues that the changes currently occurring in the Japanese language (as a result of this foreign element, among other influences) are relevant to Japan's ongoing multiculturalization and its interface with the increasingly globalized world. An advisory panel

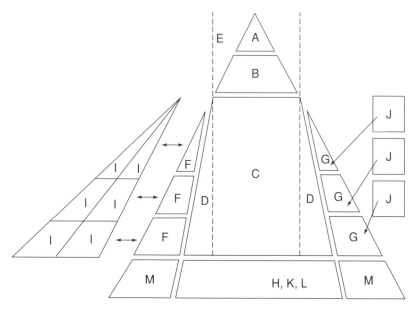

A Managers
B Middle management (including union members and non-unionists)
C Regular male employees (union members)
D Regular female employees (union members)
E Retirees and those on secondment
F Subcontracted employees
G Workers from labor dispatching firms
H Female part-timers
I Workers in small suppliers
J Entrepreneurs in independent firms
K Seasonal workers
L Student *arubaito*
M Foreign workers

Figure 6.1 The segmented labor force in Japan's large firms.
*Source:* Kumazawa (1989), p. 224.

commissioned by the prime minister to develop a vision for Japan in the twenty-first century even recommended that consideration be given to according English some status as Japan's second official language (Ono, Morimoto, and Suzuki 2001: 165–96; Suzuki 2002: 167–64).

## 6.6    The future of Japan's segmented labor markets

The above discussion highlights important ways in which the organization of work is beginning to change in Japan. A comparison between figures 6.1 and 6.2 provides some idea as to how Japan's labor market

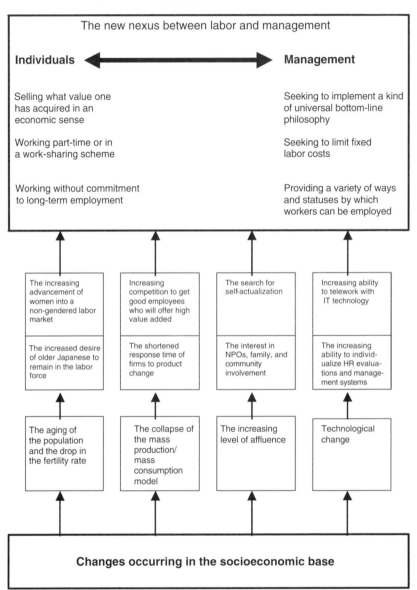

Figure 6.2 The emerging labor market in Japan (circa 2000).
*Source:* Adapted from a diagram in Hanami, Mitsuhashi, and Tachigi (2002), p. 39.

is being transformed. Figure 6.1 was developed some time ago by Kumazawa (1989) and shows how the segments depicted in figure 5.1 related to the way work was organized around the large firm. This chapter and chapter 5 suggest that Japan may be moving away from a situation in which a number of very segmented labor markets structure work around the large firms that command both the core market for Japan's elite employees and a large number of subcontractors (as shown in figure 6.1). A more fluid market seems to be emerging whereby the core market will remain a market for elite employees who will increasingly have to compete with workers in other rising markets (as shown in figure 6.2). Although the eventual outcome is difficult to predict, the new markets will accommodate the growing multiculturalization of Japanese society and the individualization of needs and wants on the supply side. Firms will increasingly be forced to search for new ways to utilize labor in order to rationalize their operations and keep the national economy internationally competitive.

The shortage of those with professional skills for the new economy will enhance the position of persons with those skills. Any decisive move to enhance the position of IT in the economy, to export more services, or to design and engineer products to be manufactured elsewhere will further improve the hand of Japan's most educated, creative, and dynamic individuals. Such people are likely to demand a loosening of corporate control over when and how they work. The consciousness of Japan's employees will continue to be influenced by Japan's relative level of affluence and by the household as a socioeconomic unit.

The dissemination by the media of information about life abroad is another factor. Another effect results from the growing amount of direct contact Japanese are having with people from overseas. This occurs through student exchanges, work-holiday programs and other work experience overseas, and through interaction with the growing number of migrants now living and working in Japan.

The second major change can be seen in a blurring of the lines of segmentation that have characterized Japan's labor market in the past. The distinctiveness of gender-specific markets is lessening. The market for graduates is becoming more diffuse, and Japanese firms are shifting to employ skilled workers who have already gained experience in the labor force. Spreading multiculturalism and the change in linguistic abilities and preferences in the broader community have been accompanied by a greater acceptance of foreign employers and foreign workers into the mainstream of many work organizations in Japan. The push for international competitiveness seems to be driving employers to extend their search for good workers far beyond the confines of the traditionally segmented labor markets upon which they have depended in the past.

What will remain most prominent are the firm size dualities and the distinction between regular and non-regular employment. While some practices first adopted in the large-scale sector will be diffused and come to characterize the world of work more generally in Japan, as long as the large firms remain dominant in the economy they will continue to reinvent difference. They will maintain a different, albeit elitist, culture for the employees of the corporate world. The distinction between regular and non-regular employment will also continue, partly because this distinction overlaps with, and is reinforced by, firm-size dualities, but also because the counterculture of the small independent entrepreneur will remain attractive to many Japanese and be economically feasible as long as the material standard of living at the bottom end of society is above a certain civil minimum. However, the most important reason these two types of segmentation will remain is that they are congruent with the major differentiations that constitute the social stratification matrix in Japan at the beginning of the twenty-first century.

When speculating about how the Japanese stratification mosaic will look in the future, two possible changes come to mind. Work sharing is one development that could considerably alter thinking about gender roles at home and at work. It would likely release many men from the long hours and the psychological pressures currently imposed upon them as regular employees and as main breadwinners. It would also allow them to reflect on the advantages of the *furiitaa* lifestyle, and to be more involved in family and community life (including participation in NPOs). While large employers may be slow to warm to the idea, the new economy will place an emphasis on the ability of firms to develop and maintain a good measure of multicultural sensitivity in terms of Japan's own subcultures.

A second critical change might result from the move away from the unilinear conception of life that has been institutionalized in Japan. Management, unions, and bureaucrats have tended in the past to conceive of life following a single path from the womb to the tomb. This approach is structured around a course taking each person through a fairly uniform childhood socialization process, a standardized schooling with further education where possible, and then employment in the best firm possible. Once employed, it was assumed that Japanese would work diligently for advancement and for the success of their firm while getting married and raising children (with or without continuing employment in the case of women). Post-career employment and then retirement on an appropriate pension ended the lifecycle. This discourse on lifecycle developed around the norms of the successful *sarariman* in the elite sector of the labor market. It rested on an assumption that was convenient for employers used to thinking of their surpluses or profit margins as being generated from economies of scale, where workers are to a considerable extent interchangeable with no unusual or unpredictable demands on them from outside the firm. In many other countries school leavers are able to work, get married and have children, and then return to the classroom in order to launch themselves in new careers and in new directions. Although a good deal of rhetoric in Japan is about lifelong learning, the institutions and the mechanisms to facilitate that kind of rotation into and out of the labor force are not in place for that to occur in any meaningful way. If, with Kelly (1998), one sees the new economy as a networked activity in which firms need to give considerably more of themselves to the social good in order to prosper, another clue to Japan's future will be found in the extent to which deregulation of the labor market is accompanied by the deregulation of the employee in Japan's large corporate sector.

*Part IV*

The broader social policy context for understanding choice at work in Japan

# 7 From labor policy to social policy: a framework for understanding labor process in Japan at the national level

All the people are equal under the law and there shall be no discrimination in political, economic or social relations because of race, creed, sex, social status or family origin

(Article 14 of the Japanese Constitution).

Every person shall have freedom to choose . . . his occupation to the extent that it does not interfere with the public welfare

(Article 22 of the Constitution).

All people shall have the right to maintain the minimum standards of wholesome and cultured living

(Article 25 of the Constitution).

All people shall have the right to receive an equal education correspondent to their ability, as provided by law

(Article 26 of the Constitution).

All people shall have the right and the obligation to work

(Article 27 of the Constitution).

The right to own or to hold property is inviolable

(Article 29 of the Constitution).

## 7.1 Approaching labor policy in Japan

The labor markets described in the preceding two chapters are embedded within a larger sociopolitical context. These passages from the Japanese Constitution provide a broad framework for work-related legislation in postwar Japan. Government policy continues to influence in numerous ways the social context in which Japan's labor markets function. In some areas, however, the policy framework has been characterized by conspicuous non-involvement. The government's indifference to horrendous pollution in the late 1960s and the early 1970s is one example. Others might be its reluctance to address various issues related to *karoshi* and illness from overwork. In other areas the government has been criticized for being over-zealous. Its control of textbooks and its battles with the

Japan Teachers' Union and other forms of left-wing unionism are well documented; so too is its active support for strategically selected industries through a system of administrative guidance. In still other cases the government has responded only after considerable international pressure has been generated; it began to deal seriously with issues concerning the right to strike in public enterprises only after the International Labor Organization (ILO) became involved.

In most areas, the government has been careful to deliberate at length and to sponsor careful comparative research on the situation in other advanced economies before coming up with its own policies. A wait-and-see approach was taken before adopting equal opportunity legislation in the mid-1980s and then tightening it at the end of the 1990s. The government's staunch resistance to radical unionism and its reluctance to concede managerial prerogatives have probably resulted in social change at the workplace lagging behind that in society as a whole. This in turn may have resulted in the initiative of many employees being restrained at work, with serious mismatching in many labor markets slowing down the restructuring processes that must occur if Japan is to successfully grapple with the new economic realities that accompany globalization.

The interest in the superior competitiveness of Japan's economy in the early 1970s shifted attention from Japan's high savings rate and capital inputs to the country's high labor productivity. This shift resulted in a focus on (i) Japanese social values, (ii) skill formation within the firm and other practices associated with internal labor markets in Japan's largest firms, and (iii) the institutions which were labeled "the three pillars" by the OECD (1977) and the "Three Sacred Emblems" by Yakabe (1977). The three pillars were lifetime or career employment (*shushin koyo* or *shogai koyo*), seniority wages (*nenko joretsu chingin*), and enterprise unions (*kigyobetsu kumiai*). Although these three practices had been noted earlier by Abegglen (1958) and Hazama (1959 and 1962), reference to the "three sacred treasures" (*sanshu no jingi*) became common in the academic literature on Japan's industrial relations in the early 1970s. Accepting them as widespread practices and the norm, many authors sought to systematize their understanding of those practices in terms of a unique set of Japanese cultural values that were seen as underpinning these institutions (e.g. Hazama 1971; Tsuda 1977 and 1980; Iwata 1974 and 1975).

These company-level practices have not been mentioned or regulated, let alone enshrined, in any legislation. Rather they have evolved out of understandings at the plant level, and labor process at the micro level has resulted in a good deal of creativity and variety among Japan's firms. To some extent the government's policy with regard to work has been one of minimal involvement. Firms (and enterprise unions) in the large-scale private sector have been allowed to develop internal personnel practices most suited to their own economic circumstances, an approach that has resulted in the institutionalization of the inequalities and inefficiencies associated with labor market segmentation.

Although more sophisticated discussions mention some of the variations in practice that have arisen from dualities in the labor market, most discussions have overlooked or downplayed the role of the government in shaping the broader context in which labor markets and work practices exist. The general absence of comprehensive legislation in the early postwar years in the domain commonly referred to in Japan as "social policy" (*shakai seisaku*) may have contributed to this oversight. So too might the tendency of outside observers to dismiss what social policy there was as not being sufficiently significant compared to the comprehensive social welfare systems found in many Western countries. In any case, the interest in policy and legislation related to work (i.e. minimal working conditions) came to be circumscribed within "labor policy" (*rodo seisaku*), a construct which incorporated a much narrower range of concerns related to work itself and the collective bargaining relationship. These were the traditional concerns of the discipline of industrial relations (or labor–management relations) and industrial sociology as they had developed in the United States.[1] Another reason for this narrow focus might also have been the general reluctance of policymakers in Japan to become involved in the affairs of companies at the private level.

In the early postwar years legislation was enacted to stop some of the prewar exploitative practices and this can be seen as having provided important regulatory guidelines. Until the 1970s the concern with labor law was focused primarily on three laws (known as the "*rodo sanpo*"): the Labor Standards Law (1947), the Trade Union Law (1945 and 1949), and the Labor Relations Adjustment Law (1946 and 1948). Until the early 1970s labor law was debated primarily in terms of how those laws should be interpreted and how changes to those laws might affect the overall functioning of the labor economy in terms of Japan's high rates of economic growth. In the early years there was a concern that an enhanced

---

[1] It should be noted that the United States government actively funded the establishment of a program designed to bring a large number of promising young Japanese scholars to American universities in the 1960s to study industrial relations and labor economics as an alternative to the Marxist approach to work organization. The program was part of the cold-war strategy developed by the United States, and reflected the concern of American policymakers with the influence of Marxist and other left-wing scholars in Japan on public debate and on the setting of agendas for the union movement and other grassroots organizations in postwar Japan. This was an important factor shaping how industrial relations research and industrial sociology developed in postwar Japan.

Trade Union Law should ensure a democratic balance between the forces for distributive justice and those for firm-based economic efficiency. The OECD reports on Japan's manpower arrangements and many other writings in the 1970s praised Japanese-style management practices for their contribution to maintaining a highly motivated labor force committed to serving the firms that employed them.

The emergence of mass society served to legitimate the Japanese model. The outcomes of these changes seemed to obviate the need for more legislation either to regulate work or to alter the distribution of income. Those were the years of the Japanese economic miracle and the *moretsu shain* who was later to receive international acclaim in the management literature of the late 1970s and the 1980s. A belief that rapid growth would result in across-the-board improvements in everyone's standard of living had taken root.

Following the successive oil shocks in the mid-1970s, Japan faced considerable unemployment for the first time in nearly three decades. Over the preceding decade Japanese had come to enjoy a lifestyle with various new conveniences that included time-activated rice cookers, washing machines, vacuum cleaners, cars, a range of high-quality audio-visual goods and various leisure-oriented services. Many Japanese wanted more than pollution and long hours of overtime. Anti-war movements, the anti-pollution movements, and consumer movements were active. Women were becoming more independent and wanted more at work. The family was changing, and the need for in-home care for the aged was beginning to be felt. Soon there would be foreign workers, the homeless, and the *furiitaa* who were not following the normal paths into the labor force.

## 7.2     Notions of labor law

With these changes in the 1970s the concept of labor law began to broaden. During the 1980s and 1990s labor law came to embrace an expanding range of concerns. This development is reflected in the list of Japan's postwar labor legislation (table 7.1). The common basis for all legislation is the Civil Code and the Constitution (table 7.2). Japan's labor laws need to be understood in relation to other legislation, especially with regard to social welfare, as this chapter and the next argue. The ILO conventions provide points of reference in the background.

Basic textbooks on labor law, including those recently reviewed by Obata (2000), map the changing terrain. Older textbooks emphasize how employment is defined and what constitutes a union. The delineation of legal rights and obligations in setting working conditions or in collective bargaining was an important issue involved with the introduction of more

Table 7.1 *Japan's postwar labor legislation*

| Date | Japanese | English |
|------|----------|---------|
| 22.12.1945 | (Kyu) Rodo Kumiai Ho | (First) Trade Union Law |
| 27.09.1946 | Rodo Kankei Chosei Ho | Labor Relations Adjustment Law |
| 7.04.1947 | Rodo Kijun Ho | Labor Standards Law |
| 30.11.1947 | Shokugyo Antei Ho | Employment Security Law |
| 21.12.47 | Shitsugyo Hoken Ho | Unemployment Insurance Law |
| 7.04.1948 | Rodosha Saigai Hosho Hoken Ho | Workmen's Accident Compensation Insurance Law |
| 20.12.1948 | Kokyo Kigyotaito Rodo Kankei Ho | Public Corporation and National Enterprise Labor Relations Law |
| 31.05.1949 | Rodo Sho Setchi Ho | Ministry of Labor Establishment Law |
| 1.06.1949 | Rodo Kumiai Ho | (Second) Trade Union Law |
| 28.12.1949 | Koyo Hoken Ho | Employment Insurance Law |
| 7.08.1953 | Denki Jigyo Oyobi Sekitan Kogyo ni Okeru Sogi Koi no Hoko no Kisei ni Kansuru Horitsu | Law Concerning the Control of Disputes in the Electric Power and Coal Mining Industries |
| 2.05.1958 | Nihon Rodo Kyokai Ho | Japan Institute of Labor Law |
| 15.04.1959 | Saitei Chingin Ho | Minimum Wage Law |
| 9.05.1959 | Chusho Kigyo Taishokukin Kyosai Ho | Law Concerning Mutual Aid Among Smaller Enterprises for Retirement Allowance |
| 25.07.1960 | Shintai Shogaisha Koyo Sokushin Ho | Physically Handicapped Persons' Employment Promotion Law |
| 29.06.1964 | Rodo Saigai Boshi Dantai Ho | Industrial Injury Prevention Organization Law |
| 21.07.1966 | Koyo Taisaku Ho | Law on Measures to Maintain Employment |
| 18.07.1969 | Shokugyo Kunren Ho | Vocational Training Law |
| 16.05.1970 | Kanai Rodo Ho | Law Concerning Persons Employed at Home |
| 1.06.1971 | Kinrosha Zaisan Keisei Sokushin Ho | Law for the Promotion of Workers' Property Accumulation |
| 8.06.1972 | Rodo Anzen Eisei Ho | Industrial Safety and Health Law |
| 1.07.1972 | Kinro Fujin Fukushi Ho | Working Women's Welfare Law |
| 28.12.1974 | Koyo Hoken Ho | Employment Insurance Law |
| 1.05.1975 | Sagyo Kankyo Sokutei Ho | Working Environment Measurement Law |
| 27.05.1976 | Chingin no Shiharai no Kakuho Nado ni Kansuru Horitsu | Security of Wage Payment Law |

(*cont.*)

Table 7.1 (*cont.*)

| Date | Japanese | English |
|------|----------|---------|
| 15.05.1983 | Tokutei Fukyo Gyoshu Nado Kankei Rodosha No Koyo Ni Kansuru Tokubetsu Sochi Ho | Law for Employment Security for Workers in Specified Depressed Industries |
| 17.05.1985 | Danjo Koyo Kikai Kinto Ho | Law Concerning the Promotion of Equal Opportunity and Treatment Between Men and Women and Other Welfare Measures for Women Workers |
| 5.07.1985 | Rodo Haken Ho | Law for the Worker Dispatching Industry |
| 31.03.1987 | Chiiki Koyo Kaihatsu Sokushin Ho | Law to Promote Employment in Local Areas |
| 2.07.1992 | Rodo Jikan Tanshuku Sokushin Ho | Law for Temporary Measures to Promote Shorter Working Hours |
| 1.04.1992 | Ikuji Kyugyo Ho | Law on Maternity Leave |
| 18.06.1993 | Paato Rodo Ho | Law Concerning Part-Time Workers |
| 9.06.1995 | Ikuji Kyugyo Ho | Law for Workers with Family Care Responsibilities (revised) |
| 1.04.1999 | Danjo Koyo Kikai Kinto Ho | Law Concerning the Promotion of Equal Opportunity and Treatment Between Men and Women and Other Welfare Measures for Women Workers (revised) |
| 1.04.1999 | Rodo Kijun Ho | Labor Standards Law (revised) |
| 1.12.1999 | Rodosha Haken Ho | Law for the Worker Dispatching Industry (revised) |
| 1.12.1999 | Shokugyo Antei Ho | Employment Security Law (revised) |

*Notes:* (1) There is a slight inconsistency in the dates given. Some are for enactment, while others are for promulgation or enforcement.

(2) The laws listed here may be consulted in Japanese in Kosei Rodo Daijin Kanbo Somuka (2001). An English version of most items may be found in Ministry of Labor (1995).

democratic work practices and the move of Japan away from fascist structures and socially "feudal" relationships which were seen as defining work in the prewar era. This narrow focus on legal interpretations of Japan's new postwar labor laws characterizes many textbooks produced in the 1960s (e.g. Hokao 1965 and successive editions into the 1990s). Introductory textbooks in the 1980s (e.g. Yasueda and Nishimura 1986)

Table 7.2 *Legislation and conventions affecting the formulation of labor law in Japan*

|  | Date | Japanese | English |
|---|---|---|---|
| **Prewar** | | | |
|  | 27.04.1896 | Mimpo | Civil Code |
|  | 24.04.1910 | Keiho | Criminal Code |
|  | 10.04.1926 | Boryoku Koi To Shobatsu ni Kansuru Hoitsu | Law Concerning Violence and its Control |
| **Postwar** | | | |
|  | 3.05.1947 | Nihonkoku Kempo | Constitution of Japan |
| **International** | 1919 to 1940 and 1951 to present | Kokusai Rodo Joyaku | Conventions of the International Labor Organization. Japan has ratified thirty-three conventions: nos. 2, 5, 7, 8, 9, 10, 15, 16, 18, 19, 21, 22, 26, 27, 29, 45, 49, 58, 69, 73, 81, 87, 88, 96, 98, 100, 102, 115, 119, 121, 131, 134, and 139. |

began to reflect sociopolitical changes that started in the 1970s. In addition to providing an interpretative overview covering "the basics" in a traditional sense, these textbooks had chapters dealing with issues being addressed in a raft of new legislation: employment security, unemployment and retrenchment, equal employment opportunity (for women), outsourcing through employment dispatching agencies, and aged workers.

By the late 1990s the shift to a broader conceptualization of labor law was firmly established. Shimoi (2000), Suwa (1999), Yasueda (1998), and the first volume in a new series edited by the Japan Association for Labor Law (Nihon Rodo Ho Gakkai: 2000) all placed labor law in the broader social context. They incorporated an understanding of how globalization and the spread of international standards were affecting labor law in Japan. They also referred to some of the unresolved sociopolitical tensions within contemporary Japan to highlight how a careful review of past legislation may provide some useful lessons in responding to social change. Tanaka's (2000) textbook combines the approach of the late 1980s and early 1990s (which was to add new chapters to the basic framework of the 1960s), with an introduction to the real issues confronting policymakers. In giving special attention to the legal situation of foreign workers in Japan (a loose group of individuals whose status is not defined by any specific piece of work-related legislation), the book recognizes that the circumstances arising out of globalization have presented the country with the need to redefine the domain associated with labor law. Tanaka's volume also discusses the legal issues posed by the recent increase in work-related suicides from the point of view of Japan's Accident Compensation Insurance Law of 1947 (and revised nearly every year thereafter).

Changes in labor policy can easily be discovered by surveying the annual issues of the Labor White Paper, major journals in this area, and various annual reviews which summarize longer-term trends. Discussions in the late 1950s and early 1960s focused on urban/rural dualities, occupational wage differentials, regional income inequalities, the *dekasegi* (migrant laborers), and poverty. In the early postwar years there was a distinct difference between (i) conservative academics, management representatives, and bureaucrats and (ii) left-leaning scholars, labor leaders, and human rights or civil rights advocates and activists. The former group tended to argue that growth would result in a broadly spread affluence that would result in the importance attached to various inequalities diminishing over time, and that business needed a free hand to "get on with the job." That view was consistent with the widely held perception that 90 percent of Japanese were part of a broadly based middle class. The latter group tended to emphasize how entrenched social inequalities defined reality for most working-class Japanese. They argued that such inequalities supported an approach to work organization in Japan that provided for the systematic generation of surplus for Japan's large firms. They tended to believe that more active state involvement was needed to achieve more equal power relations at work and a more egalitarian distribution of Japan's newly created wealth. Here the socialist-inspired unionists faced a fundamental contradiction: the majority of unionists were employed in Japan's large-scale sector; as Japan's aristocracy of labor, they enjoyed privilege at the expense of many workers in Japan's smaller firms and those who labored as casuals.

Japan's new affluence seemed to vindicate the view that workers would achieve even higher standards of living by continuing to work long hours for their firm. The metaphor of the 1960s and 1970s was the "economic pie." Debate revolved around the relationship between policies designed to enhance the size of the pie in absolute terms and policies that would redistribute the pie. Those involved in developing labor and social policy during this period invariably gave priority to enhancing size, often believing the affluence produced by growth would flow down to everyone, that income inequality would "automatically" diminish over time, and that efforts to alter the distribution of social rewards would undermine the growth process.

As the pie grew, the focus of labor and social policy shifted away from issues of inequality and social justice. From the early 1970s the main issues for labor policy became Japan's labor shortage, human resource development, and labor mobility through internal labor markets: areas linked to Japan's international competitiveness. By the mid-1970s there was a widespread belief that the Japanese approach had created the most egalitarian society in the industrialized world.

At the same time the mercantilist mentality continued to dominate the minds of many policymakers. It was common in the 1970s for policy-makers to call upon another of Japan's postwar metaphors which likened the Japanese economy to a small rowing boat in danger of being sunk by larger boats in hostile international waters. In the early 1970s the European discourse on incomes policy was introduced in the context of the "task in hand": maintaining Japan's international competitiveness. Wage inflation and militant unionism were portrayed as symptoms of the dreaded "British disease" which had ravaged a country that once headed a great empire and later came to embrace too much social welfare. The Japanese approach was framed in terms of self-restraint on the part of unions. It was presented as a uniquely Japanese approach arising out of a national ethos that placed a value on conciliatory industrial relations, on the loyalty of employees to their firm, and on employees having a strong sense of national identity and purpose.

Following the "Nixon shocks" and the oil crises in the 1970s, conser-vative policymakers focused on training, responsible unionism, and the need to adjust employment levels. Leftists were still demanding social welfare and better safety nets. In 1974 Sohyo, the left-leaning national center for organized labor, fought its annual Spring Offensive as "the People's Offensive." Its slogans demanded social welfare that would serve the interests of many in the non-unionized peripheral labor force. Sohyo's demands were deflected by (i) its continuing commitment to obtaining the right to strike in the public sector, (ii) the lack of interest among unionists in the large-scale private sector (who tended to iden-tify more with the conservative national center Domei), and (iii) the fact that the conservative government suddenly took the initiative to intro-duce bills that were plugged as opening a new era of social welfare (*fukushi gannen*). The capacity of the government to fund welfare was presented by conservatives as having been made possible only by ongoing rapid growth. The perception that growth was threatened by the oil shocks reinforced the view that everyone would benefit from (i) sensible wage restraint,

(ii) a certain leniency when it came to implementing the new welfare policies, and (iii) the constraining of irresponsible left-wing unionism that pushed for social justice at the expense of the economy's competitiveness.

In the late 1970s and early 1980s concern shifted to other issues such as the role of working women and hours of work. Sizable balance-of-payments surpluses brought international pressure on Japan to share some of its largesse abroad. Continued growth into the 1980s contributed to a tighter labor market and rising labor costs. Japan's larger firms began to develop global production and marketing strategies, and an increasing number of Japanese began to travel, study, and live overseas. The conditions for Japanese society to internationalize were further improved by legislation related to the position of women – one law altering the basis for citizenship in 1984 and another in 1985 raising public awareness of the various forms of gender-based discrimination at work. As immigration increased, international marriages became more common, and Japan became more connected to the world through the spread of international culture and other phenomena such as AIDS. The Japanese adopted a more multicultural outlook and became more informed about the world beyond Japan. Domestically, proportional representation was introduced for the Diet's Upper House electoral districts in 1983; Japan National Railways was disaggregated and privatized in 1987; the tunnel connecting Hokkaido and Honshu was completed in 1988; and the general consumption tax (*shohizei*) was introduced from April 1989. These developments further consolidated the national economy and prepared it for being more globally competitive.

In the 1990s initiatives were taken to deregulate the labor market and to improve the interface between work and family life. While some of those changes were motivated by a desire to improve the competitiveness of firms, they were also facilitated by a greater awareness of social change abroad and by the absorption of "international standards" into the work culture of Japan.

## 7.3     From labor policy to social policy as a framework for understanding the organization of work in Japan

Despite the long concern with "labor policy" (*rodo seisaku*), the term is still difficult to define. Although it usually includes various aspects of manpower planning, it is generally not used in a manner so comprehensive as to include issues related to compulsory education or to social welfare per se. However, an understanding of the choices which the Japanese make in choosing to engage with one or more of Japan's labor markets, and to work for a given employer, requires a full appreciation of how policy (or its absence) serves to reinforce social arrangements that delimit the options available to ordinary Japanese when they think about work. Here we are talking about their "conditions of possibility," to use a term employed by Derrida, the "discourse" which in Foucault's vocabulary defines their options, or simply the "superstructures" in Marxist terminology. Accordingly, when thinking about the legislative framework shaping choices at work it is useful to consider the wider setting that is the concern of social policy (*shakai seisaku*). The domain of social policy is more inclusive than that of labor policy, and it too is being transformed owing to the changes in Japanese society.

Three general approaches to social policy are relevant to understanding the organization of work in contemporary Japan. One focuses on the *objects of social policy*, identifying those for whom and by whom the policies are enacted. Central to this approach is the delineation of various interest groups and underprivileged social strata. With the shift in public consciousness the existence of new strata has been acknowledged: working women who still bear a disproportionately large share of the responsibility for children, housework, and the care of other family members; the handicapped; those who suffer from various forms of harassment and/or intimidation; foreign workers; part-timers and other casuals; aged workers; and workers who find themselves homeless.

These new strata exist only at the margins of public consciousness. When the economy was growing rapidly, isolated cases of extreme poverty could be covered by some sort of monetary consideration. Today, however, many who require attention are not poor in absolute terms; rather, they are citizens concerned about social recognition and discrimination arising from social attitudes that diminish their dignity. They are asking for a fundamental renegotiation of their social status. They are critical of the way status is inherited through a process that was markedly shaped by their parents' differential access to societal rewards and the relatively small number of good jobs.

These issues are essentially linked to the provision of social security, safety nets, and civil minimums. One concerns what the minimal standards might be; another concerns the locus of responsibility for ensuring that agreed standards are maintained. For a long time successive conservative governments have taken the view that firms and individuals (i.e. families) should take the major responsibility for looking after these matters. This has given way over time to a piecemeal approach in formulating social welfare legislation, and the percentage of Japan's GNP generated for health, pensions, and other welfare is lower than in most other similarly industrialized nations (table 7.3). This is consistent with the policy objectives of many conservatives who believe that the potential

Table 7.3 *Percentage of national income spent on social welfare in six nations (circa the mid-1990s)*

| Country | Year | A Medical care | B Pensions | C Other welfare | D Total | E Percentage of the population aged over 70 in 2002 | F Per capita income (US$) at ¥132/US$1 |
|---|---|---|---|---|---|---|---|
| Sweden | 1993 | 10.0 | 20.1 | 23.3 | 53.4 | 17.43 | 24,632 |
| France | 1994 | 9.0 | 18.3 | 10.1 | 37.4 | 15.97 | 23,217 |
| Germany | 1993 | 8.7 | 14.3 | 10.3 | 33.3 | 16.40 | 24,655 |
| United Kingdom | 1993 | 7.3 | 10.8 | 9.1 | 27.2 | 15.75 | 17,814 |
| USA | 1992 | 7.1 | 8.7 | 3.6 | 19.4 | 12.30 | 25,775 |
| Japan | 1993 | 5.9 | 7.8 | 1.6 | 15.2 | | 28,146 |
| | 1998 | 6.7 | 10.1 | 2.2 | 18.9 | 17.34 | 28,043 |
| | 1999 | 6.9 | 10.4 | 2.3 | 19.6 | | 29,043 |

*Source:* The data were compiled by the Kokuritsu Shakai Hosho Jinko Mondai Kenkyujo (The National Research Center for the Study of Social Security and Population), and appeared in Ichi-en (2002), p. 658 and Hamada and Okuma (2002), p. 474. The data for 1998 and 1999 and in column E are from Kosei Rodo Daijin Kanbo Tokei Joho Bu (2002b), pp. 24 and 313.

for economic growth is seriously compromised by expenditure on social welfare. Hirakawa (2002: 18–22) writes about this at some length, arguing, perhaps optimistically, that policymakers may be changing their views in this regard. The tendency to leave the responsibility for social welfare to the private sector has meant that workers have had to rely to a considerable extent on the willingness of their employers to develop corporate welfare programs. In this regard table 7.4 suggests that welfare benefits provided by employers have slowly risen from 13.6 percent of total labor costs in 1975 to 18.4 percent in 1998. However, considerable differences exist between large and small firms. In 1998 take-home pay was 1.62 times greater for workers in firms with over 5,000 employees than in firms having 30–99 employees; when company welfare benefits were added to take-home wages, the figure grew to 1.75 (Kosei Rodo Sho Daijin Kanbo Tokei Joho Bu 2002a: 187–8).

A second approach to social policy is concerned with the *publicly stated goals of social policy*. To some extent motives – as understood in the goals they set – may be detected from the legislation itself. However, to understand fully the dynamics of policy formation one needs to look further for patterns that reveal longer-term commitments to given ideological positions. To some extent policy has been shaped by subtle shifts in the complicated balance of power. Unification of the labor movement at the end of the 1980s had a political impact in the early 1990s, even though the major labor organization (Rengo) embraced fewer than one-fourth of all employees. Rengo has struggled to develop policy recommendations over a wide range of areas of concern to working Japanese. With conservatives floundering through a succession of coalition governments in the 1990s, the process of formulating welfare policy has been marked by uncertainty. The extended recession in the 1990s, a general concern with rationalizing public expenditure, and political inertia delayed fundamental reform.

Kume (2000) notes, nevertheless, that a fundamental change has been occurring. Reasons to replace disparate schemes with a single unified system are now receiving greater recognition. Questions have also been raised about transparency and the strong commitment to a corporatist approach. The segmented approach has served to create and maintain inequalities that came to be more entrenched and socially reproduced over time. In the 1980s public attention was diverted from these issues by the frequent media coverage given to those proclaiming that Japan was the ultimate middle-class society. Without a strong mandate, political leaders lacked the confidence necessary to initiate open public discussion of many social policy issues that impinge directly on aspects of Japan's stratification matrix.

Table 7.4 *Percentage breakdown for labor costs and the amounts spent on non-wage welfare benefits by private firms in Japan, 1975–98*

| | 1975 | 1985 | 1998 | | |
| --- | --- | --- | --- | --- | --- |
| | | | For all firms | For firms with 5,000+ employees | For firms with 30–99 employees |
| TOTAL LABOR COSTS | 100.0 | 100.0 | 100.0 | 100.0 | 100.0 |
| A. Wages | 86.4 | 84.6 | 81.6 | 78.5 | 84.6 |
| B. Non-wage costs | 13.6 | 15.4 | 18.4 | 21.5 | 15.4 |
| 1. Retirement pay | 3.1 | 3.9 | 5.4 | 7.7 | 2.7 |
| 2. Payment in kind | 0.5 | 0.0 | 0.3 | 0.4 | 0.3 |
| 3. Legally stipulated welfare | 6.1 | 7.7 | 9.3 | 8.7 | 10.3 |
| 4. Welfare benefits not required by law | 3.1 | 2.8 | 2.7 | 4.1 | 1.8 |
| 5. Education and training | 0.3 | 0.3 | 0.3 | 0.3 | 0.2 |
| 6. Recruitment | 0.2 | 0.2 | 0.2 | 0.1 | 0.1 |
| 7. Other costs | 0.2 | 0.6 | 0.2 | 0.2 | 0.1 |

*Source:* Kosei Rodo Sho Daijin Kanbo Tokei Joho Bu (2002a), pp. 187–8.

The concern with inequality connects to a third emphasis: the *social or structural origins of social policy*. There seems to be agreement about many of the greater changes driving recent shifts in social policy. They include feminism and its impact on how women think about work, child rearing, and their own sense of fulfillment. The increasing emphasis in Japanese society on human rights is another (Ogawa *et al.* 2002). These shifts are reflected in the term "barrier-free society," which has become a key Japanese term in recent years. Changes are also occurring in the structure of the family (including a greater acceptance of various types of family structures) and in the age profile of the population. The hollowing out of key industries as major firms move production overseas has been accompanied by the diversification of the labor force in terms of the needs, wants, or aspirations of those who labor. Few want to follow a standardized life-course. The opening of the Japanese market to cheaper goods of considerable quality, and to greater flows of information about choices elsewhere, further promotes the individuation of lifestyles in Japan.

Behind these changes looms globalization. Based on his comparison between the ways in which social welfare has been evolving in Japan and China during the 1990s, Nakae (1998: 319–31) provides an interesting overview of how capitalism and the capitalist welfare state have evolved. He argues that three major conditions have sustained the welfare state over the past century: continuing economic growth, the ideological cleavages between socialist and capitalist regimes, and the absolute sovereignty of the nation state. Financial crises, the rising cost of oil, and the hollowing out of industries as production is moved abroad are seen as major threats to future growth and prosperity. Since the cold war the need to compete ideologically in terms of social justice issues has declined. The new movements of finance, capital, goods, people, and information compromise the integrity of the nation state and its ability to control or regiment its citizens. In the new global era the future of social policy will increasingly be influenced by the development of international standards that are shaped by the pushing and shoving of national governments in the international arena, and in largely closed meetings organized by the Group of Eight, the WTO, certain NGOs, the ILO, and various other world economic forums sponsored by the private sector.

In this regard, the debate that was begun in the 1930s by Kazahaya Yasoji (1973) and Okochi Kazuo (1970) is of considerable interest. The former argued that social policy can best be understood as an instrument of the establishment to appease and to control members of the working class; the latter argued that progressive social legislation was in the interests of capitalists narrowly defined and in the interests of management groups more broadly defined.

Kazahaya's position was that governmental action, supported by a strong working-class political movement, was necessary for the economic interests of workers to be realized. Studies of Japan's anti-pollution policies and the move to deregulate the labor market, for example, have involved close consultation and tacit agreement between government and business without much input from union leaders and others of a socialist bent.

Okochi believed that enlightened policy would be the inevitable outcome when firms strove to be competitive in a healthy capitalist economy. He attached importance to having an integrated social policy sensitive (a) to the tradeoff between participation and efficiency, and (b) to the requirement that successful management strategies must take account of existing social customs and cultural values. These views would later be articulated by Nakayama (1974), who called for a balance between the emphasis on efficiency and the weight attached to having socially just outcomes. The writings of Tsuda (1977 and 1980), Iwata (1974 and 1975), and many others associated with this stream of thinking in the late 1970s and early 1980s argued that the uniqueness of Japanese-style management and Japan's approach to industrial relations lies in the very fact that such a balance had indeed been achieved.

Given the emphasis on the importance attached to the continuity of cultural values in much of the literature on Japan's work practices and industrial relations which emerged in the 1970s and 1980s, it is important to note that many practices, such as seniority wages, enterprise unions, and long-term employment, were institutionalized only during the Pacific War and in the immediate postwar years. In the past, *nihonteki* (typically Japanese) values were seldom treated as being connected to desired outcomes in the discussions of labor policy theorists. "Culturalists" and even many "institutionalists" highlighted such values as the central link supporting the "three pillars." However, to the extent that the existence of such values has been acknowledged, they have as often as not been seen as constraints retarding efforts to rationalize work practices.

In discussions of *nihonteki keiei* (Japanese-style management practices) scholars such as Nakayama and Tsuda emphasized ways in which the importance attached to the related set of Japanese values bound management to a vocabulary or rhetoric impelling them to implement certain democratic values and civil minimums. In their view, by paying attention to the egalitarian concerns of ordinary workers, management was able to heighten significantly the motivation of employees to work. However, while spouting a group-oriented ideology, the socialist implications of groupist values have consistently been downplayed by conservatives, and labor market segmentation has resulted in a sizable proportion of the labor force not enjoying permanent long-term employment or the benefits associated with seniority in Japan's large-scale sector. References to "groupism" and related values were translated into appeals calling for the maintenance of national economic independence at all costs. Central to achieving economic goals was the maintenance of social stability (e.g. not engaging in disruptive labor disputes) and a strong work ethic (e.g. the willingness to work long hours at the discretion of management). At the same time, the diversification of the labor force in the 1990s led management to search for new ways to legitimate its push for further rationalization as notions of "the good life" and the nature of social justice evolved.

## 7.4    Social class, labor market segmentation and inequality

In many advanced and newly industrializing economies the amount of social inequality increased during the 1990s. Japan's widening income and wealth differentials have been accentuated by a drop in intra- and intergenerational mobility. Only infrequently does one now encounter in the media the rhetoric so popular in the 1970s and 1980s that Japan was one large homogeneous middle-class society. The discussion of inequality in contemporary Japan revolves around at least four issues: declining levels of social (mainly occupational) mobility, the distribution of income and wealth, the way the system of education reproduces social class, and the significance of Japan's newcomers on the stratification matrix. Competing views on these issues have been compiled by the editors at Bungei Shunju (2000) and Chuo Koron Henshu Bu (2001). Views on income distribution appeared in a special issue of the *Nihon Rodo Kenkyu Zasshi* (no. 480: July 2000) and a recent publication of the Japanese Association of Labor Sociology (Nihon Rodo Shakai Gakkai) (2002).

The wartime experience and subsequent Occupation radically altered Japanese society. Japanese debate in the 1950s and early 1960s revolved around the extent to which Japan had democratized. Although a sizable literature about poverty and the working class was produced during those years, the spread of Japan's rapid economic growth led many to believe by the late 1970s and early 1980s that Japan had become a mass society. Surveys seemed to show that 90 percent of Japanese were middle class, and that serious pockets of poverty or wealth did not exist. It was commonly assumed that the distribution of income in Japan was more egalitarian than in other similarly developed economies, an outcome partially attributed to the leveling effect of the seniority wage system.

Assumptions concerning equality in Japan continued to be widely accepted well into the 1990s, even as restructuring and redundancies further highlighted the stratified nature of Japanese society. They held despite a good deal of research documenting (a) the extent to which Japan's labor market was segmented, (b) the extent to which wages and income were distributed according to criteria fairly similar to those operating elsewhere, (c) the increasing diversification of consumer markets from the late 1970s onwards, and (d) the high cost of private education. However, during the 1990s several global developments may have contributed to Japanese recognition of these inequalities. The end of the cold war reduced pressure on conservatives to proffer the view that Japan was more egalitarian than other societies. Greater flows of information and people contributed to a growing awareness that most other advanced economies are similarly stratified. Managers in many Japanese firms and a growing Japanese diaspora often found it advantageous to associate themselves with views that integrated their interests with those of similarly positioned people abroad by emphasizing the similarities Japan shared with other societies.

### 7.4.1    Economic inequality

In the 1990s a new generation of scholars began to rearticulate concerns about social justice. Their careful analyses of objective Japanese government data showed that income differentials had widened significantly over time. The early work of Ishikawa and Kawasaki (1991) was built on, and in 1998 Tachibanaki published his well-documented claims that income differentials had expanded considerably in the 1980s and early 1990s. He argued that in the 1990s the distribution of income in Japan was no more equal than it was in the United States. The arguments in Ishikawa and Kawasaki (1991) had focused not just on income. They also drew attention to the accumulation of wealth. Earlier Mouer (1975) had used disaggregated data from the Family Income and Expenditure Survey (FIES) to reveal structures and mechanisms reinforcing patterns of income inequality over time. The stability of occupationally based differentials was conspicuous. Those findings pointed to eight major variables determining income distribution in Japan which formed the basis for a comparison with the US in table 7.5.

A later study of the FIES data by Mouer (1991) established that "income mobility" among households had declined over time, indicating that household income at one point in time had become a more reliable predictor of income at a later point in time. Although wage differentials did not widen much over the same period, it is likely that the cumulative effect of having stable differentials over extended periods of time contributed to wealth inequality. The argument resulting from such research

Table 7.5 *A comparison of the effect of eight variables on the distribution of income in Japan and the United States circa the mid-1980s*

| Stratification subsystem | The nature of variation: rank order correlation of average income for system categories in Japan and the United States | Comparison of the amount of inequality owing to the particular subsystem in Japan and in the United States |
| --- | --- | --- |
| City-size groupings | High | Lower in Japan |
| Geographical regions | n.a. | Lower in Japan |
| Industries | Low | Lower in Japan |
| Occupation | High | Similar |
| Firm size | High | Higher in Japan |
| Age | High | Similar |
| Level of education | High | Slightly lower in Japan |
| Gender | High | Similar |

*Source:* Mouer and Sugimoto (1986), p. 127.

is not that Japan has particularly high levels of income or wealth inequality. Rather, it was (i) that the distribution in Japan is much less egalitarian than previously believed, and (ii) that levels of inequality were similar in type and extent to those found in most other similarly developed societies.

Two facets of the debate are particularly important. One was highlighted by the observations of Ota (2000), Otake (2000), and Shirahase (2002), who have suggested that part of the increase in levels of inequality resulted from a growth in the aged population. The distribution of income is more unequally spread among those in that age group than for any other in the population. This points to the importance of thinking about lifetime earnings when evaluating remuneration and working conditions for younger generations. In terms of one's working life and the living provided to workers as a result of their years in the labor force, a pension is, like bonuses and retirement allowances, a kind of delayed payment for work done earlier. For this reason pensions are considered in the next chapter, together with other types of socialized returns to work.

The other window opened by the debate on income distribution is on Japan's poor. Blue tarpaulin tent communities in parks and river basins are conspicuous and point to pockets of hardcore unemployment. The appalling living conditions of many foreign workers have also attracted the media's attention. The conditions of many impoverished Japanese are a result of the casualness with which they are employed. In construction, for example, Fowler (1996) and Gill (2001) have provided a fairly up-to-date and reliable description of Japan's day laborers, and Gill argues that they continue to form an invisible underclass supporting Japan's construction industry. This underbelly of the Japanese labor force shifts attention to the safety net stretched beneath not only those who labor at the bottom of the Japanese labor market, but also those higher up the ladder who have further to fall when made redundant and forced to take "early retirement." Hence, Japan's safety nets are also considered in the next chapter.

### 7.4.2    Social mobility

Accepting that income inequalities in objective terms have widened, the more challenging questions now concern the subjective side and the impact of objective inequality on the consciousness of those who work in Japan. By the end of the 1990s several studies squarely challenged prevailing perceptions about the homogeneity of Japanese society in terms of its middle-class consciousness. Sato (2000), for example, argued that Japanese society was no longer the mass society that underpinned social organization throughout most of the postwar era. The issues raised by Sato are fundamental to our understanding of Japan as a civil society, and to how we assess the conditions now shaping that society's conditions of possibility as it becomes increasingly exposed to globalization. Sato's analysis was based primarily on a small amount of data taken from the Survey of Social Stratification and Mobility (known as the "SSM Survey"), conducted every ten years since 1955. The survey has grown over time and now provides a huge range of data related to social inequality in Japan from over 5,000 respondents. A full report on the 1985 survey can be found in four volumes (Naoi et al. 1990); and on the 1995 survey, in six volumes (Kyujugonen SSM Chosa Kenkyukai 2000). These provide considerably more analysis than was allowed by the 1975 SSM survey (cf. Tominaga 1979).

Sato argued that Japan has become a society in which elites are increasingly rewarded for qualifications acquired through inherited access to higher education. The relatively secure, long-term employment for male householders has been eroded as male employment becomes more casualized and able women increasingly compete in the shrinking labor markets associated with the secure employment that was previously the preserve of male householders. Sato's analysis begins with the finding that many Japanese wish that effort (doryoku) were the criterion determining socioeconomic status, while also pointing out that performance (jisseki) has become the actual criterion. His analysis reveals further that those in higher-status occupations attach more weight than others to ability as a norm – an ideological stance which, not surprisingly, legitimates their being in positions of relative privilege. He concluded that the composition of Japan's intellectual elites has increasingly come to be determined through a process of class reproduction.

This has been accompanied by a decline in relatively high levels of intergenerational and intragenerational mobility (a) between blue-collar and white-collar categories – a view consistent with the ideas of Koike and Inoki (1987 and 1990) about skill formation – and (b) from skilled blue-collar work to self-employment. Sato argued that this mobility was facilitated by Japan's rapid economic growth – development that provided everyone with opportunities for upward mobility and created the basis for Japan's widespread middle-class consciousness. His major concern is that a marked decline in mobility will undermine the work ethic for many Japanese. It is a view that assumes there is, or should be, a monocultural focus on "getting ahead" in occupational terms. However, although motivation has been shaped by a sense of national identity in much of the postwar era, embourgeoisement, multiculturalization and globalization/internationalization have contributed to the articulation of other concerns about family life, community service (voluntary work), further enjoyment of material goods already acquired, and opportunities in the world beyond Japan. Sato also lamented the way in which Japan's present elites have come to associate their positions with the rights of their firms and with their own personal success rather than a deep and abiding sense of social responsibility. Although he does not write about the motivation of those who constitute this "aristocracy of labor," perhaps there is an assumption that a greater upward mobility into those positions will bolster a sense of responsibility among Japan's elites.

A major issue related to work organization in Japan concerns the design of occupational systems that will motivate employers to develop fully the skills of their employees. The casualization of work and dualities in the labor market lower the motivation to do so. Here the organization of work impinges upon the role of the family, the acquisition of knowledge and cultural literacy in society at large, the room for being creative and taking on responsibility at work, the nature of each individual's motivation to be socially active, and the distribution of rewards in contemporary Japan. Sato worries that just below the surface lurks alienation on a massive scale and its social consequences. He does not claim that this is unique to Japan, and one might note that similar tensions are coming to the fore in Australia as its egalitarian ethos has come to accommodate greater inequality and the increasing restriction of opportunity over the 1990s (see the editorial in *The Sunday Age* [Melbourne], 18 August 2002, p. 16).

Cynical catchphrases in Japan reflecting the awareness of inequality in grassroots discourses have been noted for some time. Although the collapse of left-wing unionism may have resulted in the perception that disgruntled labor no longer has a coherent discourse, disenfranchised workers continue to exist. As Hashimoto (2001) and others suggest, the real questions concern the processes through which the subjective sense of *Klasse fur sich* (class for itself) emerges from the objective inequalities associated with *Klasse an sich* (class in itself). It is in that domain that the dynamics for change in Japan and the nature of Japan as a civil multicultural society are likely to be more fruitfully understood.

The effects of education-linked career paths on the age-wage earning profile of white-collar and blue-collar occupational groupings have been known for some time. Although scholars such as Koike and Watanabe (1979) argued that the importance attached to one's place of education had diminished in Japan and that demonstrated ability at work had become a more important consideration determining promotion in Japan's corporate world, others wrote that such change was occurring only at the lower levels of management. In the early 1980s it still made sense for Kitagawa and Kainuma (1985) to write about the continuing influence of Japan's prewar elites as a potential force sitting on top of Japanese society. As indicated above, regional differentials have been marginal and gender-based differentials have been narrowing, while occupational differentials have remained fixed and have reinforced the cumulative class effect. That effect is apparent not only in the creation of wealth but also in the acquisition of education.

### 7.4.3    *Education as a conduit for inheritance*

A growing number of studies have pointed to education as the main area in which social class is being reproduced in Japan. Kariya (2001) has found that school outcomes for middle-class children have come to depend more and more on the educational backgrounds of their mothers and less on competition in the classroom. Related to Sato's concerns about alienation and the loss of motivation to work hard is Kariya's argument that many students now see little point in studying hard because they feel their ability to achieve academically is determined largely by the socioeconomic status of their parents. Ishida's (1999) report on a comparative study of Japan, the US and the UK also lends further support to the notion that social class in Japan is reproduced through the system of education in a manner similar to that found in the other two societies. Sons from families with higher socioeconomic status have more access to a better education. The quantitative study further reveals that educational attainment then determines the son's own socioeconomic status. Positive correlations for both linkages were found in the data from each of the three countries, although this correlation does not seem as strong in Japan as it is in the US and Britain. Using roughly the same data to compare Japan, the US and Germany, Ishida and Yoshikawa (2003) report that educational credentials determine occupational status and income to a similar extent in each country, although the income differentials seem to be greater in the US. In other words, the belief that educational credentials carry more weight in Japan is not supported by their data. One further observation based on this data is that the economic return from postgraduate education is considerably above that from an undergraduate degree. This finding would seem to dislodge the warnings of Dore (1976) and others (see Iwauchi 1980: 17–21), who coined the term *obaadokatora* (literally, over-doctored) to describe Japan and other countries in danger of having an overeducated labor force.

Another factor is the place of education. It has commonly been accepted that Japan's elite bureaucrats and businessmen had fairly consistently graduated from a very small number of public and private universities. In 1979, however, Koike and Watanabe analyzed the educational background of middle-level managers (*kacho*) in Japan's established firms, and argued strongly that the importance of graduating from a famous university had declined considerably. Others commented that such changes were limited to the lower levels of management where the competition for promotion had increased. The argument was that graduation from a prestigious university was still a necessary, although no longer sufficient, condition for promotion to higher levels of management (e.g. to the position of *bucho*). Authors such as Nakamura (2002) argued that the fierce competition to enroll at Japan's best universities would continue because it was seen as being the best way to join Japan's corporate elite. Nakamura pays particular attention to the great divergence between schools in terms of their success in getting graduates into top universities.

The effects of education are not just in occupational terms. Gender differences in the courses of study chosen by female and male students have often been noted at the secondary and the tertiary level. Although Okano and Tsuchiya (1999) and others have noted that education is one of the domains in Japanese society where gender-based discrimination is least institutionalized, at least in terms of the choice of study paths in a formal sense, Blackwood (2003) and Murao (2003) argue that sexist cultural norms work informally to encourage female students to take "female subjects" and take part in female extra-curricular activities.

Another important mechanism is the employment placement service. While some seem to evaluate favorably the role of school placement services in facilitating the transition into the labor force, others have noted

Table 7.6 *The percentage of students receiving private education*

|  | 1980 | 2001 |
|---|---|---|
| Primary schools (grades 1–6) | .38 | .92 |
| Middle schools (grades 7–9) | 2.30 | 5.96 |
| Secondary schools (grades 10–12) | 25.85 | 41.47 |
| Universities | 74.90 | 73.42 |

*Sources:* Sori Fu Tokei Kyoku (1981), p. 291.
Somu Sho Tokei Kyoku (2002), p. 297.

that students are often shunted directly from an educational institution into the labor force before they are fully aware of all the opportunities available. Another type of channeling occurs in terms of the private–public school divide. As table 7.6 shows, private education is particularly important at the tertiary level, with 75 percent of university students attending a private institution. Between 1980 and 2001 the preference for private education strengthened at all other levels. The shift was most noticeable at the secondary level where the critical steps are taken to prepare for university entrance. This is in line with the view that public education has deteriorated, especially in terms of discipline. In both private and public sectors a considerable gap exists between the top institutions and those considered to be third or fourth rate, and it is likely to increase as the privatization of national universities moves ahead and the lesser private universities face stiffer competition in attracting academically solid and financially viable students.

The quality of education is also pertinent. Writers on one of Japan's more conservative economic and financial dailies (Sankei Shimbun Shakai Bu 2002) pointed in particular to the decline both in the quality and the quantity of what is taught in Japan's schools. A team of writers on Japan's largest daily (Yomiuri Shimbun Osaka Honsha 2002) recently raised similar questions about the ability of Japanese universities to provide quality education. Again, the "sorting out" that is likely to accompany privatization and greater competition in an open market will result in greater distance between the best universities and those further down the ladder. In the future Japan's labor markets will only become more sensitive to these kinds of educational inequalities. In this regard, it is interesting to note that a number of the more established universities are moving to entrench further their status as world-class institutions through an active program of internationalization. This is likely to reinforce any tendency for a bilingual elite competent in Japanese and one other language (mainly English) to be set off from the rest of the largely monolingual population.

### 7.4.4 Multiculturalism

Japan's "foreign" population has always been small. Including naturalized Koreans and Chinese, it has traditionally been below 1–2 percent of Japan's total population. However, the number of foreigners living in Japan began to increase markedly from the late 1980s, owing in part to labor shortages. Komai (2001) hints that Japan's newcomers are now reaching a critical mass that could fundamentally change Japanese society. While much has been written about Japan's globalization in terms of economic restructuring and its highly publicized attempts to internationalize, Komai's (2001) discussion of Japan's migrant population focuses on some of the softer cultural changes now occurring in Japanese society. While the significance of those changes was not readily apparent when his earlier volume on migrant workers in Japan was published (1995), the more recent volume points to at least three ways that multiculturalization will affect the way work is conceived and organized. First is in terms of national identity. A greater appreciation of Japan's increased ethnic diversity and the richness of such diversity around the world will weaken the commitment to older notions of working for the Japanese state. It will also affect aspects of the work ethic tied to an ideological insistence on the need for the national economy to be internationally competitive.

Second, many of the challenges posed by newcomers at work have been presented to the Japanese public largely in terms of human rights in the broadest sense. Such rights are conceived in terms of certain standards of living, access to minimal medical care and other benefits associated with safety-net legislation. The publicity given these matters has struck a chord with Japanese sympathetic to more universal notions of workers' rights. In arguing that Japan's legal and illegal migrants ought to be treated better by the government, Komai (2001) does not appeal to hard legalistic interpretations of Japan's commitment to UN declarations or ILO conventions. Rather, he focuses on optimistic assessments of social and cultural change at the grassroots.

The third impact of multiculturalization is in the initiatives of local governments and NPOs. Yabuno (1995) describes the period after the oil shocks of the 1970s as a time during which peripheralized local communities experienced depopulation, rapid aging, feminization, unemployment, and various other changes. Yabuno argues that many local communities established their own international relations, thereby circumventing the national government in activities traditionally seen to be within the exclusive domain of the government. This grassroots diplomacy expanded the horizons of many Japanese. Both Komai and Yabuno conclude optimistically that the Japanese have generally been positive concerning newcomers and the multicultural directions in which their society is heading. These conclusions are consistent with those in Kuwahara (2001) which were introduced in chapter 6. Although Komai's (2001) review of the literature on Japan's newcomers reveals that the public discourse has evolved in an ad hoc manner in both political and academic spheres, his volume reveals that some form of critical mass has been achieved which will fundamentally alter Japanese society, and, *ipso facto*, the way it is stratified and the way work is organized.

These changes are reflected in notions of Japanese identity. Both Mouer and Sugimoto (1995) and Fukuoka (1996) observed in the mid-1990s that citizenship, blood, language, and ethnicity no longer went together in defining Japaneseness. The country's new wealth attracted a growing number of foreign workers to Japan who were single temporary residents. By the 1990s, however, families started to arrive and longer-term settlement began. While this influx was first felt in factories, several rural areas sought to overcome shortages of household labor by "importing" brides from overseas. Burgess (2003) reports that about one out of every twenty Japanese entering matrimony today marries a non-Japanese, up from one in every 200 only thirty years ago. He also notes that in about 80 percent of those marriages the Japanese partner is male, a reversal of the situation in the early 1970s. Most significant perhaps are his findings that foreign-born wives in Japan are not simply assimilating into Japanese society in an official sense. Rather, he found them to be actively participating in civil society and shaping the way officially recognized social institutions were evolving around them. One result is a greater openness to a diverse range of lifestyles and career choices.

## 7.5     Employment creation and employment policy

Employment security has been a particularly sensitive issue in postwar Japan. The highlights of that history, which are set out in this section, have been amply recorded and discussed by Koshiro (1995). Following the war large numbers of soldiers and civilians were repatriated to Japan. With Japan's infrastructure seriously damaged, the prewar jobs of many returnees no longer existed. Women and young people mobilized during the war were also released from paid employment. Reforms were pushed through for industrial relations, and the Labor Standards Law was enacted in July 1947. The legislation was designed to burden employers with as few disincentives to employ others as possible. The Employment

Table 7.7 *Percentage of employees by industrial sector, 1960–2000*

| Year | Primary industry | Secondary industry | Tertiary industry |
|------|------------------|--------------------|-------------------|
| 1950 | 48.3 | 21.9 | 29.7 |
| 1960 | 32.6 | 29.2 | 38.2 |
| 1970 | 19.3 | 34.0 | 46.6 |
| 1975 | 13.8 | 34.0 | 51.8 |
| 1980 | 10.9 | 33.5 | 55.4 |
| 1985 | 9.3 | 33.2 | 57.3 |
| 1990 | 7.1 | 33.3 | 59.0 |
| 1995 | 6.0 | 31.5 | 61.9 |
| 1999 | 5.1 | 31.2 | 63.4 |

*Source:* Rodo Sho (1999), p. 56; Kosei Rodo Sho (2002a), p. 303; and Yano Tsuneta Ki-nenkai (2001), pp. 80–1.

Security Law was passed the following November to establish Japan's first unemployment insurance system. At the same time, the Yoshida government moved to lower the number of government employees from 1.65 to 1.41 million. This led to a reduction of 95,000 employees in the National Railways, 26,500 in the postal and telephone services, 25,845 in the national civil service, and 27,000 in local governments (Kawanishi 1986: 30). The unions vigorously opposed these moves, whereupon the government obtained GHQ support to withdraw the right to strike from unions in the public sector.

The economy rebounded quickly during the Korean War, owing largely to US military procurements and other associated expenditure. Soon Japan had embarked upon two decades of high economic growth (1955–73). The Basic Agricultural Law (Nogyo Kihon Ho) was introduced in 1961 to promote the amalgamation of inefficient small-scale plots in rural Japan, forcing small farmers to leave the land and seek employment in the cities. The rural labor surplus was steadily absorbed as cities clamored for more permanent employees and *dekasegi* for their factories and large construction projects. During the 1960s regional industrial *kombinaato* were established to create employment nearer to those who had remained behind to farm (and perhaps to disperse the negative diseconomies associated with growing amounts of pollution). New technologies were introduced, the exchange rate remained at ¥360 to the US dollar, and Japan began to develop sizable export markets. Throughout this period the proportion of the labor force in primary industry declined rapidly (table 7.7).

The period of high growth came to an end with the first oil shock in 1973. Production in manufacturing dropped about 20 percent over a fifteen-month period. From 1974 to 1979 the number of regular employees in Japan's large firms declined by nearly 12 percent. While the reduction in employment during this period was particularly noticeable in Japan's large firms, employment increased in the service sector, predominantly in small and medium-sized firms and particularly for female part-timers. In December 1974 the Employment Insurance Law replaced the 1947 legislation. It brought in some innovative features, starting in April 1975. One was the provision of incentives for employment creation, training, and welfare. Another was the benefits available for up to 50 days for seasonal workers and young women who had previously not qualified for them. A third was the period for which benefits could be received: 90 days for those aged under 30; 180 days for those aged 30–45; 240 days for those aged 45–55; and 300 days for those aged over 55 (Koshiro 1995: 104). This partially recognized age as a factor determining the chances for reemployment. The most notable change, however, was the mechanism allowing employers in designated recession-hit industries to receive for up to 75 days a subsidy of up to two-thirds (in small firms with fewer than 300 employees) of the wages of each employee who would otherwise have been made redundant (Nishikawa and Shimada 1980: 137–41).

During the interval between the two oil shocks, the percentage of the labor force in the tertiary sector topped 50 percent for the first time (table 7.7). It continued to increase as manufacturing became more automated, the distribution system was overhauled, and services continued to expand. This restructuring was facilitated by the willingness of private sector unions, especially those affiliated with the IMF-JC and Domei, to see wisdom in wage restraint (Kawanishi 1992a: 374–7). Having moved quickly "to get its house in order," Japan was one of the few economies to come through the second oil shock without serious disruptions. Between 1975 and 1980 economic growth averaged 4.7 percent; from 1980 to 1985 the figure was 3.7 percent. It was during this period that the Japanese model of industrial relations started to receive acclaim. Despite growing trade friction with the United States, the economy continued to expand. Japan's huge balance-of-payments surpluses generated large outflows of capital. While direct foreign investment alleviated pressures generated by trade friction with Europe and North America, it was also stimulated by high labor costs in Japan, symbolized during the bubble years by the reluctance of Japanese workers to engage in work characterized by the three Ks. One response was to import labor from abroad, both legally and illegally. Another was to raise the retirement age. Concerns began to surface about the need to consider employment policy in terms of rising life expectancy, the aging of the population, and the restructuring of the pension scheme in 1986.

The 1990s saw major companies in financial trouble, and unemployment rose from under 3 percent in the 1980s to over 5 percent by 2002. Initially firms sought to cope with the Heisei recession in the 1990s by reducing overtime, a strategy in line with successive government initiatives to reduce annual hours of work following the Maekawa Report in September 1987. The government revised the Labor Standards Law to lower the standard workweek and encourage firms to adopt the two-day weekend and other measures to move Japan toward the target of 1,880 hours of work annually by 1997, as laid out in the Five Year Economic Plan adopted by the Miyazawa cabinet in 1992. Employment policies designed to deregulate the labor market for casual and dispatched workers were described above in chapter 5. Policies for older workers revolved around efforts to raise the compulsory retirement age to at least 60 in all firms. Changes to the pension system are discussed in chapter 8. The Equal Employment Opportunity Law of 1986 (revised in 1997) and the maternity leave legislation of 1992 (replaced in 1999 by the Carers' Leave Law) are important for understanding the changing role of women in the labor force and changes in how the family conceives of itself as an economic unit.

## 7.6    The legal framework at the meso level

The Labor Standards Law (LSL) of 1947 has provided a legal underpinning for work organization at the national level over the past half-century (for a history of the LSL see Mori 1999). The Labor Standards Law Research Group (Rodo Kijun Ho Kenkyukai) and the Central Labor Standards Consultative Council (Chuo Rodo Kijun Shingikai) has advised on amendments to the legislation roughly every two years. Substantial revisions were made in 1987, 1993, and 1997, as new legislation was introduced to replace sections of the LSL, and the labor market came to be more deregulated.

Araki (2002: 48) notes that the LSL is based on four overriding principles. One is that minimum guidelines are necessary. Second is that the employment relationship is to be based on individual contracts. Third is that work rules are to be established by employers and reflect the needs of the business. Finally, as far as possible collective agreements should form the basis for defining working conditions in firms where workers can be collectively represented. There has also been general recognition of the fact that firm size (and the ability to pay) should guide the way the LSL is implemented. Some recognition is also given to the very special needs of a few occupations and industries.

Collective agreements (either with union leaders or with employee representatives) are sanctioned by law, provided that they do not call for working conditions below those set in the LSL. Minimum standards set by law (e.g. regarding wage payments, the use of dispatched labor, various health and safety matters, hours of work, and the treatment of minors and women) are overseen by inspectors from Labor Standards Inspection Offices established around the country by the Ministry of Labor (now the Ministry of Welfare and Labor). Enforcement has depended on inspection and gazetting, small fines, civil opprobrium, and criminal provisions. Although the law sets parameters for employment contracts, most regular long-term workers do not have written contracts and depend on an oral agreement. Instead, they and their employers are commonly bound by work rules (*shugyo kisoku*). These are usually spelled out in some detail in a written document covering nine or ten areas of concern, and must be given to all employees by management in all firms with ten or more employees.

The LSL is generally seen as giving employers the right to discriminate freely in hiring (subject to restrictions related to union membership or gender as stipulated in other legislation), and the courts often treat as legal a firm's decision to cancel a promise of employment based on a reemployment agreement (*saiyo naitei*). It does, however, limit the ability of an employer to discriminate among those who are its employees. Nevertheless, it is easy to differentiate among employees for many valid reasons, and much alleged discrimination has been difficult to substantiate in the courts as discrimination per se. The right to dismiss an employee is even more restricted, and this is fairly clearly laid out in case law. In general, the LSL does not prescribe how remuneration is determined. Although it is generally accepted that younger employees are paid below their productivity (earnings which they may later recoup through seniority-linked wage payments, lighter work loads, and retirement allowances), they have no legally recognized claim on that surplus.

Particularly relevant to the discussion of hours of work in chapter 4 are provisions for annual leave. Article 39 of the LSL provides for annual leave to increase according to the number of years in the job, as shown in table 7.8, and workers who have been with the same employer for 10.5 years are entitled to a minimum of 20 days. Overall, the legislation has provided employees with a comprehensive package of minimal standards. Though many have questioned the ability of employees to enforce all their rights, this approach to setting labor standards has led to long-term compliance. Women are moving more freely in the labor market,

Table 7.8 *Minimum days of annual leave set by Article 39 of the Labor Standards Law*

| Length of employment (in years) | 0.5 | 1.5 | 2.5 | 3.5 | 6.5 | 7.5 | 8.5 | 9.5 | 10.5 |
|---|---|---|---|---|---|---|---|---|---|
| Annual paid leave entitlement (number of days) | 10 | 11 | 12 | 13 | 16 | 17 | 18 | 19 | 20 |

*Source:* Article 39 of the Labor Standards Law as published in Ministry of Labor (Rodo Sho) 1995, pp. 84–5.

and serious industrial accidents have steadily declined over the postwar period, as have hours of work.

The Trade Union Law (TUL) of 1945 was the first work-related law to be enacted immediately after the war. It gives concrete meaning to guarantees provided in Article 28 of the Constitution, providing for employees to have the right to organize, to bargain, and to act collectively. The law does not prescribe any form of organization for unions. Nor does it require them to register. Although the enterprise union is the most common type of union, there are industrial unions, trade or occupationally based unions, regional unions, position-tied unions, and gender-based unions. Most enterprise unions embrace all employees at a given place of business, but Araki (2002: 162) reports for 1995 that 13 percent of enterprises had two or more unions competing for members amongst the same pool of employees (a figure similar to that recorded by Kawanishi [1992a: 37] for the mid-1970s). Any two or more individuals are allowed to constitute a union (Kawanishi 1981b). The TUL excludes directors, executives, and others representing the employer's interests from joining a union and generally requires that unions receive no financial support from the employer (except the provision of a small room for a union office, contributions to union-run welfare funds, and the payment of wages for those engaged in union activities on the shop floor during working hours).

The right to bargain is less clearly spelled out. Management is legally bound to bargain in good faith about working conditions and personnel practices, and is subject to penalties for failing to do so. However, management is not required to negotiate concerning matters related to the political system. The law does not impose an obligation on either party to come to an agreement. What constitutes "bargaining in good faith" is not defined. Collective agreements may be made for periods of up to three years. To be effective, collective agreements must be set down in a written document signed by both parties.

In 1996 nearly 90 percent of Japan's unions had concluded collective agreements and 57 percent of those called for union shops (Seisho and Kikuchi 2002: 240). Collective agreements may provide for a check-off system. Most agreements call for full-time union leaders to be paid by the union, but guarantee that union officials may return to their previous positions after serving their union. Unions may engage in various shop-floor activities (including the organization of meetings, recruitment activities, and the display of slogans and posters) that do not interfere directly with the running of the business. Case law suggests that the legality of such activity has to be judged on a case-by-case basis (Seisho and Kikuchi 2002: 225). The wearing of arm bands and badges is a gray area. Although management is prohibited from behavior designed to undermine union activity, enforcement is difficult. There are many stories of extended disputes involving various forms of harassment (see the accounts given in Hanami 1973). The law protects unionists from criminal prosecution and civil liability when they are engaged in appropriate (*seito na*) disputative activity. "Appropriate" has been defined in the context of the objectives and behavioral choices available to unions (Seisho and Kikuchi 2002: 250). The Public Corporations and National Enterprise Labor Relations Law of 1948 withdrew the right to strike from public sector unions. In the 1960s and 1970s a number of disputes were waged unsuccessfully in an effort to restore that right. The right-to-strike issue was partially resolved with the privatization of public enterprises such as the Japan National Railways.

When disputes cannot be settled, they may be referred to one of a number of Labor Relations Commissions under provisions in the Labor Relations Adjustment Law. Seisho and Kikuchi (2002: 261–2) report that only 3 percent of all disputes are referred to the Labor Relations Commission. Of those that go to the commission, 93 percent are resolved through conciliation, 5.4 percent through mediation, and only 1.6 percent through arbitration. The current legal framework provides quite a protective environment for unions and unionists. Even with that protection, however, unions are in decline. With that decline has come a profound shift in the power relations between management and its workforce. The legal framework also leaves a good deal to be resolved between labor and management through direct negotiation, and contrasts with systems that build in compulsory arbitration. Given that employees have become increasingly independent of the need to join unions (as well as the need to toe the line for management), unions are challenged to locate and to articulate whatever collective interests remain. Whether another legal framework would assist unions in that regard is today a moot point. However, it is a central consideration in any assessment of the potential of the union movements in advanced economies to resurrect themselves within the confines of civil society. Management, on the other hand, does not require individuated employees to have such a collective set of interests in order to weld them into a highly productive unit. If in the past labor unions were allowed to exist so that some of the excessive power accruing to employers during the industrial revolution could be offset, then some thought needs to be given to the type of collective representation needed by Japanese workers in the coming years as income differentials widen, employment is casualized, and workers are further differentiated.

# 8    Social security and safety nets

## 8.1    Social security (*shakai hoken*): income protection for workers

Although Japan first provided medical insurance to some workers in the 1920s, in line with Okochi's view that capitalists would support such moves to protect their own interests, the idea of providing basic minimum guarantees to all citizens in a number of livelihood areas did not take root in Japan until the postwar period. As indicated at the beginning of chapter 7, the Constitution of 1947 built in the compulsion to do so. Influenced by America's Social Security Act (1935), by the wartime Beveridge Report in the UK, by the ILO, and by the recommendations of WHO, Article 25 of the Constitution committed the government to providing social security in a number of areas. With a very limited base from which to start after the war, the government systematized and oversaw a range of private schemes that were already in place. One outcome of that approach was low portability and considerable variation in terms of the benefits offered by each system. By the early 1960s a framework was in place to ensure that all Japanese would have some measure of security in terms of general medical care, accidental injury, unemployment, and special needs in old age.

The government strengthened its commitment to social security and welfare in the 1970s. Tamai (2000) writes that promises made at the time resulted from political opportunism rather than a firm commitment to redistribute economic surplus or far-sighted planning. Nevertheless, today the system provides for medical care, pensions, employment, accident and disaster relief, child welfare, home care, subsistence payments to the indigent, public hygiene, and a range of social services.

With the further aging of the population and growing unemployment in the 1990s, welfare systems came under severe fiscal pressure. The number of persons relying on benefits from the schemes increased, while those paying premiums into the system declined. In 2001 alone the overall cost of pensions and other welfare services was ¥17.55 trillion, up

4.7 percent from 2000. About 80 percent of that outlay was to cover shortfalls in the social insurance systems. Changes sought by the Obuchi government in its push for administrative reform included the merger of the Ministry of Labor and the Ministry of Health and Welfare early in 2001. At the same time it disbanded the Social Security System Deliberative Council (Shakai Hosho Seido Shingikai) which had been affiliated to the Prime Minister's Office for fifty years. A Social Security Advisory Council (Shakai Hosho Shingikai) was established to advise the new ministry. It will take some years for concrete changes to be implemented and for social security and social welfare to be put back on a stable financial footing.

Japan's first serious threat of postwar unemployment followed the floating of the US dollar and the first oil shock in the early 1970s. A novel approach subsidized employers in critically affected industries who retained redundant employees on their payrolls. That strategy was generally applauded both at home and abroad as the Japanese model came to attract growing attention. However, the message to employees was clear: employers would retrench workers in large numbers if pressed far enough and left to the wiles of markets, which are in turn subject to unpredictable forces of the many interconnected business cycles.

Looking back a quarter of a century later, there may be reason to reevaluate that strategy. Rather than solving the unemployment problem, it served to disguise it. The 1970s was a delicate time politically, and the ruling Liberal Democratic Party bought time by announcing its commitment to welfare. In that environment, policymakers satisfied themselves with total employment rather than full employment. Rather than training for the jobs just being created by the IT revolution, many workers continued to stay in old jobs. This reflected the preference of conservative policymakers for social stability, having nearly lost control of the Diet's Lower House in the December 1972 elections owing to considerable popular unhappiness with high inflation, severe pollution, and other distortions accompanying unbridled growth in the 1960s and early 1970s, and left-wing unionism which was still a force (although the ideologically more conservative movement associated with Domei was making headway with its emphasis on productivity).

The systems that emerged for dealing with unemployment, minimum wages, and pensions were unnecessarily complex and difficult for the average worker to understand. To administer them, a private bureaucracy of certified private agents was created. Known as *shakai hoken romushi*, these agents were needed to advise firms and individuals on the complex array of systems and concomitant paperwork, a service supplied at no small cost for many individuals wishing to qualify for the benefits. The overall effect of minimal income support and difficult access placed many individuals under tremendous pressure either to hang onto whatever employment they currently had or to return to useful employment as soon as possible. As Abe (2002), a former president of Hitotsubashi University, has recently noted, Japanese society is organized in ways that stigmatize people who are not gainfully employed. Such questioning extends to the nature of work and to the way Japan functions as a civil society.

If deregulation is to have its intended effect, attention must be given to the disincentives to labor mobility that are built into the way social security is administered in contemporary Japan. The risk of changing jobs is considerable. A good deal has been made of voluntarism and the work ethic in explaining Japan's growth over nearly half a century following Japan's defeat in the Pacific War. This volume has argued that for many Japanese the decision to work has not simply been a reflection of the workers' commitment to their firms. It identifies how various mechanisms, including the segmentation of the labor market, have functioned first to move workers out of non-productive employment and then to force them quickly back into the labor force in different, often less rewarding, positions. Other strategies may now be required to motivate employees to work smartly in an economy trying to regain its competitive edge. Here three aspects of the social safety net are discussed: minimal income guarantees for those without income, pensions, and medical services.

## 8.2     Income support schemes

### 8.2.1     The minimum wage system

A minimum wage system was introduced in 1959 with the Minimum Wage Law (MWL). Although the legislation has been amended several times, it has continued to operate without substantive change for nearly half a century. The minimum wage rate is set each year by the Ministry of Labor based on recommendations from a Central Minimum Wage Deliberative Council and forty-seven such councils at the prefectural level. Each of the councils consists of an equal number of members representing workers, employers, and the public interest (Articles 26–32).

Article 3 of the MWL stipulates that minimum wages should be based on three considerations: the cost of living, comparisons with the wages of those doing similar work, and the capacity of employers to pay. The result has been a complex system involving forty-eight separate deliberative councils and the attached administrative support. The result is marginally different rates for each major industrial category in each prefecture. It is a system that reflects the times in which it was established, when the concern with meeting the livelihood needs of families took precedence over the productivity concerns of management. In the late 1950s the *Densangata* wage system (cf. Kawanishi 2001; 1992b; 1992a: pp. 102–4 and 141–4) still formed the basis of the wage packet in most Japanese firms. Socialist-inspired unionists and sympathetic intellectuals were concerned with poverty in absolute terms, and small differences were still important to most union members.

The minimum wage system has been criticized on several grounds. One is that minimum wage levels have been set too low to achieve the social justice aims set down in Article 1 of the MWL. Apologists would argue that the low levels at which minimum wages are set serve to promote employment when coupled with restrictions on unemployment benefits. The minimum wages set for Tokyo at the beginning of 2001 are given in table 8.1. The amounts are only slightly over two-thirds of the average starting salary for male and female high school graduates. They were about a third of the average salary earned by household heads aged 25–9, hardly a wage that would stabilize the household finances of a normal family. One view is that the minimum wage today exists largely for part-time female workers, an outlook that points to the pressure on married males to compete to stay in good full-time regular employment in order to be a household head. It also highlights how dim the prospects are for Japan's *furiitaa* as they age. A further concern has been for the many foreign workers who are more easily subjugated to exploitative working conditions (Matsubara 2002) without the literacy necessary to expose their situation. A final feature of this legislation is the light penalties imposed for failing to pay the minimum wage (a fine of up to ¥10,000).

### 8.2.2   Unemployment insurance

What happens to Japanese who become unemployed? In augmenting the Unemployment Insurance Law of 1947, the Employment Insurance Law of 1974 shifted emphasis from the provision of individual benefits to the provision of incentives to firms that continued to employ people they would otherwise feel compelled to retrench. The law also provides unemployed individuals with several types of benefit: (i) a basic livelihood allowance (Articles 13–35), (ii) skill acquisition and lodgings allowances (Article 36), and (iii) a sickness and injury allowance (Article 37).

The most important of these is the basic livelihood allowance. Unemployed workers receive a benefit equal to 60–80 percent of the employment income received immediately prior to becoming unemployed, the percentage varying according to the individual's income prior to becoming unemployed. The daily minimum payment is ¥2,580, and the

Table 8.1 *Minimum wage rates set for Tokyo (at 1 January 2001)*

| Industry | A<br>The hourly wage<br>rate (in ¥) | B<br>The daily wage rate<br>(in ¥) |
|---|---|---|
| Publishing | 776 | 6,157 |
| Steel industry | 789 | 6,192 |
| Machinery manufacturing | 779 | 6,139 |
| Manufacturing electrical<br>equipment | 774 | 6,240 |
| Automotive industries | 778 | 6,248 |
| Retailing | 756 | 6,053 |
| All other non-designated<br>industries | 703 | 5,559 |
| C The monthly minimum wage for workers from all industries as<br>a percentage of the starting salary for newly employed male<br>graduates from senior high schools in Tokyo (¥168,100) | | 68.45% |
| D The monthly minimum wage for workers from all industries as<br>a percentage of the starting salary for newly employed female<br>graduates from senior high school in Tokyo (¥164,000) | | 70.17% |
| E The monthly minimum wage for workers from all industries as a<br>percentage of the average income of all household heads aged<br>25–29 in the Kanto Region (¥338,200) | | 34.02% |
| F The monthly minimum wage for workers from all industries as a<br>percentage of the average income of all household heads in the<br>Kanto Region (¥494,200) | | 23.28% |

*Notes:* (1) The calculations converting the daily minimum wage to a monthly figure com-
parable to the salary data for other employees were based on the assumption that
they worked the same number of days per month (i.e. 20.7 days).
(2) The percentages for C, D, E, and F were calculated as (100B × 20.7)/(income
provided for each type of person as given in parentheses for C–F).
*Sources:* Columns A and B: Fuse (2001), p. 101.
Rows C and D: *Chingin Kozo Kihon Tokei Chosa* (The Basic Survey of the Wage
Structure) as reported in Kosei Rodo Sho Daijin Kanbo Tokei
Joho Bu (2002c), p. 195.
Rows E and F: *Kakei Chosa* (The Family Income and Expenditure Survey)
as reported in Kosei Rodo Sho Daijin Kanbo Tokei Joho Bu
(2002c), pp. 275 and 277.

maximum is ¥17,790. Payment, however, is restricted to a period of
time determined by the person's age upon becoming unemployed and
the length of tenure with their previous employer. The length of time for
which payment may be received is shown in table 8.2. To receive the benefit one must have been previously employed (and thereby a member of
the insurance scheme) and be actively searching for work (as determined

Table 8.2 *Number of days for which benefits are available for the unemployed (at 1 January 2001)*

| Employability | Age at the time of leaving one's previous employer | Length of time employed by previous employer | | | | |
|---|---|---|---|---|---|---|
| | | 6–12 months | 1–5 years | 5–10 years | 10–20 years | Over 20 years |
| Persons who are considered to be employable | −30 | | 90 | 120 | 150 (180) | n.a. |
| | 30–45 | 90 | 90 | 120 (180) | 150 (210) | 180 (240) |
| | 45–60 | | 90 (180) | 120 (240) | 150 (270) | 180 (330) |
| | 60–65 | | 90 (150) | 120 (180) | 150 (210) | 180 (240) |
| Persons who are considered to be unemployable | −45 | 150 | 300 | | | |
| | 45–65 | | 360 | | | |

*Source:* Fuse (2001), pp. 310–11. Figures in parentheses are for regular employees.

by the Ministry of Welfare and Labor). This contrasts with the situation in countries like Australia where someone merely needs to show that they are currently looking for work and are therefore unemployed. Those in Japan who have worked for less than six months receive no benefit.

The benefit is now officially designated as a benefit for those actively looking for work (*kyushokusha kyufu*) and is no longer seen simply as an unemployment benefit (*shitsugyo teate*). The employment insurance system is run by the government, and the insurance premium is set at 1.01 percent of each individual's wages, with 0.06 percent paid out of the individual's wages and 0.95 percent paid by the employer. Coverage is compulsory for all employees and must be taken out by employers. The data in table 8.3 suggests, however, that only about two-thirds of all employees are covered, and that ratio has been fairly constant over the last thirty years. Those who come to be employed after the age of 65 are not eligible for the insurance; nor are full-time students or certain types of casual employees.

### 8.2.3 *Ongoing indigence*

What happens to Japanese for whom the basic unemployment benefit lapses or for whom illness or other circumstances make it impossible to

Table 8.3 *The number and percentage of employees covered by unemployment insurance and the percentage of insured employees who receive benefits, 1970–2000*

| Year | 1970 | 1980 | 1990 | 2000 |
|---|---|---|---|---|
| A Total number of all employees (1000s) | 33,060 | 39,710 | 48,350 | 53,560 |
| B Number of employees insured (1000s) | 21,118 | 25,339 | 31,569 | 33,905 |
| C Percentage of employees covered (100B/A) | 63.9 | 63.8 | 65.3 | 63.3 |
| D Percentage of insured employees who received the basic livelihood benefit | 2.3 | 2.6 | 1.6 | 3.1 |
| E The overall unemployment rate for the entire labor force | 1.1 | 2.0 | 2.1 | 4.7 |
| F The ratio of the percentage of benefit recipients to official unemployment rate (100D/E) | 209.1 | 130.0 | 76.2 | 66.0 |

*Source:* Columns B and D Kosei Rodo Sho Daijin Kanbo Tokei Joho Bu (2002a), p. 237.
Column A and E Kosei Rodo Sho Daijin Kanbo Tokei Joho Bu (2002a), p. 32.

find work? In 1950 the Livelihood Protection Law (Seikatsu Hogo Ho) proclaimed the right of Japanese to receive assistance when they could not look after themselves financially. While debate continues internationally on how best to define that inability and what the poverty line might be, it is generally accepted that the mark has been fixed at a very low level in Japan compared to the levels set in other similarly developed countries. This is not so much the case in absolute terms, but in terms of the relative needs of individuals to participate at a meaningful level in the cultural and social life of the community.

Reflecting Japan's economic growth, the figures in table 8.4 show that the number of people receiving this kind of assistance declined from 1970 to the mid-1990s. The gradual increase in unemployment and in homelessness is reflected in the figures for the late 1990s. The figures in table 8.4 also suggest that the average size of households receiving aid declined in the early 1990s, perhaps owing to the exodus of persons from assisted households. This would be in line with the idea that many of the homeless are males who lost permanent employment in the privileged sector as a result of restructuring and left their matrimonial home because they were unable to face that reality in the context of their own households. The abandoned households would be smaller and would require the basic livelihood allowance. Yoshimura (2000: 151) cites research by Hoshino in 1995 that suggested that only 40 percent of households and only 25 percent of individuals qualifying for this form of assistance

Table 8.4 *Changes in the number of households and individuals receiving basic livelihood assistance, 1970–2000*

| Year | A Number of households receiving livelihood maintenance benefits (1000s) | B Number of individuals receiving livelihood maintenance benefits (1000s) | C Percentage of individuals receiving livelihood maintenance benefits as a percentage of the Japanese population | D Average number of persons in recipient households receiving benefits (B/A) |
|------|------|------|------|------|
| 1970 | 658 | 1,344 | 1.30 | 2.04 |
| 1980 | 747 | 1,427 | 1.22 | 1.91 |
| 1990 | 624 | 1,015 | 0.82 | 1.63 |
| 1995 | 601 | 882 | 0.48 | 1.47 |
| 1997 | 631 | 906 | 0.72 | 1.44 |
| 1998 | 662 | 947 | 0.76 | 1.43 |
| 1999 | 708 | 1,004 | 0.79 | 1.42 |
| 2000 | 750 | 1,072 | 0.84 | 1.42 |

*Source:* Kosei Rodo Sho Daijin Kanbo Tokei Joho Bu (2001b), pp. 17 and 215–17.

actually receive it. Many simply fall through this safety net. One difficulty to be addressed is the large number of foreign workers (including long-term Korean residents) who do not qualify for such assistance. To qualify they need a permanent address, a medical certificate, evidence that they are searching for work, and evidence that they meet a very strict means test. For most Japanese there is also a certain stigma attached to receiving such assistance from the public purse, and many forgo the benefits to avoid that stigma. A law enacted on 31 July 2002 provides for self-help measures to encourage the homeless to integrate themselves back into society.

The system provides for eight types of allowance for basic living, education, housing, medical care, childbirth, unemployment, funerals, and nursing care. The amount received for each varies according to the recipient's location. There are six geographical categories that reflect differences in the consumer price index (CPI) and the local lifestyle. The general basic living allowance was ¥163,970 per month in 2000 and 2001, about 40 percent of the average wage earned in enterprises of thirty or more employees (down from 47.15 percent in 1990).

In 2000 the annual education allowance for a primary schoolchild was ¥2,150; ¥4,160 for a middle school student. As senior high school is not compulsory in Japan, upper secondary students do not receive an allowance. Although Japan is largely in line with the minimums called for in the WHO guidelines, which have since the early 1990s called for states to provide not only for basic physical needs but also for the literacy necessary to participate culturally, economically, and politically in social life, Yoshimura (2000: 164–6) argues that the contribution to social participation in Japan falls short in a number of ways. In particular he comments that the digital divide will become increasingly pronounced in Japan. The problems facing the system of social security in Japan have less to do with guaranteeing subsistence in physiological terms and more to do on the cultural and psychological side with questions concerning society's continuing openness to social mobility and the reproduction of social class.

## 8.3     Pensions

The Japanese system of pensions is extremely complex. Although severance pay is usually considered as a working condition and participation in pension funds, superannuation schemes, and retirement plans is often compulsory for employees in many societies, pensions are often associated with retirement from the labor force and therefore not discussed in many accounts of work organization. This gap also exists in many of the self-help books in Japan that advise young people on how to change jobs. Most focus on the skills and attributes one needs to satisfy employers who command the scarce supply of good jobs. A recent volume encouraging those in their twenties to change jobs mentions three risks which accompany a change in employers: a drop in pay, difficulties settling into a new set of human relationships, and the loss of skills already acquired with the current employer (Sato 2003: 102–4). The book does not mention the consequences in terms of pension benefits, the waiting period for unemployment benefits or other aspects related to company welfare benefits. Nevertheless, that this is a topic of interest to many is evident in the many pension advice columns in Japan's newspapers and weekly magazines. Many are written by *shakai romushi*, the welfare and labor issue specialists mentioned above (e.g. see the series in *Shukan Asahi* in 2002 by the S-WAVE group of *sharoshi*). Clearly, some knowledge of the pension system is fundamental to understanding how Japanese think about their motivation to work.

The linkage between work and the pension system is often not direct. It is felt in terms of the premiums paid, the age at which the main breadwinner can retire from the labor force, the need to earn supplementary income to augment one's pension, and the way a household plans to use or invest its savings. In 2000 the compulsory retirement age was set at 60 in 91.6 percent of firms with over thirty employees. Many who officially retired from those firms continued to work at the same firm or elsewhere for a much reduced wage. The complexity of the system and the constant changes to the system have made it difficult for many individuals to plan accurately or with certainty.

A voluntary pension scheme existed for employees in Japan's larger firms and for public servants in the early 1950s. The government moved in 1960 to put in place a scheme which in principle would cover every citizen. Since then policy has been conceived in terms of three major groupings: the self-employed, the unemployed, and other dependants of the self-employed (Insured Group I), employees of private firms (Insured Group II – section A), public servants (Insured Group II – section B), and the full-time housewives of those in Group II (Insured Group III). Those in Group III are insured via their spouse's employment but do not pay premiums. The result was a pension system that was a combination of numerous schemes, some based wholly on contributions and others partially based on fiscal allocations from national or local governments.

The amalgamated system was put together in an ad hoc manner. The financial bases on which most of the schemes rest were not carefully vetted actuarially and had to be re-jigged in major ways in 1985, 1989, 1994, and 2001. A recent study by the Nomura Research Institute (1999) argues that further changes must occur in 2004 if the system is to remain solvent.

One debate concerns the extent to which these schemes should be self-funded. Tamai (2000: 104) mentions the unfairness felt by many families of women who are fully employed. Both the woman and her spouse pay premiums into a fund for Group II persons, whereas the full-time housewife gets her coverage from her husband's single payment. This unfairness is also there for single persons. Their premium results only in coverage for themselves, while the same premium covers a colleague's spouse and under-age children.

In 1985 parts of several independent pension schemes were pooled to form a compulsory fund to which all Japanese in Insured Groups I and II contribute so that deficits in the poorer funds would be offset by the wealthier funds. That fund was called the "National Pensions Basic Fund" (Kokumin Kiso Nenkin). From the beginning those in the second group were allowed to have a second tier of pension funds (known as the "Welfare Pension Fund" [Kosei Nenkin]). In 1989 provisions were made for those in the first insured group to have second-tier pension funds over and above those in the compulsory fund, although less than 5 percent of the self-employed in Insured Group I have established funds under those provisions (the exceptions being doctors and similar professionals). The result was that seventy-two additional funds were created for this scheme – forty-seven for local governments to administer and twenty-five more for distinct occupational groups to manage.

Table 8.5 *The ratio of subscribers to beneficiaries for the National Pensions Basic Fund, 1993–9*

| Year | A<br>Number of persons receiving benefits | B<br>Number of persons paying contributions | C<br>Support ratio (B/A) |
|------|-----------|-----------|-----------|
| 1993 | 28,981 | 69,276 | 2.39 |
| 1994 | 30,417 | 69,548 | 2.29 |
| 1995 | 32,363 | 69,953 | 2.16 |
| 1996 | 33,940 | 70,195 | 2.07 |
| 1997 | 35,765 | 70,344 | 1.98 |
| 1998 | 37,404 | 70,502 | 1.88 |
| 1999 | 39,062 | 70,626 | 1.81 |

*Sources:* The data in columns A, B, and C were taken from Kosei Rodo Sho Daijin Kanbo Tokei Joho Bu (2002b), pp. 300–6.

In theory every Japanese aged between 20 and 60 is covered; those aged under 20 and not working are excluded from paying premiums, as are those aged over 60–65 (depending upon their date of birth) who are no longer employed and already receiving their benefits. The numbers of those receiving pensions out of the National Pensions Basic Fund increased much more rapidly in the 1990s than did those paying premiums (see table 8.5). Accordingly, in 2001 even more dramatic changes were introduced. The formula determining the sliding scale for benefits was shifted from the average increase in wages to increases in the CPI. The age for drawing a pension was to be gradually increased from 60 to 65. Those born after April 1949 (April 1954 for women) will be the first cohort to wait until 65 before receiving their pensions. Those aged over 65 had previously been able to work and keep their full pension benefit. Now they will have their benefits discounted according to the amount earned. Those on a pension who are employed will now pay premiums, whereas before they did not. Changes were also made to the way second-tier funds would be run for employees in the private sector, and the current premium rate for the Welfare Pension Fund will be increased every five years so that the current rate of 13.58 percent of salaries will rise to 24.8 percent by 2025 (*YSC*, 25 June 2002: 27).

Tamai (2000) has been particularly critical of the reforms. He argues that publicity surrounding them has been designed to cover up the true financial situation of the fund by portraying them as novel and progressive. To the extent that the system is funded through the public purse, it involves a redistribution of income. Many workers have strong feelings about changes that might benefit or undercut their financial position by even small amounts, especially when they have planned for retirement for a long time on a certain amount of income. While not overlooking the political maneuvering and the element of national pride involved in having a national pension system, such systems become vulnerable when dramatic demographic change occurs owing to improved life expectancy and falling birth rates. From the mid-1980s advanced nations in Western Europe began to have serious fiscal difficulties as a result of earlier commitments to a welfare state. Japan's experience simply confirms further what industrial relations experts abroad have reiterated for many years: in any society institutions are extremely difficult to change fundamentally even when they are seen to be in crisis. Such change often requires a massive build-up of contradictions and the kind of sea change in the socio-political landscape that occurs only once every fifty to a hundred years. The fact thus remains that the Japanese system continues to be two-tiered for some and not for others, with funds in the second tier varying considerably from one scheme to another.

Table 8.6 provides figures on the number of subscribers, the number of beneficiaries, and the total annual and average monthly amounts paid out in benefits by each major first-tier (Kokumin Kiso Nenkin) fund and by the second-tier (Kosei Nenkin) funds for employees (in Insured Group II). From the National Pensions Basic Fund public servants (in Insured Group II-B) on the average received three and a half times what those in Insured Groups I and III receive from their funds. Ordinary employees in the private sector (in Insured Group II-A) received 70 percent more than those in the other two groups. Here it should be noted that the "unified" National Pensions Basic Fund consists of various accounts which keep separate the affairs of those in each of the three insured groups. Accordingly, their benefits are different when they reach the qualifying age. If we add benefits from the second-tier funds to those from the Basic Fund, the disparities become even more pronounced (as shown in columns G and H). These disparities can be fathomed by calculating a Gini coefficient using the data in columns B and G in table 8.6. The coefficient is 0.3455, above what it is for the data for ordinary employees taken from the Family Income and Expenditure Survey. Using income-ranked categories from that data (which will in statistical terms always produce a higher value for the Gini coefficient than when it is calculated from other types of averaged groups), Otake (2000) found the Gini coefficient to be just over 0.28 (up from around 0.25 in the early 1970s). In this regard, the inclusion of accumulated wealth in retirement funds for roughly the same period results in an even less equal distribution of income. Those with the highest retirement benefits are also in many cases those who

Table 8.6 *The benefits paid from the National Pension's Basic Fund to those in Insured Groups I, II, and III, 1999*

| Type of fund | Category of insured | A Number of subscribers paying contributions (1000s) | B Number of beneficiaries (1000s) | C Amount paid in benefits (in ¥100 million) | D Average annual amount received in benefits (C/B) | E Monthly average (D/12) | F Ratio based on the monthly average from the first-tier fund for groups I and III | G Monthly average benefit with second-tier benefit included (from the bottom of column E) | H Ratio for monthly average of total pension benefits from first and second tiers |
|---|---|---|---|---|---|---|---|---|---|
| The National Pensions Basic Fund (the first-tier fund) | I and III Self-employed and housewives | 32,861 | 18,233 | 108,075 | 588,580 | 49,048 | 1.000 | 49,048 | 1.000 |
| | II-A Employees in the private sector | 32,481 | 17,233 | 204,634 | 1,187,454 | 98,955 | 2.074 | 195,893 | 3.994 |
| | II-B Public servants | 5,273 | 3,296[a] | 66,411 | 2,014,896 | 167,908 | 3.423 | 340,781 | 6.048 |
| | Welfare pension | | 171 | 705 | 412,281 | 34,357 | 0.696 | 34,357 | 0.696 |
| | Totals | 70,615 | 39,062 | | | | | | |
| Welfare Pension Scheme | II-A | 37,754 | 18,571 | 216,024 | 1,163,255 | 96,938 | | | |
| | II-B | 835[a] | | 17,331 | 2,074,478 | 172,873 | | | |

*Note:* (a) The figures for the Welfare Pension System (*Kosei Nenkin*) for those in group II-B are only for those who had been working for the National Public Service. That accounts for the difference between the 3,296,000 receiving benefits from the National Pensions Basic Fund and the 835,000 receiving benefits from the Welfare Pension Scheme. The vast majority of those in this category had been working for the public service at the local level, and received even larger benefits on a per capita basis. In other words, the pension benefit estimates used here for all public servants are on the conservative side. In this regard, it is also important to remember that many of the higher paid and better positioned civil servants (at the national level in particular but also at the local level to some extent) retire early through a practice known as *amakudari* (whereby they obtain employment in sinecures in the private sector and some quasi-public enterprises through connections they made as bureaucrats). This lowers their pensions from the system, but in fact probably results in their after-retirement resources being even larger than they would have been had they remained in the public service.

*Sources:* The data in columns A, B, and C were taken from Kosei Rodo Sho Daijin Kanbo Tokei Joho Bu (2002b), pp. 300–6. The other columns were all calculated by the authors from the first three columns.

have been able to accumulate savings and other assets quite apart from the public pension scheme.

The second-tier funds in table 8.6 actually consist of 1,737 separate funds for private sector employees, some quite adequately endowed and some with more humble endowments. The figures in table 8.6 average out variations for each fund. Moreover, some of the wealthier funds have used their surpluses to establish ski lodges, hot spring lodges, and other recreational facilities for the use of their members. If these variations were taken into account, the spread of the benefits would be much greater than is shown in table 8.6. The discomfort felt by many in Groups I and II should be obvious. As Tamai (2000: 13) notes, the minimal full benefit available to those who work the full forty years to obtain their maximum monthly entitlement was still only ¥67,000 per month in 2000, a figure which is below the amount paid to those receiving the basic livelihood benefit. It is considerably below the minimum wage mentioned above in section 4.4.1.

## 8.4     The national health system for workers

The medical insurance system is also complex. As table 8.7 shows, medical insurance has been provided through a series of funds amalgamated into four major insurance schemes: (i) the health insurance schemes for employees in the private sector which cover them and their non-employed family members (schemes A–D), (ii) schemes for public sector employees (but including teachers in private institutions) (schemes E–G), (iii) the catch-all schemes for others including entrepreneurs and workers not covered by the schemes in (i) or (ii) above (schemes H–I), and (iv) special arrangements put in place to provide additional benefits for persons aged 70 or over (scheme J). The funding and management arrangements vary from scheme to scheme (column 2) as do the levels of benefits received (as shown in the two columns to the right of the table). Employees in the private sector are subscribed to over 1,700 insurance union plans. As with pensions, it is likely that the actual variation among funds in some categories is considerable. Comparing the figures for 1991 and 1999, the differentials seem to be increasing over time. Data on benefits provided under the national health scheme (schemes H and I) is not given in the table, but would be lower than for schemes A–G.

The payment of medical benefits is fairly straightforward: 70 percent (for outpatients) or 80 percent (for hospitalized patients) of medical costs are covered for all citizens regardless of the fund. Additional coverage for those aged over 70 provided by scheme J means that they are not out of pocket for medical treatment. However, there is considerable variation

Table 8.7 *An overview of the major medical insurance schemes in Japan, March 2000*

| Insurance scheme | Insurer | Number covered (000s) | | Average ¥ value of benefits received by each member | |
|---|---|---|---|---|---|
| | | Subscribers | Family members also covered | 1991 | 1999 |
| A Government-Managed Health Insurance Scheme (Seifu Kansho Kenko Hoken) | State | 19,528 | 17,794 | 263,696 (1.00) | 290,719 (1.00) |
| B Union Managed Health Insurance Scheme (Kumiai Kansho Kenko Hoken) | 1,780 health insurance unions | 15,394 | 16,721 | 326,079 (1.24) | 369,209 (1.27) |
| C Health Insurance Scheme for Special Groups under Article 69 for the Kenko Hoken | State | 34 | 17 | 11,385 | 13,563 |
| D Seamen's Health Insurance Scheme (Sen-in Hoken) | State | 89 | 155 | 339,888 (1.29) | 374,737 (1.29) |
| E National Public Service Health Insurance Scheme (Kyosai Kumiai Hoken) | 24 health insurance cooperatives | | | 346,749 (1.32) | 410,578 (1.41) |
| F Local Public Service Health Insurance Scheme (Kyosai Kumiai Hoken) | 54 health insurance cooperatives | 4522 | 5570 | 305,765 (1.16) | 366,889 (1.26) |
| G National Private School Teachers' Health Insurance Scheme (Kyosai Kumiai Hoken) | 1 health insurance organization | | | 315,351 (1.20) | 376,110 (1.29) |
| H National Health Scheme for farmers, entrepreneurs, etc. (Kokumin Kenko Hoken) | 3,245 local authorities and 166 national health insurance unions | | | n.a. | n.a. |
| I National Health Scheme for the Unemployed (Kokumin Kenko Hoken) | 3,245 local authorities | 46,581 | | n.a. | n.a. |
| J National Health Scheme for the Aged (Rojin Hoken) | As established by local authorities | 14,502 | | n.a. | n.a. |

*Note:* The figures in the parentheses in the last two columns show the ratio of benefits received by scheme subscribers to those received by persons who are covered by the government-managed fund for private sector employees (in scheme A).
*Source:* Hamada and Okuma (2002), p. 471; and Kosei Rodo Sho Daijin Kanbo Tokei Joho Bu (2001b), p. 283.

for other kinds of benefits, reflecting variations in the relative "health" of the different funds. The government-run fund for private employees concentrated in Japan's smaller firms (scheme A) reimburses those who are off work for health-related reasons with a benefit equivalent to 8.5 percent of their regular salary, plus 1.0 percent of their bonuses. The health insurance unions covering employees in Japan's more established and larger firms cover 3.0–9.5 percent of their already much higher salary. In principle, employers and employees contribute to the funds on a 50–50 basis, but employers may contribute a larger proportion (Tsuchida 2002: 967).

It is generally agreed by those in the field that the health insurance system is financially shaky. Hamada and Okuma (2002: 468) report that the collective funds were in the red by ¥199.2 billion in 1999 and ¥127.3 billion in 2000, with a deficit of ¥500 billion anticipated in 2001. They also note that 90 percent of Japan's 1,780 health insurance unions for private sector employees are in the red. Table 8.8 shows a rise in health insurance payouts as a percentage of national income over the past half-century. The population aged 70 and over rose from 5.3 percent of the total population in 1955 to 16.7 percent in 1999. Outlays for the aged population from the special old age fund (scheme J in table 8.7) accounted for about a third of the medical costs covered by health insurance schemes. Thirty percent of those costs incurred by scheme J are covered by allocations from national and local governments, but the remaining 70 percent are covered by transfers out of schemes A–I to which they previously belonged. Because coverage varies from scheme to scheme, benefits are determined by place of employment (i.e. working conditions). The government has moved over the past few years to tighten its controls on "over-doctoring" and on other practices which unnecessarily inflate costs and to limit the liability of funds by shifting from a system accepting "open claims" to one based on a fixed, predetermined and capped fee. Many fear that this will ultimately mean the creeping privatization of medical services, greater variation in what health insurance schemes provide, and gaps between actual fees and the standard maximums. It is our unsubstantiated hypothesis that workers will have strong views about how well their health will be cared for after forty to fifty years in the labor force, and that those views will influence their motivation to work and their evaluation of the choices they have at work.

## 8.5    Social security, working conditions, and civil society

The discussion above has centered on pensions and healthcare as "hidden returns" to the Japanese worker. It is common to think of national systems

Table 8.8 *Percentage of national income paid out by medical insurance funds as benefits and the percentage of the population aged over 65, 1955–99*

| Year | Percentage of national income paid as health insurance benefits | Percentage of the population aged over 65 |
|---|---|---|
| 1955 | 3.42 | 5.3 |
| 1965 | 4.18 | 6.3 |
| 1975 | 5.22 | 7.9 |
| 1985 | 6.15 | 10.3 |
| 1995 | 7.10 | 14.5 |
| 1999 | 8.08 | 16.7 |

*Note:* Table 7.3 gave slightly different figures.
*Source:* Hamada and Okuma (2002), p. 468; and Kosei Rodo Sho Daijin Kanbo Tokei Joho Bu (2001b), p. 19.

of welfare as serving in some way to ameliorate inequalities arising from the initial distribution of wage/salary incomes. While a good deal is written about social welfare (*shakai fukushi*) and social security (*shakai hoken*) in Japan, most accounts tend to describe the complex way in which benefits are dispersed to abstractly defined beneficiaries without linking benefits to each person's position in the labor market. Employees try to do this in a piecemeal fashion, and their choices at work cannot be understood apart from that.

The realities discussed in this chapter are buttressed by a moral presumption that individuals should not receive benefits from the public purse unless they have paid for them or have fully exhausted their own privately held assets (as noted by Abe 2002). The stigma this perspective attaches to those looking to the public purse for assistance causes many citizens to simply forgo applying for welfare benefits. Coupled with the very low income individuals are given even when they decide to exercise their right to receive benefits, the consequences are considerable in terms of wealth accumulation and the reproduction of social class. Once overall income falls below a certain level, the financial position of a family becomes quite shaky. With life expectancy at about 80, and working life extending roughly from about the age of 20 to 65, the pension system magnifies through the last quarter of adult life the inequalities experienced during the working years. Given these realities, one can better appreciate the despondency of those who have lost out in restructuring, the resignation of the *furiitaa* who look for other meanings and opportunities, and the high suicide rate among the aged in Japan. The argument here is that one cannot begin to fathom how good the good jobs described by Koshiro some twenty years ago (see section 6.1 above) really are without having a full understanding of the post-retirement income differentials. The competition for those scarce good jobs starts in middle school and underscores much of the stress felt by Japan's permanently employed when they cogitate on the consequences of losing the security of their present position and having to move to the peripheral labor force.

Policy in these areas affects not only the ways in which the systems redistribute income and wealth. The debates accompanying the preparation, passage, and implementation of legislation also shape the way individual Japanese think about society and the ability of work organizations to accommodate a wider range of lifestyles and lifestyle needs within the community. While part of this may be seen in how workers think about their basic rights at work, the more important changes may be in terms of how gender-linked and age-linked roles are conceived in the context of changes in family life and in the nature of Japan's civil society. The broader connection to civil society is seen, for example, in the rise of voluntary work over the past decade. About 60 percent of Japan's 8,000 NPOs are concerned with the provision of medical care and other social welfare services. The changes brought by the expansion of the welfare/social security sector seem to further open the way for a shift in the meaning attached to work, as some Japanese begin to reorient themselves away from work that focuses attention on their individual career success to work that allows them to be socially significant.

## Part V

The power relations shaping the organization
of work in Japan

# 9 The state of the union movement in Japan

## 9.1 Labor and management as a power relationship

Life at work in postwar Japan has been shaped to a considerable extent by shifts in the balance of power between labor and management. Immediately after the war, the unionization rate surpassed 50 percent. The movement was organized around strong industrial unions with a socialist-inspired leadership. A few unions took over the management of some firms as part of the "production control movement" (*seisan kanri undo*). Densan (the Electric Power Union) fought to establish the *Densangata* wage system which tied wages to the lifecycle needs of each employee. These efforts to "democratize" the organization of work were in line with the American-led Occupation policy to democratize Japan, but bore fruit only because the collective force of workers could be brought to bear on management through mechanisms sanctioned by the state.

Management groups vehemently resisted, and ultimately the gains of labor were undermined following the reversal of US policy. The cold war brought a sharper distinction between communist and socialist regimes with controlled markets and the liberal democracies with free markets. Moore (1983) accurately conveys an assessment commonly made by Japan's liberal intellectuals in the 1950s and 1960s that Japan was in the late 1940s on the verge of becoming a socialist society. Kawanishi (1992a: chapter 4) described the next twenty years in Japan as a massive struggle between organized labor and organized management for the soul of Japan's workers. It was a struggle waged at the national level and at the enterprise level.

The key determinant was power. Leftists would argue that management was unfairly bolstered by a conservative state determined to destroy assertive unionism. Conservatives would point to the limitations of formula-driven demands based on egalitarian principles in a society increasingly characterized by differentiated lifestyles, a heterogeneous labor force, and a desire for a higher standard of living (i.e. higher productivity). At the national level the ideological conflict often appeared to be between the forces for national competitiveness (which required wage restraint and the deferral of social welfare benefits) and those for across-the-board safety nets. The tensions often revolved around management initiatives to replace the *Densangata* wage system with schemes more attuned to individual productivity. The outcomes were determined by power relations between labor and management and defined the larger setting for organizing work. Since the mid-1970s the resultant shift in power has been symbolized by declining unionization rates.

### 9.2     Declining unionization rates and the Japanese labor movement within the global setting

After remaining at about 35 percent over the twenty years prior to 1975, the unionization rate in Japan declined to just 20.7 percent in 2001 (table 9.1). Unionization rates have similarly fallen in the UK, the US and Germany (table 9.2). A report by the ILO in the late 1990s suggests that this reflects a worldwide trend and identifies a number of factors contributing to that: legislation affecting unionism, new technologies, changing labor-force participation among particular groups, casualization, downsizing, and growing unemployment. Labor has also been fragmented by the ongoing conflict between more action-oriented left-wing unionists intent on confronting management and the state at the meso level and more conservative unionists committed to working with management at the micro level. As the micro-level unionists became more influential, the firm-level branches of industrial unions gave way to independent enterprise unions, and the union movement's indifference to workers in the peripheral labor force became institutionalized.

Japanese unions have had to respond to the new logic of global capitalism, with parts of the Japanese model (e.g. just-in-time arrangements, subcontracting and the extensive use of casualized labor) integrating well into capitalism's new mode of production. Industrial restructuring has been accompanied by the growing importance of tertiary industry and the "hollowing out" of manufacturing. Given these challenges to their competitiveness, many firms have committed themselves to reorganizing work so that they can adjust overall employment levels quickly as the short-term financial fortunes of the firm fluctuate and as the concomitant need to move quickly into new product markets emerges. In the past, mechanisms such as the "convoy system" (the collective bailing-out of firms having difficulty in a particular industry by other firms in the industry and in *keiretsu* groupings) and the involvement of *sokaiya* (racketeers used to control annual meetings of stockholders) supported a complex maze of "hidden subsidies" that covered up unprofitable initiatives

Table 9.1 *Long-term trends in the unionization rates in Japan, 1946–2001*

| Year | A<br>Number of<br>unions | B<br>Number of<br>unionists<br>(in millions) | C<br>Number of<br>employees<br>(in millions) | D<br>Unionization<br>rate<br>(100B/C) | E<br>Average number of<br>members per union<br>organization (B/A) |
|---|---|---|---|---|---|
| 1946 | 12,006 | 3.680 |  | 40.0 | 306.5 |
| 1947 | 23,323 | 5.692 | 12.56 | 45.3 | 244.1 |
| 1948 | 33,926 | 6.677 | 12.59 | 53.0 | 196.8 |
| 1949 | 34,688 | 6.655 | 11.93 | 55.8 | 191.9 |
| 1950 | 29,144 | 5.774 | 12.51 | 46.2 | 192.1 |
| 1951 | 27,644 | 5.680 | 13.36 | 42.6 | 205.5 |
| 1952 | 27,851 | 5.720 | 14.21 | 40.3 | 205.4 |
| 1953 | 30,129 | 5.927 | 14.47 | 41.0 | 196.7 |
| 1954 | 31,456 | 6.076 | 15.34 | 39.6 | 193.2 |
| 1955 | 32,012 | 6.286 | 15.78 | 39.8 | 196.4 |
| 1956 | 34,073 | 6.463 | 17.42 | 37.1 | 189.7 |
| 1957 | 36,084 | 6.763 | 18.25 | 37.1 | 187.4 |
| 1958 | 37,823 | 6.984 | 19.54 | 35.7 | 184.6 |
| 1959 | 39,303 | 7.211 | 21.68 | 33.3 | 183.5 |
| 1960 | 41,561 | 7.662 | 23.16 | 33.1 | 184.4 |
| 1961 | 45,096 | 8.360 | 23.61 | 35.4 | 185.4 |
| 1962 | 47,812 | 8.971 | 24.77 | 36.2 | 187.6 |
| 1963 | 49,796 | 9.357 | 25.94 | 36.1 | 187.9 |
| 1964 | 51,457 | 9.800 | 27.01 | 36.3 | 190.5 |
| 1965 | 52,879 | 10.147 | 28.10 | 36.1 | 191.9 |
| 1966 | 53,983 | 10.404 | 29.39 | 35.1 | 192.7 |
| 1967 | 55,351 | 10.476 | 29.99 | 35.2 | 189.3 |
| 1968 | 56,535 | 10.863 | 31.59 | 34.4 | 192.1 |
| 1969 | 58,812 | 11.249 | 31.96 | 35.2 | 191.3 |
| 1970 | 60,954 | 11.605 | 32.77 | 35.4 | 190.4 |
| 1971 | 62,428 | 11.798 | 33.88 | 34.8 | 189.0 |
| 1972 | 63,718 | 11.889 | 34.69 | 34.3 | 186.6 |
| 1973 | 66,448 | 12.098 | 36.59 | 33.1 | 182.1 |
| 1974 | 67,829 | 12.464 | 36.76 | 33.9 | 183.8 |
| 1975 | 69,333 | 12.590 | 36.62 | 34.4 | 181.6 |
| 1976 | 70,039 | 12.509 | 37.10 | 33.7 | 178.6 |
| 1977 | 70,625 | 12.437 | 37.46 | 33.2 | 176.1 |
| 1978 | 70,868 | 12.383 | 37.96 | 32.6 | 174.7 |
| 1979 | 71,780 | 12.309 | 38.99 | 31.6 | 171.5 |
| 1980 | 72,693 | 12.369 | 40.12 | 30.8 | 170.2 |
| 1981 | 73,694 | 12.471 | 40.55 | 30.8 | 169.2 |
| 1982 | 74,091 | 12.526 | 41.02 | 30.5 | 169.1 |
| 1983 | 74,486 | 12.520 | 42.09 | 29.7 | 168.1 |

(*cont.*)

Table 9.1 (*cont.*)

| Year | A<br>Number of<br>unions | B<br>Number of<br>unionists<br>(in millions) | C<br>Number of<br>employees<br>(in millions) | D<br>Unionization<br>rate<br>(100B/C) | E<br>Average number of<br>members per union<br>organization (B/A) |
|------|------|--------|-------|------|-------|
| 1984 | 74,579 | 12.464 | 42.82 | 29.1 | 167.1 |
| 1985 | 74,499 | 12.418 | 43.01 | 28.9 | 166.7 |
| 1986 | 74,183 | 12.343 | 43.83 | 28.2 | 166.4 |
| 1987 | 73,138 | 12.272 | 44.48 | 27.6 | 167.8 |
| 1988 | 72,792 | 12.227 | 45.65 | 26.8 | 168.0 |
| 1989 | 72,605 | 12.227 | 47.21 | 25.9 | 168.4 |
| 1990 | 72,202 | 12.264 | 48.75 | 25.2 | 169.9 |
| 1991 | 71,685 | 12.397 | 50.62 | 24.2 | 172.9 |
| 1992 | 71,881 | 12.541 | 51.39 | 24.4 | 174.5 |
| 1993 | 71,501 | 12.663 | 52.33 | 24.2 | 177.1 |
| 1994 | 71,674 | 12.698 | 52.79 | 24.1 | 177.2 |
| 1995 | 70,839 | 12.613 | 53.09 | 23.8 | 178.1 |
| 1996 | 70,699 | 12,451 | 53.67 | 23.2 | 176.1 |
| 1997 | 70,821 | 12.285 | 54.36 | 22.6 | 173.5 |
| 1998 | 70,084 | 12.093 | 53.99 | 22.4 | 172.6 |
| 1999 | 69,387 | 11.825 | 53.25 | 22.2 | 170.4 |
| 2000 | 68,737 | 11.539 | 53.67 | 21.5 | 167.9 |
| 2001 | 67,706 | 11.212 | 54.16 | 20.7 | 165.6 |

*Note:* The figures in column A represent the number of independent union organizations (including the federations and all of their subordinates). At a firm with four enterprise unions and one company federation to which all four enterprise unions belong, the latter would be counted as unit unions, but not the federation. However, the figures in column B include all members in the four enterprise unions plus the officials in the federation, as well as officials in industrial federations, other confederations, and the national centers.
*Source:* Various editions of the *Rodo Tokei Nenpo* (Yearbook of Labor Statistics) which is updated and published annually by the Romu Gyosei Kenkyujo for the Ministry of Labor, and now for the Kosei Rodo Daijin Kanbo Tokei Joho Bu. These figures can also be gleaned from the annually released *Rodo Undo Hakusho* (White Paper on the Labor Movement) prepared by the Ministry of Labor and then the Ministry of Welfare and Labor.

by management and even the channeling of "slush funds" to cronies by a small number of corrupt managers. The surpluses required for these practices have ultimately been generated through some form of social dumping, often made possible by the careful orchestration of tightly knit *keiretsu* arrangements and by tacit understandings among those who form the business–bureaucratic–political elite. Critical to this shifting of resources have been understandings concerning the segmented labor

Table 9.2 *A comparison of unionization rates in four countries, 1985–2000*

| Country | 1985 | 2000 |
| --- | --- | --- |
| Japan | 28.9 | 21.5 |
| United States | 18.8 (1984) | 13.5 |
| United Kingdom | 53.1 (1983) | 29.9 |
| West Germany/Germany | 41.5 (1983) | 32.2 (1998) |

*Sources:* For 1985:  Rodo Sho Rosei Kyoku (1986), p. 523.
   For 2000: Kosei Rodo Sho Daijin Kanbo Tokei Joho Bu
   (2002a), p. 250.

market and entrenched inequalities between a privileged aristocracy of unionized employees and a large peripheral labor force.

Many writing about industrial relations and work organization in Japan have emphasized the importance of allegedly unique features: long-term employment, seniority wages, and the enterprise union. Although the research by Koike (1989) and others has helped to put the first two into comparative perspective, showing that neither is peculiar to Japan, only a few writers such as Kawanishi (1989 and 1992a) have examined in detail the way the enterprise union functions. From the outside it has been assumed by many observers that the enterprise union and the consultative practices associated with it have facilitated the attainment of high levels of productivity with social justice. In the 1970s the OECD (1972), Taira (1977), Yakabe (1977), and many others praised Japan's internal labor markets as a major factor accounting for the highly motivated and committed labor force that contributed greatly to Japan's rapid economic growth. Such writers often concluded that the enterprise union had facilitated the smooth operation of Japan's labor market by cooperating extensively with management.

Given this positive assessment, the drop in Japan's unionization rate is ironic. If the enterprise union had indeed been an important force facilitating Japan's extremely flexible response to the successive oil shocks of the mid-1970s, as many allege, the enterprise-based union movement in Japan should have strengthened. Even accepting the common claim that the enterprise union is more suited to the functioning of large firms with vertically structured internal labor markets, one would expect unionization rates to rise in the large-scale sector. They have not. Nor has the labor force moved from medium-sized to large-scale enterprises as some might have expected. Moreover, by the 1990s the union movement had still done little to incorporate those two-thirds of the labor force in the private sector who were employed in firms with fewer than 100 employees (Rodo Daijin Kanbo Seisaku Chosa Bu 1996a: 52).

In considering the decline of the union movement in Japan, one must consider at least three elements: economic restructuring (e.g. the shift from secondary to tertiary industry) and the push within enterprises to achieve competitive best global practice; the shift of power from unions to management; and the distancing of unions from their members and many others in the labor force. Before considering each of these, it is useful to review briefly the organization of the union movement in postwar Japan.

## 9.3    The structure of the union movement in postwar Japan

Although much attention has been given to the role of the enterprise union in Japan's postwar industrial and employment relations, there is, as figure 9.1 shows, more to the labor movement than the enterprise union.

### 9.3.1    National centers

The left in Japanese politics has long been ideologically fragmented. One consequence is that Japan has not had a unified labor movement. Early in the twentieth century radical intellectuals were divided in their support for communism, various brands of socialism, and anarchism. Reading various sources, even in English, one senses this factionalism in discussions of the left in Cole, Totten and Uyehara (1966) on the history of the socialist parties, in Smith (1972) on the student movements, in Packard (1966) on the anti-security-treaty demonstrations in 1960, in Scalapino (1967) on the history of the Japanese Communist Party, in Ui (1968 and 1972) on the anti-pollution movements, in Hoston (1986) on the evolution of Japanese Marxism, in Mackie (2003) on the feminist movement, and in Large (1982) on the socialist leadership. The factors promoting fragmentation include the high cost of strategic failure, the secrecy and suspicions and the emotional commitment associated with efforts to foster change in the face of social opprobrium and repression by the state; the tensions between the theorists at their desks and those organizing on the ground; personal rivalries and the reliance on individual and group loyalties; the strong, even idiosyncratic personalities required by a commitment to fundamentally change society; outside pressures from Comintern, from looser groupings of Christian socialists, and from competing sides when the Sino-Soviet split occurred; and the gaps between foreign prognoses and grassroots realities in Japan, and incongruence between the *etic* and the *emic*, as foreign terms were introduced by competing

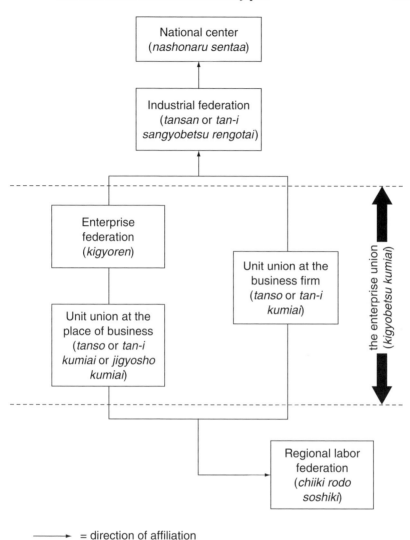

——————▶ = direction of affiliation

Figure 9.1 The three tiers of organized labor in Japan.

activists to legitimate their own ideological positions. Repeated attempts by the prewar Japanese authorities to repress the various "isms" on the left forced many to go underground, a situation which further contributed to poor communications and to the splintering of the labor movement.

It is not surprising, then, that numerous groupings emerged and began to jostle for position at the national level when unions were first legalized

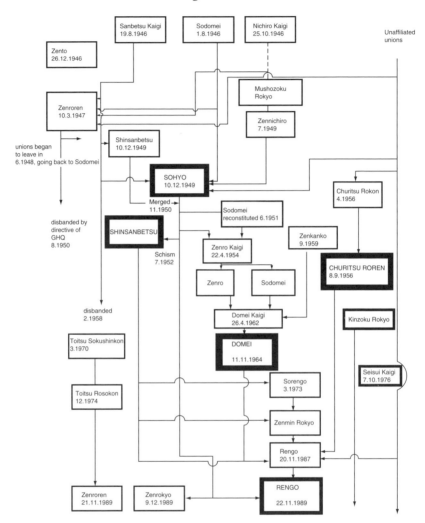

Figure 9.2  A genealogy of the postwar labor movement in Japan.

by the Occupation in December 1945. Figure 9.2 provides a genealogy beginning with the four national centers that were formed in 1946. From the early 1960s onwards, however, two national centers dominated the union movement until they merged in 1989, Sohyo on the left and Domei on the right. Though much smaller, Churitsu Roren was also a significant center, in part owing to its independent ideological stance somewhere between the other two. As table 9.3 indicates, in 1970 each center had

Table 9.3 *The national centers and their major industrial affiliates, 1970*

| National center | English rendition | Membership | | Industrial federation | |
| --- | --- | --- | --- | --- | --- |
| | | Number of members (in 000s) | Percentage distribution | Japanese name | English rendition |
| Sohyo | General Council of Trade Unions of Japan | 4,282 | 36.9 | Tekko Roren | Japanese Federation of Iron and Steel Industry Workers' Unions |
| Domei | Japanese Confederation of Labor | 2,060 | 17.7 | Zenzosen | General Federation of Shipbuilding and Engineering Workers' Unions |
| | | | | Jidosha Roren | Japan Federation of Automobile Workers' Unions |
| Churitsu Roren | Federation of Independent Unions | 1,400 | 12.1 | Denki Roren | All-Japan Federation of Electric Machine and Tool Industry Workers' Unions |
| Shinsanbetsu | National Federation of Industrial Organizations | 74 | 0.6 | | |
| Other national federations | | 1,124 | 9.7 | | |
| Other unions | | 2,829 | 24.3 | | |
| Total | | 11,605 | 100.0 | | |

*Source:* Rodo Daijin Kanbo Tokei Joho Bu (1972), pp. 326–9.

a large industrial federation from one of Japan's major manufacturing industries.

A major function of the national centers has been to provide competing ideological foci for unions at the industrial and local level. The two major centers did this by acquiring an array of industrial federations that were in turn constituted by their affiliated branches or enterprise unions (figure 9.1). The ideological thrust was most evident in each center's links with the international labor movement, Sohyo affiliating with the World Federation of Trade Unions (WFTU, centered around the socialist bloc in Eastern Europe) and Domei with the International Confederation of Free Trade Unions (ICFTU, centered around the countries in Western Europe and supported by many of the industrial federations in the US). The WFTU and the ICFTU each had its own network of international industrial confederations. When the communist regimes in Eastern Europe collapsed, the WFTU lost its ability to function in a meaningful fashion.

Formed in 1951, Sohyo sought to foster a sense of working-class consciousness by organizing an annual Spring Offensive (Shunto) that incorporated May Day demonstrations and slogans supporting working-class solidarity. Created as a center for a more conservative social democratic movement in 1964, Domei subscribed to economic unionism and waged its own "Wage Offensive" (Chinto) in conjunction with Sohyo's Spring Offensive. Annual success each spring resulted in a certain ritualization of the proceedings, and by the 1970s the negotiations with management at the industrial level had come to result in fairly predictable outcomes determined largely by changes in the consumer price index (Sano 1980). During the 1980s the commitment to Sohyo's militant unionism waned, particularly in the private sector, and several of Sohyo's strongest affiliates in the public sector (which organized teachers and employees of the Japan National Railways) were crushed following a concerted campaign by the government and the media against left-wing unions. Increasingly emphasis shifted to the ability of individual firms to meet the demands of their unions, an approach given further impetus by the recessions of the 1990s.

### 9.3.2    Industrial federations and the move to unify the national centers

Industrial federations and industrial unions perform important research functions. They promote the sharing of information among their affiliates and foster among their members a sense of industry-wide standards and an industry-level culture that Clark (1979) referred to as a "society of industry." Through their international affiliations they also obtain information necessary to link their demands to some notion of an international standard. Information gathering also allows them to assess overseas practices they do not like and to view their movement in an overall social context characterized by low unemployment, high levels of education, minimal crime, and the absence of tensions caused by having sizable ethnic minorities. While the number of industrial unions has declined over time and most industry-level organizations have come to be federations, some significant industrial unions remain (e.g. the Seamen's Union [Kaiin Domei] and the Japan Teachers' Union [Nikkyoso]).

Industrial unions and federations have tended to mirror the ideology of the national centers at the industrial level and to diffuse their views through affiliates at the shop- and office-floor level. Nevertheless, in the early 1960s the four major industrial federations listed in table 9.3 formed the Japan Council of the International Metal Workers' Federation to enable them to take a united stance in dealings with the European-oriented organization. Given their dominant position, these unions often led the Spring Offensive and had the pooled finances necessary to support a concerted research effort. The Japan Council exerted a powerful influence on the union movement and served to bridge the three ideologically opposed centers.

By the end of the 1960s working conditions in Japan's large firms had improved immensely, and private sector workers who identified with Sohyo's political unionism decreased. Having the right to strike themselves, they lost interest in the high priority placed by employees in the public sector on obtaining the right to strike. By 1970 Domei came to represent the majority of unionists in Japan's private enterprises. In the December 1972 Lower House elections the Liberal Democratic Party, in government continuously since 1955, suffered a huge loss, picking up only 46.8 percent of the popular vote, although it still managed to win a reduced majority of the seats (55.2 percent) (*ASC*, 12 December 1972: 1–2). Attention focused on the difficulties faced by a fractured union movement (with its support divided among the Japan Socialist Party, the Democratic Socialist Party, and the Japan Communist Party). Behind the scenes leaders in some of the major private sector industrial federations centered around the IMF-JC began discussions on how to unify the labor movement. In the early 1980s they formed Zenmin Rokyo – a liaison body which formed the basis for Rengo to be established in November 1987 by affiliates from three of the four national centers. Two years later Sohyo and many of its affiliates followed suit. Some unions on the left formed Zenrokyo and some formed Zenroren as competing national centers (table 9.4).

Table 9.4 *Union members affiliated to each national center, 1998–2000*

| National center | English nomenclature | 1998 | 1999 | 2000 | Percentage distribution for 2000 |
|---|---|---|---|---|---|
| Rengo | Japan Union Confederation | 7,476 | 7,334 | 7,173 | 61.0 |
| Zenroren | National Confederation of Trade Unions | 837 | 827 | 802 | 6.8 |
| Zenrokyo | | 270 | 265 | 258 | 2.2 |
| Other national federations | | 2,668 | 2,579 | 2,514 | 21.4 |
| Other unions | | 1,078 | 1,044 | 1,005 | 8.6 |
| Total | | 12,329 | 12,049 | 11,752 | 100.0 |

*Source:* Kosei Rodo Sho Daijin Kanbo Tokei Joho Bu (2002a), p. 298.

### 9.3.3    The enterprise union

Japan's postwar labor movement has been structured around organizations at the enterprise level, and the enterprise union continues to be the most basic autonomous unit in the union movement. The predominant unit of organization is the business firm (*kaisha*) or the place of business (*jigyosho*). Both are "enterprises" (*kigyo*). The term is used to distinguish clearly between the company union (which is seen as being in the service of the firm) and the enterprise union that consists of members drawn wholly from the same firm. Restricting membership to employees of a given enterprise does not mean that the enterprise union necessarily embraces all employees at a single enterprise or that it is the only union organizing workers at that enterprise.

The enterprise union (*kigyo betsu kumiai*) may be either a "unit union" (*tanso* or *tan-i kumiai*) at a single place of business or in an entire firm or in a firm-wide federation (*kigyoren*). Many large firms carry on activities at several places of business (i.e. enterprises), each with a distinct legal identity. It is common for each enterprise to have its own union, with a coordinating firm-wide federation (known as a *kigyoren* or *kigyonai rodo kumiai rengotai*). Some *kigyoren* have come to supersede their affiliates and become the enterprise union, with their affiliates then becoming branches. This complicates the collection of statistics on unions and makes the tabulations difficult to assess.

The Trade Union Law allows any two persons to form a union in Japan. Accordingly, very small unions sometimes form around the special interests of a limited number of employees. In the 1950s and 1960s second unions were formed at many enterprises to compete with the enterprise affiliate of a powerful left-wing industrial union. In many firms Japan's postwar industrial and employment relations have been colored by the presence of two unions – a "number one union" (*daiichi kumiai*) (often a left-wing union associated with Sohyo) and a "number two union" (*daini kumiai*) (often a conservative business-oriented union affiliated with a Domei industrial federation). Up to 20 percent of organized enterprises had two such unions when the practice was at its height in the late 1960s and early 1970s. The tensions this created at work often extended far beyond enterprises that had the two unions. Some of the day-to-day tensions have been described by Fujita (1968) and Kawanishi (1977 and 1990). The organizational outcomes are shown in figure 9.3. The tensions were exacerbated by the extremely competitive situation found in most firms as described by the novels mentioned above in chapter 6.

Enterprise unions maintain a strong sense of independence and possess their own assets. They receive information and support, but not orders, from their industrial federations. Most enterprise unions focus narrowly on achieving better working conditions for their members, but negotiate with management across a broad range of issues. Table 9.5 lists issues that have recently arisen in the course of company restructuring. They give some idea of the issues considered important by many enterprise unions. With labor market deregulation, a major concern is the discretion of management to shift employees among the various enterprises run by the firm. The merits and demerits of the enterprise union have been debated for some time along with arguments about its uniqueness.

## 9.4    Structural change and the social framework

It is commonly argued that high-tech and service industries require a flexibility that makes employees difficult to organize. However, Freeman and Rebick (1989), Ito and Takeda (1990), and Tsuru (1994) also suggest that only between a fourth and a fifth of the drop in unionization rates in Japan is due to the shift of employees into such industries. Fujimura (1997: 300–3) argues strongly that the drop in unionization rates has occurred across nearly all industries and in large firms as well as small ones.

The impact of technological change has been more in terms of work practices (e.g. labor process) in all industries and at all levels within already established firms. As discussed in chapters 5 and 6, changing work practices seem to be associated with further segmentation of the labor market, making it more difficult for the enterprise union to appeal to a wide range of employees. Firms continue to seek a competitive edge

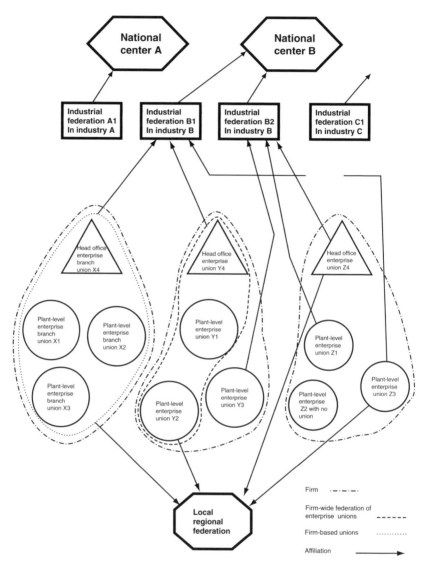

Figure 9.3 The structuring of the union movement with competing enterprise unions.

by peripheralizing their labor force. In 1996 41.8 percent of all women employees worked part-time, and 23.3 percent of Japan's total labor force was hired on a non-regular basis. Table 9.6 shows that unionization is high among regular employees in Japan's largest enterprises and much lower in smaller firms where about 60 percent of Japan's employees work. The

## Table 9.5 *Percentage of unions attaching importance to different matters raised by management in the course of their firm's restructuring, 2000*

| Aspect of restructuring | Percentage of unions concerned about the specific item |
|---|---|
| Temporary transfers and temporary change of employer | 38.6 |
| Change in the place of work with a relocation of residency | 27.8 |
| Change in the place of work without a relocation of residency | 26.2 |
| Freezing annual wage increases and other measures to restrain wages | 22.7 |
| Establishment of an early retirement scheme providing for preferential treatment for those taking voluntary early retirement | 22.3 |
| Dismissals and heavy-handed pressure to take early retirement | 20.3 |
| Reconsideration of overtime rates and other allowances | 13.0 |
| Reviews of retirement allowances and corporate pensions | 12.4 |
| Reconsideration of company welfare provisions | 11.6 |
| Restraints on the hiring of new graduates and mid-career workers | 10.8 |
| Measures to reduce the pay of managerial staff | 8.6 |
| Compulsion for employees to receive education and training oriented to changing jobs | 7.1 |
| Changes to the normal working day | 6.1 |
| Changes to the number of days off (weekly and annually) | 5.8 |
| Lowering the compulsory retirement age or other measures to reduce the employment of "over-age" employees | 2.6 |

*Source:* Taken from the *Survey on Labor Union Activities in 2000* (Rodo Kumiai Katsudo Jittai Chosa Heisei Juninen) as reported in Kosei Rodo Sho Daijin Kanbo Tokei Joho Bu (2002c), pp. 302–3.

## Table 9.6 *Unionization rate by firm size, 2000*

| A Firm size (number of employees) | B Number of unions | C Number of union members (in 1000s) | D Percentage drop in membership (1999–2000) | E Number of employees (10,000s) | F Unionization rate [100 × (C/E)] |
|---|---|---|---|---|---|
| 0–29 | 4,839 | 47 | 6.0 | 2,596 | 1.4 |
| 30–99 | 10,012 | 314 | 3.6 | | |
| 100–299 | 9,922 | 842 | 3.6 | 1,197 | 19.5 |
| 300–999 | 8,472 | 1,403 | 2.0 | | |
| 1,000+ | 20,071 | 5,274 | 2.5 | 974 | 57.2 |
| Total | 56,538 | 8,975 | 2.6 | 4,796 | 19.4 |

*Source:* Kosei Rodo Sho Roshi Kankei Tanto Sanjikan Shitsu (2002), p. 486.

enterprise union continues to define itself in terms of employees in the core labor force.

Japan's large firms have taken three steps to be more competitive. The first has been to push for the liberalization of the economy: deregulating the labor market; moving production overseas (most noticeably to China); and "freeing up society." In the past employers have wanted to isolate the social relationships relevant to their firms' operations from other processes of economic rationalization. In 1997 Nikkeiren (the Japan Federation of Employers' Associations) argued that it was important to the motivation and cohesion of their employees that Japanese firms continue practices that embraced traditional work norms, maintain traditional work force discipline, and ensure egalitarian outcomes. It cautioned firms not to move away from *Densangata*-type arrangements too quickly for fear of upsetting understandings with (organized) labor. At the same time, however, it also sought changes in the social relations that had characterized work in Japan for nearly half a century. The increased discretion of management to regulate workloads will likely result in core employees working longer and more intensely. This will make it more difficult for women to compete with men on an equal footing, for men to be involved in domestic duties to the extent necessary for wives and mothers to enter the labor force as core employees, and for employees to engage in voluntary community-oriented activity. The enhanced capacity for management to redefine workloads for its white-collar employees in terms of output rather than the time actually required to get the output will shift the basis for wage rates from labor input to labor output. That will in turn mean that employers no longer need to assume responsibility for assessing the value of labor per se or for enhancing its value as human capital. By purchasing the output rather than the labor, firms will be able to convert each employee into an independent subcontractor.

This segmentation of the core labor force corrects a certain inequality, while creating another that divides the membership of the enterprise union. As Araki (1996) explains, the current system, tied to hours of input, tended to subsidize slower or less productive employees at the expense of more able workers. Because the less able employee will need overtime to complete his work, he attracts overtime pay beyond the normal salary he would otherwise receive for working more productively and completing his work within the normal hours. This fundamental change in work relations will challenge unions to find common ground for their increasingly differentiated membership.

Unions will also be affected by changes to the labor contract for core employees. The longer contract period of three to five years will allow management to remove professionals, other highly skilled employees, and technical workers from the category of core employees (Nihon Kei-eisha Dantai Renmei 1995: 32), further reducing the pool from which the enterprise union has traditionally drawn its committed membership. Even though unions may move to broaden their definition of employee to embrace contract workers, such employees will now have to think carefully about how union affiliation might affect their chances for contract extensions, as management seeks to respond to globally generated pressure to be more competitive. One outcome is the growing ambivalence of many skilled white-collar workers toward schemes that subsidize fellow employees and others who are less productive. It is thus possible that the enterprise union may come to center itself around a shrinking core labor force. This will produce a smaller union movement with a more cohesive subgroup within the labor market – an amalgam narrowly committed to serving its own interests as Japan's aristocracy of labor. However, it is also conceivable that the aristocracy will fracture further, with cleavages emerging between blue- and white-collar, administrative and technically skilled employees. In any case, the openness of each grouping to women will critically shape Japan's union movement.

A major concern for those interested in a more broadly based union movement is that that aristocracy has supplied much of the leadership in many enterprise unions and industrial federations. As Kawanishi (1992a: 35) and others have documented, the enterprise union has come to be led by the better-educated workers (many of whom were already in managerial track positions). However, such unionists are served by the move from labor-input- to product-output-based schemes that better reward them for their higher productivity by widening intra-firm wage differentials initially between the unionists (as core employees) and non-unionists (in the peripheral labor force), and then between more productive unionists and less productive ones. The commitment of many enterprise unions to an ideology that puts productivity first is one source of apathy and anxiety among those in the second tier of the permanent labor force. This undermines notions of labor solidarity and the influence of the peak organizations at the national level.

These new cleavages sit uncomfortably with the egalitarian heritage left by the militant industrial unions that dominated Japan's employment relations immediately after the war, when unions worked to remove invidious status distinctions between workers and to inject livelihood guarantees into the wage system. The enterprise union later emerged as a response to what many skilled employees saw as excessive egalitarianism once the material standard of living rose above subsistence levels. The push for productivity shifted attention from the relative size of income shares to their absolute size. The important thing was simply that the material standard of living was improving at least a little for everyone. To the extent (i) that the driving force behind Japan's ever expanding economy was the large unionized firm and its core labor force, and (ii) that consumerism (the desire for a higher material standard of living) came to be the paramount value for most workers, the enterprise union made sense. There was a kind of social contract.

However, the validity of that social contract has come to be questioned. The high cost of living and the absence of safety nets has bolstered the sense of economic insecurity and reinforced the perception of many Japanese employees that they need to work even more competitively. The conditions for worker solidarity have changed; if unions cannot respond to the needs of both the core and the non-core labor force, unionization rates will continue to decline. The ever present linkage between wage levels, job security, and competitiveness reflects an overall weakness in the position of labor within an economy structured around extensively segmented labor markets. That weakness will continue to undermine the ability of the enterprise union to build a broadly based union movement capable of raising the unionization rate and exerting its influence at the national level.

## 9.5     Fluctuations in the political influence of the union movement

The emphasis on cooperative industrial relations has shifted attention from Japan's history of industrial conflict at the national, industrial, and enterprise levels during the postwar period. That history entailed conflict between number one and number two unions at the enterprise level, ideological divisions in the Diet and elsewhere in the political arena, several "red purges," the refusal of the Japanese government to interact with the Japan Teachers' Union, and Spring Wage Offensives.

The shift in power from Japan's industrially based unions to enterprise unions was the result of a thirty-year power struggle. The struggle had several dimensions. One involved the efforts of management and successive conservative governments to contain unionism, especially Japan's strong industrial unions. On another level were tensions between core (unionized) and non-core (non-unionized) labor. On yet another level elitist white-collar permanent (unionized) employees in Japan's large firms lined up against the less-educated and less-skilled permanent (unionized) employees in their own firms.

At this point perhaps the connection of the enterprise union to the internal labor market also requires brief comment. Although the enterprise union is often seen as an approach facilitating "internal transfers" in Japan's large firms, many transfers have been out-placements to sub-contracting and other related firms. If there is merit in arguments linking the enterprise union to the functioning of labor markets, *keiretsu* unions might have been more effective than enterprise unions. While this would present enterprise unions with the challenge of having to incorporate an even more heterogeneous cross-section of employees, it would also provide a larger critical mass and offset the ability of management to weaken the union by shifting its workforce to subcontractors or other related firms. However the enterprise union is organized, its future will be shaped significantly by the position it takes on inequalities which now differentiate each firm's labor force. Although many enterprise unions have distanced themselves from simplistic Marxist concepts and their associated symbols (Fujimura 1998: 7), they have not yet found another unifying concept. They have maintained an ongoing commitment to function as a protective organization, yet have not been able to influence significantly a number of areas which affect working conditions such as the speed of conveyor belts, the rotation of employees between jobs or shifts, and the promotion process. This contrasts, for example, with many of the workers' councils (*Betriebsrat*) in Germany, or the strong protection given by many American unions to seniority rights.

Keeping those comments in mind, Fujimura (1998) reminds us that the influence of the enterprise union at the firm level should not be underestimated. The enterprise unions were instrumental in removing CEOs from several large Japanese firms in the early 1990s: the Mainichi Newspaper Corporation, the Tokyo Broadcasting Corporation, Yamaha Corporation, Toyo Keizai Shimposha (a leading publisher of business-related books and reference works), and Tokyo Shoko Research. This may not be the production control (*seisan kanri*) gained by some unions immediately after the war, but in each case employees were dissatisfied with excessively authoritarian decision-making, management's lack of vision, and the poor performance of their firms. Benson's surveys (1994 and 1996) of small and medium-sized firms also indicate that the enterprise union has made a difference. Other data shows that 81 percent of unionized firms have arrangements for joint labor–management consultations, compared with only 32 percent of non-unionized firms (Rodo Daijin Kanbo Seisaku Chosa Bu 1996a: 232). The 2000 Survey on Labor Union Activities revealed that union size may bring greater influence (part B in table 9.7) in Japan's largest firms (part A). Part C, however, suggests that unions that do a better job of monopolizing the sale of labor in a firm have more influence. This finding is consistent with the proposition that a single enterprise union is stronger than two at the same firm.

Table 9.7 *Percentage of unions having an influence on restructuring in their firm, 2000*

A. By firm size

| Size of the firm by number of employees | Percentage of unions which have had a say in the restructuring process |
| --- | --- |
| 100–299 | 68.4 |
| 300–499 | 72.0 |
| 500–999 | 81.7 |
| 1,000–4,999 | 84.1 |
| 5,000+ | 91.3 |

B. By size of the union

| Size of the union by number of members | Percentage of unions which have had a say in the restructuring process |
| --- | --- |
| 100–299 | 78.2 |
| 300–499 | 86.9 |
| 500–999 | 88.5 |
| 1,000–4,999 | 91.4 |
| 5,000+ | 96.3 |

C. By percentage of employees unionized in the firm-based union organization

| Percentage of employees unionized at the enterprise | Percentage of unions which have had a say in the restructuring process |
| --- | --- |
| 10–30 | 55.7 |
| 30–50 | 64.3 |
| 50–70 | 77.8 |
| 70–90 | 79.0 |
| 90+ | 90.2 |

*Source:* Taken from the Survey on Labor Union Activities (2000) (Rodo Kumiai Katsudo Jittai Chosa Heisei Juninen) as reported in Kosei Rodo Sho Daijin Kanbo Tokei Joho Bu (2002c), p. 299.

There is another side to union size. The fortunes of the union movement can also be viewed in terms of the average size of its smallest independent unions. Column E in table 9.1 yields a different approach to periodization than simple reference to the unionization rate per se (as used by Fujimura 1997: 298–9). During the period of strong industrial unions, the average size of Japanese unions remained at about 190 members, dropping to about 185 following the split of many unions which

Table 9.8 *Distribution of unions by membership size, 2000*

| Size of the union in terms of membership | Number of unions | Number of members | Average number of members |
|---|---|---|---|
| 1–29 | 8,683 | 123,441 | 14.2 |
| 30–99 | 10,101 | 589,673 | 58.4 |
| 100–299 | 7,177 | 1,218,594 | 169.8 |
| 300–499 | 1,930 | 742,835 | 384.9 |
| 500–999 | 1,598 | 1,113,349 | 696.7 |
| 1,000–4,999 | 1,381 | 2,865,964 | 2,075.3 |
| 5,000+ | 315 | 4,884,701 | 15,507.0 |
| All unions | 31,185 | 11,538,557 | 370.0 |

*Source:* Kosei Rodo Sho Daijin Kanbo Tokei Joho Bu (2002c), p. 298.

accompanied the first serious push for enterprise unions in the mid-1950s. The average size came back to 190 as union membership and the strong industrial unions were bolstered by the expansion of manufacturing, legitimated by the vocabulary of the socialist-inclined free speech movements and anti-Vietnam War movements around the world, and centered increasingly around the large-scale sector in the 1960s. During the 1970s, however, as conservative enterprise unionism came to the fore in Japan, average size steadily dropped to around 165 during the 1980s when the adulation of Japanese-style management and the move away from industrial unions became more pronounced. Though unionization rates continued to fall, and a growing number of employees came to feel that they had been left behind by the bubble years, the average size of Japan's labor unions rose from a low of about 165 members in 1986 to 176 by 1996. This reflects the concerted efforts from the late 1980s to reunify the labor movement and the falling away of weaker unions as more firms were pressured by the recession.

Table 9.8 provides information on the membership of unions. Rather than the unit union counted in table 9.1, the unit of analysis in table 9.8 is the *kigyoren* (rather than its constituent unit unions). The table shows a huge disparity between unions in terms of their members and the resultant capacity to acquire a professional leadership team, to effect disputative action, and to supply leadership and other resources to its industrial federation.

The shifts in the average size of unions (in the range of 5–10 percent) over time are quite small, but are fairly significant in terms of their financial viability. One shortcoming of the enterprise union identified some time ago by Shirai (1983: 141) is its weak financial base. Based on an international comparison, Naito (1983: 146–7) argued that this is reflected in very high subscription fees paid in Japan, a factor which connects to some of the cynicism enterprise unionists feel toward their union. In recent years a number of unions have had to draw on reserves from their strike funds to finance day-to-day operations. The decision of large industrial federations such as Tekko Roren (the Japanese Federation of Steel Workers' Unions) and Denki Rengo (the Japanese Electrical, Electronic, and Information Unions) to move from annual to biennial wage negotiations is an attempt to rationalize their activities by preparing better for fewer bargaining sessions.

At the industrial level, most leaders come up from affiliated enterprise unions, and serve the industrial federation at the pleasure of their home union (and firm). Because most union leaders have to retain their employment status with their original employer in order to qualify for health and retirement benefits, they are anxious about being able to return to their firm upon completing their stint in the union movement. To have a place upon returning to their firm and to be able to draw at least part of their salary from the firm during their involvement in union affairs, the employer's support is also often necessary. Accordingly, few career union leaders at the industrial level can fully commit themselves to egalitarian causes for the more disadvantaged members of the labor force. Although there are, as Iwasaki (1993) notes, variations in this regard and some industrial federations do hire professional staff, those who have come up through the ranks from enterprise unions tend to be reined in by "the forces back home."

Rengo now attaches importance to union organization at the industrial level and recognizes the need for a critical mass of committed leaders who are financially independent. It is taking steps to train and develop such a leadership. At the same time, there is a firmly entrenched commitment to the idea that strong enterprise unions are the best guarantee that democracy will be maintained in the movement, and the move to create an independent professional leadership will take time.

A major goal in forming Rengo was to pool resources and end the forty years of continuous conservative government. Union leaders scrutinized a number of visions for achieving that aim before deciding to rebuild the Social Democratic Party of Japan (SDPJ) and the Democratic Socialist Party (DSP). Following their poor performance in the July 1992 Upper House elections, the possibility of creating an entirely new political party was also entertained. Then, as Nitta (1993) relates, the Rengo leadership was instrumental in achieving a seven-party ruling coalition following the July 1993 Lower House elections. Nitta attaches importance to (i) the decision of industrial unions to move away from single-party support, (ii) Rengo's contribution in controlling factional brawling within the

SDPJ, and (iii) its calming influence on the DSP which had considered joining the conservatives to form a different coalition. Important also was their ability to form a coalition without the Japan Communist Party (which had won only 15 of the 511 seats with 7.7 percent of the popular vote). Significant was the union movement's conscious decision to move away from left-wing ideologies and to focus on realistic democratic socialist policies to advance the welfare of the average employee.

Shinoda (1995) argues that Rengo's combined resources allowed it to develop much more sophisticated policy briefs than had previously been possible. This allowed it to have a much greater input into policy deliberations at the bureaucratic level and in the shaping of public opinion. However, as the recession extended into the 1990s, many workers were finding it difficult to make ends meet, a situation fostering cynicism and alienation among many working Japanese. While Rengo had distanced itself from the left-wing politicians, support for middle-of-the-road democratic socialism eroded and the October 1996 Lower House elections returned the main conservative party to government.

## 9.6 The enterprise union and growing diversity of needs among its members

The enterprise union's emphasis on productivity first has tended to focus attention on the material standard of living. "Wages on a par with those in Europe!" was a popular slogan in the late 1960s and early 1970s. In the mid-1970s, the demand for shorter hours of work was a demand only for the standard workweek so that more overtime pay could be earned with the same or even expanded hours. From 1975 to 1990 hours of work did not shrink.

The acquisition of basic consumer durables in the 1960s and 1970s fostered a belief that any Japanese could join the middle class simply by working hard. However, from the late 1970s there was a slowly growing realization that income differentials were widening as the mass consumer market became increasingly segmented. As workers came to build their standard of living around less tangible status symbols and style in the late 1980s, they became less interested in political activity, and the benefits of union membership came to be taken for granted. However, the ability of enterprise unions to guarantee employment came to be questioned. Instead of fighting for jobs, they often assisted management in implementing early retirement schemes and administering retrenchment packages. Once the economic bubble burst in the early 1990s and firms began to downsize, the enterprise union appeared unable or unwilling to protect the jobs of all its members. It had no answer when females were laid off, when new graduates found it hard to locate suitable employ-ment, and when those in the semi-core male labor force were transferred to smaller subcontracting firms. In the mid-1990s a growing number of middle managers found themselves unemployed, and the anxiety caused by job insecurity began to receive some prominence in the media.

Another concern among employees has been the way firms regulate their lives in terms of the life–work balance. In the heady days of the late 1980s *karoshi* (death from overwork) began to receive attention, and workers began to ask why their hours of work needed to be so long and why they had so little say in setting their own work schedules. At the same time, the economic slowdown of the 1990s allowed many employees to reflect for the first time on fatherhood and the needs of the family, and the plight of the absentee father was frequently taken up in the media. Firms responded quickly by being more flexible in determining work schedules, a move welcomed by many employees (Sato 1997a). Morishima (1997) also reported that employees took to these initiatives and appreciated having a choice between earning more income with longer hours of work and enjoying family life more fully. Embourgeoisement has been accom-panied by global flows of information and greater exposure to intellectual and ideological developments abroad. To the extent management is seen to be taking the initiative in responding to the diversification of lifestyle needs among individual employees, the value of union membership will continue to be questioned.

### 9.7    Toward new forms of unionism in Japan

The union movement has traditionally been driven by full-time male employees in Japan's large firms, predominantly in enterprise unions, but also in industrial, trade, and general unions. Departing from that pattern, several new forms of union (*shingata rodo kumiai*) have emerged over the past twenty years. Three types are discussed below. In recent years Rengo and the other national centers have promoted such unionism in an effort to stem the downward slide in unionization rates. In September 1997 Rengo announced plans to increase its membership by 1.1 million over three years. Part-timers and employees in small and medium-sized firms in medical and welfare services, financial services, construction, printing, and airport services were targeted.

### 9.7.1    *Regional unions*

The enterprise union has difficulty organizing workers without a sta-ble base in the single firm. Given that the number of *paatotaimaa* (part-timers), *arubaito* (student casuals), *friitaa* (long-term casuals), *haken rodosha* (dispatched workers), and others hired on an irregular basis has increased, Rengo focused on establishing regionally based unions (*chiiki yunion*). By June 1997, however, Rengo had managed to recruit only about 150,000 new members in 10–20 prefectures.

The union movement as a whole had not been involved in a membership drive for some time and was not well prepared for the rigors of such a campaign. Organizers had difficulty explaining the benefits of union membership to part-timers and to the dispatched workers who believed the movement primarily served the interests of Japan's core labor force. Rengo decided to fund its organization efforts more adequately and began to train organizers. It also moved to assist those looking for work by establishing a kind of job exchange for those facing unemployment and anxious about job insecurity.

### 9.7.2   Unions for managers

Under trade union legislation in Japan supervisors and other lower-level managers (*kanrishoku*) are placed outside the union's domain. A growing number of those in this stratum of management have been required to accept wage cuts, redeployment, or even "voluntary" retirement as restructuring occurs. Because voluntary retirement is seen by executives as a better outcome than having to fire employees, lower-level managers have had to put up with considerable psychological pressure and various forms of intimidation designed to push them out. Without a union, middle-aged managers have become easy targets.

In December 1993 the Tokyo Union of Managers (Tokyo Kanrishoku Yunion) was formed by fifteen individuals. By mid-1997 it had 700 members (Anonymous 1996a). Branches were formed in Nagoya (1995) and in the Osaka–Kobe–Kyoto area (Anonymous 1997b). Their most important activity has been the "labor hot line" for those who feel their rights are being abused by management (Shidara, Ito, and Kawahito 1997). The involvement of the Nihon Rodo Bengo Dan (Labor Lawyers' Association of Japan) has been critical. During ten days in 1995, 1,700 calls were received from people seeking advice about their rights at work. Two-thirds of them concerned deteriorating working conditions owing to restructuring; the other third concerned workplace intimidation designed to induce resignation or the acceptance of a major relocation within the firm. Calls from women and young workers increased over time. Half of the callers were managers; the other half were ordinary employees seeking independent job advice before entering the lower ranks of management. Calls came from large and small firms. The Tokyo Union of Managers has been critical of the enterprise union's "excessive" concern with cooperation to achieve corporate goals benefiting a small group of employees. It plans to broaden its activities and to become a general union seeking to free individual employees from the social confines of the firm.

Rengo's think tank recently surveyed 2,000 office staff (of whom about 50 percent were departmental and divisional heads). It indicated that more persons were having to negotiate their working conditions individually as annual salary systems were introduced more widely. Many, particularly managers seconded to other firms, felt that they could not depend on the enterprise union to assist in those negotiations. As the line between employees and the lower level of management blurs further, there will likely be more pressure to revise the trade union law which currently places lower-level managers outside the domain of the labor union (Anonymous 1997d and 1997e).

### 9.7.3    Unions for women

Women constitute another group of employees not well served by the male-dominated enterprise union, and in February 1995 six women formed the Tokyo Women's Union (Josei Yunion Tokyo). Its membership had grown to 250 by May 1997, and included women aged from 20 to 70. Its centrally located office is a place for women (members and non-members alike) to chat and to support each other. In its first two years the union advised about 1,000 women on retrenchment, forced retirement owing to maternity and childcare commitments, sexual harassment and other forms of intimidation, shortfalls in pay and pay cuts, and difficulties in taking annual leave (Shidara, Ito, and Kawahito 1997).

The first year of the women's union was an eye-opener for many of the union's members. For the first time they studied Japan's labor laws, and many engaged in some form of bargaining with management. They also received advice from the Labor Lawyers' Association of Japan. Ms. Nakano Mami, a lawyer assisting the union, commented that male–female wage differentials widened over the ten years following the implementation of Japan's Employment Equal Opportunity Law in April 1986 (Anonymous 1996b). In 1994 twelve women in Osaka formed their own union and obtained a court ruling that male–female wage discrimination was unlawful (Anonymous 1994b). Upset that their enterprise union would not concern itself with the dismissal of non-regular (women) workers, five women working in the Osaka office of Japan Railway Shikoku formed their own minority enterprise union and obtained a court ruling that overturned the dismissals (Anonymous 1994a).

## 9.8    Toward a more ambivalent appraisal of enterprise unionism

From the late 1940s to the Miike dispute in 1960, unions were concerned primarily with the democratization and modernization of Japanese society and with the need to establish an independent consciousness in workers (Hidaka 1984: 21–2). Such goals were conceived primarily in American and Western European terms, and a number of "feudalistic" aspects were identified by Okochi (1952: 9; 1954: 17–18), Sumiya (1950), and others who felt that agricultural workers working seasonally in urban industries were unable to articulate their interests vis-à-vis management. They directed attention to client–patron relations in the labor market, the failure of the union movement to achieve true parity with management, and the segmentation of the labor force.

In the early 1960s many came to argue that familial relations at work were integral to the maintenance of social cohesion and high levels of motivation and commitment within the firm. This shift was reinforced by the growing ideological concern with economic development. Matsushima (1962) concluded that the Japanese approach to employee relations had injected certainty into the hand-to-mouth existence of many workers. Hazama (1964) argued that the ability of managers to transplant the vocabulary of the family to the firm produced high levels of motivation and commitment among Japanese workers.

In the literature highlighting the dynamics of the internal labor market in Japan's large firms (Shirai 1980; Koike 1977; Koshiro 1982a and 1995) and Japanese-style management (Tsuda 1980 and 1981) as mechanisms promoting both efficiency and democratic involvement, the enterprise union was described as a support for the internal labor market and the development of the high skill levels and technological sophistication among employees. By the late 1980s many were portraying human resource management practices in Japan as postmodern or post-Fordist (Womack *et al.* 1990; Florida and Kenny 1993; and Coriat 1992). These assessments tended to overlook many of the tradeoffs built into the Japanese approach to enterprise unionism. When the economic bubble burst, some of its demerits became more apparent. Although the material standard of living had improved considerably over the previous forty years, it was argued that the system had still not produced a satisfactory lifestyle for ordinary employees. Housing was still inadequate and expensive; hours of work were seen as being excessively long and regimented. As attention shifted from lean production and product processes (e.g. in terms of zero defects, the large number of product lines, QC circles and the *kanban* system), the "real" labor process at many firms became more apparent. For many work was characterized by a considerably weakened sense of solidarity among employees, by overwork, and by the failure of the enterprise union to curb excessive authoritarianism at work.

### 9.9    Future directions for the union movement in Japan

The future of unions in Japan has by no means been cast. Chapter 7 stated that a vacuum in economic leadership in Japan has left the door open for labor to return as a significant actor on the national stage. In some ways the competitiveness of the Japanese economy in the 1970s and 1980s tended to vindicate the enterprise union, lending it a *raison d'être* and its proponents a false sense of security. Seen as universal best practice overseas, certain aspects of "Japanese-style management" (e.g. outsourcing, just-in-time, enterprise bargaining) had come to be widely accepted by managements abroad as part of the global drive to improve competitiveness. In the 1990s, however, global changes were accompanied by a renewed push for international competitiveness that has taken work organization far beyond the horizons of Japanese-style management. In this context the future of the Japanese union movement will be shaped by (i) the dynamic interaction of the peculiarly Japanese social milieu and ethics and the trends associated with global capitalism, (ii) the power relationship between labor and management, both in the political/organizational strength of the union movement vis-à-vis management bodies and in the labor market, and (iii) the changing consciousness of Japan's employees.

While some attention must be paid to changes in technology and to the structure of the economy as a contributing factor, the movement of workers from one industry to another does not appear to have been the major cause of the drop in unionization rates. However, technology has had an impact across the full range of industries in terms of workways and the nature of the labor market, which is now becoming more segmented with the demand for increased flexibility. This has placed increased pressure on the enterprise union (i) to broaden its membership to incorporate many non-core employees, (ii) to examine a broader range of issues relevant to the peripheral labor force as the core labor force becomes more diverse, and (iii) to move from the enterprise base to a *keiretsu* or other multi-firm basis for defining its membership.

The cultural/ideological shifts accompanying embourgeoisement, the restratification of Japanese society, and higher levels of affluence and education are affecting (i) notions of what the good life (the desired standard or mode of living) is, especially in terms of the role of male household heads within the family, and (ii) the sense of fairness or social equity.

Left-wing unionism has given way to more "mature" or "sophisticated" dialogue between labor and management. Nakamura's case study (1996) of the privatization of Nippon Telegraph and Telephone Public Corporation in 1985 provides an optimistic assessment of how such dialogue has developed out of "economic necessity." The cooperation of enterprise unions has often facilitated the successful implementation of "voluntary" retirement programs in many companies. How this will affect the awareness of the cleavages that stratify Japanese society remains to be seen.

The need to be tentative here is underlined by the complexity of political alignments at the present time. How the labor movement will ultimately align and interface with the multitude of political parties is not clear. During the 1990s unions have tended to support whoever supports labor, an approach that is unlikely to produce a cohesive political force for the union movement.

The internal dynamic of the union movement itself is between different levels of organization. National centers have the highest profile in the national political arena and will ultimately shape the images that ordinary Japanese have of unionism. The movement as a whole must eventually be seen as legitimate in philosophical or trend terms if ordinary employees are going to step forward to join. The industrial federation will likely continue to play a major role in setting standards and norms for working conditions. The enterprise union is likely to retain its prime interest in the implementation of work rules and in the regulation of work practices on the shop floor. Here a tradeoff exists between the concern for social justice and that for productivity when progressing from the national center to the enterprise union.

Despite the Union Identification Movement, which sought to change symbols used by the unions to foster and reinforce the identity of union members with the union movement, as a means of broadening the base for enterprise unionism in Japan (Fujimura 1997: 305–11), many of the more recently formed unions with different ideas about organizational structures will continue to be driven from outside the enterprise union by the national center or by groups emerging spontaneously from the grassroots. One difficulty has been that the Union Identification Movement has come down from the top, and many ordinary workers still have difficulty identifying with the union movement as a whole. The commitment of many aristocratic enterprise unionists to the movement is likely to be questioned. Change to the enterprise union is likely to come only if professional leadership is injected at the enterprise level and the core labor force fractures.

In this regard Kawanishi (1992a: 423–40) and Mouer (1992: xxv–xxvi) have noted the functional specialization that occurred with dual unionism in the past. In the 1960s and 1970s competing enterprise unions existed at up to 20 percent of Japan's unionized firms. One was a left-wing union concerned largely with social justice issues. The other was a conservative union concerned mainly with productivity issues. Each competed to keep its set of interests at the fore. While such competition may have lessened the political clout of the union movement as a whole, it also meant that unions worked harder to do what they are established to do: represent the interests of the workers as effectively as possible. The emphasis on reunification has seen many competing unions merge. However, the expected gains at the ballot box have not materialized, and union membership has fallen. Moreover, though competing unions may have merged, in many unions a delicate balance has been maintained between union members who support the social justice thrust and those who support the "productivity first" approach. Perhaps one lesson is that to be viable unions will have to balance both interests.

Considering the dynamics at work with the deregulation of internal and external labor markets, the functional approach might lead in other directions, with one type of union evolving out of the enterprise union as we know it today. Drawn largely from the elite employees in career tracks leading to managerial positions, this type of union might function as a fairly closed masonic-type organization. A second type might include those currently in the permanent core labor force who have highly specialized skills that have immediate, but not necessarily long-term, utility for a firm. Should such employees end up on medium-term contracts in the future, they could conceivably organize into strong professional, guild-type unions and perhaps be national in scope. A third type would revolve around those currently in the peripheral labor force and might be a kind of general union organized on an industry or regional basis. Its members might well develop a proletarian-type consciousness. The first type would be most concerned with productivity, the third type with social justice issues. To constitute a viable union movement, however, some sort of accord would need to be reached between these groupings with a negotiated balance being struck between the push for further improvements in productivity and the interest in social justice. The formation of unions to represent in a collective manner would have huge social and political implications. However, a union movement without a vision of labor process at the meso level will remain weak. It is likely that the trend toward greater social inequality will continue and release another set of dynamic forces. Despite prophecies about the end of ideology and the end of history, there are still a number of chapters to be written before the story of Japanese capitalism is completed.

# 10 Management organizations and the interests of employers

## 10.1 The sparse literature on management organizations in Japan

A number of organizations represent the interests of employers. It is our impression that the academic research on management organizations has been limited compared with that on labor organizations. Some time ago Aonuma (1965) analyzed the socioeconomic background of senior management in Japan's large firms. Mannari (1974) followed with a similar study but did not comment or build upon Aonuma's findings. This style of research was later picked up by Koike and Watanabe (1979), who stirred a vigorous debate on how open Japan's large firms were to making managers out of graduates from Japan's less prestigious universities (see Iwauchi 1980 and Takeuchi and Aso 1981). In this fact there is a certain paradox. On the one hand, there are many faculties of business studies (*kei-ie gakubu*) in Japan, but no faculty of labor studies (*rodo gakubu*). At the same time there is a sociology of labor (*rodo shakaigaku*), but no sociology of management (*kei-ei shakaigaku*). Over twenty years ago Hazama (1981) commented on this and pushed to establish a sociology of management. His view was that the study of industrial relations required both a sociology of labor and a sociology of management as subdisciplines.

Despite Hazama's pitch for such a sociology, the focus of studies in the sociology of work has tended to be heavily on the side of labor. Books on the sociology of work in Japan (e.g. Inagami 1981; Inoue 1997; Kawanishi 2001) have tended to describe and to analyze workers in their organizations, but have overlooked the other side of the power dynamics that determine working conditions. Although Shunto was a union-led initiative to concentrate collective bargaining into the spring months each year, the bargaining occurs between labor *and* management at the firm level, and the "battleground" is often prepared at the national level and the tone set by early skirmishes between the union movement's national centers and their constituent industrial federations, on the one hand, and management's national center and its constituent employer associations

229

Table 10.1 *References to unions and management associations in the index to Takanashi Akira's* Shunto Wage Offensive

| | Unions | | Management associations | |
|---|---|---|---|---|
| | Number of organizations cited | Total number of places referred to in the book | Number of organizations cited | Total number of places referred to in the book |
| Mention of organization at the national level | 18 | 36 | 4 | 10 |
| Mention of organization at the industrial level | 25 | 51 | 1 | 4 |
| Mention of organization at the international level | 2 | 4 | | |
| Total | 45 | 91 | 5 | 14 |

*Source:* Compiled by the authors from Takanashi (2002), pp. 123–8.

at the industrial level, on the other. Much of the writing about Shunto, however, focuses on the role of the unions. A brief look through the index of a recent book about the Spring Wage Offensive (Takanashi 2002), for example, shows that the references to unions far outweigh those to management groups (table 10.1). Particularly interesting is the number of entries referring to the internal workings of the unions (eight) compared with those for the internal affairs of management groups (none).

This impression is further confirmed by a look at the encyclopedic surveys of issues defining debate in Japan at the end of each year. Edited to reflect the issues currently picked up in the media, the annual compendium for 2003 of *Nihon no Ronten* (Bungei Shunju 2002) consisted of 134 essays on the most important topics/issues defining Japanese society at the end of 2003. The articles were sorted into eighty major categories from politics, employment relations, and America's role in the world to sports and culture. Not one dealt with the implications of the merger of Japan's two most influential employers' federations in May 2002.

It should be noted that there is a large supply of books on *kei-eigaku* (management studies) and on *nihongata* or *nihonteki kei-ei* (Japanese-style management). However, Hachiyo Publishing's series of over ten volumes on management, including Inaba's *The Firm in Society* (2002) and Futagami's *Enterprise and the Economy* (2000), make no mention of the three or four national centers that have been instrumental in setting the agenda for national policy affecting how work is organized in

Japan. The same is true of Mineruva's series on management studies (e.g. Kataoka and Shinozaka 1998). Even when the focus is on the future of management in Japan at the beginning of the twenty-first century (e.g. as in Takagi 2000 or Minami and Kameda 2000), the role or contribution of national or regional management associations in the running of Japan's firms is not mentioned. One can conclude that *kei-eigaku* in Japan is concerned wholly with what happens within the firm at the micro level. Having noted the sparse attention given to management associations in the currently available literature on work organization in Japan, this chapter provides a brief overview of how management is linked at the meso level.

Some time ago Hazama (1981: 8) proffered several reasons for the relative absence of research on the associations representing corporate Japan. One was that management organizations are much more tightly structured than their labor counterparts and more closed to outside scrutiny. Japan's unions have depended on a certain openness to mass participation, and their *raison d'être* is in democratically representing a diverse cross-section of workers. Management forms a much more cohesive group and may perhaps have a certain discipline that accompanies the sharing of a common corporate culture and a sense of elitist purpose. To borrow a term first made popular by Mills (1956), this allows for management to function around a range of "tacit agreements" and to debate many critical issues while keeping differences "in-house." Another factor cited by Hazama is the greater willingness of unions to make information available to the public through their publications. To some extent this has been necessary in order to involve a wide range of intellectuals in various study groups and research projects (many on a voluntary basis) and to form joint fronts on specific issues with various citizens' groups. Union activities have involved large numbers of people, thereby resulting in many of the union's activities being more newsworthy in the mainstream media than a small committee reporting on its meeting with government officials to hammer out small points of policy.

The legal status of unions also draws attention to their affairs. The Trade Union Law gives workers certain rights to behave collectively, but also regulates what unions can and cannot do. It provides a yardstick against which to assess their performance. Management, however, has more of a free hand. The way management might associate for mutual benefit is not touched upon in the law (except in the 1954 legislation that provides guidelines for the Japanese Chamber of Commerce and Industry). Generally, management groups have been able to invoke the norms of privacy to shroud their discussions and activities. This can be seen not only in management's dealings with unions, but also in its reaction to concerns about pollution in the 1970s (cf. Ui 1968 and 1972), in the practice of collusion in contract bidding (McCormack 1996), in the political contributions by specific firms to specific politicians or bureaucrats (a matter constantly reported as scandalous in the print media), and in the general lack of transparency in the overextension of credit (i.e. bad loans) in the banking sector.

## 10.2    Toward a sociology of management

"Management organization" is a direct translation of the Japanese term *kei-eisha dantai*. Another term, *shiyosha dantai* (employers' associations), is also used. The latter term is generally more inclusive of a broader range of firms and tends to refer to the owners or entrepreneurs who are ultimately responsible for the running of the firm and guarding its assets against the demands of labor. In this sense the term *shiyosha* refers somewhat loosely to Japan's capitalists (*shihonka*), but without the class connotations associated with the Marxist academic tradition. As such it focuses attention on the wage-for-labor nexus and on the firm and its owners in terms of how paid labor is utilized to generate profits. The term *kei-eisha* refers more broadly to the managers or executives whose responsibilities extend over a wider range of concerns than just managing human resources and generating profits. Although the adjectives "top," "middle," and "lower" have been used in English to suggest that there are three categories of management, in Japanese Hazama (1997a: 130–63) distinguishes between *kei-eisha* as directors and executive officers at the top of a corporate organization, *kanrishoku* (administrative officers) as equivalent to middle management in English nomenclature, and *kantokusha* (supervisors) as lower-level management. This is consistent with the practice of *kantokusha* belonging to Japan's enterprise unions, and the recognition given to *kanrishoku* as being in a kind of no-man's land – neither in the ranks of the *kei-eisha* nor in the union.

In an earlier book Hazama (1981) wrote about *shiyosha dantai*, but later called for a sociology of *kei-eisha* – a strategy that would allow for a more integrated approach to the study of decision-making in Japan's larger organizations. This move suggests a subtle distinction in usage between *kei-eisha* who work as a team of *shiyosha* collectively fulfilling a range of functions and the small entrepreneur (*ji-eigyosha*) who as a *shiyosha* is the single manager of a small company and covers by himself or herself all of the functions from strategic planning, marketing, and purchasing to the management of a handful of employees.

Hazama's sociology of management incorporated the study of management ideology and behavior both within the firm and in various management associations. Hazama tended to see the structuring of work as the outcome of power relations between labor and management. From his viewpoint those relations were determined largely, though not wholly, by the power internally generated out of the ideology and behavior of those in each grouping. Accordingly, for Hazama the study of industrial relations and employment relations constituted an overarching discipline that was concerned primarily with the resultant structural arrangements. It built on the integration of the two sociologies – a sociology of labor and a sociology of management – and incorporated research on labor law, social policy, and the politics of government. Within that larger context this chapter focuses on management ideology and behavior at the meso level by considering how management is organized vertically and horizontally beyond the confines of the firm.

## 10.3    Enterprise groupings and the vertical integration of management

Many of Japan's firms are vertically grouped together in one of two ways. The *keiretsu* group is a tier of contracting and subcontracting firms. They have been conspicuous in manufacturing. The interaction among *keiretsu* firms is based on unilateral hierarchical linkages rather than on mutual interaction. The *keiretsu* reduce the fixed labor costs associated with the manufacture of goods that are only assembled at the final stages by workers in the larger firms at the top of the subcontracting pyramids. Those lower down the hierarchy are often played off against each other, and contractors lower costs by shifting them further down the subcontracting chain. The success of just-in-time schemes has contributed to the maintenance of considerable differences in working conditions between those in Japan's large firms and those in smaller firms. The pressures felt in subcontracting firms and the exploitative dimensions built into *keiretsu* are well documented in business novels (for a full list see Tao 1996). However, the *keiretsu* have enhanced the flow of capital, technology, and personnel while also contributing to the trickling down of industrial standards, particularly in terms of quality control and the discipline associated with professional work habits.

Another type of enterprise grouping, the *kigyo shudan*, has worked to maintain linkages among Japan's larger firms that were affiliated with the *zaibatsu* groups in prewar Japan. After the war, the affiliated companies regrouped around a number of financial institutions. Six major enterprise groups were commonly recognized in the late 1990s (table 10.2). In 1994 these six groups accounted for about 15 percent of Japan's corporately owned capital and roughly 20 percent of net profits (down from around 24 percent in 1993 but up from 12 percent in 1988). In the late

Table 10.2 *Major enterprise groupings in Japan in 1995*

| Grouping | Number of companies in the grouping | Name of regular presidents' meeting | Main bank | Main trading company |
|---|---|---|---|---|
| Mitsui | 27 | Nimokukai (October 1961) | Sakura | Mitsui Bussan |
| Mitsubishi | 28 | Kin-yokai (1954) | Mitsubishi | Mitsubishi Shoji |
| Sumitomo | 20 | Hakusuikai (April 1951) | Sumitomo | Sumitomo Shoji |
| Fuyo | 29 | Fuyokai (January 1966) | Fuji | Marubeni |
| Sanwa | 44 | Sansuikai (February 1967) | Sanwa | Nichimen Nissho Iwai |
| Ichikan | 48 | Sankinkai (January 1978) | Daiichi Kangyo | Itochu Nissho Iwai |

*Source:* Hazama (1997a), pp. 118–19; and Toyo Keizai Shimpo Sha (2000), pp. 10–11.

1990s they did that with only 3.6 percent of Japan's labor force, down from just over 4 percent at the beginning of the 1990s (Hazama 1997b: 121; Toyo Keizai Shimpo Sha 2000: 13). These groupings each have at least one affiliated firm in each important manufacturing industry. However, each group extends far beyond the major corporations that form its core. For example, Toray belongs to the Mitsui Group of twenty-seven companies, but heads a group of 204 other companies, most of which are 80–100 percent owned by Toray. Each of the nearly 200 companies in the Big Six controls a large number of subsidiaries and other related companies. The empires extend into every region and nearly all industrial sectors.

To some extent each grouping functions as a very large diversified corporation. The presidents of the major companies meet on a regular basis, and in many of these groups there are separate regular meetings between vice-presidents, planning executives, public relations officers, and those looking after other important functions. Because of their mutual holdings of stocks, and tight interfirm networks, the firms in each group have worked to cross-subsidize each other. One result has been the diffusion of a certain standard of treatment across the group in terms of working conditions and personnel practices, so that many typical male employees could identify themselves with a larger grouping as a Mitsubishi or Sumitomo man.

Toyo Keizai Shimpo Sha (2000) lists about twenty-five other enterprise groupings. Most are concentrated in specific industries. They include Toyota (with 200 firms), Matsushita (281 companies, including 42 manufacturing companies and 85 retail companies), and Sony (1,174 subsidiaries, including 48 in related manufacturing). Kojima (2000) has examined how the internet and the spread of IT are resulting in the creation of new networks and new businesses. Biggu Pen (2002) has taken a different approach, looking at fifty-seven industries and identifying thirty-five industrially based groupings without specifically highlighting the Big Six. Their presentation suggests that there are other ways of thinking about enterprise groupings and that the groupings are multidimensional and not just vertical in the strict sense.

## 10.4    Management organizations and the horizontal integration of management at the national level

After the war the main goal of the Occupation was democratization. The immediate strategy was to strengthen the independence of Japan's ordinary workers both individually and collectively. It did this through land reform, the dissolution of the *zaibatsu* and the purging of key industrial leaders, and the legalization of labor unions. It also disbanded the powerful Japan Federation of Economic Organizations (Nippon Keizai Renmeikai, formed in 1922), the socially influential Industrial Club of Japan (Nihon Kogyo Kurabu, formed in 1919), the Chamber of Commerce (Shoho Kaigisho, formed in 1878), the Industrial Patriotic Society (Sangyo Hokokukai, formed in 1939), the *zaibatsu* cliques, and other prewar organizations controlling economic activity and work organization in ways directly contributing to the war effort. One outcome was the sudden jump in Japan's unionization rates as shown in table 9.1. The story of Japan's management associations in the postwar years (see table 10.3) is largely one of their efforts to regroup, to reassert their control over Japan's economic agendas, and to limit the influence of the union movement.

The first national organization to form after the war was the Keizai Doyukai (the Japan Association of Economic Executives). Formed in April 1946, Doyukai consisted of a new generation of leaders. Able to mouth the Occupation's vocabulary of democracy, these leaders were more progressive than their elders and were able to see the sense of having a more open society. Their charter (*kaiin kiyaku*) explicitly limited membership to progressive businessmen (Koga 2000: 266). Committed to building a new Japan, they soon gained the support of the Occupation authorities. Many of its members were open to reading both the Marxist-inspired literature being produced by academics at Japan's leading universities in the years immediately after the war and the literature on the virtues of democracy being produced in America and Western Europe. In the 1950s and 1960s the Association functioned as a study group, and its members produced a number of important position papers which provided visions for a democratic approach to business management and industrial relations.

The organization gave younger leaders an opportunity to extend their networking skills before moving on to Nikkeiren and Keidanren, the two major employers' federations. Koga (2000: 262–70) provided a long list of individuals who first headed Doyukai or had important positions there before becoming top leaders in the other two senior organizations. In Doyukai they were trained to think about business activities within a larger social framework. Koga concluded that Doyukai lost much of its early influence as a progressive force as its members aged and graduated to leadership roles in Keidanren and Nikkeiren. More significantly he points to Doyukai's loss of mission – its early commitment to an intellectually and academically oriented concern with the future of Japan as a socioeconomic entity – as it evolved into being a kind of holding pen for prospective business leaders.

The second of these changes may have resulted from the institutionalization of the *keiretsu* and the way the business world functioned. The result was a degree of certainty that brought with it a fairly clear idea of how a businessman's career would fit into the overall picture. This may have resulted in a certain overall conservatism. Many employees became strongly attached to the goals of their firm and did not cultivate the ability to incorporate either their family or the wider community into their thinking. The weeding-out of left-wing socialist-inspired educators from Japan's top universities also resulted in university graduates not being challenged to think critically about issues of social justice, the environment, and social organization outside the firm. This is not to say that this generation would oppose moves to change gender relations or the role of newcomers in Japanese society. It does, however, underline the absence of a drive to proactively and creatively explore alternative ways to organize social affairs and to take the lead in formulating new visions for Japanese society. On that basis Koga (2000) argued that Doyukai was seen by many as having outlived its usefulness. He concludes his discussion (pp. 269–70) by considering whether the appointment of Kobayashi Yotaro as its new leader (*daihyo kanji*) in April 1999 would give Doyukai renewed momentum. Kobayashi was an outspoken graduate of Keio and Pennsylvania universities with extensive experience in

America. He is the first head of a foreign-owned corporation to step into that position.

Immediately after the end of the war, in September 1945, government leaders took the initiative to call together leaders from Japan's main pre-war business organizations. One result was the creation of a new organization, Keizai Dantai Rengokai (Keidanren), initially as a body to facilitate communication among the doyens of the prewar groups. Although some of the wartime leadership had been purged by the SCAP directives, those in the second line moved quickly to form the Keizai Dantai Rengokai to fill the vacuum. They offered the new organization as the most effective means by which the GHQ could communicate with Japan's new industrial leaders. With the idea that it would be a body independent of the government and the old *zaibatsu* groupings, Occupation authorities approved the launching of Keidanren in August 1946. Following a good deal of jostling, Keidanren came to be the national center representing large-scale manufacturing and heavy industry, the sector that became the driving force behind Japan's rapid economic growth in the 1960s and 1970s.

Over time Keidanren came to be known for running the corporate office of Japan Incorporated. Its strength came from its ability to mobilize committees of businessmen from Japan's major firms to dovetail into the work of the government ministries (particularly those responsible for finances and industrial and trade policy). It supplied a constant stream of able leaders to participate on a wide range of government consultative councils (*shingikai*), and the term *minryo* (the private sector and the bureaucracy) came to be used as a label designating the close working relationship between the two groups. In the 1990s Keidanren turned its attention to business ethics in order to bolster the image of the business community following a spate of scandals and spectacular bankruptcies involving prominent firms following the collapse of the economic bubble in the early 1990s. Toyota Sho-ichiro headed the organization from 1994 to 1998, and actively promoted the development of a charter of business ethics and corporate responsibility. The charter publicly underlined a commitment to the social good and to transparency. At the beginning of the twenty-first century words such as "transparency," "restructuring," and "disclosure" appeared frequently in media discussions concerning ways to move the economy forward.

In regional Japan leaders of commerce and local industry continued to use the wartime organizational framework of local chambers of commerce and industry (*shokokaigisho*) to communicate among themselves regarding issues of common interest. In September 1946 the Law Concerning Commercial, Industrial and Economic Associations was repealed, and

Table 10.3 *An overview of five major employers' federations, 1950–2003*

| | Keizai Doyukai | Keizai Dantai Rengokai | Nihon Shoko Kaigisho | Nihon Kei-eisha Dantai Renmei | Nippon Keizai Dantai Rengokai |
|---|---|---|---|---|---|
| Acronym | Doyukai | Keidanren | Nissho | Nikkeiren | Nippon Keidanren |
| Common English rendition | Japan Association of Corporate Executives | Japan Federation of Economic Organizations | Japan Chamber of Commerce and Industry | Japan Federation of Employers' Associations | Japan Business Federation |
| Dates established | April 1946 | August 1946 → May 2002 → | November 1946 | April 1948 → May 2002→ | May 2002 → |
| Membership criteria | Individuals (managers, officials of economic federations, lawyers, accountants) who have a progressive outlook | | Incorporated companies and organizations and owners of smaller firms | | Companies become affiliated through belonging to industrial associations (*gyokai*) or regionally based associations (*chikibetsu keizai dantai*) |
| Number of members | 1,321 persons (July 2002) | | 527 chambers with 150,000 members | | 1,541 companies, 127 industrial federations and 54 regional associations |
| Financial obligation of members | Individual subscription | | Varies according to the capitalized value of the member | | Affiliation fee depends on the size of the firm, ranging from ¥3–5 to 100 million |

| Major functions | To consider the role of business in socio-economic development | To represent the interests of large manufacturing firms in the context of national/state interest | To look after interests of the commercial sector in the context of liberalizing a rather complex and protected distribution system | To consolidate the views of affiliated employers' associations in recommending employment policy and in countering the influence of unions | This body was formed to combine the functions of Keidanren and Nikkeiren |
|---|---|---|---|---|---|
| | (progressive in principle) | (conservative) | (conservative) | (conservative) | |
| Industrial-level organizations | None | | None | | 127 industrial federations are affiliated, but no special organizational arrangement within Nippon Keidanren |
| Regionally based organizations | None | | 527 chambers around the country and overseas | | 54 regional associations with a special organization of association heads |
| Annual budget in 2002 (¥million) | 878 | | 3,569 | | 3,641 |
| Amount of budget per member (¥) | 664,648 | | 22,306 | | 2,362,751 |

*Source:* Information publicly made available by each of the organizations.

the involvement of the state in their affairs (which accompanied the special legal protection they enjoyed) came to an end. With a new spirit of independence, the local chambers joined together in November 1946 to form a national body to coordinate their activities. The organization was later to be once more defined by legislation in 1954 (the Shoko Kaigi Sho Ho).

Somewhat delayed was the formation of an employers' association to coordinate the interests of employers vis-à-vis labor at the national level. Initially concerned that such moves would undermine its efforts to strengthen the union movement, Occupation authorities came to appreciate how radical some unions had become and to see value in having an employers' organization to deal with labor and employment relations. Formed in August 1948, mainly as a body to deal with Japan's militant union movement and the forces for socialism in Japan, Nikkeiren fitted in with the reversal of American policies for the democratization of Japan and its decision to constrain the union movement and give priority to Japan's economic recovery as part of its larger strategy to contain communism in Asia.

By 1950 the lines were drawn between labor and management in Japan. By the late 1980s management had a dominant say in the nation's economic affairs, a position further reinforced in May 2002 when Nikkeiren and Keidanren merged to form Nippon Keidanren. An overview of the four postwar associations is provided in table 10.3. A quick glance at the table reveals that Nissho is the most broadly based organization, with 527 regional affiliated offices (including a large number of overseas branches) and 160,000 members, a number equivalent to about 2.58 percent of all enterprises in Japan and nearly 10 percent of those with five or more employees (based on the figures in table 10.3). With 1,233 affiliated companies, Nippon Keidanren represents only a minuscule percentage of Japan's 6.2 million enterprises and only 2.53 percent of those with 100 or more employees. Doyukai's membership consists of individual business leaders.

## 10.5    Networked families and the *keibatsu*

The relative power of management is enhanced by another set of networks based on horizontal ties: interpersonal relationships that are facilitated by family connections, sometimes referred to as *keibatsu*. Many studies have described how Japan's elites are linked through a complex series of marriages. Hazama (1997b: 142–3) provides a two-page diagram detailing the mosaic of intermarriages that connected the founder of Matsushita Electric with an extensive range of other influential individuals (including

Table 10.4 *Distribution of firms in Japan by firm size, July 1999*

| Firm size (number of employees) | Number of firms | Percentage |
|---|---|---|
| 0 | 2,062,858 | 33.25 |
| 1–4 | 2,367,874 | 38.17 |
| 5–29 | 1,511,460 | 24.37 |
| 3–99 | 212,272 | 3.42 |
| 100–499 | 45,063 | 0.73 |
| 500+ | 3,722 | 0.06 |
| Total | 6,203,249 | 100.00 |

*Source:* Kosei Rodo Sho Daijin Kanbo Tokei Joho Bu (2002a), pp. 50–1.

the head of the Bank of Japan, a member of the Upper House of parliament, and the presidents of Sanyo Electric, Suntory, and many other corporations in Japan). The family tree also reveals that many of Matsushita's companies have been run by relatives of one sort or another. Kitagawa and Kainuma's study (1985: 142–3) of elites provides a similar mapping of another intertwined lineage connecting through an array of interlocking marriages several postwar prime ministers and industrialists at the top of Japan's business world. It is generally accepted that these networks and alliances have facilitated the formation and maintenance of the types of tacit agreement associated with the real "behind-the-scenes" decision-making of elites around the world.

## 10.6 Management in Japan's smaller firms and the Shoko Kaigisho

Management of Japan's smaller firms with, say, fewer than 100 employees (which, as noted in chapter 5, engage the majority of Japan's workforce: see table 10.4) is generally not represented by the major *kei-eisha dantai*. Like most of their employees, the vast majority of those owning and operating Japan's small businesses are left without adequate representation, especially at the meso level. This is not to say that owners of small businesses and their management teams do not belong to associations. Apart from belonging to a local chamber of commerce and industry, many small entrepreneurs affiliate with the Japan Association of Small and Medium-Sized Businesses (Nihon Chusho Kigyo Dantai Renmei), an organization which makes representations to the Office for Small and

Medium-Sized Businesses (Chusho Kigyo Cho) and other sections of the government. Such groups have not always effectively protected the interests of small firms from the rationalism associated with the economies of scale enjoyed by Japan's larger enterprises. In the 1960s and 1970s small retailers obtained legislation limiting the inroads of supermarkets and other large-scale high-volume chains with much smaller margins and much more competitive prices. By the 1980s, however, the legal protection they enjoyed had gradually eroded, and many small retailers now face very severe competition from the larger players. The political clout of small entrepreneurs is more often seen in terms of local politics and is often consolidated through organizations such as local shopping arcade associations (*shotenkai*) found throughout Japan. While local associations with an industrially defined basis may be considered as *shiyosha dantai*, they are not usually considered as *kei-eisha dantai* unless they are organized at the regional level, and the term *shiyosha dantai* is not generally used to include Rotary Clubs or similar associations in which local businessmen, shopkeepers, and other professionals often discuss their "business."

## 10.7    Nikkeiren's half century

The change in US policy in the late 1940s allowed management to take the offensive in the struggle to reestablish its authority in the workplace, to expel left-wing radicals from its workforce, and to move the fundamentals of employment relations negotiations from the industrial level back to the enterprise. With the tacit support of the Occupation authorities, the first "red purge" was carried out in 1950. A decade later a second clampdown on radical unionism resulted in the prolonged struggle with and ultimate defeat of the union movement at the Mitsui Miike coalfields in 1960.

The years between 1960 and the mid-1970s were characterized by the steady introduction of American management philosophies, a brief interlude with an emphasis on Japanese-derived solutions in the 1980s, and then a further borrowing from the US as the recession of the 1990s set in and a growing number of managers came to accept that ultimately globalization would be driven by the adoption of American standards and approaches in dealing with market forces. A careful analysis of the push and shove between labor and management over the first four postwar decades would reveal that the tensions were mainly about the union's push for greater distributive justice and management's emphasis on the need to be internationally competitive (i.e. more efficient by containing labor costs and generating more surplus that could be invested back into the operations of the firm).

The emphasis on pay according to the immediate livelihood needs of the employee, as imposed by Japan's powerful industrial unions in the late 1940s, gave way to seniority wages and a longer-term view of life-cycle needs in the 1950s. In the 1960s the push was to adjoin criteria linked to the employee's job designation and qualifications. By the 1980s payments according to performance-linked task assignments had become widespread and in the 1990s companies began to introduce schemes that would more tightly tie wage income to actual output over the short term. As Kusuda (2000) describes in some detail, the evolution of the wage system was an incremental process whereby new determinants were added on to an existing system, thereby reducing the relative importance of previous criteria over time.

The ongoing concern of Nikkeiren with high wages is evidenced in a series of reports and pronouncements. One of the best known is *Japanese Management for the New Age* (Nihon Kei-eisha Dantai Renmei, 1995). Although Nikkeiren has for some time emphasized the necessity of trading off job security for higher wages, in this report it underlined the high fixed costs associated with having a large permanent labor force. The report suggested that it was time to disaggregate the core labor force as it was then conceived in most of Japan's established corporations. More recently a similar line has been publicly pushed by Fukuoka Michio, one of Nikkeiren's executive directors. He has argued that Japan's economic woes resulted from a loss of international competitiveness owing to excessively high wage rates and too much of a commitment to protective or safety-net provisions. He pushed for the deregulation of the labor market, greater use of part-time and other casual labor, and a shift from pay linked to age, position, and other personal traits to pay for work actually accomplished, stating that such a move would help to eliminate discrimination based on gender and age (*SRN*, 13 May 2002: 3).

Two reports released in 2002 corroborate this general assessment of Nikkeiren's stance on these matters (Nihon Kei-eisha Dantai Renmei 2002a and 2002b). The first details the vision for a new wage system that would match output with wage payments at regular intervals. By removing seniority as a consideration in determining remuneration, the proposed arrangements would pave the way for firms to acquire more readily suddenly needed skills from the external labor market. The approach is seen as a means of shifting the fixed costs of human capital formation (and the associated risks) more squarely onto the individual employee before he or she is even employed. Decisions about the skills to invest in and the ability to make such an investment are likely to be determined by parents through processes reproducing social class.

While the first report points to an ongoing attachment to disciplined management and a fairly simplistic view of the nexus between labor output and labor cost, the second report points to a new wave of thinking aimed at creatively managing an increasingly diverse labor force. Produced by a group of about thirty people, each responsible for the management of younger employees in their respective firms, the report calls for a move away from personnel practices that treat all employees as though they were from the same mold. This is in line with various calls from outside business (e.g. Paku 2002; Hayashi 1996 and 2003; and Wakisaka 2002) for a more balanced approach to organizing life around work, family, and community. The experience of companies such as Matsushita Denki, P & G, Isetan, and Benedix Corporation is cited to introduce innovative ways of shortening hours of work, implementing work sharing and telecommuting schemes, and contributing in meaningful ways to the diverse career needs of individual employees. Particularly noticeable is the report's invitation to unions to play an active role in providing information on worker needs and proactively proposing better ways that management can embrace its work force.

Some unionists have seen the proposal as a Trojan horse. They argue that unions have for many years been in touch with their members' views and have had their input largely ignored by management. While the top leadership of Rengo seems to welcome the suggestion that their views might carry more weight in the future, after decades of representing their members' interests other unionists see as presumptuous the invitation to begin performing an information gathering function within the confines of each firm's personnel management program. They are particularly alarmed at the suggestion that enterprise unions might want to evolve into employees' consultative councils. The suggestion nevertheless underlines the major dilemma facing the union movement as unionization rates continue to fall and the mission of unions in an affluent Japan is no longer clear to anybody.

## 10.8    The newly formed Japan Business Federation

Nippon Keizai Dantai Rengokai was formed in May 2002, and Okuda Hiroshi (chairman of Toyota Motor Corporation) became its first chairman. Okuda had been chairman of Nikkeiren since May 1999. He brought with him a reputation for the tough but quick and fair decision-making that was credited with revitalizing Toyota in the mid- to late 1990s, and Toyota achieved a record profit in 2001. Many hoped he would work the same magic for Japan's economy. The merger was conceived as a means of consolidating the position of Japan's large business community in the wake of bankruptcies, questionable managerial practices, and scandals at some of Japan's largest and most prestigious firms. Many felt that a more unified front would give business circles more weight in influencing legislation and government policy on economic reform, taxes, social welfare, and employment practices. The new executive board consisted of nine directors from Keidanren, four from Nikkeiren, and two new directors. All directors were presidents of large corporations. In addition it established a new umbrella organization to coordinate the various prefectural-level organizations (known as *chi-ikibetsu keizai dantai*).

Where is Okuda likely to lead Nippon Keidanren? At Toyota he moved quickly to treat what has been called "the big company disease" (the slow and complex decision-making machinery associated with Japan's large organizations). In a series of annual keynote addresses as president of Nikkeiren (as reported in the *SRN*, 30 August 1999: 4; 7 August 2000: 4; and 1 August 2001: 4), Okuda provided some insight into his thinking. While embracing globalization based on the spread of American capitalism, American standards, and a heavy dependence on free market forces, he argued that Japan needed to ensure that its own brand of capitalism had a human face. In saying that, he hinted that the deregulation of markets should be welded to the history, cultural orientation, national character, and existing institutions associated with work organization in each country. In the case of Japan, he seems to place a great emphasis on employment security and the role of internal labor markets. His view is that the approach of Japanese-style management to developing and retaining human resources and to looking after employees is the key to reinvigorating the economy and regaining Japan's international competitiveness. Nonetheless, while arguing that it is immoral and short-sighted to expose excess labor to the whims of the labor market, Okuda also endorses moves to deregulate the labor market and trim the core labor force. His belief is that the hard decisions that firms must quickly adopt can be humanized by statesmanlike leadership.

Is management likely to follow Okuda's lead? Although Nippon Keidanren is still in its early days, one can already sense a certain discomfort with the notion of humanized markets among CEOs in many affiliated companies. They continue to downsize their own work forces as they see fit, and argue that Okuda's humanist approach is a luxury that only the rich companies like Toyota can afford. Even regarding the introduction of work sharing schemes – about which Okuda met directly with the head of Rengo, Sasamori Kiyoshi, in March 2003, and achieved an accord – many businesses have concluded that work sharing would only frustrate their efforts to promote the most rational use of personnel. Business leaders have also been critical of his support for the proposals of the Koizumi government to reform the medical and pension schemes, arguing that such reform would shift too much of the financial burden back on their firms.

Despite the apparent agreement between the heads of Nippon Keidanren and Rengo concerning work sharing, management and unions are likely to remain at loggerheads over a number of other issues, many of which continue to be highlighted during the Spring Offensive at the beginning of each financial year. Okuda has claimed that employment security ought to be the goal of management and unions, that talk of wage hikes in any form was irresponsible regardless of a firm's ability to pay in the short term, and that any surpluses generated at this time should be ploughed back into the firm's future. He has stated that wage hikes have become increasingly out of line with improvements in productivity over the past decade, and that labor and management need to return to the parity existing a decade ago. Rengo's recent White Paper for the Spring Offensive reveals (i) an abiding commitment to Keynesian policy and (ii) a continued insistence that unions need to be consulted more fully at the firm level. However, the union movement has not been proactive in putting forth its own visions of how work should be organized, and for the foreseeable future it is likely that management groups such as the Nippon Keidanren will, however presumptuously, take the lead in defining a role for the union movement.

The dominance of management's national center arises from its ability to be involved in policymaking deliberations. This means having a conspicuous presence on the government's many consultative bodies (*shingikai*) and in the various private advisory groups established by leading politicians. Central to that involvement is its wide range of committees and subcommittees. Its prospectus for 2002–3 (Nippon Keizai Dantai Rengokai 2003: 10–15) lists thirty-four committees dealing with different aspects of domestic policy, each led by one or two heads of major corporations. The time of the chairmen and committee members is supplied gratis by their companies. Eight of the committees are of particular relevance to labor process: those on (i) management and labor policy, (ii) employment, (iii) personnel management, (iv) labor–management relations, (v) labor legislation, (vi) regional revitalization, (vii) corporate behavior, and (viii) the national standard of living and lifestyles. The work of most committees is carried out by subcommittees or working parties. Because those involved either command their enterprises or, in the case of junior executives, have considerable support from their enterprises, they are able to mobilize many resources within their companies to prepare reports and to facilitate participation in outside meetings and even the occasional overseas mission. With 1,262 companies (including 70 with foreign ownership), 125 industrial associations and over 50 regional associations affiliated under its umbrella, the pool of talent is huge. Related to its involvement in policymaking is the Federation's involvement in international forums. It takes an active interest in ILO activities and was instrumental in the establishment of the Confederation of Asia-Pacific Employers (CAPE) in 2001 and is affiliated with the International Organization of Employers.

Another source of strength is in the activities of its regional affiliates. At the local level they provide many kinds of advice to local businessmen and maintain channels of communication between Japan's largest firms and its medium-sized and smaller firms. The larger affiliates employ legal and other professions to provide specialized advice. While smaller offices are unable to do so, they are plugged into a network through which the appropriate counsel can be sought on most issues.

Nippon Keidanren's presence is further reinforced by its ability to produce a constant stream of publications. Its newspaper, *Nippon Keidanren Taimusu*, has been published every Thursday since 1946. It conveys the organization's views on all aspects of employment relations. As a kind of clipping service, *Keizai Clippu* is a monthly magazine. *Keizai Trend* (Economic Trends) is a glossy monthly with a lead article explaining Keidanren's stance or proposals regarding a major issue, and then a number of articles on issues that may be of general interest to managers at affiliated firms. The Federation has a publishing house that stocks 120–150 different titles offering advice on how to look after certain aspects of business (in particular, personnel affairs) and suggestions for managers seeking ways to grow.

Finally, the role of political contributions should be considered. In 1990, Koga (2000: 109) reports, Keidanren coordinated the contribution of some ¥13 billion from business to the Liberal Democratic Party. Although Keidanren argued that such pooled money was clean because it could not be tied to the interests of particular firms, the contributions were heavily criticized in the media. Most ordinary people could not be convinced that such large amounts of money would be given to a political party without strings. Keidanren decided in 1993 that the association should stop coordinating political contributions, but in 2003 the newly formed Nippon Keidanren decided to again coordinate such contributions, and the media has widely warned in its editorials that Nippon Keidanren must take care not to misuse the influence that comes from such activity. At the same time, the Federation has also been active in gathering and channeling donations for a wide range of public events that are in the broader interests of society and the nation's standing as a whole.

## 10.9     The future for management associations

Japan has a range of organizations to which firms can affiliate. Industry, regional and firm-size differences, the large proportion of small firms
in the economy, and the domination of most national organizations by
representatives from Japan's largest corporations mean that several management cultures coexist in Japan. At the same time, the hierarchical
organization of work at the meso level, the status attached to the scarce
jobs identified by Koshiro (1982b), the nature of the enterprise groupings, and the involvement of Nippon Keidanren in setting the nation's
economic agenda all contribute to a trickle-down effect resulting in the
diffusion of a commonly understood and distinctly Japanese culture of
work. Accordingly, to understand labor process at the meso level, it is
important to be abreast of trends occurring in the groups mentioned in
this chapter. Over the next decade major changes will take place in Japan's
economic leadership. One of those will be a "changing of the guard" and
the emergence of a new generation that has grown up with Japan's affluence and has come through the top ranks of their companies after the
bubble years. They will likely have to implement the restructuring that
is now being talked about and then legitimate and live with the logic on
which the new arrangements come to rest.

The leadership of the 1950s, 1960s, and even the 1970s was born out
of a tradition of national sacrifice, the sense of social justice associated
with scarcity, and some of the elements of socialist thinking associated
with the notion of democratic capitalism (*shusei shihonshugi*). The next
generation, reigning from the late 1970s into the 1990s, however, were
apprenticed at a time when Japan was emerging as a powerful force in
the world economy. They inherited the model associated with Japanese-
style management and helped to circulate ideas about its overall superiority, along with the cultural essentialist view that Japan was an ethnically
homogeneous middle-class society without major disparities in lifestyle.
Based on assumptions about the distinctiveness of Japan's own brand of
capitalism, this second generation of leaders tended to be committed to
"more of the same" and to the firm as a castle which should be defended
at all costs. Sometimes that involved a system of mutual interdependence
and a tightly knit coterie of "corporate warriors" who tended to cover up
poor individual performance in order to maintain the outward appear-
ance of great collective strength.

The late 1990s brought with it recognition of the need for a new generation. At the beginning of the new century one editorial in Nikkei
Bijinesu's influential monthly, *Associe* (vol. 10: February 2003: 7) called
for such a change. Noting that 10 percent of Japan's CEOs of major

companies were aged under fifty and that many firms were giving able young employees challenging managerial projects once reserved for more senior managers, it mentioned a survey reported in *Nikkei Bijinesu* (1 July 2002) showing that major firms listed on Japan's upper stock market headed by men in their thirties and forties outperformed similar firms led by presidents in their fifties.

The age difference reveals itself not just in terms of energy and the high levels of concentration required to run complex organizations in the constantly changing global environment. To restructure firms, managers will need to be in tune with the new generation of young people coming into the labor force. Part of the challenge is in understanding aspects of lifestyle about which employees are most concerned. There is a spreading interest in being more involved in family and community life at all levels. Potential employees are also looking more carefully at employment options. The weekly *Shukan Toyo Keizai* (25 January 2003: 82–91) reported that over 20 percent of university graduates have decided not to work during the first year after graduation. Whereas graduates used to line up to get a job at the best firm possible (as judged by the likely financial benefits for themselves and the firm's size, status, and stability), with major firms having the pick from a large number of aspirants, firms are now finding that graduates are becoming more choosy. Reflecting this fact, weeklies such as *Shukan Toyo Keizai* and *Shukan Daiyamondo* (e.g. as revealed in their 25 January 2003 issues) are now publishing rankings of companies informing them of the criteria they must meet in order to employ the best scarce graduates.

Management is also having to respond to watchdogs. Over the past decade the Asahi Shimbun has annually surveyed Japan's largest employers to gather data for its index on corporate responsibility (*kigyo no shakai kokendo*). It ranks companies in terms of their efforts to provide for (i) a fair and transparent workplace, (ii) gender equality, (iii) employment for the handicapped and non-Japanese residents, (iv) a framework for implementing global standards, (v) a framework for ensuring the welfare of consumers, (vi) contributions to the broader society, (vii) environmental guarantees, (viii) a moral basis for running the firm, and (ix) the disclosure of basic information (Asahi Shimbun Bunka Zaidan Kigyo no Shakai Kokendo Chosa Iinkai 2002).

Large firms are now considering how to retain and to motivate a competitive but malleable labor force by integrating better employees recruited mid-career from outside, reducing the size of their permanent labor force, and blurring the lines between permanent and non-permanent employment. The new generation of managers will have to develop new visions to legitimate the heavy demands placed on their elite labor force. It is too early to judge whether the new visions will share certain common assumptions accepted across the board or whether they will vary greatly from company to company. When thinking about business ethics, governance, and notions of social responsibility, the new generation of business leaders will need to balance considerations internal to each firm, industry, and regional locale with those raised by the diffusion of global standards, the logic of free markets and the new social consciousness emerging in Japan. As Teramoto and Sakai (2002) indicate in their volume on corporate governance, the outcome of structural reform must not be simply to stop the scandalous behavior of managers in a few firms. Change must bring with it more dynamic ways to create and use information so that firms can create added value in an increasingly global, competitive, and fluid environment. The ability of the new generation to do that will go a long way to determining the power relationship they have with labor in the future.

*Part VI*

# The future

# 11 The future of work in Japan

## 11.1 The end of the model

Not long ago Japan was seen as offering both the fully industrialized and the newly industrializing world a viable model for organizing work. Following the OECD's two reports on Japan's industrial relations in the 1970s, Dore's comparative study praising the running of Japanese factories compared with the way the British managed theirs (1973), and Vogel's popular volume drawing attention to Japan's across-the-board success (1979), a series of volumes applauding Japanese management practices appeared at the beginning of the 1980s. "Japanese-style management" became a key referent in a new literature on corporate culture in the 1980s. Japan seemed to be going from strength to strength as its economy entered what have become known as the bubble years in the late 1980s.

By 2003, however, the awe engendered by Japanese employment practices had given way to skepticism. The bubble years were followed by recession. The management of many firms seemed to be buffeted not only by forces attributed to globalization, but also by unforeseen changes within Japanese society, especially in terms of the labor supply it had previously taken for granted. Unemployment more than doubled in just over a decade, and the growth rate fell from over 5 percent into negative territory. While only one firm on the upper stock market had gone bankrupt in 1985 and none had done so in 1989, twenty-nine did so in 2002. By 2003 references to the Japanese model were hard to find, whereas allusions to "the Japanese disease" had come to the fore. Many observers came to speak of the "lost decade," a term first used in 1974 by Hazama to refer to a Japan plagued by workaholism. Today it is used to refer to the particular difficulties Japan has had in coming to grips with globalization and the higher degree of competition and rationalization global development has brought to Japan. One observer has suggested that Japan's economy was beset by a kind of narcolepsy – an illness punctuated by periods of inattention – that allowed debt to freely rise and other areas in need of attention to go unheeded. The Japanese seem to have entered "their century" without confidence, groping about for a way forward out of the current recession.

How could the decline from the heady days of the late 1980s have occurred so rapidly and on such a scale? Observers have pointed to Japan's own financial crisis and to the bad debts that had accumulated behind a veil that hid the true situation from the public – indeed from many of the employees in the very firms experiencing the most trouble. The first in a series of articles on *nihonbyo* (the Japanese disease) published prominently on the front page of Japan's leading economic newspaper (the *NKSC*) throughout January 2003 highlighted four major sources of the problem: (i) the failure to implement many of the much-talked-about structural reforms in terms of how corporate society is organized and run in Japan; (ii) an innately conservative attachment of Japan's leaders to the ways which appeared to have brought Japan so much economic growth over four decades; (iii) an apparent imperviousness to the full extent of the crisis besetting Japan in terms of how globalization is progressing, the main features of change in the nature of Japanese society including its move toward multiculturalism, and the fall in levels of universal literacy; and (iv) a loss of confidence in risk taking following the sudden collapse of the bubble economy in the early 1990s.

Our view is that the Japanese economy is suffering from a much more basic contradiction which has been visible since the mid-1970s and is seen in the paradox sensed by many Japanese over the past quarter of a century and noted at the beginning of this volume – the contradiction of being so rich and yet feeling so poor. Japanese worked long hours to get to where they are today in a material sense, and many continue to work hard. In this context it should be noted that the national economy remains competitive and has continued to generate sizable balance-of-payments surpluses. For that very reason, perhaps, one is struck by the title of McCormack's (1996) volume, *The Emptiness of Japanese Affluence*. The puzzlement which is felt by many Japanese in subjective terms has been born out of major contradictions in the objective life circumstances we have tried to document throughout this volume. The contradictions are between the rhetoric describing Japan as an egalitarian society, on the one hand, and the reality of social inequality on the other.

In discussing Sato's (2000) volume on the end of Japan's middle-class mass society, we noted the surprise of many Japanese in the recent "discovery" of inequality in Japan at the end of the 1990s, and commented that it should not have been any surprise at all, given the objective dimensions of inequality in Japan, and that the facts showing that Japan had become less egalitarian had been publicly documented for some time. The subjective denial of that reality as part of the cold-war ideology on the conservative side of politics served to isolate critical scholars on the left within Japan and meant that the country had to wait an unnecessarily long time until established scholars of a more conservative hue felt moved to pronounce that inequality was indeed a major feature of Japanese society.

## 11.2    The ongoing crisis of inequality

In considering the future of work in Japan, it is useful to keep the Japanese paradox in perspective. Rifkin (1996: 14), for example, has written in a similar vein about the confusion of the relatively well-off people in other similarly industrialized societies: "In every industrial country, people are beginning to ask why the age-old dream of abundance and leisure, so anticipated by generations of hardworking human beings, seems further away now, at the dawn of the Information Age, than at any time in the past half century." Basic to his argument about the looming crisis in advanced capitalist societies is the view that inequality is an endemic problem – a contradiction in objective terms which will sooner or later surface and result in a subjective awareness that gives way to fundamentally revolutionary tendencies. For Rifkin it is the unequal distribution of employment that will seriously exacerbate the situation. Without accepting fully Rifkin's vision concerning the likelihood that technological advance will lead to catastrophic levels of unemployment, it is nonetheless instructive to revisit Hazama's data showing that the net profits of major companies in Japan's major enterprise groupings increased over the 1990s, while the size of their labor force decreased.

One key to understanding work in Japan over the next decade will be in the way unemployment is handled. Japan's enviably low unemployment rates over the forty years leading up to the 1990s have risen. In the meantime, something has changed so that many of Japan's more productive employees no longer see value in subsidizing less able employees. The work force has been trimmed even in firms belonging to Japan's enterprise groupings with their strong communitarian ethos. The drive to rationalize should not be seen simply as a response to the pressures firms feel to be more competitive. There is also a materialism that attracts the more capable workers to seek the monetary rewards associated with the desirable lifestyles they increasingly see on television, on the internet, and on trips overseas for business and pleasure. This push to rationalize comes with advocacy for transparency – exposure of the subsidies for "underperformers."

The challenge facing Japan and other societies in these regards is in finding and designing ways of dealing with the underemployed (i.e. society's "underperformers"), some of whom are in the better jobs and some of whom miss out completely. Some may believe that the next major technological revolution will create new employment. They perhaps have a fairly strong case based on past history. Nevertheless, if we accept that the IT revolution is likely to create considerable employment on or just above the poverty line (not Koshiro's scarce jobs mentioned above in chapter 5, but jobs nonetheless), the outcome will still be the entrenchment of social inequality and solidification of the lines between social classes as those inequalities are socially reproduced.

The clash between Okuda, who heads Toyota and Nippon Keidanren, and has pushed for the Toyota way of retaining employees at all costs, and managers in many firms that have decided to retrench workers (as discussed in chapter 10) points to the fundamental dialectic at work in Japanese capitalism today. The shift of the world's "last great socialist economy" from market-conforming but nonetheless socialist structures which resulted in intricate patterns of cross-subsidization to a more rationalist capitalist format is a sociopolitical choice. While this view may seem contrary to a more economic determinist view, or even the sociopolitical arguments of Fukuyama that such changes are inevitable (even though temporarily slowed down by the cold war), the experience of Japan over the last few decades suggests that the relationships between capitalism, socialism, and globalization are symbiotic. Although the generation of huge balance-of-payments surpluses may have inevitably drawn Japan into the global capitalist system, the power struggles in the background have been real and the outcomes have not always been inevitable.

Related to these challenges are shifts in Japan's demographics. New ways of estimating demographic change suggest that life expectancy in Japan is likely to continue rising for both women and men as the median age for the population rises from 41.5 in 2000 to 51.1 in 2025, and the dependency ratio increases. Some have suggested that the retirement age might be raised to 75. This would institutionalize the already high labor-force participation rate for Japanese aged 65–75, and result in a newly defined "aged population" accounting for only 17–18 percent of Japan's population in 2025, a dependency ratio equivalent to that now cited for those in Japan's population aged over 65 in 2000. However, if Rifkin (1996) is right in arguing that current levels of production can be achieved globally with a smaller labor force, another option is to discourage those aged 65–75 from working and to shift the newly unemployed to servicing them in ways that will enhance the leisure they enjoy as a reward for their hard work during their years in the labor force. The redistributive consequences of adopting either approach are not obvious, but will be hotly debated in a society seeking to balance productivity concerns with those of social justice.

## 11.3    The policy framework

It is too early to know how employment will evolve in Japan over the first few decades of the twenty-first century. However, employment practices and the organization of work will be shaped by forces at the three levels introduced in chapter 1: the macro or global level; the meso, national, or societal level defined in geopolitical terms; and the micro level where practices are hammered out within the firm, family, school, and/or local community. It is the interaction of forces generated by each of these domains that will shape the behavior and relative bargaining power of employees (as suppliers of labor both in their own right and on behalf of their families) and employers (as buyers of labor). Their interaction will influence greatly the way work is organized.

An approach cognizant of labor process on those three levels has been adopted for this volume, but with attention being focused on the meso level. Our contention is that social and cultural trends, policies, the segmentation of the labor market and the power relations between organized labor and organized management at that level impinge greatly upon the choices that employers and employees make at the micro level. It is further posited that realities at the meso level are increasingly shaped by developments at the global level – developments that also open up possibilities for employers and employees to work around the forces generated at the meso level. Those propositions remain to be tested.

These propositions are not meant to suggest that the influence of industrial relations institutions or other work-related legislation at the national level is diminishing. Rather, they are built upon recognition that much of the impact of globalization on local events will continue to be mitigated by intervention at the national level. They do, however, suggest that the environment in which national institutions function is evolving and that the outcomes are uncertain. While reference to international standards may become more common, national systems of employment and industrial relations will be further shaped and honed by the way workers navigate through the "windows of opportunity" that remain after interaction in order to achieve work environments suitable to their needs. Changes at the meso level will provide clues as to how the global and the local impinge upon each other in shaping work organization.

## 11.4    The end of the *sarariiman* and established employment practices?

From the mid-1990s a number of observers have speculated about whether the *sarariiman* has a future in a more globalized Japanese economy. In putting the salaried employee (blue-collar and white-collar) under the microscope, they have questioned not only the survival of Japanese-style management, but also the lifestyle of a nation that had been ordered around the needs of the business firm, especially the large corporation. The reference was to the structures that drove competition among employees in the firm, to long-term employment practices, and to the application of several criteria in determining wages (including seniority, ability, educational attainment, and job description). It was also to the expectation that, at worst, redundant male employees could and would be relocated through an internal labor market existing either within the same firm or among related firms in an enterprise grouping. Finally, the reference was to the segmentation of the labor market.

Forces now shaping work organization in Japan include the aging of the population, heightened international competition, and the changing outlook or consciousness of those in the labor force (especially in terms of the role of women). They are reflected in the establishment of venture capital firms, in the spread of the *furiitaa* and the parasitic singles lifestyle (which is accompanied by the postponement of marriage and children), in the free-agent schemes for individual employees, in the extension of the mandatory retirement age, in the high turnover of those in their first job following graduation, in the "slow life movement," and in the general romanticism associated with alternative lifestyles. At the same time, some of the attraction associated with these kinds of developments lies in the difficulties faced by those who choose to follow the "road less traveled." There is, then, a quixotic element in the new lifestyle that is seen as positive, while the tough realities and structural constraints facing those who choose that path are also fully recognized.

Some writers (e.g. Yomiuri Shimbun Keizai Bu 2001) have concluded that the old system of long-term employment and senior wages is coming to an end. They see a different type of Japanese employee emerging, one who wants to test his or her own value in the market and then be remunerated accordingly. These observers see change coming in free-agent schemes and in raising the retirement age. These changes, they argue, will promote employment security for a small number of the most proficient employees while assigning a growing proportion of the less proficient workers to the peripheral labor force where decisions to employ and to maintain employment are more at the whim of the employer. The high rate of unemployment among Japan's youth, casualization, and the increased use of dispatched workers are cited as indicators of this new trend. The Yomiuri editors mention a survey taken by Denki Rengo showing that only a fourth of its members were interested in providing their employers with a high level of commitment. The findings indicated that levels of commitment are considerably below those existing two decades earlier and below the levels registered by workers completing the survey in thirteen other countries (including South Korea, France, and America). While noting that few Japanese employees are enamored of the idea of their income being determined solely by market value (an arrangement seen as going hand in hand with the high turnover rates and the wide income disparities associated with the American labor market), the Yomiuri writers argue that these changed circumstances are producing a new type of employee (the *shinshu sarariiman*), who is much more willing to work for foreign firms if the pay is higher and in accordance with their market value. This will induce many large Japanese firms to offer competitive salaries to keep Japan's most capable employees on their payrolls.

Inagami (2003) reports on a group project examining the situation in this regard at major firms in Japan's key industries between 1960 and 2000. The findings show that between 1960 and 1990 the firms were able to maintain their commitment to long-term employment guarantees through secondment and other practices involving firms in the same enterprise grouping, and that this commitment served to maintain high morale in the workplace. By 2000, however, those mechanisms were no longer able to cope with the number of employees needing to be redeployed. The result has been a spillover of unwanted labor from large firms to many smaller firms having a business relationship with the larger firm (which resulted in a broadening of the internal labor market) and to the external labor market in general. Inagami concludes that employers are moving away from long-term employment practices (*choki antei koyo*) and seniority-based personnel practices to performance-based management. In a recent interview at the beginning of 2003, Yashiro Masamoto, president of Shinsei Ginko (formerly the Long-Term Credit Bank of Japan), commented positively on his bank's move away from its earlier reliance on academic credentialism in the bank's approach to hiring and its commitment to function internationally by injecting Japan's own brand of English-language proficiency into its personnel management schemes (Yashiro and Hanami 2003).

Those critical of that position recognize some of these trends, but argue that major changes in the employment system are confined mainly to Japan's small and medium-sized firms and to certain industries. Even if there is movement away from seniority-based salary systems, they posit, the practice of long-term employment guarantees will remain for core employees in Japan's largest firms. They argue that Inagami's analysis is based on an amalgam of all employees in Japan's large firms and does not distinguish between those in different career tracks. They argue that the shift in the overall average occurs as semi-core employees are moved further from the ideal associated with a shrinking group of core employees.

Here Toyota's commitment to long-term employment guarantees is relevant. Its enterprise union federation made news during the Spring Offensive in 2003 by not demanding any wage rise at all in its negotiations with management. Moreover, the strong attachment of core employees to those guarantees has recently been described by Ono (2002) and Ihara (2003). The situation is the same at Honda (Wada 2003), and at Nissan whose CEO (Carlos Ghosn), a French national with immense experience in Europe, has also indicated support for the practice (Nishii 2003). The president of Canon (Mitarai 2003), with thirty years at the helm of its North American operations, has also argued that the pattern of long-term employment is most appropriate in the Japanese context. One could cite many other firms where support for the practice remains strong among both management and elite employees.

In recent months a number of firms such as Fujitsu have attracted considerable attention in the media with the announcement that they are stepping back from performance management for several reasons. One is the difficulty of objectively measuring an individual's productivity and the effects of the resultant arbitrariness on morale. The focus on individual output also tends to undermine the team work so critical to the success of on-the-job training, QC circles, and many other practices associated with the generation of high efficiency in Japan. Still others such as Ono (1997), Takanashi (2001), and Koseki (2002) continue to emphasize the ongoing link between seniority and the ability to perform in higher positions. Important to those taking this view is the claim that certain features of Japanese-style management have always outlived the doomsday predictions which have surfaced in the past when Japan was faced with challenges similar to those posed by globalization today (e.g. trade liberalization in the 1960s, the floating of the US dollar in the early 1970s, the oil shocks in the mid-1970s, and the sharp appreciation of the yen in the 1980s). It is not surprising, then, that a number of popular books (e.g. Tanaka 2002) confidently predict that the Japanese-style *sarariiman* will continue to dominate the scene at work in many of Japan's firms.

Our view is that the practice of long-term employment will likely remain in Japan's large firms in traditional manufacturing industries for members of each firm's core labor force. At the same time, this core is likely to shrink, and firms will have to compete for scarce good labor as other industries (e.g. information technology or services) and smaller firms gain the advantage by linking remuneration to short-term assessments of each employee's market value. Japan's large firms too will increasingly come to treat their non-core labor force in a similar manner. They will be especially inclined to do so when obtaining the services of professionals with highly developed but very specialized skills that are costly to impart and only needed in specific situations. All firms will respond with more family-friendly practices and various work-sharing schemes to secure the services of family-oriented workers and other "directed" individuals.

Books such as the one by Sekine (2002) will continue to appeal to the adventurous spirit of the Japanese *sarariiman* and to many of the young people not yet in the labor force. Kosugi (2003) documents how the number of *furiitaa* has increased, with subgroupings now discernible. Older Japanese will be critical of the way the values of Japan's young people have changed, many lamenting that the work ethic of the 1960s and 1970s has given way to a commercial materialism that is undermining the very fabric of Japanese society and the way work has been organized in Japan over the past fifty years. Our view is that the processes are more complex, and that throughout the postwar period many Japanese have worked very hard over many years to attain the material affluence associated with the upper middle-class lifestyle in many Western societies. While affluence has not necessarily brought happiness, it has been a goal of many older Japanese. However, affluence was achieved in Japan without the concomitant change in lifestyles. We would argue further that long hours of work resulted from structures which made those hours a prerequisite for advancement – a necessary, though not sufficient, condition for achieving affluence in Japan. In a sense a significant measure of lifestyle equality was achieved, albeit in a somewhat mechanical fashion. The confusion of affluence with lifestyle shrouded the myth of social equality and homogeneity that underpinned the belief that by hard work alone anyone in Japan could somehow "make it." The awakening to structured social inequality in the 1990s cannot be understood apart from the above-mentioned paradox of being so rich and feeling so poor. Both have contributed to many Japanese reassessing the way they work and the options they have regarding work at the beginning of the twenty-first century.

## 11.5   The future of work in Japan

This volume began with one major concern: the broader socioeconomic context in which Japanese employees make choices about work. It considered the tradition of working long hours and sought to delineate factors at the meso level that impinged upon the willingness of employees to put in such hours, some of which were even "donated" to their employers as "service overtime." In looking for reasons behind the motivation of Japanese employees to toil long and hard, we sought to steer away from structural conspiracy theories which rested on simplistic notions of capitalist exploitation, while also eschewing dependence on cultural factors such as an innate work ethic or an entrenched loyalty to the firm as a surrogate family or primordial group. We also strove to avoid the temptation to focus on Japanese-style management and firm-based techniques designed to enhance the loyalty of employees to their firms by creating at the micro level a corporate culture revolving around long-term employment, seniority wages, and the enterprise union. Although these elements may be important at the firm level, as the first step in assessing the motivation to work, we felt it was important to first paint the backdrop against which employees end up in a particular firm – be it a large firm or a small one – and attempt to make rational choices on the job. That setting included images of power relations between organized labor and organized management and the social and labor policy frameworks which sometimes ameliorate and sometimes exacerbate inequalities shaping the assets individuals take to work and some of the socialized rewards they receive for their efforts at work once they have retired from the labor force. Brush strokes were added to suggest how social values and thoughts about work are changing in ways that are reshaping the supply side of the labor market.

Work is an arena in which we can glimpse images of the new Japan that is emerging at the beginning of the twenty-first century. It is a Japan in which a new work ethic is emerging. For the first twenty or thirty years after the war, many Japanese sought a new purpose in life. The goals and the symbols associated with serving the empire had been dashed. Some turned to Japan's new religions; others turned to work, blindly committed to carrying out their jobs within a certain firm as their contribution to rebuilding a nation and a civilization worth saving. The *nihonjinron* literature as folklore helped to validate that goal. However, commitment and hype are not enough. Japan was successful in no small measure because structures were put in place at both the meso level and the micro level that in mechanical and functional terms made workways more efficient. Some of the mechanisms relied on the introduction of technology; others on work intensification. For a decade or two this may have been acceptable. Many workers voted with their feet, crossing over from left-wing unions with their banners promoting collectivistic egalitarianism to the more conservative enterprise unions advocating productivity first and materialistic benefits from cooperating with management. The attention shifted from the rebuilding of the national economy to the building of *maihomu* (an independent house on a privately owned plot of land), to enhancing the educational credentials of offspring and to achieving other consumerist goals associated with embourgeoisement.

With work intensification, however, came overwork and overregimentation. Hours of work even rose slightly as casualization spread in the 1980s. The immediate outcomes were still greater affluence and exhaustion, as evidenced in the pathological effects of overwork (e.g. *karoshi*). The shift to wage systems rewarding actual performance represented for many an attempt to squeeze further effort out of exhaustion. Retrenchment and the threat of unemployment provided another incentive for those still employed to give that one last ounce. Taken together, these factors contributed to the Midas phenomenon – unimagined wealth with a new form of poverty. The search for meaningful work led some to seek employment as *furiitaa*. Others have sought meaning in voluntary work and community involvement. Multiculturalization has meant that firms have had to become more accepting of multiple lifestyles and to adopt increasingly sophisticated strategies to motivate employees. With those thoughts in mind, employers seem to be pulled in one direction by those who advocate a kind of socialist capitalism with secure employment for all and in another direction by those advocating the logic of open markets. Out of the tensions produced by these kinds of ideological differences a new form of Japanese capitalism will likely emerge. As the outcome will in part be a response to the global context, the old debate on similarity and difference will continue. Despite the apocalyptic prophecies, the end of history is not yet in sight. Any revival of the labor movement can only serve to underline further one basic fact of life: Japanese capitalism, like other capitalisms, will continue to generate its own contradictions from which partisan support will emerge for organizing work in one way or another. The challenge will be to generate surplus through labor processes which also allow for a reasonable distribution of the fruits of that labor.

# References

Abe, Kin-ya 2002, "Nihon no Seken wa 'Mushoku' o Yurusanai" (The Japanese Society Which Will Not Accept Persons Not Working), *Chuo Koron* (no. 1418: July), pp. 108–11.

Abegglen, James C. 1958, *The Japanese Factory: Aspects of its Social Organisation* (Glencoe, IL: The Free Press).

1973, *Management and Worker: The Japanese Solution* (Tokyo: Sophia University).

Ago, Shin-ichi 1996, *Kokusai Rodo Kijun Ho – ILO to Nihon-Ajia* (Toward an International Labor Standards Law: The ILO in Japan and Asia) (Tokyo: Sanseido).

Ando, Masakitchi 1947, *Saitei Seikatsuhi no Kenkyu* (Research on the Cost of Maintaining a Minimal Standard of Living) (Tokyo: Koseikan).

1944, *Kokumin Seikatsuhi no Kenkyu* (Research on the Cost of Maintaining the People's Standard of Living) (Tokyo: Sakai Shoten).

Anonymous 1994a, "Paato no Josei no Sosho" (The Continuing Lawsuits Concerning Part-time Women Employees), *Asahi Shimbun* (morning edition), 3 July, p. 15.

1994b, "'Shokaku' de Dansei to Sabetsu – Sumitomo-Keiretsu Sansha OL ga Chotei Shinsei" (Women from Three Sumitomo Firms Apply for Mediation Concerning Sex Discrimination in their Promotion), *Asahi Shimbun* (morning edition), 26 March, p. 25.

1996a, *Oshigoto no Nazo Hen* (A Volume About the Realm of Work) (Tokyo: Obunsha).

1996b, "Working Time in Europe: Part One," *European Industrial Relations Review* (no. 278: March), pp. 14–20.

1997a, "Soshikika ni yotte Beikoku Rodo Undo Saisei" (Reviving the American Labor Movement by Increasing the Membership), *Shukan Rodo Nyusu*, 14 April, p. 1.

1997b, "Kanrishoku Yunion – Kansai de mo Hataage" (The Union for Managerial Staff: Now Lifting Off in the Kansai Area), *Shukan Rodo Nyusu* (no. 1719: 2 June), p. 3.

1997c, "Daikigyo de no Roso Yumu o Kohyo" (Unions to Publicize the Names of Large Firms Which Remain Non-Union), *Shukan Rodo Nyusu* (no. 1701: 13 January), p. 1.

1997d, "Rengo Soken Chosa: Yowamaru Roso no Kyushinryoku" (Survey of Rengo Soken: The Declining Attraction of Unions), *Shukan Rodo Nyusu* (no. 1728: 4 August), p. 3.

1997e, "Rengo Soken: 'Rodo Hosei' de Hokoku" (Rengo Soken's Report on Labor Law), *Shukan Rodo Nyusu* (no. 1711: 31 March), p. 3.

Aonuma, Yoshimatsu 1965, *Nihon no Keieiso: Sono Shusshin to Seikaku* (A Portrait of Management in Japan: The Origins and Characteristics of Japan's Managers) (Tokyo: Nihon Keizai Shimbunsha).

Apter, David 1965, *The Politics of Modernization* (Chicago: University of Chicago Press).

Araki, Takashi 1996, "Regulation of Working Hours for White-Collar Workers Engaging in 'Discretionary Activities,'" *Japan Labor Bulletin* (vol. 35, no. 7: July), pp. 4–8.

2002, *Labor and Employment Law in Japan* (Tokyo: Japan Institute of Labor).

Asahi Shimbun Bunka Zaidan "Kigyo no Shakai Kokendo" Chosa Iinkai, ed. 2002, *Yuryoku Kigyo no Shakai Kokendo 2002* (The Social Responsibility Index for Japan's Biggest Corporations 2002) (Tokyo: PHP Kenkyujo).

Asakura, Mutsuko and Konno, Hisako 1997, *Josei Rodo Hanrei Gaido* (A Guide to Court Cases Concerning Working Women) (Tokyo: Yuhikaku).

Asakura, Takashi, Yamazaki, Yoshihiko, Kondo, Michiko, and Hirai, Yoichi 1990, *Daitoshi Kinrosha no Rodo Seikatsu no Shitsu to Kenko – Kito Kodo to Kenko Shukan* (Health and the Quality of Working Life of Workers in Large Cities: The Return Trip Home and Matters of Health) (Tokyo: Tokyo Toritsu Rodo Kenkyujo).

Athos, Anthony G. and Pascale, Richard Tanner 1981, *The Art of Japanese Management* (New York: Simon and Schuster).

Atsumi, Reiko 1979, "*Tsukiai* – Obligatory Personal Relationships of Japanese White-Collar Employees," *Human Organization* (vol. 39, no. 1: Spring), pp. 63–70.

Ayusawa, Iwao F. 1966, *A History of Labor in Modern Japan* (Honolulu: East-West Center Press).

Azumi, Koya and Hull, Frank 1982, "Technology, Organization and Alienation in Japanese Factories: A Contradiction of the Blauner Thesis," a paper presented to the International Colloquium on the Comparative Study of Japanese Society (Noosa Heads, Queensland, Australia: 29 January – 6 February).

Ballon, Robert J., ed. 1969, *The Japanese Employee* (Tokyo: Sophia University in cooperation with the Charles E. Tuttle Company).

Bell, Daniel 1960, *The End of Ideology* (Glencoe, IL: The Free Press).

Benders, Joe 1994, "Leaving Lean? Recent Changes in the Production Organisation of Some Japanese Car Plants," *Economic and Industrial Democracy* (vol. 17), pp. 9–38.

Bennett, John W. and Ishino, Iwao 1963, *Paternalism in the Japanese Economy: Anthropological Studies of Oyabun-Kobun Patterns* (Minneapolis: University of Minnesota Press).

Benson, John 1994, "The Economic Effects of Unionism in Japanese Manufacturing Enterprises," *British Journal of Industrial Relations* (vol. 32, no. 1), pp. 1–21.

1996, "Management Strategy and Labour Flexibility in Japanese Manufacturing Enterprises," *Human Resource Management Journal* (vol. 6, no. 2), pp. 44–57.

Beynon, Huw 1984, *Working for Ford*, second edition (Harmondsworth: Penguin).

Biggu Pen 2002, *Gyokai Keiretsu Chizu* (A Mapping of Japan's Industrial Groupings) (Tokyo: Kanki Shuppan).

Blackwood, Thomas 2003, "The Reproduction and Naturalization of the Sex-Based Separate Sphere in Japanese High Schools: The Role of Female 'Managers' of High School Baseball Teams," *Social Science Japan* (no. 25: February), pp. 22–6.

Bungei Shunju, ed. 2000, "'Shogeki Repooto' – Shin Kaikyu Shakai Nippon" (The New Class Society in Japan: An Up-Front Report), a special issue of *Bungei Shunju* (May).

2002, *Nihon no Ronten 2003, Setogiwa no Sentaku* (The Issues Defining Japan in 2003: Critical Decisions for the Future) (Tokyo: Bungei Shunju).

Burgess, Christopher 2003, "(Re)Constructing Identities: International Marriage Migrants as Potential Agents of Social Change in a Globalising Japan," Ph.D. thesis submitted to Monash University, Melbourne.

Chalmers, Norma J. 1989, *Industrial Relations in Japan: The Peripheral Workforce* (London: Routledge).

Chuma, Hiroyuki 1994, *Kensho Nihongata 'Koyo Chosei'* (The Inspection System: The Japanese Approach to Adjusting Employment Levels) (Tokyo: Shueisha).

Chuo Daigaku Kigyo Kenkyujo (The Chuo University Enterprise Research Centre), ed. 1991, *Nihon no Kigyo-Keiei to Kokusai Hikaku* (A Comparative Study of Japan's Enterprises and Management) (Tokyo: Chuo Daigaku Shuppanbu).

Chuo Koron Henshu Bu, ed. 2001, *Ronso – Churyu Hokai* (The Debate on the Collapse of the Middle Class) (Tokyo: Chuo Koronshinsha).

Chusho Kigyo Cho (The Agency for Small and Medium-Sized Enterprises) 2001, *Chusho Kigyo Hakusho 2001 Nenban: Mezame Yo! Jiritsu shita Kigyo e* (The 2001 White Paper on Small and Medium-Sized Enterprises: Time to Wake Up and Build Strong Firms) (Tokyo: Gyosei).

Clark, Rodney C. 1979, *The Japanese Company* (New Haven, CT: Yale University Press).

Clark, Robert L. and Ogawa, Naohiro 1997, "Transitions from Career Jobs to Retirement in Japan," *Industrial Relations: A Journal of Economy and Society* (vol. 36, no. 2: April), pp. 255–70.

Cole, Allan B., Totten, George O., and Uyehara, Cecil H. 1966, *Socialist Parties in Postwar Japan* (New Haven, CT: Yale University Press).

Cole, Robert E. 1971, *Japanese Blue Collar: The Changing Tradition* (Berkeley: University of California Press).

1979, *Work, Mobility and Participation: A Comparative Study of American and Japanese Industry* (Berkeley: University of California Press).

Coriat, Benjamin 1992, *Gyakuten no Shiko – Nihon Kigyo no Rodo to Soshiki* (For a Change in Thinking: Organization and Work in the Japanese Enterprise), translated from French (*Penser à l'envers. Travail et organisation dans l'entreprise japonaise*) by Hanada Masanori and Saito Yoshinori (Tokyo: Fujiwara Shoten).

Corneau, Guy 1995, *Otoko ni Narenai Musukotachi* (Absent Fathers, Lost Sons), translated into Japanese by Hirai Misa (Tokyo: TBS Buritanika).

Cornfield, Daniel B. and Hodson, Randy, eds. 2002, *Worlds of Work: Building an International Sociology of Work* (New York: Kluwer Academic/Plenum Publishers).

Dalby, Liza Crichfield 1985, *Geisha* (New York: Vintage).

Deery, Stephen, Plowman, David and Fisher, Christopher 1981, *Australian Industrial Relations* (Sydney: McGraw Hill).

Dore, Ronald P. 1973, *British Factory – Japanese Factory: The Origins of National Diversity in Industrial Relations* (Berkeley: University of California Press).

1976, *The Diploma Disease* (London: George Allen and Unwin).

Dore, Ronald P. and Sako, Mari 1989, *How the Japanese Learn to Work* (London: Routledge).

Drucker, Peter 1993, *Managing for the Future: The 1990s and Beyond* (New York: Truman Talley Books/Plume).

Dunlop, John T. 1958, *Industrial Relations Systems* (New York: Holt).

Florida, Richard and Kenny, Martin 1993, *Beyond Mass Production: The Japanese System and its Transfer to the US* (New York: Oxford University Press).

Fowler, Edward 1996, *San'ya Blues: Laboring Life in Contemporary Tokyo* (Ithaca, NY: Cornell University Press).

Freeman, Richard B. and Rebick, Marcus E. 1989, "Crumbling Pillar? Declining Union Density in Japan," *Journal of the Japanese and International Economies* (vol. 3, no. 4: December), pp. 578–605.

Fujimoto, Takeshi, Shimoyama, Fusao, and Inoue, Kazue 1965, *Nihon no Seikatsu Jikan* (The Time for Living in Japan) (Tokyo: Rodo Kagaku Kenkyujo Shuppan Bu).

Fujimura, Hiroyuki 1993, "Rodo Kumiai Josei Yakuin no Kokusai Hikaku" (Women in the Union Hierarchy: An International Comparison of Union Officials), in *Gendai no Josei Rodo to Shakai Seisaku* (Working Women and Social Policy in the Contemporary World), edited by Shakai Seisaku Gakkai (Tokyo: Ochanomizu Shobo), pp. 125–44.

1997, "New Unionism: Beyond Enterprise Unionism?" in *Japanese Labour and Management in Transition: Diversity, Flexibility and Participation*, edited by Mari Sako and Hiroki Sato (London: LSE/Routledge), pp. 296–314.

1998, "The Future of Trade Unions in Japan," *Japan Labor Bulletin* (vol. 37, no. 7), pp. 5–8.

Fujita, Wakao 1968, *Daini Kumiai* (The Number Two Union), new edition (Tokyo: Nihon Hyoronsha).

Fukuoka, Yasunori 1996, *Zai-nichi Kankokujin/Chosenjin* (Koreans Residing in Japan) (Tokyo: Chuo Koronsha).

Fukuyama, Francis 1993, *The End of History and the Last Man* (New York: Avon Books).

Fuse, Naoharu 2001, *Rodo Ho: Hayawakari Jiten* (Labor Law: A Handy Dictionary), new revised edition (Tokyo: PHP Kenkyujo).

Futagami, Kyo-ichi 2000, *Kigyo to Kei-ei* (The Enterprise and the Economy), vol. 1 in the series *Gendai Keieigaku Koza* (The Complete Survey of Modern Management) (Tokyo: Yachiyo Shuppan).

Galenson, Walter and Odaka, Konosuke 1976, "The Japanese Labor Market," in *Asia's New Giant*, edited by Hugh Patrick and Henry Rosovsky (Washington, DC: The Brookings Institute), pp. 587–672.

Garten, Jeffrey E. 1997, "Can the World Survive the Triumph of Capitalism?" *Harvard Business Review* (vol. 75, no. 1: January–February), pp. 144–50.

Gee, Ellen M. and Gutman, Gloria M., eds. 2000, *The Overselling of Population Aging: Apocalyptic Demography, Inter-Generational Challenges, and Social Policy* (Oxford: Oxford University Press).

Gill, Tom 2001, *Men of Uncertainty: The Social Organization of Day Laborers in Contemporary Japan* (Albany, NY: SUNY Press).

Goldthorpe, John H. *et al.* 1968, *The Affluent Worker: Industrial Attitudes and Behaviour* (Cambridge: Cambridge University Press).

1969, *The Affluent Worker in the Class Structure* (Cambridge: Cambridge University Press).

Goodman, Roger 1992, *Japan's "International Youth": The Emergence of a New Class of School Children* (Oxford: Oxford University Press).

Hamada, Hideo 2002, "Koreika Shakai" (The Aging of Society), in *Asahi Gendai Yogo CHIEZO 2002* (The 2002 Asahi Treasury of Knowledge Concerning Key Words), edited by the Jiten Henshu Bu (Tokyo: Asahi Shimbunsha), pp. 459–63.

Hamada, Hideo and Okuma, Yukiko 2002, "Shakai Hosho·Shakai Fukushi" (Social Security and Social Welfare), in *Asahi Gendai Yogo CHIEZO 2002* (The 2002 Asahi Treasury of Knowledge Concerning Key Words), edited by the Jiten Henshu Bu (Tokyo: Asahi Shimbunsha), pp. 464–74.

Hamaguchi, Eshun, ed. 1993, *Nihongata Moderu to wa Nanika* (What is the Japanese Model?) (Tokyo: Shin-yosha).

Hampden-Turner, Charles and Trompenaars, Fons 1994, *The Seven Cultures of Capitalism: Systems for Creating Wealth in the United States, Britain, Japan, Germany, France, Sweden and the Netherlands* (London: Judy Piatkus).

Hanami, Hiroaki, Mitsuhashi, Hideyuki, and Tachigi, Nami 2002, "Hatarakikata-Mitsuketa Kojin to Shakai no Atarashii Kankei" (Work Ways: Toward a New Relationship Between the Individual and Society), *Nikkei Bijinesu* (no. 1139: 29 April), pp. 26–40.

Hanami, Tadashi A. 1973, *Rodo Sogi Roshi Kankei ni Miru Nihonteki Fudo* (Industrial Disputes: The Japanese Element in Industrial Relations) (Tokyo: Nihon Keizai Shimbunsha).

1979, *Labor Relations in Japan Today* (Tokyo: Kodansha International).

1985, *Labor Law and Industrial Relations in Japan*, second revised edition (Boston: Kluwer Law and Taxation Publishers).

Hashimoto, Kenji 2001, *Kaikyu Shakai Nihon* (The Class Society in Japan) (Tokyo: Aoki Shoten).

Hayashi, Michiyoshi 1996, *Fusei no Fukken* (Restoring Fatherhood) (Tokyo: Chuo Koronsha).

2003, *Kazoku no Fukken* (Revitalizing the Family) (Tokyo: Chuo Koronshin-sha).

Hazama, Hiroshi 1959, "Chinrodosha no Keisei to Kazoku" (The Nature of Wage Labor and the Family), in *Ie – Sono Kozo Bunseki* (The Family: A Structural Analysis), edited by Kitano Seiichi and Okada Ken (Tokyo: Sobunsha), pp. 259–82.

1962, "Gijutsu Kakushin to 'Nihonteki' Romu Kanri – A Sekiyu O Seiyujo Chosa Hokoku" (Technological Change and "Japanese-Style" Management: A Report on the Survey at the O Refinery of A Petroleum), in *Romu Kenkyu Shiryo*, no. 60 (Research Material on Personnel Management) (Tokyo: Nihon Romu Kenkyuakai).

1963, "Ootomeeshon to Romu Kanri" (Automation and Personnel Management), *Nihon Rodo Kyokai Zasshi* (no. 52: July), pp. 12–19.

1964, *Nihon Romu Kanri Shi Kenkyu* (Research on the History of Personnel Management in Japan) (Tokyo: Daiyamondosha).

1967, "Rodosha no Kigyo Ishiki to Kumiai Ishiki" (The Consciousness of Workers Concerning their Company and Union), in *Gendai Rodo Mondai Koza Roshi Kankei* (Lecture Series on Contemporary Issues Concerning Labor: Industrial Relations), edited by Okochi Kazuo (Tokyo: Yuhikaku), pp. 181–96.

1971, *Nihonteki Keiei: Shudanshugi no Kozai* (Japanese-Style Management: The Merits and Demerits of Japan's Strong Group-Oriented Ethos) (Tokyo: Nihon Keizai Shimbunsha).

1981, *Nihon no Shiyosha Dantai to Roshi Kankei* (Japan's Employers' Associations and Labor–Management Relations) (Tokyo: Nihon Rodo Kyokai).

1986, *Keizai Taikoku o Tsukuriageta Shiso: Kodo Keizai Seichoki no Rodo Etosu* (The Thought and Behavior Making an Economic Superpower: The Workers' Ethos During the Period of High Economic Growth) (Tokyo: Bunshindo).

1989, *Keiei Shakaigaku: Gendai Kigyo no Rikai no tame ni* (The Sociology of Management: Toward an Understanding of the Modern Enterprise) (Tokyo: Yuhikaku).

1997a, *The History of Labour Management in Japan*, translated by Mari Sako and Eri Sako (London: Macmillan).

1997b, *Keiei Shakaigaku Shinpan* (The Sociology of Management, new edition) (Tokyo: Yuhikaku).

Hazama, Hiroshi, ed. 1994, *Kodo Keizai Seichoka no Seikatsu Sekai* (Living Under the Regime of High Economic Growth) (Tokyo: Bunshindo).

Hazama, Hiroshi *et al.*, eds. 1986, *Aruga Kizaemon Kenkyu: Ningen, Shiso, Gakumon* (Research on Aruga Kizaemon: People, Intellect and Learning) (Tokyo: Ochanomizu Shobo).

Hazama, Hiroshi and Kitagawa, Takayoshi 1985, *Keiei to Rodo no Shakaigaku* (The Sociology of Work and Management) (Tokyo: Tokyo Daigaku Shuppankai).

Hidaka, Rokuro 1984, *The Price of Affluence: Dilemmas of Contemporary Japan* (Tokyo: Kodansha International).

Higuchi, Yoshio 1991, *Nihon Keizai to Shugyo Kodo* (Employment Behavior and the Japanese Economy) (Tokyo: Toyo Keizai Shimposha).

Hirakawa, Takehiko 2002, "Fukushi Gai-nen no Hen-yo to Shakai" (Society and the Changes in how the Welfare Society is Defined), in *Guroobarizeeshon to Iryo-Fukushi* (Welfare, Medical Services and Globalization), edited by Hirakawa Takehiko *et al.*, vol. IV in the series, *Guroobarizeeshon to Nihon no Shakai* (Globalization and Japanese Society) (Tokyo: Bunka Shobo Hakubunsha), pp. 12–25.

Hirakawa, Takehiko *et al.*, eds. 2001, *Guroobarizeeshon to Iryo-Fukushi* (Welfare, Medical Services and Globalization), vol. IV in the series, *Guroobarizeeshon to Nihon no Shakai* (Globalization and Japanese Society) (Tokyo: Bunka Shobo Hakubunsha).

Hiromatsu, Takashi, Sato, Shin, Kodaira, Kazuyoshi, and Shinohara, Kyo 2002, "Kaware, Chusho Kigyo – Nihon no Yataibone ga Abunai" (Small and Medium-Sized Firms Face Pressure to Change as Japan's Foundations are in Danger), *Nikkei Bijinesu* (no. 1140: 6 May), pp. 26–41.

Hirose, Yoshinori 1983, *Jutaku Roon Shokogun* (The Rise and Fall of the Housing Loan) (Tokyo: Kadokawa Shoten).

1989, *Daishosen* (The Great Commercial Confrontation) (Tokyo: Tokuma Bunko).

Hokao, Ken-ichi 1965, *Rodo Ho Nyumon* (An Introduction to Labor Law) (Tokyo: Yuhikaku, with a fifth edition appearing in 1999).

Hoston, Germaine A. 1986, *Marxism and the Crisis of Development in Prewar Japan* (Princeton: Princeton University Press).

Huntington, Samuel P. 1992, "The Clash of Civilizations?" *Foreign Affairs* (vol. 72, no. 3: Summer), pp. 22–49.

Ichibangase, Yasuko and Kobayashi, Shizuka 2002, "Shakai Fukushi" (Social Welfare), in *Gendai Yogo no Kiso Chishiki 2002* (Encyclopedia of Contemporary Words 2002), edited by Ichiyanagi Midori (Tokyo: Jiyu Kokuminsha), pp. 984–90.

Ichi-en, Mitsuya 2002, "Shakai Hosho" (The Social Security System), in *IMIDASU '02* (Innovative Multi-Information Dictionary, Annual Series), edited by Shogo Sha (Tokyo: Shuei Sha), pp. 657–64.

Ihara, Ryoji 2003, *Toyota no Rodo Genba* (The Workplace at Toyota) (Tokyo: Sakurai Shoten).

Iijima, Nobuhiko 2002, "Guroobarizeeshon to Fukushi Kokka·Fukushi Shakai" (Globalization, the Welfare State and the Welfare Society), in *Guroobarizeeshon to Iryo-Fukushi* (Welfare, Medical Services and Globalization), edited by Hirakawa Takehiko *et al.*, vol. IV in the series, *Guroobarizeeshon to Nihon no Shakai* (Globalization and Japanese Society) (Tokyo: Bunka Shobo Hakubunsha), pp. 26–44.

Imaizumi, Reisuke, ed. 1999, *Tenkanki ni Okeru Shakai Fukushi: Shakai Fukushi to Enjo Gijutsu* (Social Welfare at a Turning Point: Social Welfare and the Art of Helping) (Tokyo: Chuo Hoki Shuppan).

Inaba, Motokichi 2002, *Shakai no Naka no Kigyo* (The Firm in Society), vol. III in the series *Gendai Keieigaku Koza* (The Complete Survey of Modern Management) (Tokyo: Yachiyo Shuppan).

Inagami, Takeshi 1981, *Roshi Kankei no Shakaigaku* (The Sociology of Industrial Relations) (Tokyo: Tokyo Daigaku Shuppankai).

1983, *Labor–Management Communication at the Workshop Level* (Tokyo: Japan Institute of Labor).

1988, *Japanese Workplace Industrial Relations* (Tokyo: Japan Institute of Labor).

1995, *Seijuku Shakai no Naka no Kigyobetsu Kumiai* (The Enterprise Union in a Developed Society) (Tokyo: Nihon Rodo Kenkyu Kiko).

2003, *Kigyo Guruupu Kei-ei to Shukko-Tenseki Kanko* (Managing in the Enterprise Group and the Practice of Inter-Company Transfers) (Tokyo: Tokyo Daigaku Shuppankai).

Inagami, Takeshi, *et al.* 1994, *Neo-Koporateizumu no Kokusai Hikaku* (A Comparative Study of Neo-Corporatism) (Tokyo: Nihon Rodo Kenkyu Kiko).

Inagami, Takeshi and Kawakita, Takashi, eds. 1988, *Yunion Aidentiti: Do Hiraku Rodo Kumiai no Shorai* (Union Identity: How Can Unions Make a Future for Themselves?) (Tokyo: Nihon Rodo Kyokai).

Inose, Naoki *et al.* 1988, *Naze Nihonjin wa Hatarakisugirunoka* (Why Are the Japanese Overworked?) (Tokyo: Heibonsha).

Inoue, Masao 1997, *Shakai Hen-yo to Rodo – "Rengo" no Seiritsu to Taishu Shakai no Seijuku* (Social Change and Labor – The Establishment of Rengo and the Maturation of Japanese Society) (Tokyo: Bokutakusha).

Inoue, Shun *et al.*, eds. 1996, *Jikan to Kukan no Shakaigaku* (The Sociology of Time and Space), vol. VI in the series *Gendai Shakaigaku* (Contemporary Sociology) (Tokyo: Iwanami Shoten).

Isa, Kyoko 2002, "Kokoro ni Yutori demo Tairyoku wa Shimpai" (The Heart is Willing, But Women Worry About their Physical Strength), *ASC*, 3 May, p. 22.

Ishida, Hiroshi 1993, *Social Mobility in Contemporary Japan: Educational Credentials, Class and the Labour Market in Cross-National Perspective* (Stanford, CA: Stanford University Press).

1999, "Gakureki Shutoku to Gakureki Koyo no Kokusai Hikaku" (A Comparative Study of Educational Attainment and the Impact of Education on Socio-Economic Attainment), *Nihon Rodo Kenkyu Zasshi* (no. 472: October), pp. 46–58.

Ishida, Hiroshi and Yoshikawa, Yumiko 2003, "How Profitable is Japanese Education? An International Comparison of the Benefits of Education," *Social Science Japan* (no. 25: February), pp. 3–7.

Ishida, Isoji 1967, "Kei-eisha Dantai no Soshiki to Kino" (The Organization and Function of Management Associations), in *Roshi Kankei*, edited by Okochi Kazuo, vol. IV in the series *Gendai Rodo Mondai Koza* (A Complete Guide to Contemporary Labor Issues) (Tokyo: Yuhikaku), pp. 307–25.

Ishikawa, Akihiro and Kawasaki, Yoshimoto, eds. 1991, *Nihon Shakai wa Byodo ka: Chuken Sarariiman no Imeeji* (How Egalitarian Is Japanese Society? Images of the Stable Salaried Employee) (Tokyo: Saiensusha).

Ishikawa, Tsuneo 1991, *Shotoku to Tomi* (Income and Wealth) (Tokyo: Iwanami Shoten).

Ishikawa, Tsuneo, ed. 1994, *Nihon no Shotoku to Tomi no Bunpai* (The Distribution of Income and Wealth in Japan) (Tokyo: Tokyo Daigaku Shuppankai).

Ito, Masanori and Takeda, Yukihiko 1990, "Rodo Kumiai Soshikiritsu no Suii to Sono Henka Yoin" (Trends in the Unionization Rate and Factors

Affecting those Changes), *Rodo Tokei Chosa Geppo* (Monthly Labor Statistics and Research Bulletin) (vol. 42, no. 6: June), pp. 6–14.

Iwasaki, Kaoru 1993, "Union Leaders' Attitudes and Career Development," *Japan Labor Bulletin* (vol. 32, no. 2: February), pp. 5–8.

Iwasaki, Nobuhiko 1984, "Jidosha Sangyo Rodosha ni Okeru Rodo Seikatsu to Sogai" (Alienation and the Working Life of Workers in the Auto Industry), *Kobe Daigaku Bungakubu Kiyo* (no. 11).

1985, "Rodosha Teichaku Seisaku to Rodo Seisaku" (Strategies to Build Loyalty Among Workers and Life at Work), in *Kyodai Kigyotaise to Rodosha* (Workers and the Large Enterprise System), edited by Oyama Yoichi (Tokyo: Ochanomizu Shobo), pp. 522–41.

Iwata, Ryushi 1974, *Nihonteki Keiei no Hensei Genri* (The Underlying Organizational Principles of Japanese-Style Management) (Tokyo: Bunshindo).

1975, *Gendai Nihon no Keiei Fudo* (The Management Ethos of Modern Japan) (Tokyo: Nihon Keizai Shinposha).

1980a, *Nihonteki Sensu no Keieigaku* (Management According to the Japanese Sense) (Tokyo: Toyo Keizai Shinposha).

1980b, *Gakureki Shugi wa Hokai Shitaka* (Has Credentialism Really Come to an End?) (Tokyo: Nihon Keizai Shimbunsha).

1982, *Japanese-Style Management: Its Foundations and Prospects* (Tokyo: Asian Productivity Organization).

1989, *Nihon no Kogyoka to Jukuren Keisei* (The Industrialization of Japan and the Formation of a Skilled Labor Force) (Tokyo: Nihon Hyoronsha).

Japan Institute of Labor 1983, *Highlights in Japanese Industrial Relations: A Selection of Articles from the Japan Labor Bulletin* (Tokyo: Japan Institute of Labor).

1992, *Japanese Working Life Profile: Labor Statistics 1992–1993* (Tokyo: Japan Institute of Labor).

Kagiyama, Yoshimitsu and Ota, Shigeru 2001, *Nihon ni Okeru Rodo Joken no Tokushitsu to Shihyo 2001 Nenban* (Characteristics and Indices that Define Working Conditions in Japan: the 2001 edition) (Tokyo: Hakuto Shobo).

Kagoyama, Takashi 1943, *Kokumin Seikatsu no Kozo* (The Structure of Life Amongst the Japanese People) (Tokyo: Nagatoya Shobo).

1953, *Hinkon to Ningen* (Poverty and Human Existence) (Tokyo: Kawade Shobo).

Kahn, Herman 1970, *The Emerging Japanese Superstate: Challenge and Response* (Englewood Cliffs, NJ: Prentice-Hall).

Kajita, Takamichi 2002, "Nihon no Gaikokujin Rodosha Seisaku" (Policy for Foreign Workers in Japan), in *Kokusaika Suru Nihon Shakai* (Japanese Society in the Process of Internationalization), vol. I in the series *Kokusai Shakai* (International Society), edited by Kajita Takamichi and Miyajima Takashi (Tokyo: Tokyo Daigaku Shuppan), pp. 15–44.

Kamata, Satoshi 1973, *Jidosha Zetsubo Kojo: Aru Kisetsuko no Nikki* (The Auto Factory of Despair: The Diary of One Seasonal Worker) (Tokyo: Gendai Shi Shuppankai).

1982, *Japan in the Passing Lane: An Insider's Account of Life in a Japanese Auto Factory*, translated and edited by Tatsuru Akimoto (New York: Pantheon Books; London: Allen and Unwin).

1986, *Nihonjin no Shigoto* (Japanese at Work) (Tokyo: Heibonsha).

Kanamori, Hisao, ed. 1990, *Sengo Keizai no Kiseki* (The Position of Japan's Postwar Economy) (Tokyo: Chuo Keizaisha).

Kaneko, Yoshio 1980, "The Future of the Fixed-Age Retirement System," in *The Labor Market in Japan: Selected Readings*, edited by Nishikawa Shunsaku and translated by Ross Mouer (Tokyo: Tokyo University Press), pp. 104–23. Originally published as "Tei-nensei no Shorai," *Nihon Rodo Kyokai Zasshi* (vol. 15, no. 5: May 1973), pp. 2–10.

Kanomata, Nobuo 1990, "Fubyodo no Susei to Kaiso Koteika Setsu" (Trends in Inequality and the Theory of Status Crystallization), in *Gendai Nihon no Kaiso Kozo* (The Social Stratification of Contemporary Japan), vol. I of *Shaikai Kaiso no Kozo to Katei* (The Processes of Social Stratification), edited by Naoi Atsushi and Seiyama Kazuo (Tokyo: Tokyo Daigaku Shuppankai), pp. 151–67.

Kariya, Takehiko 1991, *Gakko-Shokugyo-Senbatsu no Shakaigaku: Kosotsu Shushoku no Nihonteki Mekanizumu* (A Sociology of School, Work and Competition: The Japanese Mechanism by which High School Graduates Gain Employment) (Tokyo: Tokyo Daigaku Shuppankai).

2001, *Kaisoka Nihon to Kyoiku Kiki – Fubyodo Saiseisan kara Iyoku Kakusa Shakai e* (The Crisis in Education and the Stratification of Japan: From Inequality in Class Reproduction to a Difference in Incentives) (Tokyo: Yushindo Kobunsha).

Karoshi Bengodan Zenkoku Renraku Kaigi (The National Defence Council for Victims of Death from Overwork) 1991, *Karoshi – When the "Corporate Warrior" Dies* (Tokyo: Madosha).

Kassalow, Everett M. 1983, "Japan as an Industrial Relations Model," *Journal of Industrial Relations* (vol. 25, no. 2: June), pp. 201–19.

Kataoka, Shinshi and Shinozuka, Tsuneo 1998, *Atarashii Jidai to Kei-eigaku* (Management Studies and the New Era), vol. I in *Sosho Gendai Kei-eigaku* (The Library of Management Studies) (Tokyo: Mineruva Shobo).

Kato, Tetsuro and Steven, Rob 1991, *Is Japanese Capitalism Post-Fordist?*, Occasional Papers of the Japanese Studies Centre, no. 16 (Melbourne: Japanese Studies Centre).

Kato, Tetsuro and Steven, Rob, eds. 1993, *Is Japanese Management Post-Fordism?* (Tokyo: Madosha).

Kato, Yuji 1989, "Kaikyu-Kaiso Kosei no Henka to Rodosha Kaikyu" (Changes to the Class-Strata Structure and the Working Class), in *Gendai Nihon Keizai no Kozo to Seisaku* (Policy and the Structure of the Economy in Contemporary Japan), edited by Teruoka Shuzo and Seiyama Takuro (Kyoto: Mineruvia Shobo), pp. 214–37.

Kawaguchi, Akira 2000, "Dagurasu=Arisawa Hosoku wa Yuko na no ka" (Does the Douglas–Arisawa Effect Still Hold?), *Nihon Rodo Kenkyu Zassahi* (no. 501: April), pp. 18–21.

Kawanishi Hirosuke 1977, *Shosuha Rodo Kumiai Undoron* (View on the Labor Movement in Minority Unions) (Tokyo: Kaien Shobo).

1979, "Sangyo-Rodo Shakaigaku no Kenkyu Doko to Kadai" (The History and Challenges of a Sociology of Industry and Labor), in *Kikan Rodo Ho* (no. 113: Fall), pp. 202–13.

1981a, *Kigyobetsu Kumiai no Jittai* (The Situation of the Enterprise Union) (Tokyo: Nihon Hyoronsha).

1981b, "Tenkan Subeki Rodo Undoron no Shiten – 'Futari no Rodo Kumiai' no Soshutsu o" (Looking at Strategies for the Labor Movement in Transition – Promoting the Two-Person Labor Union), *Gekkan Rodo Mondai* (no. 294: December), pp. 58–61.

1984, "Daisanki Rodo Shakaigaku no Seika" (The Formation of a Sociology of Labour: The Third Period), *Keizai Hyoron* (special issue of "Rodo Nenkan 84" [Labor Annual 1984]) (Tokyo: Nihon Hyoronsha), pp. 233–45.

1986, *Japan in Umbruch* (Japan in Transition), translated into German by Wolfgang Seifert (Cologne: Vund-Verlag).

1989, *Kigyobetsu Kumiai no Riron: Mo Hitotsu no Nihonteki Roshi Kankei* (A Theory of the Enterprise Union: The Other View of Japanese-Style Industrial Relations) (Tokyo: Nihon Hyoronsha).

1990, *Shinban-Shosuha Rodo Kumiai Undoron* (Views on the Labor Movement in Small Minority Unions: The Revised Edition) (Tokyo: Nihon Hyoronsha).

1991, "Roshi Kankei Kenkyu to Rodo Shakaigaku" (Industrial Relations Research and Labor Sociology), in *Shakai Seisaku Kenkyu no Hoho to Ryoiki* (Social Policy: Its Method and Problem Consciousness), edited by the Shakai Seisaku Gakkai (The Society for the Study of Social Policy) (Tokyo: Keibunsha), pp. 131–57.

1992a, *Enterprise Unionism in Japan*, translated from Japanese by Ross Mouer (London: Kegan Paul International).

1992b, *Densangata Chingin no Sekai – Sono Keisei to Rekishiteki Igi* (The Densan Wage System – Its Formation and Historical Significance) (Tokyo: Waseda Daigaku Shuppan Bu).

1993, *Kikigaki-Densai no Gunzo* (A Portrait of Densan Through its Records) (Tokyo: Heigensha).

1997, *The Human Face of Industrial Conflict in Post-war Japan* (London: Kegan Paul International).

2000, *Nihon no Rodo Shakaigaku* (Labor Sociology in Japan) (Tokyo: Waseda Daigaku Shuppan Bu).

2001, "Rodo Kumiai wa Sonzoku Dekiru ka" (Can Labor Unions Survive?), *Campus Now* (Waseda University) (no. 121: April), p. 8.

Kazahaya, Yasoji 1973, *Nihon Shakai Seisaku Shi* (The History of Social Policy in Japan), 2 vols. (Tokyo: Aoki Bunko).

Keizai Kikaku Cho (The Economic Planning Agency) 2001, *Kokumin Seikatsu Hakusho – Heisei Juninenban: Boranteia ga Fukameru Koen* (The 2000 White Paper on the People's Lifestyle: Good Relationships from the Growing Interest in Voluntary Activity) (Tokyo: Okura Sho Insatsu Kyoku).

Keizai Kikaku Cho, Kokumin Seikatsu Kyoku (The Economic Planning Agency, Office of the People's Livelihood) 1996, *Kokumin Seikatsu Senkodo Chosa: Yutaka na Shakai no Kokumin Ishiki* (A Survey of the People's Attitudes Toward Everyday Life: National Public Opinion in Affluent Society) (Tokyo: Okura Sho Insatsu Kyoku).

Kelly, Kevin 1998, *New Rules for the New Economy* (New York: Penguin Books).

Kenny, Martin and Florida, Richard 1993, *Beyond Mass Production: The Japanese System and its Transfer to the US* (Oxford: Oxford University Press).

Kensy, Rainer 2000, *Keiretsu Economy – New Economy* (New York: Palgrave).

Kinoshita, Jun 1993, "Kigyo Shakai" (The Enterprise Society), in *Shinpan Shakai Seisaku – o Manabu Hito no Tame ni* (The Revised Social Policy Edition – For Those Wanting to Know About Social Security), edited by Tamai Kingo and Omori Maki (Kyoto: Sekai Shiso Sah), pp. 72–92.

Kishimoto, Shigenobu 1978, *"Churyu" no Genso* (The Illusion of the Middle) (Tokyo: Kodansha).

Kitagawa, Takayoshi 1956, "Rodo Kumiai Kenkyu ni Okeru Jakkan no Kihonteki Mondai ni Tsuite" (A View of some Basic Problems in the Research on the Union Movement), in *Nihon Shakaigaku no Kadai* (Challenges for Sociology), a *Festschrift* in honor of Professor Hayashi Megumi, edited by Fukutake Tadashi (Tokyo: Yuhikaku), pp. 233–45.

1965, *Rodo Shakaigaku Nyumon* (An Introduction to the Sociology of Labor) (Tokyo: Yuhikaku).

1968, *Nikkeiren – Nihon no Shihai Kiko* (Nikkeiren – The Apparatus that Controls Japan) (Tokyo: Rodo Junpo Sha).

Kitagawa, Takayoshi and Kainuma, Jun 1985, *Nihon no Eriito* (Japan's Elite) (Tokyo: Otsuki Shoten; reprinted 1993).

Koga, Jun-ichiro 2000, *Keidanren – Nihon o Ugokasu Zaikai Shinku Tanku* (Keidanren – The Think Tank that Moves Japan) (Tokyo: Shincho Sha).

Koike, Kazuo 1969, "Nihonjin wa Naze Yoku Hataraku ka" (Why Do the Japanese Work So Hard?), in *Nihonjin no Keizai Kodo* (The Economic Behavior of the Japanese), edited by Sumiya Mikio (Tokyo: Toyo Keizai Shimposha), pp. 9–19.

1977, *Shokuba no Rodo Kumiai to Sanka* (Participation and the Union on the Shop Floor) (Tokyo: Toyo Keizai Shimposha).

1978, *Rodosha no Keiei Sanka* (Worker Participation in Management) (Tokyo: Nihon Hyoronsha).

1983a, "Internal Labor Markets: Workers in Large Firms," in *Contemporary Industrial Relations in Japan*, edited by Taishiro Shirai (Madison: University of Wisconsin Press), pp. 29–61.

1983b, "Workers in Small Firms and Women in Industry," in *Contemporary Industrial Relations in Japan*, edited by Taishiro Shirai (Madison: University of Wisconsin Press), pp. 89–115.

1988, *Understanding Industrial Relations in Modern Japan*, translated by Mary Saso (London: Macmillan).

1989, "Some Conditions for QC Circles: Long-Term Perspectives in the Behaviour of Individuals," in *Constructs for Understanding Japan*, edited by Yoshio Sugimoto and Ross Mouer (London: Kegan Paul International), pp. 94–129.

1991, *Shigoto no Keizaigaku* (The Economics of Work) (Tokyo: Toyo Keizai Shimposha).

1994, *Nihon no Koyo Shisutemu: Sono Fuhensei to Tsuyomi* (Japan's Employment System: Its Universality and Strength) (Tokyo: Toyo Keizai Shimposha).

1995, *The Economics of Work in Japan* (Tokyo: LTCB International Library Foundation).

1997, *Human Resource Development*, Japanese Economy and Labor Series, no. 2 (Tokyo: Japan Institute of Labor).

Koike, Kazuo and Inoki, Takenori 1987, *Jinzai Keisei no Kokusai Hikaku: Tonan Ajia to Nihon* (A Comparative Study of the Formation of Human Capital: Japan and Southeast Asia) (Tokyo: Toyo Keizai Shimposha).

Koike, Kazuo and Inoki, Takenori, eds. 1990, *Skill Formation in Japan and Southeast Asia* (Tokyo: University of Tokyo Press).

Koike, Kazuo and Watanabe, Ikuro 1979, *Gakureki Shakai no Kyozo* (The Myth of Education-Based Credentialism in Japan) (Tokyo: Toyo Keizai Shimposha).

Kojima, Ikuo 2000, *"Zukai de Wakaru e-Kigyo Keiretsu" to Gyokai Saihen no Shikumi* (The Electronically Linked Enterprise Groups and a Map of the Restructured Industrial Groupings) (Tokyo: Subaru Sha).

Komai, Hiroshi 1989, *Japanese Management Overseas: Experiences in the United States and Thailand* (Tokyo: Asian Productivity Organization).

1995, *Migrant Workers in Japan* (London: Kegan Paul International).

2001, *Foreign Migrants in Contemporary Japan*, translated by Jens Wilkinson (Melbourne: Trans Pacific Press).

Komatsu, Ryuji 1994, "The Labour Movement and the Government in Japan," in *Industrial Relations in Australia and Japan*, edited by Jim Hagan and Andrew Wells (Sydney: Allen and Unwin), pp. 116–22.

Kondo, Dorinne 1990, *Crafting Selves: Power, Gender and Discourses of Identity in a Japanese Workplace* (Chicago: University of Chicago Press).

Korzeniewicz, Roberto Patricio and Moran, Timothy Patrick 1997, "World-Economic Trends in the Distribution of Income: 1965–1992," *American Journal of Sociology* (vol. 102, no. 4: January), pp. 1000–39.

Kosaka, Kenji, ed. 1994, *Social Stratification in Contemporary Japan* (London: Kegan Paul International).

Kosei Rodo Daijin Kanbo Somuka (Department of General Affairs, Minister's Secretariat, Ministry of Health, Labor and Welfare) 2001, *Rodo Ho Zensho* (The Compendium of Labor Law) (Tokyo: Romu Gyosei Kenkyujo).

Kosei Rodo Sho (The Ministry of Welfare, Labor and Health) 2000, *Rodo Hakusho Heisei Juni Nenban* (The 2000 White Paper on Labor) (Tokyo: Nihon Rodo Kenkyu Kiko).

2001a, *Rodo Keizai Hakusho Heisei Jusan Nenban: Joho Tsushin Gijitsu (IT) no Kakushin to Koyo* (The 2001 White Paper on the Labor Economy: Employment and the IT Revolution) (Tokyo: Nihon Rodo Kenkyu Kiko).

2001b, *Kosei Rodo Hakusho Heisei Jusan Nendo: Shogai ni Watari Kojin no Jiritsu o Shien suru Kosei Rodo Gyosei* (The 2001 Welfare and Labor White Paper: Toward a Labor and Welfare Policy which Will Support the Development of the Individual Throughout their Life) (Tokyo: Gyosei).

Kosei Rodo Sho Daijin Kanbo Tokei Joho Bu (Statistics and Information Department, Minister's Secretariat, Ministry of Health, Labor and Welfare) 2002a, *Rodo Tokei Yoran Heisei Jusan Nendo* (The 2001 Handbook of Labor Statistics) (Tokyo: Zaimu Sho Insatsu Kyoku).

2002b, *Kosei Tokei Yoron – Heisei Jusan Nendo* (Handbook of Health and Welfare Statistics for Fiscal Year 2001) (Tokyo: Kosei Tokei Kyokai).

2002c, *Rodo Tokei Nenpo Heisei Ju-ni Nen* (Year Book of Labor Statistics 2000) (Tokyo: Romu Gyosei Kenkyujo).

Kosei Rodo Sho Koyo Kinto-Jido Katei Kyoku (Ministry of Welfare, Labor and Health, Bureau of Equal Employment and Child–Family Affairs) 2001, *Josei Rodo Hakusho – Heisei Jusan Nenpan* (The 2001 White Paper on Working Women) (Tokyo: Nijuisseiki Shokugyo Zaidan).

Kosei Rodo Sho Roshi Kankei Tanto Sanjikan Shitsu (Office of the Adviser on Industrial Relations, Ministry of Welfare, Labor and Health) and Nihon Rodo Kenkyu Kiko (The Japan Institute of Labor) 2002, *Rodo Undo Hakusho Heisei Jusannenban: "Koyo no Seefuteinetto" Tsukuri to Roso no Yakuwari* (The 2001 Labor Movement White Paper: Establishing an Employment Safety Net and the Role of Unions) (Tokyo: Nihon Rodo Kenkyu Kiko).

Koseki, Tomohiro 2002, *Hataraku Koto wa Ikiru Koto* (Work is Living) (Tokyo: Kodansha).

Koshiro, Kazutoshi 1980, *Labour Management Relations in Japanese Public Enterprises* (Bochum: Studienverlag Brockmeyer).

1981a, "The Path for Unionism in the Eighties," *Japan Echo* (vol. 8, no. 1: Spring), pp. 20–9.

1981b, "Koyo Kyushuryoku wa Teika Suruka" (Will the Capacity to Absorb Labor Decrease?), *Keizai Seminaa* (no. 1: October), pp. 219–31.

1982a, *Nihon no Roshi Kankei* (Industrial Relations in Japan) (Tokyo: Yuhikaku).

1982b, "Ryoko na Koyo Kikai no Kishosei to Nihonteki Roshi Kankei" (The Scarcity of Good Jobs and Japanese Industrial Relations), *Nihon Rodo Kyokai Zasshi* (vol. 24, no. 1: January), pp. 4–13.

1995, "Sengo Nihon Rodo Kumiai Undoshi Gaisetsu" (An Overview of Japan's Labor Movement in the First Fifty Years After the War), in *Sengo Gojunen: Sangyo Koyo Rodoshi* (The First Half Century After the War: A History of Labor, Employment and Industry), edited by the Nihon Rodo Kenkyu Kiko (Tokyo: Nihon Rodo Kenkyu Kiko), pp. 1–176.

2002, *A Fifty-Year History of Industry and Labor in Postwar Japan*, edited by Charles Weathers, Japanese Economy and Labor Series no. 6 (Tokyo: Japan Institute of Labor).

Kosugi, Reiko 2003, *Furiitaa to iu Ikikata* (Freelancing as a Way of Life) (Tokyo: Keiso Shobo).

Krauss, Ellis 1974, *Japanese Radicals Revisited: Student Protest in Postwar Japan* (Berkeley: University of California Press).

Kruger, David and Fuyuno, Ichiko 2002, "Innovate or Die: Reinventing Japan," *Far Eastern Economic Review* (vol. 165, no. 16: 25 April), pp. 28–33.

Kumazawa, Makoto 1976, *Kokka no naka no Kokka* (The State Within the State) (Tokyo: Nihon Hyoronsha).

1981, *Nihon no Rodoshazo* (Portrait of Japan's Workers) (Tokyo: Chikuma Shobo).

1983, *Minshushugi wa Kojo no Monzen de Tachisukumu* (How Democracy Stands Timid in front of the Factory Gate) (Tokyo: Tabata Shoten).

1986a, *Shokubashi no Shura o Ikite* (Learning from the Tough History of the Workplace) (Tokyo: Chikuma Shobo).

1986b, *Shinhen-Nihon no Rodoshazo* (An Updated Portrait of Japan's Workers) (Tokyo: Chikuma Shobo).

1989, *Nihonteki Keiei no Meian* (The Pluses and Minuses of Japanese-Style Management) (Tokyo: Chikuma Shobo).

1993a, *Hatarakimonotachi Naki Egao: Gendai Nihon no Rodo-Kyoiku-Keizai Shakai Shisutemu* (The Workers: The Social System and the Economy, Education, and Labor in Contemporary Japan) (Tokyo: Yuhikaku).

1993b, *Shin-Nihon no Rodosha Zo* (New Snapshots of the Japanese Worker) (Tokyo: Chikuma Shobo).

1994, *Shinhen-Nihon no Rodosha Zo* (An Updated Portrait of the Japanese Worker) (Tokyo: Chikuma Shobo).

1996, *Portraits of the Japanese Workplace: Labor Movements, Workers, and Managers*, translated from Japanese by Andrew Gordon and Mikiso Hane (Boulder, CO: Westview Press).

1997, *Noryokushugi to Kigyo Shakai* (The Commitment to Ability and the Enterprise-Centered Society) (Tokyo: Iwanami Shoten).

2001, *Risutora to Waaku Shearingu* (Restructuring and Work Sharing) (Tokyo: Iwanami Sshoten).

Kume, Ikuo 2000, "Rodo Seisaku Katei no Seijuku to Hen-yo" (The Evolution and Maturing of the Labor Policy-Making Process), *Nihon Rodo Kenkyu Zasshi* (no. 475: January), pp. 2–13.

Kusaka, Kimindo 1989, *Nihon Keizai no Koko ga Wakaranai: Yoten Kaisetsu 50 no Q&A* (Commonly Misunderstood Aspects of the Japanese Economy: Fifty Key Questions and Answers) (Tokyo: PHP Kenkyujo).

Kusuda, Kyu 2000, "Sengo Nihon no Chingin Seido no Sokatsu" (An Overview of the Wage System in Postwar Japan), in *Nihon no Chingin: Sengo no Kiseki to Shinseiki no Tenbo* (The Japanese Wage System: The Shifting Focus in Postwar Japan and a Prognosis for the New Century), edited by Nihon no Chingin 2000 nen Purojekuto [Team]) (Tokyo: Shakai Keizai Seisansei Honbu Seisansei Rodo Joho Sentaa), pp. 3–22.

Kuwahara, Yasuo 1987, "Japanese Industrial Relations," in *International and Comparative Industrial Relations*, edited by Greg J. Bamber and Russell D. Lansbury (Sydney: Allen and Unwin), pp. 211–31.

1989, *Industrial Relations System in Japan*, Japanese Industrial Relations series no. 16 (Tokyo: Japan Institute of Labor).

1993, "Are Workers Really in Short Supply?" in *Highlights in Japanese Industrial Relations: A Selection of Articles from the Japan Labor Bulletin*, vol. III, edited by the Japan Institute of Labor (Tokyo: Japan Institute of Labor), pp. 46–50.

Kuwahara, Yasuo, ed. 2001, *Guroobaru Jidai no Gaikokujin Rodosha: Doko kara Kite Doko e* (Foreign Workers in the Globalized Era: Their Origins and Future) (Tokyo: Toyo Keizai Shimposha).

Kyotani, Eiji 1993, *Furekishibiriti to wa nani ka Gendai Nihon no Rodo Katei* (What Does Flexibility Mean for Labor Process in Contemporary Japan?) (Tokyo: Madosha).

Kyujugonen SSM Chosa Kenkyukai (The 1995 Social Stratification and Mobility Research Group) 2000, *Nihon no Kaiso Shisutemu* (The Social Stratification System in Japan), 6 vols. (Tokyo: Tokyo Daigaku Shuppankai).

Large, Stephen S. 1982, *Organized Workers and Socialist Politics in Interwar Japan* (Cambridge: Cambridge University Press).

Levine, Solomon B. 1967, "Postwar Trade Unionism, Collective Bargaining and Japanese Social Structure," in *Aspects of Social Change in Modern Japan*, edited by R. P. Dore (Princeton: Princeton University Press), pp. 245–85.

Lincoln, James R. and Kalleberg, Arne L. 1996, "Commitment, Quits and Work Organization in Japanese and US Plants," *Industrial and Labor Relations Review* (vol. 50, no. 1: October), pp. 39–59.

Lipietz, Alain 1997, "Economic Restructuring: The New Global Hierarchy," in *Work of the Future: Global Perspectives*, edited by Paul James, Walter F. Veit and Steve Wright (Sydney: Allen and Unwin), pp. 45–65.

Mabuchi, Hitoshi 2001, "Discourses of Intercultural Edducation in Japan," Ph.D. thesis submitted to Monash University, Melbourne.

McCormack, Gavan 1996, *The Emptiness of Japanese Affluence* (New York: M. E. Sharpe).

McCormack, Gavan and Sugimoto, Yoshio, eds. 1986, *Democracy in Contemporary Japan* (Sydney: Hale and Iremonger).

Mackie, Vera 2003, *Feminism in Modern Japan: Citizenship, Embodiment and Sexuality* (Cambridge: Cambridge University Press).

McMillan, C. J. 1989, *The Japanese Industrial System*, second revised edition (New York: W. de Gruyter).

Mahathir, bin Mohamad and Ishihara, Shintaro 1994, *"No" to Ieru Ajia: Tai-Obei e no Hosoku* (The Asia That Can Say "No!" – At a Crossroads in Relations with Europe and America) (Tokyo: Kobunsha).

Mannari, Hiroshi 1974, *The Japanese Business Leaders* (Tokyo: University of Tokyo Press).

Marsh, Robert and Mannari, Hiroshi 1976, *Modernization and the Japanese Factory* (Princeton: Princeton University Press).

1988, *Organizational Change in Japanese Factories* (Greenwich, CT: JAI Press).

Mathews, Gordon 1996, *What Makes Life Worth Living? How Japanese and Americans Make Sense of their Worlds* (Berkeley: University of California Press).

Masataka, Nobuo 2002, *Chichioyaryoku: Boshi Mitchaku Gata Kosodate kara no Dasshutsu* (The Power of Fatherhood: Getting away from the Mother-Centered Approach) (Tokyo: Chuo Koronshinsha).

Matsubara, Hiroshi 2002, "Economic Gloom Just Adds to Illegal Workers' Plight: Government, Devious Employers Seek to Reap Benefits Without Legal Responsibilities," *Japan Times*, 27 June, p. 3.

Matsushima, Shizuo 1951, *Rodo Shakaigaku Josetsu* (An Introduction to the Sociology of Labor) (Tokyo: Fukumura Shoten).

1956a, "Roshi Kankei" (Industrial Relations), in *Koza Shakaigaku-Kaikyu to Kumiai* (Lectures in Sociology: Class and Unions), edited by Fukutake Tadashi (Tokyo: Tokyo Daigaku Shuppankai), pp. 167–89.

1956b, "Rodo Shakaigaku no Tomen suru Mittsu no Kenkyu Kadai" (The Three Tasks Confronting the Sociology of Labor), in *Nihon Shakaigaku no Kadai* (Challenges for Sociology), a *Festschrift* in honor of Professor Hayashi Megumi, edited by Fukutake Tadashi (Tokyo: Yuhikaku), pp. 201–14.

Matsushima, Shizuo, ed. 1962, *Romu Kanri no Nihonteki Tokushitsu to Hensen* (Change and the Characteristics of Japanese-Style Personnel Management) (Tokyo: Daiyamondosha).

Matsushima, Shizuo and Hazama, Hiroshi 1962, "F Kogyo Y Tanko Chosa" (The Surveys at F Mining Company and the Y Coal Colliery), in *Romu Kanri no Nihonteki Tokushitu to Hensen* (Change and Characteristics of Japanese-Style Personnel Management), edited by Matsushima Shizuo (Tokyo: Daiyamondosha), pp. 67–158.

Meaney, Neville, Matthews, Trevor, and Encel, Sol 1988, *The Japanese Connection* (Melbourne: Longman Cheshire).

Mieno, Takashi 1990, *"Seikatsu no Shitsu" no Imi* (The Meaning of "Quality of Life") (Tokyo: Hakuto Shobo).

Mills, C. Wright 1956, *The Power Elite* (New York: Oxford University Press).

Minami, Tatsuhisa and Kameda, Hayao, eds. 2000, *Nijuissekigata Kigyo no Kei-ei. Soshiki. Ningen* (Management, Organization and People in the Twenty-First-Century Firm) (Tokyo: Bunshindo).

Ministry of Labor 1995, *Labor Laws of Japan 1995* (Tokyo: Romu Gyosei Kenkyujo).

Mitarai, Fujio 2003, "Nihon Keizai: Hikanron ni Konkyo Nashi" (The Japanese Economy: No Reason for Pessimism), *Asahi Shimbun* (morning edition), 20 April, p. 17.

Miura, Fumio, ed. 2001, *Zusetsu Koreisha Hakusho 2001 Nendoban* (The 2001 White Paper on the Aged: A Brief Overview) (Tokyo: Zenkoku Shakai Fukushi Kyogikai).

Miyajima, Takashi and Kajita, Takamichi, eds. 2000, *Gaikokujin Rodosha kara Shimin e – Chiiki Shakai no Shiten to Kadai kara* (From Foreign Workers to Citizens from the Perspective of the Local Community) (Tokyo: Yuhikaku).

Miyata, Kazuaki 1995, *Gendai Nihon Shakai Fukushi Seisaku Ron* (Welfare Policy in Contemporary Japanese Society) (Kyoto: Mineruva Shobo).

Mizukami, Tetsuo 1993, *Integration of Japanese Residents into Australian Society: Immigrants and Sojourners in Brisbane*, Papers of the Japanese Studies Centre, no. 20 (Melbourne: Japanese Studies Centre).

Mombu Kagaku Sho (Ministry of Education and Science) 2002, *Mombu Kagaku Tokei Yoran: Heisei Juyon Nenban* (The 2002 Handbook of Statistics on Education and Science) (Tokyo: Zaimu Sho Insatsu Kyoku).

Moore, Joe 1983, *Japanese Workers and the Struggle for Power, 1945–1947* (Madison: University of Wisconsin Press).

Mori, Kiyoshi 1999, *Haiteku Shakai to Rodo: Nani ga Okite iru ka* (Work and the High Tech Society: What is Happening?) (Tokyo: Iwanami Shoten).

Morikawa, Hidemasa 1973, *Nihongata Keiei no Genryu* (The Origins of Japanese-Style Management) (Tokyo: Toyo Keizai Shimposha).

Morishima, Motohiro 1997, "Changes in Japanese Human Resource Management: A Demand-Side Story," *Japan Labor Bulletin* (vol. 36, no. 11: November), pp. 5–11.

Motojima, Kunio 1965, "'Rodo Kyogyo Shudan' ni Okeru Shihai Kozo" (The Control Structure in "Joint Cooperative Work Groups"), in *Koza Gendai Shakaigaku Shudanron* (Lecture Series on Contemporary Sociology:

Groups), edited by Kitagawa Takayoshi (Tokyo: Aoki Shoten), pp. 243–79.

Mouer, Ross 1975, "Nihon ni Okeru Ka-i Taikei Betsu no Shotoku Bunpu no Jokyo: Kakei Chosa Kenkyu o Tsujite" (A Subsystems Approach to Income Distribution in the Japanese Setting: A Study of the FIES Data, 1963–1972), *Kikan Riron Keizaigaku* (Quarterly Journal of Theoretical Economics) (vol. 26, no. 1: April), pp. 30–44.

1989, "The Japanese Model of Industrial Relations: Warnings or Opportunities?" *Hitotsubashi Journal of Social Studies* (vol. 21, no. 1: August), pp. 105–24.

1991, "Income Distribution in Japan: Change and Continuity, 1962–1990," paper presented to the Sixth Biennial Conference of the Japanese Studies Association of Australia (Canberra: Australian National University, July).

1992, "Translator's Preface," in *Enterprise Unionism in Japan*, by Kawanishi Hirosuke (London: Kegan Paul International), pp. xxiii–xxvi.

1995, "Postmodernism or Ultramodernism: The Japanese Dilemma at Work," in *Japanese Encounters with Postmodernity*, edited by Yoshio Sugimoto and Johann P. Arnason (London: Kegan Paul International), pp. 32–64.

1997, "Between Modernism and Postmodernism: Comparing Japan," in *Work of the Future: Global Perspectives*, edited by Paul James, Walter Veit and Steve Wright (Sydney: Allen and Unwin), pp. 139–56.

Mouer, Ross and Sugimoto, Yoshio 1986, *Images of Japanese Society: A Study in the Structure of Social Reality* (London: Kegan Paul International).

1995, "*Nihonjinron* at the End of the Twentieth Century: A Multicultural Perspective," in *Japanese Encounters with Postmodernity*, edited by Yoshio Sugimoto and Johann P. Arnason (London: Kegan Paul International), pp. 237–69.

2003, "Civil Society in Japan," in *Civil Society in Asia*, edited by David Schak and Wayne Hudson (Aldershot: Ashgate), pp. 209–24.

Murao, Yumiko 2003, "Gender Issues in Classrooms: The Present Situation and Future Tasks," *Social Science Japan* (no. 25: February), pp. 19–21.

Naito, Norikuni 1983, "Trade Union Finance and Administration," in *Contemporary Industrial Relations in Japan*, edited by Shirai Taishiro (Madison: University of Wisconsin Press), pp. 145–59.

Nakae, Akihiro 1998, *Nijuisseki no Shakai Hosho – Nihon to Chugoku no Genjo to Kadai* (Social Security in the Twenty-First Century: The Present and Future of Social Security in China and Japan) (Tokyo: Daiichi Shobo).

Nakagawa, Kiyoshi 2001, *Nihon Toshi no Seikatsu Hendo* (Changes in the Lifestyles of Urban Japanese) (Tokyo: Keiso Shobo).

Nakagawa, Takeo 2002, "Zaikai Kaeruka Okuda Ryu" (Will the Okuda Approach Change Japan's Top Management?), *ASC*, 27 May, p. 13.

Nakamura, Chu-ichi 2002, *Eriito e no Michi wa Chugaku-Koko Erabi de Kimaru Yushuko no Kyoiku Shisutemu no Himitsu* (The Decisive Importance of Choosing the Right Middle School and Senior High School in order to Enter the Elite: The Way the Education System of the Elite Schools Works) (Tokyo: Eeru Shuppan Sha).

Nakamura, Keisuke 1996, "Transformation of Industrial Relations in the Telecommunications Industry," *Japan Labor Bulletin* (vol. 35, no. 11: November), pp. 5–10.

Nakamura, Takafusa 1995, *The Postwar Japanese Economy: Its Development and Structure*, second edition (Tokyo: University of Tokyo Press).

Nakamura, Shoichi, ed. 1986, *Shakai Byorigaku o Manabu Hito no tameni* (Learning About Social Pathology) (Tokyo: Sekai Shisosha).

Nakano, Takashi 1956, *Shitauke Kogyo no dozoku to Oyakata-Kokata* (Extended Families, Bosses and Followers in the Subcontracting Industries) (Tokyo: Ochanomizu Shobo).

Nakayama, Ichiro 1974, *Roshi Kankei no Keizai-Shakaigaku* (The Social Economics of Labor–Management Relations in Postwar Japan) (Tokyo: Nihon Rodo Kyokai).

1975, *Industrialization and Labor–Management Relations in Japan*, translated into English by Ross Mouer (Tokyo: Japan Institute of Labor).

Naoi, Atsushi *et al.*, eds. 1990, *Gendai Nihon no Kaiso Kozo* (The Nature of Stratification in Contemporary Japan), 4 vols. (Tokyo: Tokyo Daigaku Shuppankai).

Neustupny, J. V. 1991, *On Romanizing Japanese*, Japanese Language Series no. 5 (Melbourne: Japanese Studies Centre).

NHK Hoso Bunka Kenkyujo (The Broadcasting Culture Research Institute of NHK) 2002, *Nihonjin no Seikatsu Jikan 2000* (The Way Japanese Used Time in 2000) (Tokyo: Nihon Hoso Shuppan Kyokai).

NHK Kokusai Kyoku Keizai Purojekuto (The Economic Project in the International Bureau of NHK) and Daiwa Soken Keizai Chosa Bu (The Economic Research Department of the Daiwa Research Institute) 1995, *A Bilingual Guide to the Japanese Economy* (Tokyo: Kodansha International).

NHK Yoron Chosa Bu (The Public Opinion Survey Bureau of the NHK) 1992, *Nihonjin no Seikatsu Jikan 1990* (The Way Japanese Used Time in 1990) (Tokyo: Nihon Hoso Shuppan Kyokai).

Nihon Fujin Dantai Rengokai (The Japan Association of Women's Organizations) 2002, *Josei Hakusho 2001* (The 2001 White Paper on Women) (Tokyo: Horupo Shuppan).

Nihon Kei-eisha Dantai Renmei (The Japan Federation of Employers' Associations) 1969, *Noryoku Shugi Kanri – Sono Riron to Jissen* (The Theory and the Practice of Managing by Ability) (Tokyo: Nihon Kei-eisha Dantai Renmei).

1995, *Shinjidai no "Nihonteki Keiei": Chosen subeki Hoko to sono Gutaisaku* ("Japanese-Style Management" for a New Era: The Challenges and Some Practical Strategies) (Tokyo: Nihon Kei-eisha Dantai Renmei).

2000a, *Genten Kaiki – Deibaashiteii-Manejimento no Hokosei* (Returning to the Starting Point: The Orientation of Managing for Diversity) (Tokyo: Nihon Kei-eisha Dantai Renmei).

2000b, *Seika Shugi Jidai no Chingin Shisutemu no Arigata* (Approaches to Implementing a Wage System for the Era of Output-Based Management) (Tokyo: Nihon Kei-eisha Dantai Renmei, 15 May).

Nihon Kei-eisha Dantai Renmei and Kanto Kei-eisha Kyokai 1996, *"Shinjidai no Nihonteki Kei-ei" ni Tsuite no Forooappu Chosa Hokoku* (A Follow-Up Survey on Nikkei's Report on Japanese Management for a New Era) (Tokyo: Nihon Kei-eisha Dantai Renmei and Kanto Kei-eisha Kyokai).

Nihon no Ronten (The Editors of Japan's Current Debates) 2002, *Joshiki "Nihon no Ronten"* (The Basic "Debates Defining Japan") (Tokyo: Bungei Shunju).

Nihon Rodo Ho Gakkai (The Japan Association for Labor Law) 2000, *Nijuisseiki Rodo Ho no Tenbo* (The Outlook for Labor Law in the Twenty-First Century) (Tokyo: Yuhikaku).

Nihon Rodo Kenkyu Kiko (The Japan Institute of Labor) 1996, *Rodo Shijo no Henka to Rodoho no Kadai* (Changes in the Labor Market and Legal Issues) (Tokyo: Nihon Rodo Kenkyu Kiko).

2000, *Rodo Kankei Hoki Shu* (A Collection of Laws and Regulations Concerning Labor–Management Relations) (Tokyo: Nihon Rodo Kenkyu Kiko).

2001a, *Kinrosha Seikatsu* (Workers' Lives) (Tokyo: Nihon Rodo Kenkyu Kiko).

2001b, *Daitoshi no Wakamono no Shugyo Kodo to Ishiki* (The Employment and Consciousness of Young People in Japan's Big Cities), Chosa Kenkyu Hokokusho no. 146 (Tokyo: Nihon Rodo Kenkyu Kiko, October).

Nihon Rodo Shakai Gakkai (The Japan Association for the Sociology of Labor) 1990, *Rodo Shakaigaku no Kadai* (The Tasks Confronting the Sociology of Labor) (Tokyo: Jichosha).

2002, *Atarashii Kaikyu Shakai to Rodosha Zo* (A Portrait of Workers and the New Class Society), a special issue of *Nihon Rodo Shakai Gakkai Nenpo* (no. 13).

Nikkei Bijinesu, 1995, *Ichidoru-Hachijuen Kojo* (The Factory at Eighty Yen per Dollar) (Tokyo: Nihon Keizai Shimbunsha).

1997, "Sekai Kasenka no Shogeki: Go Nengo ni Nokoru Kaisha wa Koko da" (The Challenge of Global Oligopolization: The Companies That Will Still Be Around in Five Years), *Nikkei Bijinesu* (no. 892: 26 May), pp. 20–35.

2003, "Dankai no Sedai ga Taijo sureba Nihion Kigyo wa Yomigaeru" (Japan's Enterprises Will Recover When the "Inbetween Generation" of Managers Retires), *Associe* (no. 10: February), p. 7.

Ninomiya, Atsuko 2001, "Shoshika Mondai o do Toraeruka" (How Should the Trend Toward Having Fewer Children be Viewed?), in *Josei Hakusho 2001* (The 2001 White Paper on Women), edited by Nihon Fujin Dantai Rengokai (The Japan Association of Women's Organizations) (Tokyo: Horupu Shuppan), pp. 38–46.

Nippon Keizai Dantai Rengokai (Japan Business Federation) 2003, *Nippon Keizai Dantai Rengokai: 2002–2003* (Tokyo: Nippon Keizai Dantai Rengokai).

Nishii, Motoyuki 2003, "Nihon yo Tsuyomi Wasureruna" (Japan: Don't Forget Your Strengths [an Interview with Carlos Ghosn]), *Business on Sunday*, an insert in *ASC*, 5 April, pp. 1–2.

Nishikawa, Shunsaku, ed. 1980, *The Labor Market in Japan: Selected Readings*, translated by Ross Mouer (Tokyo: University of Tokyo Press).

Nishikawa, Shunsaku and Shimada, Haruo 1980, in *The Labor Market in Japan: Selected Readings*, edited by Nishikawa Shunsaku and translated by Ross Mouer (Tokyo: University of Tokyo Press, 1980), pp. 124–41.

Nishitani, Satoshi and Yoroi, Takayoshi, eds. 2000, *Rodo Ho Ni: Kobetsuteki Rodo Kankei Ho* (Labor Law, vol. II: The Law Relating to Individual Employment Relations) (Kyoto: Horitsu Bunka Sha).

Nitta, Michio 1993, "Historic Change in Japanese Politics and Labor Movement: The July 18 General Election and its Effect," *Japan Labor Bulletin* (vol. 32, no. 11: November), pp. 5–8.

1995, "Union Participation of Workers in Managerial and Supervisory Positions," *Japan Labor Bulletin* (vol. 34, no. 1: January), pp. 6–8.

Nomura, Masami 1993a, *Toyotaizumu* (Toyotaism: The Toyota Production System) (Kyoto: Mineruva Shobo).

1993b, *Jukuren to Bungyo: Nihon Kigyo to Teiraa Shugi* (Skill and the Division of Labor: Taylorism and the Japanese Enterprise) (Tokyo: Ochanomizu Shobo).

1994, *Shushin Koyo* (Lifetime Employment) (Tokyo: Iwanami Shoten).

Nomura Sogo Kenkyu Jo, Shakai-Sangyo Kenkyu Honbu (Nomura Research Institute, The Centre for Social and Industrial Research) 1999, *Kawariyuku Nihonjin: Seikatsusha Ichimannin ni Miru Nihonjin no Ishiki to Kodo* (The Changing Japanese: The Behavior and Consciousness of Japanese as Seen in a Sample of Ten Thousand) (Tokyo: Nomura Sogo Kenkyu Jo Joho Resoosu Bu).

2001, *Nisen-yonnen Koteki Nenkin Kaikaku* (The Radical Changes Coming to Public Pensions Systems in 2004) (Tokyo: Nomura Sogo Kenkyu Jo Joho Resoosu Bu).

Obata, Fumiko 2000, "Rodo Ho Nyumon" (Introductory Textbooks for Labor Law), *Nihon Rodo Kenkyu Zasshi* (no. 477: April), pp. 2–7.

Obi, Keiichiro 1980, "The Theory of Labor Supply: Some New Perspectives and some Implications," in *The Labor Market in Japan: Selected Readings*, edited by Nishikawa Shunsaku and translated by Ross Mouer (Tokyo: University of Tokyo Press), pp. 41–66. Originally published as "Rodo Kyokyu no Riron: Sono Kadai Oyobi Kiketsu no Gan-i," *Mita Gakkai Zasshi* (vol. 61, no. 1: January), pp. 1–25.

Odaka, Kunio 1941, *Shokugyo Shakaigaku* (A Sociology of Occupations) (Tokyo: Iwanami Shoten).

1944, *Shokugyokan no Henkaku* (Changing Views on Occupations) (Tokyo: Kawade Shobo).

1948, *Shokugyo to Kindai Shakai* (Occupations and Modern Society) (Tokyo: Kaname Shobo).

1952, *Rodo Shakaigaku* (Labor Sociology) (Tokyo: Kawade Shobo).

1965, *Nihon no Keiei* (Management in Japan) (Tokyo: Chuo Koronsha).

1975, *Toward Industrial Democracy: Management and the Workers in Modern Japan* (Cambridge, MA: Harvard University Press).

1984, *Nihonteki Keiei: Sono Shinwa to Genjitsu* (Japanese-Style Management: The Myths and the Realities) (Tokyo: Chuo Koronsha).

Odaka, Kunio, ed. 1956, *Imono no Machi – Sangyo Shakaigakuteki Kenkyu* (Iron Town: Research in Industrial Sociology) (Tokyo: Yuhikaku).

Ogasawara, Koichi 2002, *Rodo Gaiko: Sengo Reisenki ni okeru Kokusai Rodo Renkei* (Labor Diplomacy: Labor's International Interaction During the Cold War) (Kyoto: Mineruva Shobo).

Ogawa, Masaaki, Kitagawa, Takayoshi, Sekiya, Shinsuke, eds. 2002, *Ashita no Fukushi ni Motomerareru Mono: Fukushi no Genten o Kangaeru* (Looking for Tomorrow's Welfare: Thinking About the Origins of Welfare) (Tokyo: Chuo Hoki Shuppan).

Ogura, Kazuya 1996, "The Problem of Working Hours in Japan Today," *Studies of the Japan Institute of Labor* (no. 11: March), pp. 45–57.

Okamoto, Hideaki 1964, "Rodo Kumiai no Shakaigaku" (A Sociology of Labor Unions), in *Shakaigaku Kenkyu Annai* (A Guide to Research in Sociology), edited by Fukutake Tadashi (Tokyo: Yuhikaku), pp. 164–94.

Okano, Kaori and Tsuchiya, Motonori 1999, *Education in Contemporary Japan: Inequality and Diversity* (Cambridge: Cambridge Univeristy Press).

Okochi, Kazuo 1952, *Reimeiki no Nihon Rodo Undo* (The Early Years of the Union Movement in Japan) (Tokyo: Iwanami Shoten).

1954, *Nihon no Rodo Kumiai* (Japan's Labor Unions) (Tokyo: Toyo Keizai Shimposha).

1956, "Shinban e no Jo" (Toward a New Departure), in *Rodo Kumiai no Seisei to Soshiki* (The Formation and Organization of Labor Unions), edited by Okochi Kazuo (Tokyo: Tokyo Daigaku Shuppankai), pp. 5–8.

1970, *Shakai Seisaku Yonjunen* (Forty Years with Social Policy) (Tokyo: Tokyo Daigaku Shuppankai).

Okochi, Kazuo, Karsh, Bernard, and Levine, Solomon B., eds. 1973, *Workers and Employers in Japan: The Japanese Employment Relations System* (Tokyo: University of Tokyo Press; Princeton: Princeton University Press).

Okonogi, Keigo 1978, *Moratoriamu Ningen no Jidai* (The Age of the Moratoriamu Types) (Tokyo: Chuo Koronsha).

Okuda, Hiroshi 1999, "Okuda Kaicho Kiso Enzetsu" (The Keynote Speech of the President of Nippon Keidanren, Mr. Okuda Hiroshi), *SRN* (no. 1819: 30 August), p. 4.

Ono, Akira 1989, *Nihonteki Koyo Kanko to Rodo Shijo* (Japanese-Style Employment Practices and the Labor Market) (Tokyo: Toyo Keizai Shimposha).

1997, *Henka Suru Nihonteki Koyo Kanko* (The Changing Nature of Japanese Employment Practices) (Tokyo: Nihon Rodo Kenkyu Kiko).

Ono, Susumu, Morimoto, Tetsuro, and Suzuki, Takao 2001, *Nihon/Nihongo/Nihonjin* (Japan, the Japanese Language, and the Japanese) (Tokyo: Shinchosha).

Ono, Takeshi 2002, *Riin Seisan Hoshiki no Rodo – Jidosha Kojo no Sanyo Kansatsu ni Motozuite* (Work on the Production Line in an Automobile Manufacturing Plant: A Study Based on Participant Observation) (Tokyo: Ochanomizu Shobo).

Ono, Tsuneo and Mouer, Ross 1986, *Labour Policy in Japan: A Survey of Issues in the Eighties*, Papers of the Japanese Studies Center no. 14 (Melbourne: Japanese Studies Center).

Organization for Economic Cooperation and Development 1972, *OECD Tainichi Rodo Hokokusho* (The OECD Report on Labor in Japan), translated by the Rodosho (Ministry of Labor) (Tokyo: Nihon Rodo Kyokai).

1977, The Development of Industrial Relations in Japan: Some Implications of the Japanese Experience (Paris: OECD). A Japanese version was published in 1977, *Roshi Kankei Seido no Tenkai – Nihon no Keiken ga Imi suru mono* (Tokyo: Nihon Rodo Kyokai).

2001, *OECD Economic Surveys: Japan* (Paris: Organization for Economic Cooperation and Development).

Ormonde, Tom 1992, "Large, Lucky and Lazy: What Many Japanese Think of Australia and Australians," in *Japanese Images of Australia: A Collection of Writings on Australia 1991*, edited by Ross Mouer, Asian Perceptions of Australia no. 2 (Melbourne: Monash Asia Institute), pp. 27–38. Reprinted from *The Age* (Melbourne), 18 August 1990, The Saturday Extra, pp. 1 and 6.

Osono, Tomokazu 1995, *Nihon No Hensachi: Sekai ni Okeru JAPAN no Jitsuryo o Yomu* (The Statistics on Japan: Looking at How Japan Stacks up in the World) (Tokyo: Sanmaaku Shuppan).

1997, *Hitome de Wakaru Kigyo Keiretsu to Gyokai Chizu: Nihon no Sangyokai ni Harareta Tate Ito Yoko Ito o Yomu* (A Map of the Enterprise Groupings in Japanese Industry: Identifying the Vertical and Horizontal Linkages in the Japanese Business World) (Tokyo: Nihon Jitsugyo Shuppansha).

Ota, Kiyoshi 2000, "Kokusaihikaku kara Mita Nihon no Shotoku Kakusa" (A Comparative View of Income Inequality in Japan), *The Japanese Journal of Labour Studies* (no. 480), pp. 33–40.

Otake, Fumio 2000, "Kyuju Nendai no Shotoku Kakusa" (Differentials in the Distribution of Income in the 1990s), *Nihon Rodo Kenkyu Zasshi* (no. 480: July), pp. 2–11.

Otake, Fumio and Saito, Makoto 1999, "Shotoku Fugyodoka no Haikei to sono Seisakutekigan-i: Nenreikaisonai Koka, Nenreikaisokan Koka, Jinko Koreika Koa" (Assessing the Growing Amount of Income Inequality in Japan and its Implications: The Effect of Aging, and Differentials Within and Between Age Groups on the Overall Distribution), *Quarterly of Social Security Research* (vol. 31, no. 1), pp. 65–76.

Ouchi, William G. 1981, *Theory Z: How American Business Can Meet the Japanese Challenge* (Reading, MA: Addison-Wesley).

Owaki, Masako, Nakano, Mami, and Hayashi, Yoko 1996, *Hataraku Onnatachi no Saiban* (Court Cases Involving Working Women) (Tokyo: Gakuyo Shobo).

Oyama, Hiroshi, Sumitani, Shigeru, Takegawa, Shogo; Hiraoka, Ko-ichi, eds. 2000, *Fukushi Kokka e no Shiza – Yuragi Kara Saikochiku e* (A View of the Welfare State: Restructuring a Shaky System) (Kyoto: Mineruva Shobo).

Packard, George R. 1966, *Protest in Tokyo* (Princeton: Princeton University Press).

Paku, Joan Sukkucha (Joanna Sook Ja Park) 2002, *Kaisha Ningen ga Kaisha o Tsubusu: Waaku Raifu Baransu no Teian* (The Company Man Will Destroy the Company: A Proposal for a Balanced Working Life) (Tokyo: Asahi Shimbunsha).

Pascale, Richard Tanner and Athos, Anthony G. 1981, *The Art of Japanese Management: Applications for American Executives* (New York: Simon and Schuster).

Patrick, H., ed. 1976, *Japanese Industrialisation and its Social Consequences* (Berkeley: University of California Press).

Phillimore, Jane 2002, "Women 'Childfree', but not Childless: As Men Sing the Joys of Parenthood, Women Increasingly Drop Out," in *The Observer* and appearing in *The Japan Times*, 10 May, p. 5.

PHP Kenkyujo (The PHP Research Institute) 1996, *Zatsugaku: Bijinesuman Handobukku (1997 Nenban)* (Miscellany: The 1997 Handbook for Businessmen) (Tokyo: PHP Kenkyujo).

Plath, David W., ed. 1983, *Work and Lifecourse in Japan* (Albany: State University of New York Press).

Research Project Team for Japanese Systems, Masuda Foundation, ed. 1992, *Japanese Systems: An Alternative Civilization?* (Yokohama: Sekotac).

Rifkin, Jeremy 1996, *The End of Work: The Decline of the Global Labor Force and the Dawn of the Post-Market Era* (New York: G. P. Putnam).

Rodo Daijin Kanbo Seisaku Chosa Bu (Policy Planning and Research Department, Minister's Secretariat, Japanese Ministry of Labor) 1982, *Rodo Tokei Yoran 1982* (Handbook of Labor Statistics 1982) (Tokyo: Okura Sho Insatsu Kyoku).

1985, *Rodo Tokei Nenpo Showa Gojuhachi Nen* (Year Book of Labor Statistics, 1983 [vol. XXXVI]) (Tokyo: Rodo Horei Kyokai).

1992, *Rodo Tokei Yoran 1992* (Handbook of Labor Statistics 1992) (Tokyo: Okura Sho Insatsu Kyoku).

1995, *Rodo Tokei Nenpo Heisei Roku Nen* (Year Book of Labor Statistics, 1994 [vol. XLVII]) (Tokyo: Romu Gyosei Kenkyujo).

1996a, *Rodo Tokei Yoran 1996 Nenban* (Handbook of Labor Statistics, 1996) (Tokyo: Okura Sho Insatsu Kyoku).

1996b, *Shugyo Keitai no Tayoka ni Kansuru Sogo Jittai Chosa Hokoku* (Survey on the Increasing Variety of Employment Systems) (Tokyo: Okura Sho Insatsu Koyoku, 1 April).

1996c, *Heisei Roku Nen Chingin Rodo Jikan Seido Nado Sogo Chosa Hokoku* (Report on the 1994 General Survey of Systems for Wages and Working Hours) (Tokyo: Rodo Daijin Kanbo Seisaku Chosa Bu).

Rodo Daijin Kanbo Rodo Tokei Chosa Bu (Labor Statistics and Research Department, Minister's Secretariat, Japanese Ministry of Labor) 1970, *Rodo Tokei Nenpo Showa Yonjuyon Nen* (Year Book of Labor Statistics, 1969 [vol. XXII]) (Tokyo: Rodo Horei Kyokai).

Rodo Daijin Kanbo Tokei Joho Bu (Statistics and Information Department, Minister's Secretariat, Japanese Ministry of Labor) 1972, *Rodo Tokei Nenpo Showa Yonjuroku Nen* (Yearbook of Labor Satistics 1971 [vol. XXIV]) (Tokyo: Rodo Daijin Kanbo Tokei Joho Bu).

1976, *Rodo Tokei Nenpo Showa Goju Nen* (Yearbook of Labor Statistics 1975 [vol. XXVIII]) (Tokyo: Rodo Daijin Kanbo Tokei Joho Bu).

1982, *Rodo Tokei Yoran 1982 Nenban* (Handbook of Labor Statistics: 1982) (Tokyo: Okura Sho Insatsu Kyoku).

Rodo Kagaku Kenkyujo (Institute for the Science of Labor) 1943, *Chingin Kettei ni Kansuru Rodo Kagakuteki Kenkai* (A Perspective from the Science of Labor Concerning the Setting of Wage Rates) (Osaka: Osaka Yako Shoten).

1954, *Saitei Seikatsuhi no Kenkyu* (Research on the Minimum Standard of Living) (Tokyo: Rodo Kagaku Kenkyujo).

1960, *Nihon no Seikatsu Suijun* (The Standard of Living in Japan) (Tokyo: Rodo Kagaku Kenkyujo).

Rodo Sho (The Ministry of Labor) 1992, *Rodo Hakusho, Heisei Yon Nenban: Rodoryoku Fusoku, Rodo Ido no Kappatsuka to Kigyo no Taio* (The 1992 Labor White Paper: The Labor Shortage, Increased Labor Mobility and the Responses of Firms) (Tokyo: Nihon Rodo Kenkyu Kiko).

1995, *Labor Laws of Japan 1995* (Tokyo: Romu Gyosei Kenkyujo).

1996, *White Paper on Labor 1996: Summary* (Tokyo: Japan Institute of Labor).

1999, *Rodo Hakusho Heisei Junenban* (The 1998 White Paper on the Labor Economy) (Tokyo: Nihon Rodo Kenkyu Kiko).

2002, *Rodo Keizai Hakusho Heisei Jusan Nenban* (The 2001 White Paper on the Labor Economy) (Tokyo: Nihon Rodo Kenkyu Kiko).

Rodo Sho Rosei Kyoku (Ministry of Labor, Labor Policy Division) and Nihon Rodo Kyokai (Japan Institute of Labor) 1986, *Rodo Undo Hakusho Showa 61 Nenban: Nijuisseiki o Tenbo Suru Rodo Undo no Taido* (The 1986 White Paper on the Labor Movement: The Movement as it Prepares for the Twenty-First Century) (Tokyo: Nihon Rodo Kyokai).

Rohlen, Thomas P. 1974, *For Harmony and Strength: Japanese White-Collar Organisation in Anthropological Perspective* (Berkeley: University of California Press).

Roshi Kankei Chosakai (The Survey Group on Industrial Relations) 1981, *Tenkanki ni Okeru Roshi Kankei no Jittai* (The Realities of Industrial Relations in a Period of Change) (Tokyo: Tokyo Daigaku Shuppankai).

Rostow, W. W. 1959, *The Stages of Economic Growth* (Cambridge: Cambridge University Press).

Sankei Shimbun Shakai Bu Kyoiku Mondai Shuzai Han 2002, *Kyoiku Hokai* (The Collapse of Education) (Tokyo: Kadokawa Shoten).

Sano, Yoko 1980, "A Quantitative Analysis of Factors Determining the Rate of Increase in Wage Levels During the Spring Wage Offensive," in *The Labor Market in Japan: Selected Readings*, edited by Nishikawa Shunsaku and translated by Ross Mouer (Tokyo: University of Tokyo Press, 1980), pp. 216–35. Originally published as "Shunto Soba no Keiryo Bunseki," *Gendai Rodo* (no 1: July 1975), pp. 55–70.

1988, "Seven Mysteries of Long Working Hours," *Japan Quarterly* (vol. 35, no. 3: July–September), pp. 248–52.

Sato, Hiroki 1996a, "Keeping Employees Employed: Shukko and Tenseki Job Transfers – Formation of a Labor Market with Corporate Groups," *Japan Labor Bulletin* (vol. 35, no. 12: December), pp. 5–8.

1996b, "Multiple Job Holders in Japan," *Japan Labor Bulletin* (vol. 35, no. 3: March), pp. 5–8.

1997a, "Flexible Working Hours System and Conditions for its Active Utilization," *Japan Labor Bulletin* (vol. 36, no. 12: December), pp. 4–8.

1997b, "Labour–Management Relations in Small and Medium-Sized Enterprises: Collective Voice Mechanisms for Workers in Unionised Companies," in *Japanese Labour and Management in Transition: Diversity, Flexibility and Participation*, edited by Mari Sako and Hiroki Sato (London: LSE/Routledge), pp. 315–31.

Sato, Hiroki and Fujimura, Hiroyuki 1991, *Ekuserento Yunion* (Excellent Unions) (Tokyo: Daiichi Shorin).

Sato, Machiko 1993, *Shin Kaigai Teiju Jidai* (The New Era of a Japanese Diaspora) (Tokyo: Shinchosha). This is available in English as *Farewell to Nippon* (Melbourne: Trans Pacific Press, 2001).

Sato, Takao 2003, *Nijudai no Tenshoku* (Changing Jobs in your Twenties) (Tokyo: Zen-nichi Shuppan).

Sato, Toshiki 2000, *Fubyodo Shakai Nihon – Sayonara Sochuryu* (Japan, The Unequal Society – Farewell to the Mass Middle-Class Society) (Tokyo: Chuo Koronshinsha).

Sawyers, Malcolm 1976, "Income Distribution in OECD Countries," *OECD Employment Outlook Occasional Studies* (Paris: OECD).

Scalapino, Robert A. 1967, *The Japanese Communist Movement, 1920–1966* (Berkeley: University of California Press).

Seisho, Hiroshi and Kikuchi, Takashi 2002, *Rodo Ho* (Labor Law) (Tokyo: Yuhikaku).

Seiyama, Kazuo, Naoi, Atsushi, Sato, Yoshimichi, Tsuzuki, Kazuharu, and Kojima, Hideo 1990, "Gendai Nihon no Kaiso Kozo to Sono Susei" (Trends in the Structuring of Social Strata in Contemporary Japan), in *Gendai Nihon no Kaiso Kozo* (The Social Stratification of Contemporary Japan), vol. I of *Shaikai Kaiso no Kozo to Katei* (The Process of Social Stratification), edited by Naoi Atsushi and Seiyama Kazuo (Tokyo: Tokyo Daigaku Shuppankai), pp. 15–50.

Sekine, Susumu 2002, *Sarariiman Daidasso no Susume: Gojusai kara no Jinsei Saisekkei Dokuhon* (An Argument for Getting Out of the Salaried Employee's Rut: A Reader on How to Reestablish Life After Fifty) (Tokyo: Nikkei BP Sha).

Shakai Kagaku Kenkyu Jo (at Tokyo Daigaku) 1950, *Sengo Rodo Kumiai no Jittai* (The Position of Labor Unions in Postwar Japan) (Tokyo: Nihon Hyoronsha).

Shibata, Hirokatsu 1988, "Dyuaru-Inobeshonka no Rodo Kanri no Hen-yo" (Changes in Personnel Management in a Period of Dual Innovation), *Senshu Daigaku Shakai Kagaku Nenpo* (vol. 22: March), pp. 51–100.

Shidara, Kiyotsugu, Ito, Midori, and Kawahito, Hiroshi 1997, "Risutora Teichaku Jidai ni Hatarakitsuzukeru Ho" (How to Continue Working in an Era when Restructuring is a Constant), *Sekai* (no. 635: May), pp. 81–93.

Shimada, Akiko 1990, *Nihonjin no Shokugyo Rinri* (The Work Ethic of the Japanese) (Tokyo: Yuhikaku).

Shimada, Haruo 1980, *The Japanese Employment System*, Japanese Industrial Relations Series, no. 6 (Tokyo: Japan Institute of Labor).

1995, *Japan Kuraishisu – Hito o Wasureta Nihon wa Shizumu* (Japan's Crisis: A Japan Which Forgets its People Cannot Survive) (Tokyo: Kodansha).

Shimada, Haruo and Seike Atsushi 1992, *Shigoto to Kurashi no Keizaigaku* (The Economics of Work and Living) (Tokyo: Iwanami Shoten).

Shimizu, Ikko 1987, *Gappei Jinji* (The Management of a Merger) (Tokyo: Kadokawa Shoten).

1996, *The Dark Side of Japanese Business: Three "Industry Novels": Silver Sanctuary, The Ibis, Keiretsu*, translated and edited by Tamae K. Prindle (New York: M. E. Sharpe).

Shimizu, Naoko 1997, "Rodo Kumiai tte Nan Da?" (A Union? What Might That Be?), *Sekai* (no. 635: May), pp. 106–14.

Shimoi, Takashi 2000, *Rodo Ho* (The Labor Law) (Tokyo: Yuhikaku).

Shinoda, Toru 1995, "'The Tale of Cain and Abel?' A Study of Contemporary Japanese Labor Politics," *Japan Labor Bulletin* (vol. 34, no. 11: November), pp. 4–8.

Shinozuka, Eiko 1989, *Nihon no Koyo Chosei: Oiru Shokku Iko no Rodo Shijo* (Employment Adjustment in Japan: The Labor Market after the Oil Shocks) (Tokyo: Keizai Shimposha).

Shirahase, Sawako 2002, "A Study of Income Inequality for Households with Elderly Members: Comparison among Industrial Nations," *Japan Labor Bulletin* (vol. 41, no. 11: December), pp. 7–10.

Shirai, Taishiro 1980, *Roshi Kankei Ron* (A Theory of Labor–Management Relations) (Tokyo: Nihon Rodo Kyokai).

1983, "A Theory of Enterprise Unionism," in *Contemporary Industrial Relations in Japan*, edited by Shirai Taishiro (Madison: University of Wisconsin Press), pp. 117–43.

Shirai, Taishiro, ed. 1983, *Contemporary Industrial Relations in Japan* (Madison: University of Wisconsin Press).

Smith, Henry Dewitt, II 1972, *Japan's First Student Radicals* (Cambridge, MA: Harvard University Press).

SOHO Shinku Tanku (The SOHO Think Tank) 2001, *Nenpan SOHO Hakusho* (The 2001 White Paper on Small Office/Home Office) (Tokyo: Doyukan).

Somusho Tokei Kyoku 2002, *Nihon no Tokei 2002* (Statistics of Japan 2002) (Tokyo: Zaimu Sho Instatu Kyoku, 2002).

Sone, Yasunori 1989, "Interest Groups and the Process of Political Decision-Making in Japan," in *Constructs for Understanding Japan*, edited by Ross Mouer and Yoshio Sugimoto (London: Kegan Paul International), pp. 259–95.

Sorifu Tokei Kyoku 1981, *Nihon no Tokei 1981* (Statistics of Japan 1981) (Tokyo: Okura Sho Insatsu Kyoku, 1981).

Steven, Rob 1983, *Classes in Contemporary Japan* (Cambridge: Cambridge University Press).

Stockwin, J. A. A. 1980, "Understanding Japanese Politics," in *Japanese Society: Reappraisals and New Directions*, edited by Ross Mouer and Yoshio Sugimoto as a special issue of *Social Analysis* (nos. 5/6: December), pp. 144–53.

Stone, P. B. 1969, *Japan Surges Ahead: Japan's Economic Rebirth* (London: Weidenfeld and Nicolson).

Sugimoto, Yoshio 1977, "Comparative Analysis of Industrial Conflict in Australia and Japan," in *Sharpening the Focus*, edited by R. D. Walton (Brisbane: Griffith University), pp. 198–219.

1988, "'Keizai Nippon' to 'Jishuku Nippon'" (The "Economic Japan" and the "Self-Disciplined Japan"), *Sekai* (December), pp. 34–40. This was reprinted in *Tenno Hyakuwa* (One Hundred Stories About the Emperor), vol. II, edited by Tsurumi Shunsuke and Nakagawa Rokuhei (Tokyo: Chikuma Shobo), pp. 780–6.

Sumiya, Mikio 1950, "Rodoryoku ni Okeru Hokentekinarumono – Hannohanko ni tuite" (The Feudal Element in the Japanese Labor Force – Some Comments on the Part Farmer/Part Factory Worker), *Shakaigaku Hyoron* (vol. 1, no. 1), pp. 20–30.

1954, "Chinrodo no Riron ni Tsuite" (On the Theory of Wage Labor), *Keizaigaku Ronshu* (vol. 23, no. 1: October), pp. 22–69.

1965, "Shakai Kagaku Kenkyu" (Research in the Social Sciences), in *Rodo Keizai Ron* (The Theory of Labor Economics) by Sumiya Mikio (Tokyo: Nihon Hyoronsha, 1965).

Sumiya, Mikio, ed. 1969, *Nihonjin no Keisai Kodo* (The Economic Behavior of the Japanese), 2 vols. (Tokyo: Toyo Keizai Shimposha).

Suwa, Yasuo 1992, "Enterprise-Based Labor Unions and Collective Agreements," *Japan Labor Bulletin* (vol. 31, no. 9: September), pp. 4–8.

1994, "Will the Union for Middle Management Expand?" *Japan Labor Bulletin* (vol. 33, no. 7: July), pp. 5–8.

1999, *Koyo to Ho* (Employment and the Law) (Tokyo: Hoso Daigaku Kyoiku Shinkokai).

Suzuki, Hiromasa 2002, "Waakushearingu o Meguru Oshu Senshinkoku no Doko to Nihon no Kadai" (Recent Trends in Europe Related to Work Sharing and their Implications for Japan), *Sekai no Rodo* (vol. 52, no. 4: April), pp. 2–12.

Suzuki, Yohsisato 2002, *Nihongo no Dekinai Nihonjin* (The Japanese who Cannot Use Japanese) (Tokyo: Chuo Koronshinsha).

Tachibanaki, Toshiaki and Rengo Sogo Seikatsu Kaihatsu Kenkyujo, eds. 1995, *"Shoshin" no Keizaigaku: Naniga "Shusse" o Kimeru no ka* (The Economics of Promotion: What Determines Career Progression?) (Tokyo: Toyo Keizai Shimposha).

Tachibanaki, Toshiaki 1998, *Nihon no Keizai Kakkusa* (Economic Inequality in Japan) (Tokyo: Iwanami Shoten).

Taira, Koji 1977, "Nihongata Kigyobetsu Rodo Kumiai Sambiron" (An Argument in Favor of the Japanese-Style Enterprise Union), *Chuo Koron* (Year 92, issue no. 3: March), pp. 114–26. A summary translation of this later appeared as "In Defense of Japanese Enterprise Unions," *Japan Echo* (vol. 4, no. 2: Summer), pp. 98–109.

Takagi, Kiyoshi 2000, "Nihonteki Kei-ei go no Maneejimento-Sutairu" (Management Style: Going Beyond Japanese-Style Management), in *Atarashii Jidai to Kei-eigaku* (Management Studies and the New [Global] Era), edited by Kataoka Shinshi and Shinozaka Tsuneo as vol. I in *Sosho Gendai Kei-eigaku* (The Library of Management Studies) (Kyoto: Mineruva Shobo), pp. 91–116.

Takanashi, Akira 1994, *Konnichi no Koyo Shitsugyo Mondai* (Today's Employment and Unemployment) (Tokyo: Nihon Rodo Kenkyu Kiko).

2001, *Nihon no Koyo Mondai* (The Employment Problem in Japan) (Tokyo: Shakai Keizai Seisansei Honbu).

2002, *Shunto Wage Offensive*, second edition, Japanese Economy and Labor Series no. 1 (Tokyo: Japan Institute of Labor).

Takasugi, Ryo 1992, *Jinjiken* (The Right to Decide an Employee's Future) (Tokyo: Kodansha).

2000, *Shacho – Kainin Saru* (Mr. Company President – When the Choice is to Resign) (Tokyo: Kodansha).

Takeuchi, Hiroshi and Aso, Makoto 1981, *Nihon no Gakureki Shakai Kawaru – Sangyo Shakai no Henkakuki ni Mukete* (Japanese Society Based on Credentialism is Changing: Facing Change as an Industrialized Society) (Tokyo: Yuhikaku).

Takezawa, Shin-ichi 1995, *Japan Work Ways: 1960–1976–1990* (Tokyo: Japan Institute of Labor).

Tamai, Kingo 2000, "Nenkin" (Pensions), in *Shinpan Shakai Seisaku – o Manabu Hito no Tame ni* (The Revised Social Policy Edition – For Those Wanting to Know About Social Security), edited by Tamai Kingo and Omori Maki (Kyoto: Sekai Shiso Sha), pp. 96–121.

Tanaka, Hidetomi 2002, *Nihongata Sarariiman wa Fukkatsu suru* (The Japanese-Style Salaried Employee Will Rise Again) (Tokyo: Nihon Hoso Shuppan Kyokai).

Tanaka, Kiyosada 2000, *Rodo Ho no Kadai* (Issues in Labor Law) (Tokyo: Rodo Horei Kyokai).

Tao, Masao 1996, *Kigyo Shosetsu ni Manabu: Soshikiron Nyumon* (Learning from Business Novels: An Introduction to Organizational Theory) (Tokyo: Yuhikaku).

Teramoto, Yoshiya and Sakai, Taneji 2002, *Nihon Kigyo no Kooporeeto Gabanansu – "Tochi" kara "Tochi" e: Niju Seikigata Gabanasu Kozo no Gurando Dezain* (Patterns of Governance in Japanese Corporations: From Direct Political Control to Coordinated Information – a Grand Plan for an Approach to Enterprise Governance for the Twenty-First Century) (Tokyo: Seisansei Shuppan).

Teruoka, Itsuko 1990, *Yutakasa to wa Nani ka* (What Does it Mean to Be Affluent?) (Tokyo: Iwanami Shoten).

Thurow, Lester C. 1993, *Head to Head: The Coming Economic Battle Among Japan, Europe and America* (New York: William Morrow and Company).

1996, *The Future of Capitalism: How Today's Economic Forces Shape Tomorrow's World* (St. Leonards, New South Wales: Allen and Unwin).

Thurow, Lester C., ed. 1985, *The Management of Challenge: Japanese Views* (Cambridge, MA: MIT Press).

Tominaga, Ken-ichi 2001, *Shakai Hendo no naka no Fukushi Kokka: Kazoku no Shippai to Kokka no Atarashii Kino* (The Welfare State in a Period of Change: The Failure of the Family and the New Functions of the State) (Tokyo: Chuo Koronshinsha).

Tominaga, Ken-ichi, ed. 1979, *Nihon no Kaiso Kozo* (The Social Stratification of Japan) (Tokyo: Tokyo Daigaku Shuppankai).

Totsuka, Hideo and Tokunaga, Shigeyoshi, eds. 1993, *Gendai Nihon no Rodo Mondai: Atarashii Paradaimu o Motomete* (Debating the Nature of Work in Contemporary Japanese Society: Looking For a New Paradigm) (Kyoto: Mineruva Shobo).

Totten, George 1967, "Collective Bargaining and Works Councils as Innovations in Industrial Relations in Japan," in *Aspects of Social Change in Modern*

*Japan*, edited by R. P. Dore (Princeton: Princeton University Press), pp. 203–43.

Toyama, Shigeru 1987, *Nihonjin no Kinben Chochikukan* (The Views of Japanese on Work and Saving) (Tokyo: Toyo Keizai Shimposha).

Toyo Keizai Shimposha 2003, "Shushoku Burando Rankingu & Kigyo no Saiyo Doko Chosa" (Ranking Employment Openings and the Survey of Plans for Employment in Japanese Firms), *Shukan Toyo Keizai* (no. 5802: 25 January), pp. 82–93.

Toyo Keizai Shimposha, ed. 2000, *Nihon no Kigyo Keiretsu* (Japan's Enterprise Groupings) (Tokyo: Toyo Keizai Shimposha).

Tsuchida, Takeshi 2002, "Shakai Hoken" (Social Insurance), in *Gendai Yogo no Kiso Chishiki 2002* (Encyclopedia of Contemporary Words 2002), edited by Ichiyanagi Midori (Tokyo: Jiyu Kokuminsha), pp. 964–71.

Tsuchiya, Shingoro 1995, *Ajia e no Kigyo Shinshutsu to Kaigai Fu-nin – Sono Keikaku to Jikko* (The Movement of Firms into Asia and Working Overseas) (Tokyo: Nikkan Kogyo Shimbunsha).

Tsuda, Masumi 1976, *Nihonteki Kei-ei no Yogo* (The Vindication of Japanese-Style Management) (Tokyo: Toyo Keizai Shimposha).

1977, *Nihonteki Kei-ei no Ronri* (The Principles of Japanese-Style Management) (Tokyo: Chuo Keizai Shinposha).

1980, *Nihonteki Kei-ei no Daiza* (The Foundation Supporting Japanese-Style Management) (Tokyo: Chuo Keizai Sha).

1981, *Gendai Kei-ei to Kyodo Seikatsutai* (Modern Management and the Sense of Living Together in an Enterprise Community) (Tokyo: Dobunkan).

1982, *Nihonteki Kei-ei no Shinro* (The Way of Japanese-Style Management) (Tokyo: Chuo Keizai Sha).

1987, *Nihonteki Keiei wa Doko e Ikunoka* (Where is Japanese-Style Management Headed?) (Tokyo: PHP Kenkyujo).

Tsujimura, Kotaro 1980, "The Effect of Reductions in Working Hours on Productivity," in *The Labor Market in Japan: Selected Readings*, edited by Nishikawa Shunsaku and translated by Ross Mouer (Tokyo: University of Tokyo Press), pp. 67–83. This originally appeared as "Rodo Jikan Tanshuku wa Seisan o Sogai Suru ka," *Keizai Hyoron* (vol. 21, no. 12: November 1972), pp. 56–67.

1995, *Nijuisseiki no Mukete: Roshi e no Messeeji* (Facing the Twenty-First Century: A Message for Labor and Management) (Tokyo: Nihon Rodo Kenkyu Kiko).

Tsuru, Tsuyoshi 1994, "Why Has Union Density Declined in Japan?" *Japan Labor Bulletin* (vol. 33, no. 11: November), pp. 5–8.

Ui, Jun 1968, *Kogai no Seijigaku* (The Politics of Pollution) (Tokyo: Sanseido).

1972, "The Singularities of Japanese Pollution," *Japan Quarterly* (vol. 19, no. 3: July–September), pp. 281–90.

Ujihara, Shojiro 1966, *Nihon Rodo Mondai Kenkyu* (Research into the State of Labor in Japan) (Tokyo: Tokyo Daigaku Shuppankai).

Van Wolferen, Karel 1990, *The Enigma of Japanese Power: People and Politics in a Stateless Nation* (New York: Vintage).

Vogel, Ezra F. 1979, *Japan as Number One: Seasons for America* (Cambridge, MA: Harvard University Press).

Wada, Katsutoshi 2003, *Kabushiki Kaisah Saisei – Sono Riron to Honda no Tatakai* (The Revival of a Japanese Corporation – Theory and the Struggle at Honda Motors) (Tokyo: Shogaku Sha).

Wakisaka, Akira 2002, *Nihongata Waaku Shearingu* (Work-Sharing Japanese Style) (Tokyo: PHP Kenkyujo).

Wakisaka, Akira and Tomita, Yasunobu 1999, *Daisotsu Josei no Hatarakikata* (The Workways of Female University Graduates) (Tokyo: Nihon Rodo Kenkyu Kiko).

Whitehill, Arthur M. Jr and Takezawa, Shin-ichi 1968, *The Other Worker: A Comparative Study of Industrial Relations in the United States and Japan* (Honolulu: The East-West Centre Press).

Whittaker, D. H. 1990, *Managing Innovation: A Study of British and Japanese Factories* (Cambridge: Cambridge University Press).

Wigmore, John Henry 1969–75, *Law and Justice in Tokugawa Japan*, 12 vols. (Tokyo: University of Tokyo Press).

Wilcox, Claire 1966, *Economies of the World Today: Their Organization, Development and Performance* (New York: Harcourt, Brace and Jovanovich).

Womack, J. P., Jones, Daniel, and Roos, Daniel 1990, *The Machine that Changed the World* (New York: Macmillan).

Wood, Stephen 1996, "How Different Are Human Resource Practices in Japanese 'Transplants' in the United Kingdom?" *Industrial Relations: A Journal of Economy and Society* (vol. 35, no. 4: October), pp. 511–25.

Woronoff, Jon 1982, *Japan's Wasted Workers* (Tokyo: Lotus Press).

1990, *Japan as Anything but Number One* (Tokyo: Yohan).

1992, *Japanese Management Mystique: The Reality Behind the Myth* (Chicago: Probus Publishing).

Yabuno, Yuzo 1995, *Rookaru-Inishiateibu – kokkyo o Koeru Kokoromi* (Local Initiatives: Efforts to Go Beyond National Borders) (Tokyo: Chuo Koronsha).

Yakabe, Katsumi 1977, *Labour Relations in Japan: Fundamental Characteristics* (Tokyo: Ministry of Foreign Affairs).

Yamada, Masahiro 1999, *Parasaito Shinguru no Jidai* (The Age of the Parasitic Singles) (Tokyo: Chikuma Shobo).

2001, "Furiitaa Nihyakumannin ni Ashita wa nai sa" (The Two Million Floating Casuals Have No Economic Future), *Bungei Shunju* (July 2000), pp. 198–204; translated as "No Future for the Freeters," *Japan Echo* (vol. 27, no. 3: June, 2001), pp. 52–5.

Yano Tsuneta Ki-nenkai (The Yano Tsuneo Memorial Association) 1993, *Nihon Kokusei Zue 1993* (A Statistical Overview of Japan 1993), the fifty-first annual edition (Tokyo: Kokuseisha).

2001, *Nihon no Hyakunen: Niju Seiki ga Wagaru Deeta Bukku* (Japan's Twentieth Century as Seen Through a Data Handbook), fourth edition (Tokyo: Yano Tsuneta Ki-nen Kai).

Yashiro, Masamoto and Hanami, Tadashi 2003, "Ikinokoreruka Nihon Keizai, Kigyo Sarariiman" (The Japanese Economy and the Enterprise's Salaried Employee: Will They Survive?), *Shukan Rodo Nyuusu* (no. 1970: 1 January), p. 1.

Yasueda, Hidenobu 1998, *Rodo no Ho to Seisaku* (Labor Law and Labor Policy) (Tokyo: Yuhikaku).

Yasueda, Hidenobu and Nishimura, Ken-ichiro 1986, *Rodo Ho* (Labor Law) (Tokyo: Yuhikaku; sixth edition 1999).

Yomiuri Shimbun Keizai Bu 2001, *Dokyumento "Cho" Sarariiman* (Document on the Super Salaried Employee) (Tokyo: Chuo Koronshinsha).

Yomiuri Shimbun Osaka Honsha, ed. 2002, *Tsubureru Daigaku, Tsuburenai Daigaku* (The Surviving Universities and those that Collapse) (Tokyo: Chuo Koronshinsha).

Yoshida, Kazuo 2001, *Nihon Keizai Saiken – "Kokumin no Itami" wa Do Naru* (Restructuring Japan's Economy: What About the People's Suffering?) (Tokyo: Kodansha).

Yoshimura, Rinpei 2000, "Hinkonsen to Koteki Fujo" (The Poverty Line and Public Assistance for the Poor), in *Shinpan Shakai Seisaku – o Manabu Hito no Tame ni* (The Revised Social Policy Edition – For Those Wanting to Know About Social Security), edited by Tamai Kingo and Omori Maki (Kyoto: Sekai Shiso Sha), pp. 148–67.

# Author index

# General index

absentee fathers 83–5
absenteeism 85–6
aging of the population 146, 173
*amakudari* 99
annual leave
    underutilization of 86–7
aristocracy of labor 152, 215
*arubaito* 121, 123, 129, 132, 223

barrier-free society 159
Basic Livelihood Allowance 184, 248
*Basic Survey of Schools* 128, 131–2
behavioral approach 53–4
business leadership 248–9
business-first capitalism 13

capitalism
    business-first capitalism 13
    and corporatism 11–12
    emperor-first capitalism 12
    in a global context 15–19
    in Japan 248–9, 254, 256, 259, 263
    and mercantilism 153
casualization of work 165, 259, 263
    casual employment 114, 117, 121–3
    demand for casual work 123, 134, 135
    *See also arubaito* and *furiitaa*
children raised overseas 123, 132
Christmas cakes 134
Churitsu Roren 206
civil society 195
commuting 78, 83
competition
    and capital accumulation 15–16, 91,
        92
    among employees 111
    within the global context 16–19, 104–5,
        116, 146, 173
convergence and divergence 20–1, 47–8
corporate responsibility 248, 249
corporatism 11–12, 63–4
culturalist approach 54–5, 184, 248

*dekasegi rodo* (migrant labor) 37
*densangata* wage system 199, 200
designated work system 111
dispatched workers 127, 259, 263
    *Kaw fir* 115
Domei 153, 172, 179, 206, 208, 211
Douglas–Long–Arisawa effect 88, 123

economic growth
    and the affluent worker 152–3
    and capital accumulation 14
    and employment 170–3
    in the generation of economic surplus
        13–14
    Heisei recession xiii
economic inequality 161, 162–4
education
    credentialism in determining
        occupational status 167
    and social inequality 166–9
*emic* dimensions xvii, 204
emperor-first capitalism 12
employment
    employment policy 170–3, 179–80
    total employment 179
employment contract, length of 114
enterprise (*keiretsu*) groupings 200, 202,
    233–5, 236
enterprise system 60
enterprise society 62, 127, 140–1,
    257–8
enterprise union (*kigyobetsu kumiai*) 33,
    37, 48, 51, 60, 61, 62, 146, 210–11,
    225–6, 255
    and the diversity of members' needs
        221–2

family life
    conflict with work 83–5, 125
    and homeless household heads
        184–5
    and the minimum wage 181